Rethinking Jewishness in Weimar Cinema

Film Europa: German Cinema in an International Context
Series Editors: **Hans-Michael Bock** (CineGraph Hamburg); **Tim Bergfelder** (University of Southampton); **Barbara Mennel** (University of Florida)

German cinema is normally seen as a distinct form, but this series emphasizes connections, influences, and exchanges of German cinema across national borders, as well as its links with other media and art forms. Individual titles present traditional historical research (archival work, industry studies) as well as new critical approaches in film and media studies (theories of the transnational), with a special emphasis on the continuities associated with popular traditions and local perspectives.

Recent volumes:

Volume 24
Rethinking Jewishness in Weimar Cinema
Edited by Barbara Hales and Valerie Weinstein

Volume 23
Sensitive Subjects: The Political Aesthetics of Contemporary German and Austrian Cinema
Leila Mukhida

Volume 22
East German Film and the Holocaust
Elizabeth Ward

Volume 21
Cinema of Collaboration: DEFA Coproductions and International Exchange in Cold War Europe
Mariana Ivanova

Volume 20
Screening Art: Modernist Aesthetics and the Socialist Imaginary in East German Cinema
Seán Allan

Volume 19
German Television: Historical and Theoretical Pespectives
Edited by Larson Powell and Robert R. Shandley

Volume 18
Cinema in Service of the State: Perspectives on Film Culture in the GDR and Czechoslovakia, 1945–1960
Edited by Lars Karl and Pavel Skopal

Volume 17
Imperial Projections: Screening the German Colonies
Wolfgang Fuhrmann

Volume 16
The Emergence of Film Culture: Knowledge Production, Institution Building, and the Fate of the Avant-Garde in Europe, 1919–1945
Edited by Malte Hagener

Volume 15
Homemade Men in Postwar Austrian Cinema: Nationhood, Genre and Masculinity
Maria Fritsche

For a full volume listing, please see the series page on our website:
http://www.berghahnbooks.com/series/film-europa

RETHINKING JEWISHNESS IN WEIMAR CINEMA

Edited by
Barbara Hales and Valerie Weinstein

berghahn
NEW YORK · OXFORD
www.berghahnbooks.com

First published in 2021 by
Berghahn Books
www.berghahnbooks.com

© 2021, 2023 Barbara Hales and Valerie Weinstein
First paperback edition published in 2023

Every reasonable effort has been made to supply complete and correct credits for images inside this book. If there are errors or omissions, please contact the publisher so that corrections can be addressed in any subsequent edition.

All rights reserved. Except for the quotation of short passages for the purposes of criticism and review, no part of this book may be reproduced in any form or by any means, electronic or mechanical, including photocopying, recording, or any information storage and retrieval system now known or to be invented, without written permission of Berghahn Books.

Library of Congress Cataloging-in-Publication Data

Names: Hales, Barbara, 1962- editor of compilation. | Weinstein, Valerie, 1971- editor of compilation.
Title: Rethinking Jewishness in Weimar cinema / edited by Barbara Hales and Valerie Weinstein.
Description: New York : Berghahn Books, 2021. | Series: Film Europa: German cinema in an international context ; vol 24 | Includes bibliographical references and index. | Summary: "The burgeoning film industry in the Weimar Republic was, among other things, a major site of German-Jewish experience, one that provided a sphere for Jewish "outsiders" to shape mainstream culture. The chapters collected in this volume deploy new historical, theoretical, and methodological approaches to understanding the significant involvement of German Jews in Weimar cinema. Reflecting upon different conceptions of Jewishness - as religion, ethnicity, social role, cultural code, or text - these studies offer a wide-ranging exploration of an often overlooked aspect of German film history"—Provided by publisher.
Identifiers: LCCN 2020019062 (print) | LCCN 2020019063 (ebook) | ISBN 9781789208726 (hardback) | ISBN 9781789208733 (ebook)
Subjects: LCSH: Motion pictures—Germany—History—20th century. | Jews in the motion picture industry—Germany. | Jewish motion picture producers and directors—Germany. | Germany—Civilization—Jewish influences.
Classification: LCC PN1993.5.G3 R45 2021 (print) | LCC PN1993.5.G3 (ebook) | DDC 791.430943/09042—dc23
LC record available at https://lccn.loc.gov/2020019062
LC ebook record available at https://lccn.loc.gov/2020019063

British Library Cataloguing in Publication Data

A catalogue record for this book is available from the British Library

ISBN 978-1-78920-872-6 hardback
ISBN 978-1-80073-948-2 paperback
ISBN 978-1-78920-873-3 ebook

https://doi.org/10.3167/9781789208726

Contents

List of Figures   vii

Acknowledgments   ix

Introduction. The Jewishness of Weimar Cinema   1
    Barbara Hales and Valerie Weinstein

Part I. Jewish Visibility On and Off Screen

Chapter 1.   Humanizing Shylock: The "Jewish Type" in Weimar Film   25
    Maya Barzilai

Chapter 2.   Energizing the Dramaturgy: How Jewishness Shaped Alexander Granach's Performances in Weimar Cinema   44
    Margrit Frölich

Chapter 3.   The Jewish Vamp of Berlin: Actress Maria Orska, Typecasting, and Jewish Women   67
    Kerry Wallach

Chapter 4.   Jewish Comedians beyond Lubitsch: Siegfried Arno in Film and Cabaret   88
    Mila Ganeva

Chapter 5.   Alfred Rosenthal's Rhetoric of Collaboration, the Politics of Jewish Visibility, and Jewish Weimar Film Print Culture   111
    Ervin Malakaj

Part II. Coding and Decoding Jewish Difference

Chapter 6.   Two Worlds, Three Friends, and the Mysterious Seven-Branched Candelabrum: Jewish Filmmaking in Weimar Germany   131
    Philipp Stiasny

Chapter 7.	Homosexual Emancipation, Queer Masculinity, and Jewish Difference in *Anders als die Andern* (1919) Valerie Weinstein	152
Chapter 8.	Der Film ohne Juden: G.W. Pabst's *Die freudlose Gasse* (1925) Lisa Silverman	178
Chapter 9.	"The World Is Funny, Like a Dream": Franziska Gaal's *Verwechslungskomödien* and Exile's Crisis of Identity Anjeana K. Hans	196

Part III. Jewishness as Antisemitic Construct

Chapter 10.	Cinematically Transmitted Disease: Weimar's Perpetuation of the Jewish Syphilis Conspiracy Barbara Hales	215
Chapter 11.	The Einstein Film: Animation, Relativity, and the Charge of "Jewish Science" Brook Henkel	237
Chapter 12.	"A Clarion Call to Strike Back": Antisemitism and Ludwig Berger's *Der Meister von Nürnberg* (1927) Christian Rogowski	257
Chapter 13.	Banning Jewishness: Stefan Zweig, Robert Siodmak, and the Nazis Andréas-Benjamin Seyfert	278
Chapter 14.	Detoxification: Nazi Remakes of E.A. Dupont's Blockbusters Ofer Ashkenazi	300

Coda

Chapter 15.	"*Filmrettung*: Save the Past for the Future!": Film Restoration and Jewishness in German and Austrian Silent Cinema Cynthia Walk	327

Afterword Barbara Hales and Valerie Weinstein	338
Index	342

Figures

Figure 1.1. Henrik Galeen as Aaron in *Der Golem* (1914, dir. Galeen). Source: Deutsche Kinemathek. 34

Figure 2.1. Alexander Granach with Ruth Weyher in *Schatten* (1923, dir. Arthur Robison). Source: Deutsche Kinemathek. 55

Figure 3.1. Maria Orska. Portrait by Yva (Else Neuländer-Simon). Berlin, ca. 1926–27. Source: Author's private collection. 70

Figure 4.1. Siegfried Arno, publicity postcard, no date. Courtesy of Theaterwissenschaftliche Sammlung, Universität zu Köln. 93

Figure 6.1. Hermann Vallentin and Helene Sieburg in *Zwei Welten* (1930, dir. E.A. Dupont). Production still. Source: DFF-Deutsches Filminstitut & Filmmuseum. 140

Figure 6.2. Oskar Karlweis, Willy Fritsch, and Heinz Rühmann in *Die Drei von der Tankstelle* (1930, dir. Wilhelm Thiele). Production still. Source: DFF-Deutsches Filminstitut & Filmmuseum. 144

Figure 8.1. Screenshot from *Die freudlose Gasse* (1925, dir. G.W. Pabst). 179

Figure 9.1. *Peter* (1934): Eva/Peter (Franziska Gaal) and her grandfather (Felix Bressart), once again expelled from their home. Screenshot courtesy of Film Archiv Austria. 206

Figure 10.1. Scene from *Falsche Scham* (1925–26, dir. Rudolf Biebrach). Source: DFF-Deutsches Filminstitut & Filmmuseum. 225

Figure 11.1. "The Einstein-Film." Cover illustration of the four-page film program for *Die Grundlagen der Einsteinschen Relativitätstheorie*, Colonna-Filmgesellschaft, 1922. Source: Filmmuseum München/Edition Filmmuseum, used with permission. 243

Figure 12.1. Evchen (Maria Matray) appeals to Hans Sachs (Rudolf Rittner) for support. *Der Meister von Nürnberg* (1927, dir. Ludwig Berger). Courtesy of DFF-Deutsches Filminstitut & Filmmuseum, Frankfurt. 263

Figure 13.1. Willi Forst and Hilde Wagener in Robert Siodmak's *Burning Secret* (1933). Courtesy of Kreisky-Archiv, Vienna. 287

Figure 14.1. A visit by the regional nobility connects the village with the outside world in Hans Steinhoff's 1940 *Die Geierwally*. 303

Figure 15.1. Avid Media Composer: five elements. Screenshot. 328

Figure 15.2. Avid Media Composer: composite edit. Screenshot. 329

Figure 15.3. *Das alte Gesetz*, Russian export print. Title card on YouTube. Screenshot. 331

Figure 15.4. *Die Stadt ohne Juden*, French export print. Frame scan of previously missing footage. Reproduction courtesy of Filmarchiv Austria. 333

Acknowledgments

It has been a pleasure to write and edit this book, thanks to collaboration with so many marvelous friends and colleagues. Our greatest thanks go to our contributors: this book grew out of lively conversation and generous scholarly exchange. As this project developed, discussions that had been going on in print and in person for years sprang off the page, took on new life face-to-face and online, and blossomed into the chapters in the volume you hold in your hand. Most of the chapters have been read, discussed, reflected on, and revised by multiple members of our contributor community and we all have shared ideas and sources with one another. Other interlocutors whose published work graces other venues also participated in our conversations about German-Jewish filmmaking in Weimar and enriched this volume in important ways. These colleagues include Nick Baer, Darcy Buerkle, Sabine Hake, Sara Hall, Todd Herzog, Rick McCormick, Barbara Mennel, Jonathan Skolnik, Joel Westerdale, and our anonymous peer reviewers at Berghahn Books.

Thank you to all the members of the editorial and production staff at Berghahn who have eased our book's way into the world, especially Chris Chappell, Mykelin Higham, and Keara Hagerty for your clarity, support, good nature, and efficiency throughout the process.

Our home departments and institutions have made our work possible in large and small ways, including space, time, and financial support for conference and research travel and necessary production costs. Thank you to the University of Houston Clear-Lake, the University of Cincinnati, the Charles Phelps Taft Research Center, and the Niehoff Center for Film and Media Studies at the University of Cincinnati.

And of course, we both are incredibly grateful to the other friends and colleagues who support us, and to our families for their unconditional love.

Barbara Hales and Valerie Weinstein

Introduction

THE JEWISHNESS OF WEIMAR CINEMA

Barbara Hales and Valerie Weinstein

The postwar historiography of Weimar cinema blossomed from two seeds, Siegfried Kracauer's *From Caligari to Hitler: A Psychological History of the German Film* (1947) and Lotte Eisner's *The Haunted Screen: Expressionism in the German Cinema and the Influence of Max Reinhardt* (1952). Both Kracauer and Eisner delved into what have become the canonical works of Weimar cinema for evidence of a German national character: Kracauer in psychological and Eisner in aesthetic terms. In *Caligari to Hitler*, Kracauer argues that films reflect the deep layers of a national unconscious. He interprets Weimar cinema as the manifestation of a stunted and emasculated (implicitly male) German psyche that craved the mother's nurturing embrace and the leadership of a tyrannical father. In *Haunted Screen*, Eisner theorizes Weimar Expressionist cinema as the epitome of a brooding, uniquely German aesthetic, prefigured in German Romanticism.

The horror of National Socialist (Nazi) war crimes and the specter of Nazism cast long shadows on both *Caligari to Hitler* and *Haunted Screen*. Kracauer aims to explain how Weimar cinema presaged Hitler's rise. Eisner mourns a time when German angst produced great art, a time "before Hitler came to power, [when] the Germans liked to declare that their great poets, such as Goethe or Schiller, always emerged at times of national hardship."[1] In a review for *Sight and Sound*, Thorold Dickinson wrote of *Haunted Screen*, "Those who believe that film is a reflection of twentieth century history can find in this remarkable book and in the films it describes a compulsive impression of the consequences of the Treaty of Versailles."[2] Dickinson's words apply equally well to *Caligari to Hitler*.

In projecting Weimar cinema as a reflection of a tortured and menacing—even proto-fascist—German soul, Kracauer and Eisner both elide the question of the widespread involvement of Jewish film professionals in Weimar cinema and any particular effects this involvement may have had. It is difficult to ascertain how many Jewish people worked in Weimar film. According to Ofer Ashkenazi, before the Nazi takeover in 1933 around 20 percent of German film professionals were Jewish.³ Yet, a naïve reader of *Caligari to Hitler* and *Haunted Screen* might not be aware of the Jewish backgrounds of many Weimar film industry leaders, like producer Erich Pommer, whose productions Kracauer and Eisner describe as exemplary of German psychology and aesthetics. Kracauer and Eisner do not write about German film professionals of Jewish heritage as psychologically, culturally, or artistically separate from the national character that their works purportedly exemplify.

Kracauer's and Eisner's parallel experiences (as Weimar film critics driven from their German homeland because of their Jewish ancestry) no doubt influenced their postwar writings. What it meant to be Jewish and/or German in the Weimar Republic was ambiguous. To what extent Jewishness and Germanness were coextensive or mutually exclusive was unclear, at least until the Nazis came to power and racialized diverse individuals as Jews and mixed breeds (*Mischlinge*), based on ancestry rather than religious identification, and began to excise them from German culture. Kracauer emigrated to Paris in 1933 and then to New York in 1941. Some early reviewers criticized *Caligari to Hitler* as a "refugee's revenge."⁴ Eisner, who was raised Protestant by parents who had converted from Judaism, also had to flee to Paris in 1933 because of Nazi antisemitism. Richard Roud notes, "Like many 'assimilated' German Jews [Eisner] was as much (if not more) German than Jewish. 'I wrote my books out of longing for German culture and nostalgia for the 1920s,' she said in 1982 when she received the first Helmut Käutner prize endowed by the city of Düsseldorf."⁵ By absorbing Weimar-era Jewish-German film professionals seamlessly into the larger category of German, *Haunted Screen* expresses nostalgia for a time when the categories German and Jewish were not mutually exclusive, when Eisner's identification with German culture was not yet troubled by Nazi racializations, and when her longing for that culture was not yet tainted by Nazi crimes.

Refusing to distinguish between Jewish and non-Jewish German filmmakers, *Caligari to Hitler* and *Haunted Screen* react against Nazi antisemitism and film historiography. Nazis fixated on the involvement of Jewish people in Weimar cinema and blamed them for the industry's aesthetic, moral, and economic ills. A representative 1933 article in *Der Angriff*, the Berlin Nazi newspaper, claimed spuriously that 90 percent of Weimar film professionals were Jewish and that this Jewishness had infected Weimar film morally and artistically.[6] In 1935 Propaganda Minister Joseph Goebbels described the German film industry as having been "almost exclusively in non-Aryan hands" before 1933.[7] Nazi film historians exaggerated and condemned Jewish influence on Weimar cinema, combining inaccurate information and antisemitic stereotypes. For example, Carl Neumann, Curt Belling, and Hans Walther Betz's revisionist history of Weimar cinema, *Film-"Kunst," Film Kohn, Film Korruption* (Film "Art," Film Cohen, Film Corruption), detailed the Nazis' *Kampf* (struggle) to replace Jewish-corrupted "film in Germany" with an artistically and racially worthy "German film."[8] Neumann, Belling, and Betz claimed that Jews had controlled 90 percent of Weimar film studios and comprised 80–90 percent of film personnel.[9] They contended that Jewish greed had caused Weimar film's moral decadence and aesthetic bankruptcy.[10] Writing in exile, Kracauer and Eisner challenged the Nazi narrative of Weimar cinema, which treated Jewishness as if it were opposed to both Germanness and art, by arguing that works by both Jewish and non-Jewish filmmakers similarly reflected a German national character and aesthetic tradition and by praising the artistry of Jewish filmmakers alongside non-Jewish ones. In not marking German film professionals as either Jewish or not Jewish in their writings, Kracauer and Eisner wrote as if they were blind to Jewish difference, in contrast to the antisemitic visions of Nazi film historians, who saw Jews everywhere.

Working within a racist-nationalist framework that this volume wholeheartedly rejects, the Nazis were preoccupied with the contributions of Jewish people to Weimar cinema and what effects those contributions might have had. Burdened by such Nazi criticisms of Jewish filmmakers and their impact, postwar scholarship on Weimar film tended to downplay the ethnoreligious background of German-Jewish film professionals, following the lead of *Caligari to Hitler* and *Haunted Screen*. By the turn of the twenty-first century, a new approach to the Jewish presence in Weimar cinema that centered the contributions of Jewish filmmakers without reinforcing antisemitic assumptions was long overdue. In 2004 and 2005, respectively, Irene Stratenwerth and Hermann Simon's edited volume, *Pioniere in Celluloid: Juden in der Frühen Filmwelt* (*Pioneers of Celluloid: Jews in the Early Film World*) and S.S. Prawer's *Between Two Worlds: The Jewish Presence in German and Austrian Film 1910–1933* coaxed the Jewishness of many early film professionals in Germany back into the limelight. Through these books, some forgotten figures and the Jewishness of other better-known ones reentered contemporary scholarly consciousness. Increasing numbers of articles and book chapters thematized the Jewishness of Weimar film professionals and integrated tools and methods from contemporary Jewish, ethnic, and cultural studies into their scholarship on Weimar film.

In 2012, Ofer Ashkenazi's *Weimar Film and Modern Jewish Identity* reframed Weimar cinema as a major site of German-Jewish experience, which provided a "unique sphere in which Jewish 'outsiders' could influence the shaping of mainstream bourgeois culture."[11] He argued that Weimar cinema's liberal cosmopolitanism reflected experiences of and debates around Jewish assimilation through a process of double coding, which exposed its Jewishness only to the canny eye. Ashkenazi's work opened the door to new ways of thinking about the role of Jewishness in the creation of Weimar cinema as well as its indirect expressions. *Rethinking Jewishness in Weimar Cinema* supplements Stratenwerth and Simon's, Prawer's, and Ashkenazi's important contributions, offering additional historical, theoretical, and methodological approaches to Jewish involvement in the Weimar film industry, and presenting new case studies.

Writing about the Jewishness of Weimar cinema and Weimar film professionals poses thorny theoretical and methodological problems. How is it even possible to identify film professionals as Jewish? And whose guidelines do we use? Different approaches to these questions lead to the vastly different statistics cited above about the number of Jewish film professionals in Weimar and also to the different emphases on their Jewishness in the secondary literature. Believing, as this volume's editors and contributors do, that Jewishness encompasses not only religious but also secular identities and practices, how do we conceptualize it in a historically and theoretically responsible way, which not only accounts for observant Jews but also includes nonpracticing Jews and even people who may not have identified themselves as Jewish, while trying to avoid the pitfalls of historical discourses that treated Jews as a race? Answering this question requires both a historical and theoretical foundation.

The chapters in this volume consider Jewishness as both an ethnoreligious identity assigned to or embraced by various film professionals and a conceptual category within the larger framework of Jewish difference. Lisa Silverman theorizes Jewish difference as a widespread and influential signifying system in German-speaking interwar Europe.

Analogous to and intersecting with systems like gender, race, and class, Jewish difference codes people, behaviors, objects, representations, and the like as Jewish or non-Jewish. Such coding as Jewish or non-Jewish affects individuals' positions within a hierarchical social structure as well as the representations, identifications, and social structures available to them.[12]

Some Weimar film professionals openly discussed being Jewish and drew on their Jewish heritage in their work. Ernst Lubitsch, for example, began his career with comedies set in urban Jewish communities and drew overtly on Jewish traditions of humor. In a 1916 interview in the *Kinematograph* with Julius Urgiß, Lubitsch spoke about Jewish humor as central to his work and to cinema itself.[13] Not all Jewish artists in Weimar Germany, however, integrated their Jewishness into their work as overtly as Lubitsch did. Yet numerous film professionals are known to have had Jewish origins, for example actor Elisabeth Bergner and director Paul Czinner. In other cases, conversion, mixed heritage, and other factors make it difficult to decide whether to include particular artists in a study of Jewish film production or to interpret their work through that critical lens. Fritz Lang, director of Weimar classics such as *Metropolis* (1925–26) and *M* (1931), is a good example of such a problematic case. Lang was raised strictly Roman Catholic. He considered himself Catholic and it is easy to spot Catholic motifs in films like *Metropolis* and *Das wandernde Bild* (*The Wandering Image*; 1920).[14] Although Lang's Jewish-born mother had converted to Catholicism before he was born, the Nazi-era Nuremberg Laws classified Lang as a half-Jew; some later scholarship has also treated him as such.

As illustrated by the example of Fritz Lang, Jewish identity is defined and experienced differently from inside and outside and changes over time. In *Recovering Jewishness: Modern Identities Reclaimed*, Frederick Roden argues that "culturally mixed identities" and figures of cultural slippage such as Lang exemplify a modern Jewish identity that is always already split, hybrid, and liminal. Such liminality is key also for Sander Gilman. In the introduction to *Jewish Frontiers*, Gilman describes Jewishness as a border zone, characterized by intercultural contact and ambivalence. The Jews who occupy this space, according to Gilman, are those who understood themselves as Jews at a specific moment in time.[15] This would seem to return us, methodologically, to considering only individuals who self-identified as Jewish. Yet Gilman suggests that individuals' self-understanding as Jewish is not necessarily self-conscious. Gilman states, "The Jews are to be understood as a multiple yet single entity. Multiple because of the culture manifested under that label and yet unitary because of the common archeology or cultural identity they believe they share—even those who are never self-consciously part of the Jews."[16] This liminal, contradictory identity as elaborated throughout Gilman's writings is a discursive construct that has been naturalized through scientific and biomedical discourses and internalized by Jewish subjects, whether or not—as Gilman posits here—they consciously identify with it.

Together with Gilman and other contemporary scholars in German-Jewish studies, the editors of this volume understand Jewishness in the Weimar context as a permeable, malleable, and constructed category at the contested border of Germanness, a position that people may occupy whether or not they are aware of it and that images and performances can signify, whether or not the artists behind them identify as Jewish. The flexibility, fluidity, and intangibility of the boundaries between Jewishness and Germanness correspond with Leo Spitzer's account of the situational marginality experienced by people undergoing the process of assimilation, in which the social membrane that separates marginal and dominant groups remains inconsistent and permeable.[17] We propose that an understanding of how Jewishness was conceived in the Weimar Republic, filtered through a contemporary theoretical framework that emphasizes the construction, coding, and visibility of Jewishness, can provide a solid foundation for rethinking Jewishness in Weimar cinema. Such an approach considers historical rhetoric of blood and ancestry, spirituality, culture, and assimilation that were current in the Weimar Republic and applies different contemporary ways of thinking about the construction and representation of Jewishness to films produced in that context.

Identifying Jews and Identifying as Jewish in Weimar

The parameters of Jewish identity in Weimar Germany were varied and ambiguous, bound up in notions of blood and ancestry; discussions of spirituality, politics, culture, and assimilation; and experiences of antisemitism. In the period following World War I, Germany experienced a rise in antisemitism and nationalism, as is evident in the *Judenzählung* (Jew count)—an effort to expose the supposed unwillingness of Jews to participate in the war effort. It was also believed that Jews were unsupportive of Germany through the allegiance of left-wing Jews who signed the Versailles Treaty. Additionally, some Germans blamed Jews for the 1918–19 socialist revolutions and eastern European Jewish refugees for the urban blight that afflicted many German cities in the interwar years. Moreover, eugenic ideology legitimated a conception of Jews as afflicted by hysteria and prone to revolutionary ideas—not merely genetically different but also diseased.

German-Jewish intellectuals of the period including Martin Buber, Franz Rosenzweig, and Gershom Scholem found a spiritual connection in various Jewish texts with particular focus on works from the kabalistic tradition. Although each of these thinkers produced significant scholarly works, they were also clearly moved by their spiritual studies, as well as motivated to disseminate their learning to the wider Jewish community. Notably, Rosenzweig led the famous *Lehrhaus*, the Free Jewish School of adult learning in Frankfurt am Main. There was also increasing support among Jewish intellectuals for establishing a Jewish state in Palestine. Gershom Scholem would ultimately move to Palestine, while other intellectuals including Walter Benjamin seriously considered this option. Socialism, spiritualism, and Zionism each offered young disenfranchised Jewish Germans an alternative to attempting to integrate into the wider culture.

Notwithstanding those Jews who identified with socialist and Zionist causes, the majority of German Jews were committed to full participation in Weimar society with respect to custom and language. In Oskar Karbach's 1921 article "Das Princip der Assimilation" (The Principle of Assimilation), he notes that the ideas of the Enlightenment brought equal rights to Jews through a system of individualism.[18] As members of a world community, Jews shared in the same privileges and problems as the rest of society.[19] As individuals, Jews could serve a higher purpose, which would benefit all members of society—Jews and non-Jews alike.[20]

Mose Beilinson was skeptical of the idea of Jewish integration. In his 1923 "Untergang der Assimilation" (Downfall of Assimilation), Beilinson notes that assimilation is always failing—Jews live in metaphysical exile: "The Jewish people can disappear from the world without a trace. . . . The spirit of Jewishness will only become more permanent from this act."[21] According to Beilinson, after integration into the majority culture, assimilated Jews will still possess a hidden emptiness and anxiety that belies full participation.[22]

In his article "Forget Assimilation: Introducing Subjectivity to German-Jewish History," contemporary critic Scott Spector problematizes the notion of Jewish assimilation in early-twentieth-century Germany, so eloquently analyzed by Karbach and Beilinson. Spector notes that German-Jewish history is varied in the twentieth century—

individual Jewish subjectivity speaks against strong binaries of assimilation and dissimilation. Spector cites Gershom Scholem's 1966 lecture on Germans and Jews, reminding the reader that Scholem initially regards these categories as unstable in that not all Germans are Germans and not all Jews are Jews.[23] These generalizations used to categorize individuals are both dangerous and inaccurate, with an "excess of empathy" assumed by scholars who treat this problematic.[24]

Challenging the unstable categories, Spector notes that Jews who called themselves (or were called) assimilated could go beyond the term, and that we should try to capture how individuals lived in the world. Scholars should in turn look at cultural contributions in order to discuss how German Jews as subjects lived in their time period. We should not merely draw binaries in light of the destruction of the Shoah, but instead take into consideration nuance: "The historical exploration of subjectivity is a search for context."[25]

Various scholars have, in fact, studied the way in which German Jews of the early twentieth century expressed their subjectivity within the context of historical circumstances. Michael Brenner in his work *The Renaissance of Jewish Culture in Weimar Germany* mentions Jews who participated in a "particular Jewish sphere" as cultural realm, while still living in the majority culture.[26] These Jewish individuals, similar to Spector's assessment, occupied multiple subject positions, taking "inspiration from German myths and Hasidic tales."[27] The variety of practices, identifications, and cultural contributions by Jews in the Weimar Republic was in truth varied: some took part in traditional Judaism, while others were completely dissimilated from Jewish life.[28] Additionally, there were liberal Jews who sought to reform Jewish traditions into new "literary, artistic, and scholarly expressions." For these Jews, cultural associations and clubs "advanced a collective identity among German Jews" that differed from non-Jewish surroundings.[29]

The reform movement sought to refashion Jewish tradition by emphasizing spirituality over ritual. They believed they were drawing on authentic Judaism, which could serve as the foundation of genuine *Gemeinschaft* (community).[30] Obviously, not all scholarly works by German-speaking Jews contributed to this cultural tradition; Brenner notes that neither Sigmund Freud nor Albert Einstein was part of this movement, but only those Jews who were affiliated with Jewish organizations and thus consciously engaged in producing a specifically Jewish culture.[31]

Leora Auslander discusses the implicit ambivalence of constructing a Jewish identity in Weimar. German Jews at the beginning of the twentieth century were able to negotiate multiple identities within mainstream German society.[32] At the same time, Jews tended to socialize with other Jews, with whom they shared a sense of greater familiarity.[33] Auslander contends, "The majority of Berliners of Jewish origin were not divorced from Jewish sensibility, whether or not they were believers, practicing, or defined themselves as Jewish" and that German Jews had a unique relationship with "the senses, to time, to history, to the home and to the material world."[34] While fully participating in the dominant German culture, German Jews thus retained a Jewish identity in which cultural practices were transformed and transmitted, even when they were not conscious of this fact.[35] Jews have a specific relation to time and space, since various historical events such as the exodus are integrated into ritual. The past is thus transmitted and renarrated through family and the wider Jewish community.[36]

Jakob Wassermann's *My Life as a German and Jew* (1921), exemplifies the ambiguity of the Weimar Jewish sensibility. Wassermann explores his own Jewish identity while recognizing that his Jewish identity poses a threat to his Germanness. Wassermann regards his Jewishness as a racial identity rather than a conscious decision to join a religious group.[37] He believes that his Jewishness broadens his possibilities in life, intellectually and spiritually, and refuses to be judged by those who judged him on account of this: "I was a Jew; that told the whole story. I could not change it and did not wish to change it."[38] Wassermann notes that he does not have stereotypical features that are considered Jewish—he mentions his "straight nose," his "quiet demeanor" and his blond hair, but also concedes that these are primitive ideas.[39] In sum, he is proud of his Jewish heritage even if this identity comes with its own tensions and responsibilities.[40] While Wassermann notes that other Jews might desire to be "Aryan," he refuses to associate with Christian symbols out of an unconscious experience that lay in the blood.[41]

Wassermann's sense of his Jewish identity as rooted in his heredity reflects Weimar's wider discussion of Jewish identity. According to Donald Niewyk, there was a common belief among Weimar Jews that unique mental and physical characteristics were in fact passed down to each successive generation.[42] Ludwig Holländer states in his 1932 speech, "Warum sind und bleiben wir Juden?" (Why are we and why do we remain Jews?) that appeared in the *Central-Verein Zeitung*, that there lives in each Jew the totality of their Jewish elders.[43] Jewish religion and custom are carried down from one generation to the next in a "long-term memory." Holländer notes that the Jewish ideal is found in personality, religion, family, social-ethical behavior, as well as knowledge. Jews are, for Holländer, the *Ebenbild Gottes* (direct reflection of God).[44]

One must be sensitive to the ways in which Jews themselves during this period appealed to the heredity of their Jewish identity and how this sort of racial discourse would be used against them by the Nazis. Ideas of racial consciousness were popular in the Jewish community, with Jewish writers positing that the Jewish "race" belonged to the plethora of races found in the German community. Kurt Alexander, member of the Jewish fraternity Sprevia, thus affirms that Jews are members of a *Gemeinschaft* because they have a soul created by blood.[45] He further contended that the strength of the Jewish community rooted in its bloodline will allow Jewish men to lift up the fatherland from the depths of defeat in World War I.[46] The resistance to rank the Jewish "race" as compared to other races distinguished Jewish thinkers from eugenic proponents like Eugen Fischer.[47]

The notion of the blood and soul of the Jew, popular in German discourse in the 1920s is also attuned to the ever-present antisemitism following World War I. Wassermann considers himself an ancestral Jew with a sense of justice born into him from the soul of a people who have lived through many generations of suffering.[48] This sense of innate justice forces him to bristle at the supposed German hatred that he is shown. As a German Jew, Wassermann feels German himself: "In my innocence I had always been convinced that I was a part of German life."[49] He does not see the difference between the two groups, trying to fathom whether it is faith or blood that divides the two.[50]

In his work, Wassermann outlines the blatant antisemitism that he has experienced as a German Jew: "Against me he [the German] wants to set himself."[51] Wassermann's German friend explains to Wassermann that the German and Jewish spirits cannot mix because Jews could never identify with the host nation in their supposed social and religious isolation, lack of will to identify as German, and pride in tradition; the friend additionally notes that Jews are "criminals" and "usurers."[52] According to Wassermann, as a Jew living in Germany you cannot demand "full pay"—you are considered to be "pockmarked."[53] Wassermann regards the antisemitism he experienced as a character flaw in the German people.[54] For Wassermann, the German and the Jew are antagonistic figures.[55]

Antisemitism was also a common theme in Martin Buber's Jewish journal, *Der Jude: eine Monatsschrift*. In the 1925 special issue entitled "Antisemitismus und Volkstum" (Antisemitism and Jewish National Characteristics), various German authors (both Jews and non-Jews) commented on antisemitism in Germany and Europe. Writer Otto Flake in his essay "Antisemitismus und Zukunft" (Antisemitism and the Future) offers a particularly poisonous view of Jews, positing that the hatred of Jewry is a natural historical occurrence, appearing at the slightest provocation.[56] Behind the historical need to persecute the Jews is that Jews as a "race" supposedly crucified Christ. Flake maintains further that there is a price to be paid for living as a separate nation within Germany.[57] In their refusal to assimilate into the host country, Jews must give up the desire to take on a national German style of writing and expression of ideas. For Flake, Jews have no right to make demands.[58]

Coarse antisemitism like Flake's was widespread at the time in Germany. Members of all classes believed that Jews controlled the German economy and German political movements, and were the arbiters of unwholesome cultural trends.[59] In particular, antisemitism was spread by the German *völkish* (ethnic and nationalist) groups such as the League for Defense and Defiance, which considered Jews to be unpatriotic.[60] In his essay entitled "Pharisäertum," Martin Buber decries Flake's blatant stereotypes of the Jews and disagrees that Jews should be forced to assimilate into a supposed host culture. For Buber, the Jews will survive each onslaught of antisemitism: this sense of survival supposedly appears in every Jewish heart.[61]

Moritz Goldstein supports the ideas of Buber and offers the last word in the special issue. He notes that every young German Jew recognizes his condition and feels shame, together with a desire to break free of hate and mistrust, and to foster fair play.[62] Instead of interacting with those they mistrust, young Jews must recognize that they live in a world of enemies. The recipe is to protect oneself, avoid the everconsuming talk about the German-Jewish situation, and grow and accomplish something beyond the shackles of antisemitism. For Goldstein, time is too valuable to discuss this matter endlessly. Many Jewish people in Weimar Germany followed Goldstein's dictum, creating lives, cultures, and texts that transcended antisemitism, even as they reflected experiences, standpoints, and tropes that contemporary observers may or may not recognize as Jewish.

Locating Jewishness in Weimar Film

Representations of Jewishness and Jewish difference in Weimar cinema can be difficult to recognize, because they were entangled in anxieties about visibility and performance. Darcy Buerkle analyzes E.A. Dupont's 1923 film *Das alte Gesetz* (*The Ancient Law*), which follows the travails of a rabbi's son, Baruch Mayer, and his flight from a small Jewish community in order to act on the grand stage in Vienna. Buerkle examines the identity and affect of the religious Jew, balancing the laws of the Torah with that of the majority culture, and notes that modern Jewish identity in the guise of assimilation is achieved through the practice of passing. With long mirror scenes and shot-reverse-shots, Baruch interrogates himself and is in return interrogated by the audience: "[Baruch] has left the shtetl in body but as a new arrival and as an actor, he has specifically chosen an existence that cultivates an audience. . . . He will have to make daily decisions not to be seen as a Jew."[63] *Das alte Gesetz* is a film about being a Jew in a secular world with an anxious subtext of hiding one's Jewishness.

According to Buerkle, the spectator is also always aware that Baruch is a Jew, and the constant negotiation of identity makes the viewer anxious on Baruch's behalf.[64] The anxiety that this passing provokes is felt by the assimilated Jewish spectator, as well as the spectator who is not a Jew in an essentialized sense or even a self-identified Jew. It is at once present for the historical spectator who is faced with this lived experience in Weimar Germany.[65] For all the positive discourse of assimilation in *Das alte Gesetz* (Baruch becomes a star, he marries his sweetheart from the shtetl, his parents see his performance), the danger of being seen as a Jew in Weimar is a potent message. Ultimately, Baruch's most notable sign of Jewishness, his sidelocks, must remain hidden so he is not seen as laughable. When he cuts off his sidelocks, his Jewishness becomes invisible to the audience, but his constant negotiation between Jewishness and assimilated existence never ceases; he carries a Siddur in his pocket when he is forced to perform on the High Holidays. The hidden prayer book is "a central affective circumstance for German-Jews during Weimar": living an assimilated life, the Jew may at any time be unmasked.[66]

Buerkle argues that Jewishness in Weimar is "a category that is both powerful and largely unspoken," one that was frequently silenced or displaced by anxiety, shame, and the "symbolic public effacement of Jewishness."[67] Kerry Wallach's readings of diverse cultural texts in *Passing Illusions: Jewish Visibility in Weimar Germany* reveal the disclosure and concealment of Jewishness in Weimar Germany to have been an infinitely complex matter, which was governed by multiple varying factors, motivations, and dynamics between Jewish and non-Jewish performers and spectators—in life, on the page, on stage, and onscreen.

Given its inconsistent visibility, Jewishness and the corresponding conceptual frame of Jewish difference are not always easy to locate in Weimar films. Between the widespread involvement of Jewish film professionals, the multiplicities of German-Jewish identities and cultures, the tense affects around Jewish positionalities, and the complex dynamics around Jewish visibility in Germany, Jewishness circulates in Weimar cinema similarly to the "inferential ethnic presences" of Hollywood cinema, as described by Ella Shohat, which "penetrate the screen without always literally being represented by ethnic and racial themes or even characters."[68]

Ashkenazi's *Weimar Film and Modern Jewish Identity* provides important interpretive tools and historical context for locating subtle and elusive traces of Jewishness in Weimar cinema. Ashkenazi builds on the work of Henry Bial, who argues that Jewish-American identity has been shaped by the coding and decoding of Jewishness on stage and screen, by performances that are double coded, insofar as they are differently recognizable to Jewish and non-Jewish spectators.[69] By directing our attention to the performativity and double coding of Jewishness in Weimar cinema, Ashkenazi shows how Jews in the Weimar film industry could craft, albeit through hidden meaning, the hopeful process of acculturation and social mobility. Ashkenazi cites German sociologist Georg Simmel's notion of the stranger as an analogy for the Jew in the modern world: "an integrated person whose presence nevertheless articulates 'externality and opposition.'"[70] Ashkenazi theorizes that assimilation of Jews into Weimar Germany—the "absorption of bourgeois values and norms" into the modern Jewish experience—included the adoption of *Bildung* (personal cultivation and education) in crafting a liberal morality.[71] In an urban milieu that accepted various ethnicities, Jewish middle-class individuals could take part as equals in a formation of a multicultural and middle-class society.[72] Cinema was a medium whereby Jewish artists could influence the shaping of mainstream bourgeois culture and also provide the particular vocabulary that allowed for integration of the hopes and fears of Jews.[73] Through film and the double coding of Jewish difference, the contemplation of Jewish assimilation would take place in "the constitution of a multicultural, liberal community that would accept the notion of multilayered identity."[74]

Deep knowledge of context and close attention to detail are required in order to recognize such subtle articulations of Jewish difference, knowledge and skill that the contributors to this volume all showcase in their analyses of the Weimar film industry. Their analyses expand on Ashkenazi's work, introducing lesser-known films and figures, exploring the work of Jewish-identified Weimar film professionals, and analyzing different modes of Jewish visibility and the articulation of Jewish difference in Weimar cinema. Together, they offer a clear snapshot of the robust scholarly conversations taking place today.

Jewishness in Weimar Germany is a multifaceted phenomenon. Ancestry, spirituality, culture, and experiences of assimilation and antisemitism constituted core traits for people who self-identified as Jews. Discourses of Jewish difference constructed, coded, and differentiated between the Jewish and the non-Jewish. The chapters in this volume explain different ways in which this complex phenomenon manifests in and around cinema of the Weimar Republic and they offer conceptual, theoretical, and methodological tools with which to unpack it. The chapters and the tools they deploy emphasize the visibility, construction, coding, and decoding of Jewishness in Weimar cinema. Most of them center around films and figures that have received little scholarly attention. In doing so, the chapters build on contemporary work at the intersection of German-Jewish studies, film studies, and cultural studies, contribute to our scholarly archive, and introduce new sites and methods for rethinking Jewishness in Weimar cinema.

In the first part of this volume, chapters by Maya Barzilai, Margrit Frölich, Kerry Wallach, Mila Ganeva, and Ervin Malakaj consider how and to what extent the Jewishness of select Weimar film professionals was on display, on and off screen. Case studies of Jewish-identified public figures, including Henrik Galeen, Alexander Granach, Maria Orska, Siegfried Arno, and Alfred Rosenthal, offer new perspectives on casting, stereotyping, self-representation, and strategic (in)visibility. These case studies delve into different modes of visibility, including typecasting, performance, humor, and film criticism, and explain what these different modes of visibility reveal about and how they may have shaped Jewishness in the Weimar film industry. They provide methodological and theoretical insights not only for German-Jewish film studies but also for ethnic studies in other film cultures.

In the second group of chapters, Philipp Stiasny, Valerie Weinstein, Lisa Silverman, and Anjeana K. Hans demonstrate how to decode markers of Jewish difference in films that on the surface do not appear to be about Jews. The films analyzed in this section cover a broad range, from *Zwei Welten* (*Two Worlds*; 1930, dir. E.A. Dupont), which thematizes antisemitism explicitly; to lighter fare like *Die Drei von der Tankstelle* (*The Three from the Filling Station*; 1930, dir. Wilhelm Thiele) and comedies starring Franziska Gaal, which she made in exile. Chapters in this part also scrutinize melodramas: *Anders als die Andern* (*Different from the Others*; 1919, dir. Richard Oswald) and *Die freudlose Gasse* (*The Joyless Street*; 1925, dir. G.W. Pabst). Both these films are well known for their political interventions regarding gender and sexuality, but the analyses here reveal how Jewish difference plays a significant part in these films as well. The diverse film analyses in this part of the volume highlight the importance of historical context for understanding Jewish difference in Weimar cinema, because Jewishness was often repressed, displaced, or expressed through markers of other kinds of difference. The authors of the chapters in this part both elaborate on salient features of Weimar culture and explain how this background helps them recognize signifiers of Jewish difference in various films, despite its seeming absence. They trace Jewishness and its absence across dialogue, character, narrative, and other filmic elements and explain their significance in historical perspective. The close readings and careful contextualizations in these chapters illustrate how and where to look for Jewishness in Weimar cinema when that Jewishness has been masked or double coded.

Jewish-identified filmmakers and spectators, however, were not alone in coding and decoding Jewishness in Weimar cinema. Therefore, we include a third group of chapters in our volume that examines how Weimar-era antisemites coded and decoded Jewish difference and their role in constructing Jewishness in Weimar and Weimar cinema. These chapters, by Barbara Hales, Brook Henkel, Christian Rogowski, Andréas-Benjamin Seyfert, and Ofer Ashkenazi foreground antisemitism's performative function in respect to Jewishness. Just as Nazi law racialized people as Jews or *Mischlinge*, based on their ancestry, and thereby reshaped their identity and fate, antisemitic discourses made films and filmic representations Jewish by proclaiming them such. The chapters in this part explain how antisemitic discourses constructed Jewishness in and around sexual hygiene films, in the outraged reception of Hanns Walter Kornblum's *Die Grundlagen der Einsteinschen Relativitätstheorie* (*The Basic Principles of the Einstein Theory of Relativity*; 1922) and Ludwig Berger's *Der Meister von Nürnberg* (*The Master of Nuremberg*; 1927), and through the Nazi-era excision of Jewishness from *Brennendes Geheimnis* (*Burning Secret*; 1932–33, dir. Robert Siodmak) and remakes of *Die Geierwally* (*The Vulture-Wally*; 1921 and 1939–40) and *Peter Voss, der Millionendieb* (*Peter Voss: Thief of Millions*; 1932 and 1943–46). Such antisemitic constructions of Jewish difference, which were a component of Weimar cinema's complex and contradictory relation to Jewishness, would become dominant in Third Reich cinema and in Nazi film historiography.

As a coda we include Cynthia Walk's brief chapter about the process of film preservation and the restoration of E.A. Dupont's *Das alte Gesetz* and Hugo Bettauer's *Die Stadt ohne Juden* (*The City Without Jews*; 1924), followed by a more formal afterword. Walk's chapter on film preservation helps us consider how to restore Weimar cinema's Jewishness today. Film restoration grapples with questions similar to our scholarly ones: How can we reconstruct Weimar film from its remaining fragments and how do we frame it for a contemporary audience? Where was Jewishness located in that past and how was it received? How can we make it legible to audiences today? How do we balance what we think we know about the past with today's resources, interests, and needs? The pragmatic, artistic, and historically informed decisions made by *Das alte Gesetz*'s and *Die Stadt ohne Juden*'s restoration teams inspire our scholarly inquiry. Our conclusion reflects on the results of that inquiry, questions it has raised, and on future directions it might take.

Barbara Hales is a Professor of History and Humanities at the University of Houston-Clear Lake. Her publications focus on film history of the Weimar Republic and the Third Reich. She is the author of *Black Magic Woman: Gender and the Occult in Weimar Germany* (Peter Lang, Oxford, 2021). She has also co-edited a volume entitled *Continuity and Crisis in German Cinema 1928-1936* for Camden House in 2016 (with Mihaela Petrescu and Valerie Weinstein). Dr. Hales is President of the Houston based organization, Center for Medicine After the Holocaust.

Valerie Weinstein is Professor of Women's, Gender, and Sexuality Studies, Niehoff Professor in Film and Media Studies, and affiliate faculty in German Studies and Judaic Studies at the University of Cincinnati. She is the author of *Antisemitism in Film Comedy in Nazi Germany* (Indiana University Press, 2019) and numerous articles on Weimar and Nazi cinema. She is co-editor, with Barbara Hales and Mihaela Petrescu, of *Continuity and Crisis in German Cinema 1928-1936* (Camden House, 2016).

Notes

1. Lotte Eisner, *The Haunted Screen* (Berkeley: University of California Press, 1994), 310.
2. Thorold Dickinson, "Review of *The Haunted Screen, Sight and Sound*," 39 (1, Winter 1969): 52.
3. Ofer Ashkenazi, *Weimar Film and Modern Jewish Identity* (New York: Palgrave Macmillan, 2012), 159.
4. Leonard Quaresima, "Introduction to the 2004 Edition: Rereading Kracauer," *From Caligari to Hitler* (1947; reprint Princeton, NJ: Princeton University Press, 2004), xl.
5. Richard Roud, "The Moral Taste of Lotte Eisner," *Sight and Sound* 53 (2, Spring 1984): 140.
6. "Verjudung und Geschäftemacherei im 'deutschen' Film," *Der Angriff*, 1 March 1933, first insert (1. Beilage).
7. A[lbert] S[chneider], "Dr. Goebbels vor den Filmschaffenden: Ein neues Bekenntnis zum Film," *Lichtbild-Bühne*, 16 December 1935.
8. Carl Neumann, Curt Belling, and Hans-Walther Betz, *Film "Kunst," Film Kohn, Film Korruption* (Berlin: Verlag Hermann Scherping, 1937), 15.
9. Neumann et al., *Film "Kunst,"* 26, 39, 106.
10. Neumann et al., *Film "Kunst,"* 5 et passim.
11. Ashkenazi, *Weimar Film and Modern Jewish Identity*, 3.
12. Lisa Silverman, "Reconsidering the Margins: Jewishness as an Analytical Framework," *Journal of Modern Jewish Studies* 8 (1, March 2009): 103–20; Lisa Silverman, "Beyond Antisemitism: A Critical Approach to German Jewish Cultural History," in *Nexus 1: Essays in German Jewish Studies*, 27–45 (Rochester, NY: Camden House, 2011); Lisa Silverman, *Becoming Austrians: Jews and Culture Between the World Wars* (Oxford: Oxford University Press, 2012).
13. Julius Urgiß, "Künstlerprofil: Ernst Lubitsch," *Der Kinematograph*, Düsseldorf, 30 August 1916, rpt. *Lubitsch*, ed. Hans Helmut Prinzler and Enno Patalas, Munich 1984, 89–90.
14. Barry Keith Grant, ed., *Fritz Lang: Interviews* (Jackson: University Press of Mississippi, 2003), 163.
15. Sander Gilman, *Jewish Frontiers: Essays on Bodies, Histories, and Identities* (New York: Palgrave Macmillan, 2003), 25.
16. Gilman, *Jewish Frontiers*, 26.
17. Leo Spitzer, *Lives in Between: Assimilation and Marginality in Austria, Brazil, and West Africa, 1780–1945* (Cambridge: Cambridge University Press, 1989).
18. Oskar Karbach, "Das Princip der Assimilation," *Der Jude: eine Monatsschrift* 6 (9, 1921–22): 522.
19. Three-quarters of German Jews in Weimar were liberals. Liberal pressures from the outside also urged Jews to "amalgamate and disappear" as conservative critique intensified: after World War I, "thousands of Jews quietly changed their names and religion, and frequently intermarried as well." Donald L. Niewyk, *The Jews in Weimar Germany* (New Brunswick: Transaction, 2001), 96.
20. Karbach, "Das Princip," 524.
21. Mose Beilinson, "Untergang der Assimilation," *Der Jude: eine Monatsschrift* 7 (3, 1923): 174. (Das jüdische Volk kann spurlos in der Welt zerrinnen. . . . Der Geist des Judentums wird davon nur noch fester werden.")
22. Beilinson, "Untergang der Assimilation," 174.

23. Scott Spector, "Forget Assimilation: Introducing Subjectivity to German-Jewish History," *Jewish History* 20 (3–4, 2006): 350. See Gershom Scholem, "Jews and Germans," in *On Jews and Judaism in Crisis: Selected Essays, Gershom Scholem*. Ed. Werner J. Dannhauser (Philadelphia: Paul Dry Books, 2012), 71–92.
24. Spector, "Forget Assimilation," 350.
25. Spector, "Forget Assimilation," 391.
26. Michael Brenner, *The Renaissance of Jewish Culture in Weimar Germany* (New Haven, CT: Yale University Press, 1996), 2.
27. Brenner, *Renaissance*, 2.
28. Brenner, *Renaissance*, 2–3.
29. Brenner, *Renaissance*, 5.
30. Brenner, *Renaissance*, 6–7. Both cultural production as well as social welfare were a part of this collective experience.
31. Brenner, *Renaissance*, 5.
32. Leora Auslander, "The Boundaries of Jewishness, or When Is a Cultural Practice Jewish?" *Journal of Modern Jewish Studies* 8 (1, March 2009): 57.
33. Auslander, "Boundaries," 60.
34. Auslander, "Boundaries," 57, 59.
35. Auslander, "Boundaries," 48.
36. Auslander, "Boundaries," 57, 59. Auslander does not support a simplistic determined identity—"No one cultural location completely saturates an individual's mode of being"—but she does support a construct of identity that is passed on even when we are not conscious of it. We live in a world of marked categories, and we are creators/transmitters of ideas. Auslander argues not to let all Jewish history stand in the shadow of the Shoah, in order that we should not let Third Reich racial classifications "impoverish our analytical imagination and therefore the history of prewar European Jewry." Auslander, "Boundaries," 60.
37. Jakob Wassermann, *My Life as a German and Jew*, trans. S. N. Brainin (New York: Coward-McCann, 1933), 16–17.
38. Wassermann, *My Life*, 170.
39. Wassermann, *My Life*, 11–12.
40. Wassermann, *My Life*, 90.
41. Wassermann, *My Life*, 23.
42. Niewyk, *Jews in Weimar*, 100.
43. Ludwig Holländer, "Warum sind und bleiben wir Juden?" *Central-Verein Zeitung: Allgemeine Zeiung des Judentums* 11, no. 51. Berlin, 16 December, 1932, 513.
44. Holländer, "Warum sind und bleiben wir Juden?," 513.
45. Kurt Alexander, "Tendenzrede: gehalten auf dem Festkommens zum 25. Jubiläum der 'Sprevia' am 3 November, 1919," *K.C. Blätter: Monatschrift der im Kartell-Convent Korporationen* 9 (11–12; November–December 1919), 181.
46. Alexander, "Tendenzrede," 180–81. This speech was given on 3 November 1919 in a celebration of the Jewish fraternity Sprevia's twenty-fifth anniversary. The defeat mentioned here would be Germany's defeat in World War I.
47. Some of the more famous scientists involved with the German racial hygiene movement include Fritz Lenz, Eugen Fischer, and Ernst Rüdin, all with medical degrees working across a wide range of disciplines including anthropology and psychiatry. The intention of these doctors was to support the procreation of the healthy members of society, while curtailing births from groups deemed to be asocial, criminal, or mentally disabled.

48. Wassermann, *My Life*, 272–73.
49. Wassermann, *My Life*, 81.
50. Wassermann, *My Life*, 77–79.
51. Wassermann, *My Life*, 171.
52. Wassermann, *My Life*, 172, 83, 86.
53. Wassermann, *My Life*, 150.
54. Wassermann, *My Life*, 221.
55. Wassermann, *My Life*, 221.
56. Otto Flake, "Antisemitismus und Zukunft." *Der Jude: eine Monatsschrift* 1 Sonderheft, Antisemitismus und Volkstum (1925): 11.
57. Flake, "Antisemitismus," 12.
58. Flake, "Antisemitismus," 15. For Flake, Jews must be forced to suppress their Jewishness.
59. Niewyk, *Jews in Weimar*, 43.
60. Niewyk, *Jews in Weimar*, 47.
61. Martin Buber, "Pharisäertum," *Der Jude: eine Monatsschrift* 1 Sonderheft, Antisemitismus und Volkstum (1925): 131.
62. Moritz Goldstein, "Leisten, nicht grübeln!" *Der Jude: eine Monatsschrift* 1 Sonderheft, Antisemitismus und Volkstum (1925): 136.
63. Darcy Buerkle, "Caught in the Act: Norbert Elias, Emotion and The Ancient Law." *Journal of Modern Jewish Studies* 8.1 (March 2009): 93.
64. Buerkle, "Caught in the Act," 93.
65. Buerkle, "Caught in the Act," 94.
66. Buerkle, "Caught in the Act," 95–96.
67. Darcy Buerkle, *Nothing Happened: Charlotte Salomon and an Archive of Suicide* (Ann Arbor: University of Michigan Press, 2013), 3, 4. Also, Buerkle, "Caught in the Act." One example of the social and symbolic domination of both Jews and women in the Weimar Republic is the disappearance of new women coded as Jewish from advertising images in the early 1930s. See Darcy Buerkle, "Gendered Spectatorship, Jewish Women and Psychological Advertising in Weimar Germany," *Women's History Review* 15 (4, September 2006): 626.
68. Ella Shohat, "Ethnicities-in-Relation: Toward a Multicultural Reading of American Cinema," in *Unspeakable Images: Ethnicity and the American Cinema*, ed. Lester D. Friedman, 215–50 (Urbana: University of Illinois Press, 1991), 223.
69. Henry Bial, *Acting Jewish: Negotiating Ethnicity on the American Stage and Screen* (Ann Arbor: University of Michigan Press, 2005).
70. Ashkenazi, *Weimar Film*, xv. Georg Simmel, *Sociology: Inquiries into the Construction of Social Forms*, vol. 1 (Leiden: Brill, 2009), 601.
71. Ashkenazi, *Weimar Film*, 1–2. Although many German Jews in Weimar chose amalgamation into German culture, leaving Jewishness behind, the majority of liberal Jews instead supported assimilation or a mutual relationship of the majority culture and Jewish custom: "Jews would always have a separate identity, and they would be no less good Germans for it." Niewyk, *Jews in Weimar*, 99–100.
72. Ashkenazi, *Weimar Film*, 2.
73. Ashkenazi, *Weimar Film*, 3.
74. Ashkenazi, *Weimar Film*, 11.

Bibliography

Alexander, Kurt. "Tendenzrede: gehalten auf dem Festkommens zum 25. Jubiläum der 'Sprevia' am 3 November, 1919." *K.C. Blätter: Monatschrift der im Kartell-Convent Korporationen* 9 (11–12, November–December 1919): 179–81.

Ashkenazi, Ofer. *Weimar Film and Modern Jewish Identity*. New York: Palgrave Macmillan, 2012.

Auslander, Leora. "The Boundaries of Jewishness, or When Is a Cultural Practice Jewish?" *Journal of Modern Jewish Studies* 8 (1, March 2009): 47–64.

Beilinson, Mose. "Untergang der Assimilation." *Der Jude: eine Monatsschrift* 7 (3, 1923): 171–79.

Bial, Henry. *Acting Jewish: Negotiating Ethnicity on the American Stage and Screen*. Ann Arbor: University of Michigan Press, 2005.

Brenner, Michael. *The Renaissance of Jewish Culture in Weimar Germany*. New Haven, CT: Yale University Press, 1996.

Buber, Martin. "Pharisäertum." *Der Jude: eine Monatsschrift* 1 Sonderheft, "Antisemitismus und Volkstum" (1925): 123–31.

Buerkle, Darcy. "Caught in the Act: Norbert Elias, Emotion and the Ancient Law." *Journal of Modern Jewish Studies* 8 (1, March 2009): 83–102.

———. "Gendered Spectatorship, Jewish Women and Psychological Advertising in Weimar Germany." *Women's History Review* 15 (4, September 2006): 625–36.

———. *Nothing Happened: Charlotte Salomon and an Archive of Suicide*. Ann Arbor: University of Michigan Press, 2013.

Dickinson, Thorold. "Review of *The Haunted Screen*." *Sight and Sound* 39 (1, Winter 1969): 52.

Eisner, Lotte. *The Haunted Screen: Expressionism in the German Cinema and the Influence of Max Reinhardt*. France, 1952. Reprint, Berkeley: University of California Press, 1994.

Flake, Otto. "Antisemitismus und Zukunft." *Der Jude: eine Monatsschrift* 1 Sonderheft, "Antisemitismus und Volkstum" (1925): 10–17.

Gilman, Sander. *Jewish Frontiers: Essays on Bodies, Histories, and Identities*. New York: Palgrave Macmillan, 2003.

Goldstein, Moritz. "Leisten, nicht grübeln!" *Der Jude: eine Monatsschrift* 1 Sonderheft, "Antisemitismus und Volkstum" (1925): 136–37.

Grant, Barry Keith. *Fritz Lang: Interviews*. Jackson: University Press of Mississippi, 2003.

Holländer, Ludwig. "Warum sind und bleiben wir Juden?" *Central-Verein Zeitung: Allgemeine Zeiung des Judentums* 11 (51). Berlin, 16 December 1932.

Jay, Martin. "The Free Jewish School Is Founded in Frankfurt am Main." In *Yale Companion to Jewish Writing and Thought in German Culture, 1096–1996*, ed. Sander L. Gilman and Jack Zipes. New Haven, CT: Yale University Press, 1997.

Kaplan, Marion A. *The Making of the Jewish Middle Class: Women, Family, and Identity in Imperial Germany*. New York: Oxford University Press, 1991.

Karbach, Oskar. "Das Princip der Assimilation." *Der Jude: eine Monatsschrift* 6.9 (1921–22): 521–24.

Kracauer, Siegfried. *From Caligari to Hitler: A Psychological History of the German Film*. 1947. Reprint Princeton, NJ: Princeton University Press, 2004.

Lenz, Fritz. *Grundriß der menschlichen Erblichkeitlehre und Rassenhygiene. Band II: Menschliche Auslese und Rassenhygiene*. Munich: J.F. Lehmanns, 1921.

Neumann, Carl, Curt Belling, and Hans-Walther Betz. *Film "Kunst," Film Kohn, Film Korruption*. Berlin: Hermann Scherping, 1937.

Niewyk, Donald L. *The Jews in Weimar Germany*. New Brunswick, NJ: Transaction, 2001.
Prawer, S.S. *Between Two Worlds: The Jewish Presence in German and Austrian Film 1910–1933*. New York: Berghahn Books, 2005.
Quaresima, Leonard. "Introduction to the 2004 Edition: Rereading Kracauer," trans. Michael F. Moore. In *From Caligari to Hitler: A Psychological History of the German Film*, by Siegfried Kracauer, ed. Leonard Quaresima, xv–xlix. Princeton, NJ: Princeton University Press, 2004.
Roud, Richard. "The Moral Taste of Lotte Eisner." *Sight and Sound* 53 (2, Spring 1984): 139–40.
S[chneider], A[lbert]. "Dr. Goebbels vor den Filmschaffenden: Ein neues Bekenntnis zum Film." *Lichtbild-Bühne*, 16 December 1935.
Scholem, Gershom. "Jews and Germans." *On Jews and Judaism in Crisis: Selected Essays, Gershom Scholem*, ed. Werner J. Dannhauser, 71–92. Philadelphia: Paul Dry Books, 2012.
Shohat, Ella. "Ethnicities-in-Relation: Toward a Multicultural Reading of American Cinema." In *Unspeakable Images: Ethnicity and the American Cinema*, ed. Lester D. Friedman, 215–50. Urbana: University of Illinois Press, 1991.
Silverman, Lisa. *Becoming Austrians: Jews and Culture Between the World Wars*. Oxford: Oxford University Press, 2012.
———. "Beyond Antisemitism: A Critical Approach to German Jewish Cultural History." In *Nexus 1: Essays in German Jewish Studies*, 27–45. Rochester, NY: Camden House, 2011.
———. "Reconsidering the Margins: Jewishness as an Analytical Framework." *Journal of Modern Jewish Studies* 8 (1, March 2009): 103–20.
Simmel, Georg. *Sociology: Inquiries into the Construction of Social Forms*, vol. 1. Leiden: Brill, 2009.
Spector, Scott. "Forget Assimilation: Introducing Subjectivity to German-Jewish History." *Jewish History* 20 (3–4, 2006): 349–61.
Spitzer, Leo. *Lives in Between: Assimilation and Marginality in Austria, Brazil, and West Africa, 1780—1945*. Cambridge: Cambridge University Press, 1989.
Stratenwerth, Irene and Hermann Simon, eds. *Pioniere in Celluloid: Juden in der frühen Filmwelt*. Berlin: Henschel, 2004.
Urgiß, Julius. "Künstlerprofil: Ernst Lubitsch." *Der Kinematograph*, Düsseldorf, 30 August 1916, rpt. *Lubitsch*, ed. Hans Helmut Prinzler and Enno Patalas, 89–90. Munich, 1984.
"Verjudung und Geschäftemacherei im 'deutschen' Film." *Der Angriff*, 1 March 1933.
Wallach, Kerry. *Passing Illusions: Jewish Visibility in Weimar Cinema*. Ann Arbor: University of Michigan Press, 2017.
Wassermann, Jakob. *My Life as a German and Jew*, trans. S.N. Brainin. New York: Coward-McCann, 1933.

PART I

JEWISH VISIBILITY ON AND OFF SCREEN

Chapter 1

HUMANIZING SHYLOCK

The "Jewish Type" in Weimar Film

Maya Barzilai

While Jewish actors embodied a wide variety of roles on the German screens of the Weimar era, they also had to contend with the legacy of the "Jewish type," often a racial caricature. These types included, among others, the *Trödler* (Jewish merchant), the observant and bedraggled *Ostjude* (eastern European Jew), as well as the figure of Judas, a deceitful Jewish type. Even when screenplay writers and directors did not put such types to explicit use, they still often made implicit use of types, thereby falling back on racial stereotyping. Within this framework, Jewish actors nonetheless exerted a measure of freedom when it came to their performances and could, especially when enacting central roles, subvert the caricature or add complexity to the fixed type. The two actors at the focus of this chapter, Henrik Galeen (also a screenwriter and director) and Alexander Granach, were immigrants from eastern Europe who had adapted to German culture and performed on German theater stages prior to and alongside their film-acting careers. On the way to stardom, they shed linguistic and physical attributes of the past, adapting to secularized German culture. The perceived Jewishness of these actors continued, however, to shape their careers and the roles they embodied, just as they, in turn, attempted to remold the Jewish type.

Before discussing examples of Galeen's and Granach's screen performances, this chapter first explores how the term "type" was used in German film criticism of the mid-1920s by Béla Balázs and Karl Freund, up to Siegfried Kracauer's 1960 *Theory of Film*. These critics share an understanding of the importance of character typage for creating authenticity effects on the screen. They differentiate between nonprofessional actors whom directors cast in roles that match their off-screen identities, and professional actors who rely on a correspondence between the pre-filmic person (through physical or imagined attributes) and the character in front of the camera, thus projecting recognizable types. The theories discussed here do not focus on negative types or stock types, despite their prevalence on the screen. Balázs promotes, nonetheless, a correspondence between an actor's racial character and the role they enact.

Jewish actors in Weimar Germany had to negotiate between typecasting as a useful way of establishing a sense of authenticity on the screen and the more insidious presence of negative stereotypes that could turn a potentially believable character into a Jewish caricature. Jewish journalists and filmmakers wrote in alarm about the presence of such stock types, which had been drawn from vernacular theater, in Weimar film. Against this background of minor Jewish roles used for comedic effects, with an accompanying antisemitic sting, Jewish actors playing major roles could draw on preconceived types in order to call into question their characteristics and reveal greater depths and nuances to their implicitly or explicitly Jewish roles. Galeen and Granach embodied, at various stages of their film careers, stereotypical Jewish roles that nonetheless afforded opportunities for reflection on the very nature of the Jewish type and its subtending set of stereotypical characteristics.[1] The roles of Knock in *Nosferatu* (1922) and Judas in *I.N.R.I.* (1923) allowed Granach, in particular, to express his versatility as an actor who could individualize and humanize the Shylock and Judas types, shifting the normative trajectory of these roles through his expressionist style of acting.

Film Types: Classical Theoretical Approaches

In 1924 Hungarian-Jewish film critic Béla Balázs wrote, "The film director's creativity starts with his choice of actors. This gives his figures their decisive, essential substance." Balázs differentiates between casting in the theater and in cinema, arguing that while spoken language is essential for characterization on the stage, on the silver screen external appearance determines character. Therefore, the director needs to find "the character itself"—that is, an actor that suits the imagined character through his or her appearance.[2] Balázs advises directors to select actors that fit both the individual character and the *Rassencharakter* (racial character) projected on the screen, thereby allowing the actor to focus on the "personal details of a particular role." When this does not take place, the actor needs to "exaggerate and to acquire a series of stereotypical gestures that are slightly off-key," rather than acting "naturally" with "all the weight of habitual existence."[3] Within these parameters, Balázs advocated for a flexible typage: the anatomy of the actor must leave some room for their personal physiognomic interpretation so that they might perform "outward and inner transformations."[4]

Balázs's notion of a useful alignment between an actor's external, given properties and the cinematic role they embodied represented a broader understanding of film as a potentially authentic medium, or at least a medium that capitalizes on notions of authenticity. For instance, in his 1927 essay "Behind My Camera: New Possibilities for Shooting Film," German-Jewish cinematographer Karl Freund touched on the compatibility between cinematic realism and film types: "The Americans were the first to recognize that film has its own laws, that realism is much more important in film than in theater. The same American directors who invented the close-up also stressed the importance of naturalistic performances. They practically bred film types, casting even the smallest roles to make the audience believe they were witnessing real life."[5] In order to achieve naturalistic performances, casting had to rely on what Freund calls film types, finding actors that closely resemble the desired character on the screen.

According to Siegfried Kracauer, certain directors who seek to portray "wide areas of actual reality, social or otherwise," even employ nonactors, people from the social milieus they attempted to represent. Such nonprofessional actors provide directors with "authentic looks and behaviors" and they can animate a film invested in "social patterns rather than individual destinies."[6] The Hollywood star, by contrast, artificially performs what the nonactor manages to do unwittingly, acting out a character that we imagine resembles the actor in their everyday life outside of the role. In Kracauer's words, the star "uses his acting talent . . . to feature the individual he is or appears to be, no matter for the rest whether his self-portrayal exhausts itself in a few stereotyped characteristics or brings out various potentialities of his underlying nature. The late Humphrey Bogart invariably drew on Humphrey Bogart whether he impersonated a sailor, a private 'eye,' or a night club owner."[7] Audiences rely, in other words, on their perceived image of the particular Hollywood star when approaching each instantiation on the screen, whether it is a schematic or more developed character.

In their assessments of famous female actors such as Asta Nielsen and Greta Garbo, both Balázs and Kracauer resisted the notion of type, however.[8] In his 1933 essay following the release of the film *Grand Hotel*, Kracauer maintained that Garbo does not represent a specific type, but rather a generic form, that of "the Woman." The universality of her "form" "as good as erased," he contends, "all typical characteristics," enabling her acting to avoid recourse to certain specifications and features, as in the case of other actors.[9] In this way, Kracauer finds that Garbo's universality supplants any notion of type and allows our sense of her age and nationality to remain in flux. For him, gender (female) served as a universal form, and this review does not account for Garbo's whiteness as an enabling factor for her universality, which stands at a level "even higher than the type." Significantly, as Kracauer himself was about to depart from Berlin to Paris, after the burning of the Reichstag, he was writing this essay about Garbo's ability to escape the otherness of the type, which was often coded in the Weimar period as Jewish.[10]

In contrast to Garbo's universality, the Jewish actors of Balázs's and Kracauer's day could not shed their perceived ethnoracial baggage. However, rather than aspire to overcome the type, certain actors used their Jewishness to trouble the notion of cinematic authenticity, depicting identity as a form of masquerade, as in the case of Ernst Lubitsch. In other words, these actors resisted the supposedly natural correlation, advocated by Balázs, between the persona of the actor and the role they played, acting, instead, in an exaggerated and artificial manner precisely when confined to a Jewish type. Another strategy at the Jewish actor's disposal was to revisit the fixed type and inhabit it in a way that lent this character new, unexpected depth and individuality.

Jewish Types on the Weimar Screen

As both director and actor, Lubitsch attained a kind of casting middle ground—using Jewish stereotypes but, ultimately, producing complex film types through surprising and comedic plot twists. When enacting a stereotypical character such as Meyer in the film *Meyer aus Berlin* (*Meyer from Berlin*), Lubitsch portrayed this character, according to Ofer Ashkenazi, as both "the Jew" and as a typical "middle-class urbanite," young, bored with his life, and seeking new experiences and identities.[11] The coexistence of multiple types within the same character allowed a versatile actor like Lubitsch to offer a multifaceted form of typage, neither erasing specificities, as in Kracauer's image of Garbo, nor suggesting that a Jewish-coded character must remain confined to stereotypes. Lubitsch's characters defy, for instance, the notion that Jews are devoid of emotion, for they all fall blindly in love.[12] Valerie Weinstein has shown, furthermore, that Lubitsch's "blend of theatricality and problematic anti-Semitic stereotypes leads to camp-like effects," rather than to an entrenchment of well-rehearsed stereotypes. Such performances mark the site of otherness as a theatrical one, based on "superficial and often exaggerated features," thereby challenging the notion of a stable ethnic identity.[13]

In *Passing Illusions: Jewish Visibility in Weimar Germany*, Kerry Wallach discusses this duality of "appearing non-Jewish and Jewish at once," of desiring to pass as non-Jewish in certain contexts and yet remain visibly Jewish for some viewers.[14] Lubitsch turned what Wallach calls "dual legibility" into a trademark of his comedic roles, enacting Jews who try to pass as non-Jews, failing to assimilate into the non-Jewish society. Wallach further maintains that, in the early 1920s, Jewish cultural critics lauded the wide range of characters that Jewish actors could perform on the theater stage or in the cinema, thereby either ignoring or coopting the antisemitic notion of Jewish chameleonism, the ability to imitate any segment of the general population.[15] These critics also resisted the German popular theater's propensity, starting in the early nineteenth century, to lampoon assimilating Jews and caricature their unsuccessful attempts to blend into educated society. Such *Judenpossen* (Jew farces) were based, as Katrin Sieg has argued, on the conceit of the German actor's universal "ability to transcend its gendered and racial coordinates," in contrast to the Jew's unsuccessful mimicry of the Christian.[16]

Alongside the debates surrounding Jewish acting as a form of passing in the Weimar period, other film critics such as Hans Wollenberg (1893–1952) and Max Kolpenitzky (1905–98) focused on the exaggeration of Jewishness on the screen. They suggested that such performances fall back to old antisemitic stereotypes.[17] In other words, in contrast to "naturalistic performances" by nonactors or type roles that still allowed professional actors to exhibit "various potentialities," stereotypical Jewish film characters recycled stock imagery from the revue or cabaret stage, and even from the *Jargon* (dialect) theater.[18] These latter roles bypassed the duality of appearing non-Jewish and Jewish at once, and could thereby pose a threat to a secularized German-Jewish society.

Wollenberg and Kolpenitzky both titled their articles about Jewish roles on the screen "Der Jude im Film" (The Jew in Film), pointing to the fact that they were contending with a particular type that had become ossified as "the Jew."[19] Wollenberg's September 1927 piece for the German-Jewish weekly newspaper *C.V.-Zeitung* opens with general remarks on the nature of cinema. Like Balázs, Wollenberg emphasized the visual dimension of the medium that speaks to the eye through external appearances; in contrast to the former critic, though, Wollenberg did not consider the language of the body to be a nuanced and intricate one. Instead, he claims that film coarsens, since it derives from what is typical and not from the individual. When directors seek to represent a particular social group, they must do so through recourse to external attributes and gestures, ones that make recognition an obvious, simple matter for all.[20] The effect of the visual art of film is to "exaggerate the Jewishness of the Jew, that is, to show the Jew not how he is in reality, but how old, popular stereotypes envision him."[21] Wollenberg qualified this statement by explaining that some Jewish characters on the screen are based on accurate understandings of Judaism and its particularities, but he also pointed to the ease with which the medium can be harnessed to promote false prejudices.

One such example was the role of the Jewish soldier Mischka Rappaport in the 1926 *Die dritte Eskadron* (The Third Squadron), played by "the fine actor" Siegfried Arno (1895–1975). Wollenberg quotes dialogues from the film's intertitles in which the Jewish soldier claims that his legs are naturally bowed and does not profess any patriotism. Thus, the moral and physical inferiority of the Jew is not only displayed visually but also asserted verbally. Another Jewish type that Wollenberg discusses in his piece is the lawyer type that harks back, for him, to the Jewish money lender, as well as to the lowly profiteer or agent. The most despicable aspect of this "antisemitic enterprise" is that Jewish producers stand behind many of these films (in addition to the actors, writers, and directors, who might also be Jewish).[22]

In his August 1927 piece for the *Israelitisches Familienblatt*, Kolpenitzky does not find any representations of Jews on the screen that are worthy of applause. Rather, he claims that two negative Jewish types tend to appear in German films: the upwardly mobile Jew, the *Modefatzke* (fashion swellhead)—in the model of a lowly baker's apprentice that becomes a chef—or, its opposite, the "devious *Ostjude*" with his "soiled caftan and wavy side locks." Kolpenitzky appears indignant regarding the low quality of German cinema, including Universum Film Aktiengesellschaft (UFA) productions: "Still today, in the twentieth century, the Jew is fated to enact the roles of Shylock or Judas."[23] The critic recommends that when Jews are filmed, a more genuine Jewish type should be adopted, like that of the Jewish intellectual that had featured in recent literature such as *Jud Süß* (Lion Feuchtwanger's 1925 work) or theater productions such as Henry Bernstein's 1908 *Israël*. While Kolpenitzky warned against small but insidious parts that could also be acted by non-Jews, German-Jewish writer Heinz Goldberg, who cowrote the film *Dreyfus* (1930), focused in his 1931 piece on Jewish actors, contending that they are often cast in ways that appeal only to the base instincts of mass society. Goldberg identifies these cynical goals for casting, showing that rather than consider the film's aesthetic demands, casting practices are intended to demean Jewish actors and turn them into clowns. One of his central examples is the production of the 1931 film *Der Hauptmann von Köpenick* (The Captain of Köpenick), during which the Jewish author and screenplay cowriter Carl Zuckmayer insisted on casting the small role of the merchant with a Jewish actor. Goldberg had proposed that a non-Jew should play the role, to which Zuckmayer responded: "Only a Jew can be cast as the punchline."[24] In other words, the Jewish Zuckmayer subscribed to the ethnoracial casting practices of his generation, according to which the identity of the actor must align with that of the role for the punchline to be effective. In this case, the Jew must play the merchant who sells old uniforms, and is thus responsible for a cascade of misunderstandings after a German cobbler wearing a Prussian infantry captain uniform convinces guardsmen to serve under his command. The film, directed by Richard Oswald, initially screened in December 1931, featuring the German-Jewish actor Leopold Steckel (1901–71) in the small but significant role of the *Trödler*. Zuckmayer did not heed Goldberg's advice and used ethnoracial casting for comic effects.

These opinion pieces by Wollenberg, Kolpenitzky, and Goldberg share an understanding that while Jewish actors have played a wide variety of roles in German cinema, and have proven their versatility, the antisemitism of their day still expresses itself in the film medium through highly stereotyped characters. These minor roles have a sole purpose—to promote a jeering laughter and entertain the masses. All three writers encouraged actors, directors, and producers to become more aware of the effects of their films and resist this tendency. Like Wollenberg, film critic Rudolph Arnheim (1904–2007) urged Jewish actors to portray human beings, not merely Jews.[25] Kolpenitzky and Goldberg seem more skeptical about the possibility that the casting of Jews in minor roles could move beyond motivations of vindictive entertainment or even incitement.[26] As Ella Shohat and Robert Stam explain, negative stereotypes can exert their damage in varying ways, depending on the social and historical context. If "stereotypes of other communities participate in a continuum of prejudicial social policy and actual violence against disempowered people, placing the very body of the accused in jeopardy," then these Jewish critics writing in the late 1920s and early 1930s expressed a foreboding sense of the potential danger posed by film stereotypes with the intensification of anti-Jewish sentiment in Germany.[27]

The films discussed in the following sections screened during an earlier period in Weimar history, ranging from 1915 to 1923. They typify Jewish casting in central roles a decade or less prior to the indignant pieces by Kolpenitzky, Wollenberg, and Goldberg. The immediate post–World War I years witnessed a surge in antisemitic sentiment alongside a flourishing of Jewish culture and successful integration of Jewish actors.[28] In these larger roles, we still find typecasting and stereotyping: Wollenberg's "devious *Ostjude*" and Kolpenitzky's Judas appear in these films, alongside a coded version of Shylock through Alexander Granach's character of Knock. Still, Jewish actors of early Weimar film were able to inhabit their roles and individuate them, even when these roles appeared stereotypical on paper. When Granach enacted the traitor Judas in a historical film drama, he managed to elicit a range of audience reactions beyond loathing. He personalized the caricature and rendered it more human. Henrik Galeen cast himself, in turn, as a traditional Jew who ultimately acquiesces to his daughter's marriage with a German baron. Through this role, he not only projected the *Ostjude* stereotype but also used it as a costume or performance that can then be cast off and superseded, just as the clay golem itself is ultimately smashed and discarded in Paul Wegener's first golem film.

Henrik Galeen as the Eastern European Jewish Type

The 1914–15 *Der Golem*, a predominantly lost film cowritten and codirected by Henrik Galeen and Paul Wegener, contended with the issues of intermarriage and assimilation. Shot in the months leading up to World War I, the film screened during the war. Its image of the observant Jew, whose main concerns are accumulating wealth and preventing his daughter's intermarriage, helped to cement the *Ostjude* type in the Weimar period, which witnessed an influx of eastern European Jews to German cities. The screenplay details how workers dig up a golem statue in "present-day" Hildesheim, Germany, and then sell it to a Jewish antiquities and curiosities dealer, "der alte Aaron" (old Aaron), a *Trödler*.[29] After discovering how to animate the golem, "old Aaron" uses this artificial creation in his attempts to prevent the meeting between his daughter and her lover, the local baron. The film's drama and its resolution revolve around this affair and culminate with the golem's destruction and the couple's union, as the father clasps the baron's hand. The surviving screenplay accentuates the presence of types through the general avoidance of proper names: Galeen and Wegener named their characters *der Jude, die Tochter, der hungernde Gelehrte,* and *der Graf* (the Jew, the daughter, the hungry scholar, the baron). Notably, they identify the Jew in ethnic terms; the initial mention of his generic name, Aaron, enhances his Jewishness.[30]

Galeen himself appeared in this central role, using it to project an outdated (for German society) image of a religious Jew, replete with the traditional trappings of a black velvet yarmulke and sidelocks. The use of this particular Jewish type was, perhaps, an outcome of the film's plot, in which a merchant, rather than a rabbi, animates the golem. Dressed as an observant Jew, Galeen partially smooths over the transition between the "wonder rabbi" (the screenplay's term for the legendary animator of the golem) and the present-day *Trödler.* Galeen's type in the early golem film stands in contrast, for instance, with Ernst Lubitsch's protagonists in his 1914–18 German films, characters who seek to change their outer appearances and assimilate. At the same time, unlike the stereotypical Jewish characters bemoaned in the Jewish press of the late 1920s to early 1930s, "old Aaron" does not perform a comical role intended for laughs and jeers. The Jewish father in *Der Golem* represents, instead, the type, also described by Kolpenitzky, of the eastern European "caftan" Jew who clings to his outmoded dress and viewpoints. While the exact years in which the film is set remain vague, the overall studio design is a modern one, thus dating the Jew as a relic of the past, in contrast to his daughter, a modernized woman. Ironically, the dug-up statue of the medieval golem, when awakened to life, ultimately forces the *Ostjude* to move on with the times and accept the union of his daughter with the baron.

By 1913, Galeen, age thirty-five, had already established himself as a theater assistant for director Max Reinhardt (1906), actor in Swiss theater (1907–9), and director at the Volksbühne (1911). Born to a Jewish family in eastern Galicia, Galeen was an acculturated author, director, and actor who went on to write the screenplays for *Nosferatu* (1921) and *Das Wachsfigurenkabinett* (*Waxworks*; 1924), as well as to direct major film productions such as *Der Student von Prag* (*The Student of Prague*; 1926) and *Alraune* (1927). While his earlier film, *Der Golem,* presents a tale of assimilation, Galeen underwent, through the role of "the Jew," a reverse process of returning to his Galician origins for the duration of the cinematic event. The character of "old Aaron" challenged him, precisely as he collaborated with the non-Jewish actor and director Wegener, to wear his Jewishness on his sleeve, thereby also adding some authenticity to the role. Concomitantly, by enacting this Jewish type in a particular film rather than throughout his theater and stage career, Galeen could also distance himself from the figure of "the Jew" that he had long abandoned and recycle it as a mere costume that he could easily remove. The film as a whole suggests, through the plot of intermarriage, that Jewish identity is not fixed and can be remolded (figure 1.1).

A still image from the production shows Galeen bent over an old book, which contains the formula for animating a golem. His eyes peer upward and to the side, suggesting a scheme that he would like to hide from the scholar who has sold him the book—namely, that he owns a golem statue, which he plans to animate. The set designer, Rochus Gliese, casually placed a Torah scroll on the table in the foreground. It simultaneously enhances the Jewish aura of the space and its owner and desacralizes this sacred object, which is offered for sale among other antiquities and curiosities. Galeen's enactment of the Jew follows

Figure 1.1. Henrik Galeen as Aaron in *Der Golem* (1914, dir. Galeen). Source: Deutsche Kinemathek.

suit: donning the traditional garb of an observant Jew, his character appears preoccupied with earthly matters of wealth and control, rather than with spiritual matters. The first mention of Galeen as Aaron in the screenplay cements the stereotypical connection between Jews and finance: "Old Aaron sits with his horn-rimmed glasses on his nose poring over the books—calculates—writes—records."[31] While "books" refers here to accounting books, the very use of this term sets up the contrast between the learned Jew who studies the ancient books—the Torah and Talmud—and the character of Aaron. Thus, the father figure in *Der Golem* combines two different types: he is both an *Ostjude* and a merchant. This combination has an even more cynical bite since "the Jew" profits from the reselling of dug-up and seized Jewish items, some of which have ritual uses. His outward observant appearance does not stand in correlation, therefore, with his demeanor and actions.

Galeen not only played a stock Jewish type in *Der Golem*, but also, at least as far as the few surviving segments from the film reveal, exaggerated his bodily gestures. One of these segments takes place in a smithy, where Galeen instructs Wegener as golem to perform certain tasks. While the golem exerts excessive force when wielding a hammer, "the Jew" appears terrified and contorts his body. He raises his hands repeatedly, emphasizing thereby his distorted physique and cowering stature. The golem, by contrast, stands erect, unbending.[32] The discrepancy between these two figures creates a visually striking effect that exaggerates the Jewish physiognomy. The golem appeared to spectators as both manly and primitive, even Mongolian, a stark contrast to the scheming eastern European Jew.[33] If the film's plot focused on the Jewish need to integrate, through marriage, into German society, Galeen's acting further underscored the degree to which his prior ethnoreligious identity was not merely a curiosity but rather an obstacle that should be overcome. In other words, the film's narrative of assimilation told the story of Galeen and his integration into the Weimar film industry. Fittingly, while posing a temporary threat to the German social order, the monstrous golem is subdued in this film of 1914–15, and even cast aside, a relic of a Jewish past.

Alexander Granach as Knock and Judas: Revisiting the Type

Granach enjoyed a varied and prolific career on the theater stage and in film. He arrived in Berlin from Galicia as a baker's apprentice and only gradually, through his interest in Yiddish theater, began to appear on the German theater stage, first in Jewish productions and subsequently at the Reinhardt Theater.[34] In his autobiography, *Da geht ein Mensch: Roman eines Lebens* (*From the Shtetl to the Stage: The Odyssey of a Wandering Actor*), Granach relates his intense identification with the sorrows and pains of Shakespeare's Shylock through the mediation of Karl Emil Franzos's 1905 novel, *Der Pojaz* (The Clown). When reflecting on this role, which he played in a post–World War I production of *The Merchant of Venice* in Munich, Granach explains the depths of this character: Shylock is wicked, "a black fool," and an object of hate and scorn, but he is also a figure of "human greatness, spiritual strength, and tragic loneliness."[35] Shylock, for Granach, is a flesh-and-blood character who can speak in his own defense, and he proposes that Jews enact Shylock "as victim and accuser against the evil society that spits on him and persecutes him, and as a representative of the human rights of the Jews."[36]

We might begin to reconsider the difficult, scorned, and hated roles that Granach himself often played on the screen in view of his interpretation of Shylock. For Granach, Shylock is a complex character; rather than view him as a wicked "type," he considers how Shylock might be personalized and humanized. Austrian Jewish actor Fritz Grünbaum made a similar point in his 1931 contribution to the *C.V.-Zeitung*, in which he sought to differentiate between malicious and benign forms of comedic Jewish character enactment. For him, an actor who reveals how "good-hearted, prudent, and touchingly human such a comically poor Jew can be serves the Jewish cause far more than the actor who idealizes the Jewish type to the extent of bloodless unreality, intentionally challenging the non-Jew to protest against this portrayal."[37] With the phrase "a comically poor Jew," Grünbaum does not intend only a financially unfortunate Jewish character but also the inept, blundering Jew. In other words, he would rather that Jewish actors take up imperfect characters, like Shylock, and humanize them, than that they try to altogether avoid any such problematic figures for fear of mockery, and portray only idealized, impeccable Jewish types. In his own theater and film acting career, Grünbaum enacted the "fool" or the "ruthless attorney" types (see *Mensch ohne Namen*, Man Without a Name, 1932) and used Jewish stereotypes and humor to entertain audiences.[38]

A similar approach to the embodiment of Jewish (or Jewish-inflected) characters also informs the career of Granach. In the 1922 *Nosferatu*, written by Galeen who previously enacted the role of Aaron in *Der Golem*, Granach appeared as Knock, an evil and physically distorted realtor who unhesitatingly sends Hutter, the innocent male lead, into danger's way and even hints at the blood that Hutter will shed when he reaches the vampire's castle. In his analysis of Knock, Anton Kaes notes that when "distorting his face with wild grins and grimaces, [Granach's Knock] acts like a comic, lower-class copy of his master."[39] Knock thus becomes a caricature of the master, Nosferatu/Graf Orlok, implying, more broadly, that the Jew is a lower-class imitation of the non-Jew.[40] Knock's greed as a real estate agent who has sold his soul to the vampire aligns him, furthermore, with the character of Shylock. Even more so, the names of both characters end with the same syllable "ock," pointing to a kind of triangulation between Shylock, Knock, and Orlok, whereby Knock is a diminished and comic version of the tragic Shylock as well.

The fact that Granach, an actor of Jewish, eastern European extraction, was cast as Knock needs to be taken into consideration. In other words, Granach's recognizable face and persona bestowed on Knock a Shylockian dimension—especially in view of his 1920 theatrical embodiment of this role—enhancing the Jewish associations with Knock and moving audiences to ask what Jewish type this character might represent. From the first scene of *Nosferatu*, when Knock reads the letter from Count Orlok, the indecipherable code in which the letter is written implicitly recalls the notion of a secret Jewish language in which conspiracies against regimes and societies were supposedly coded. Through the course of the film, and as Orlok approaches the city of Wisborg, Knock loses all semblance of normalcy, and is jailed as a psychiatric patient, ultimately attacking his guard/caretaker and escaping. Kaes emphasizes that Knock appears "demented" in the film, "more a victim than a perpetrator," a scapegoat who is chased out of town.[41] This representation cements the implicit link to the despised and mistreated Shylock. The intertitles further speak to this issue: "The fear-ridden city searched for a victim: it was Knock."[42]

Galeen and Granach's Knock does not exhibit, however, the human greatness of Shakespeare's Shylock: rather than speak in his own defense against the accusations of murder, Knock merely jeers and runs away from the mob, appearing to enjoy the chase and the spectacle. He manages to escape because of his cunning nature, another antisemitic stereotype, rather than due to his moral qualities or physical abilities. For Kaes, the possible association of the chase with persecution and pogrom is averted and the scene becomes a slapstick act, adding a parodic quality to what would otherwise appear as an outright antisemitic characterization.[43] At the same time, Knock, who was first imprisoned, is ultimately driven out of town and, through the sacrifice of Ellen,

Orlok himself vanishes. *Nosferatu* fulfills the fantasy of the disappearance of the unwanted Jew while also asking the viewer to critically reflect on their own scapegoating desires.

Two years later, in Robert Wiene's lavish historical drama, *I.N.R.I.*, based on a 1905 novel by Peter Rosegger, Granach enacted another despised Jew, Judas Iscariot. Rather than play Judas as the treacherous traitor who betrays Christ for profit, Granach depicted an alternative Judas who, in Uli Jung and Walter Schatzberg's words, "becomes a passionate political activist . . . an underground rebel, who is devoted to Jesus because he expects him to lead the Jewish uprising against the Roman army of occupation." The film has Judas betray Jesus because of ideological motivations, rather than out of greed, in an attempt to force him to become a "revolutionary leader."[44] Jung and Schatzberg further maintain that in the first half of the film, Judas is the most dominant character alongside Jesus (Grigori Chmara). Wiene sets Judas apart from the other disciples by filming Granach in this role through close-ups and individualized scenes, showing him "passionately following his master's words."[45] Reinhold Zwick likewise contends that, rather than becoming a villain, Wiene's Judas serves as a "foil to the strong and consistent orientation of Wiene's Jesus towards non-violence and reconciliation—traits which must be seen against the backdrop of Germany's effort . . . to restore its international reputation after the First World War."[46] In other words, Judas's idealism wrongly manifests itself through political agitation and militancy, so that his betrayal at the end is misguided, rather than malicious. The lost segments of the frame narrative support this interpretation of the film, since they focus on a present-day German anarchist who plots to kill a government official and is sentenced to death, a fate he comes to accept after understanding the error of his violent ways.[47]

Hans Neumann, the film's producer, called this movie "a film of humanness," since it foregrounds the "human goals" common to all nations in the post–World War I period, when Germany was accused of "barbarism" toward other peoples.[48] In terms of the use of types and casting, this statement correlates to the way in which Judas was also humanized in the film, endowing the antisemitic type of the deceitful, betraying Jew with human motivation and a fundamentally ethical intention. Just as the censors criticized the film for its positive portrayal of a repentant anarchist, so the review of *I.N.R.I.* in the *Film-Kurier* expressed disappointment at Granach's unwillingness to follow the Judas type. Alexander Granach's Judas is too uninhibited and overdone, the reviewer protested: "His gesture remains decorative, because it is not an end to itself, not a symbol of his inner condition. . . . His Judas does not become a type, but remains a singular individual, that lacks, as such, its inner truth."[49] This anonymous critic takes issue precisely with the individualization of Judas through Granach's acting. Because Granach does not align himself with a type, and draws on his expressionist acting style, his character appears, for this reviewer, to lack "inner truth," incapable of expressing his inner condition in a symbolic manner. Ironically, to this reviewer the Judas type appears more authentic than any personalized deviation from the accepted script.

In his work on Jewish actors in German theater, Galili Shachar locates a duality or tension in Weimar culture whereby the same qualities that are viewed in an antisemitic light—the Jewish ability to adapt to different surroundings, or the supposedly deformed and diseased Jewish body—also became essential to modernist, avant-garde theater.[50] As an aspiring theater actor, Granach had his crooked legs straightened through a risky procedure, but he also, at the same time, "performed figurations of 'ugliness' and transformed the images of the *Unheimliche* into a critical form of theatrical representation." His acting style, furthermore, was ecstatic, and this quality was the very hallmark of expressionist theater.[51] Thus the propensity and openness of modern theater to express diversity and otherness allowed Jewish actors, like Granach, to convey their own experience on the stage, Shachar maintains, rather than suggest that there is something inherently Jewish about acting or theater.[52] Granach transposed some of these acting abilities to the medium of film, but here too, as the *Film-Kurier* reviewer reveals, German viewers treated his versatility and exaggerated gestures at times as insufficiencies. The notion that his portrayal of Judas lacked "inner truth" is a form of coded antisemitism: first, the Jewish actor should uphold the Christian antisemitic image of Judas as greedy traitor, rather than uncover the humanity of this figure; second, Jews, more generally, lack an "inner truth" in view of their ability to blend into the general society.

Both Galeen and Granach did not shy away from roles coded as Jewish and embodied Jewish types that often represented European stereotypes of Jews. Their parts attest to a kind of typecasting in Weimar film, whereby Jews cast themselves or were cast by others in roles that seemed to match their extrafilmic Jewish identities. Nonetheless actors like Lubitsch and Granach could also transform these roles from within, betraying the supposed truth of the type, a Shylock or a Judas, and providing their own multifaceted truths as acculturated Jewish actors.

Moreover, rather than view exaggeration or unnaturalness in the enactment of a particular role as a sign of a mismatch between actor and character, in line with Balázs and Kracauer, for whom the universalist Christian-white Garbo was an ideal, we need to also consider how this form of Jewish acting drove a wedge between personal identity and screen character, subverting assumptions about typecasting. If, by casting Jewish actors in Jewish roles, directors and producers thought that they were mitigating the negative image of the assimilated and even chameleon Jew, the actors themselves could, and did, prove them otherwise. Weimar typecasting threw acculturated actors back into Jewish roles that they themselves could no longer authentically play, resulting in the minor character portrayals that Jewish critics found extremely offensive. At the same time, Jewish roles also gave actors a chance to revisit the stock type and render it a full-fledged human being.

Maya Barzilai is associate professor of Hebrew literature and Jewish cultures at the University of Michigan. She researches Weimar film, Zionism, and translation studies, with an emphasis on German-Jewish culture and German-Hebrew literary exchanges. Her first book *Golem: Modern Wars and Their Monsters* (New York University Press, 2016) received the Jordan Schnitzer Book Award of the Association of Jewish Studies in 2017. Her book, *Golem, How He Came into the World*, devoted to Paul Wegener's 1920 film, appeared with the German Film Classics, Camden House, in 2020.

Notes

1. In her contribution to this volume, Kerry Wallach takes up the neglected issue of female typecasting.
2. Béla Balázs, *Béla Balázs: Early Film Theory*, ed. Erica Carter, trans. Rodney Livingstone (New York: Berghahn Books, 2010): 27.
3. Balázs, *Early Film Theory*, 27.
4. Balázs, *Early Film Theory*, 28.
5. Karl Freund, "Behind My Camera: New Possibilities for Shooting Film," in *The Promise of Cinema: German Film Theory, 1907–1933*, ed. Anton Kaes, Nicholas Baer, and Michael J. Cowan (Oakland: University of California Press, 2016), 511.
6. Siegfried Kracauer, *Theory of Film: The Redemption of Physical Reality* (Princeton, NJ: Princeton University Press, 1960), 99.
7. Kracauer, *Theory of Film*, 100.
8. See also Balázs's paean to Asta Nielsen as an actress who is capable of a "stupefying" "diversity of gestures" and "wealth of mimed expressions." Balázs, *Early Film Theory*, 87.

9. Siegfried Kracauer, "Greta Garbo: A Study," in *The Promise of Cinema: German Film Theory, 1907–1933*, ed. Anton Kaes, Nicholas Baer, and Michael J. Cowan (Oakland: University of California Press, 2016), 145.
10. Kracauer, "Greta Garbo," 146, 144.
11. Ofer Ashkenazi, *Weimar Film and Modern Jewish Identity* (New York: Palgrave Macmillan, 2012), 27.
12. Ashkenazi, *Weimar Film and Modern Jewish Identity*, 28–29.
13. Valerie Weinstein, "Anti-Semitism or Jewish 'Camp'? Ernst Lubitsch's *Schuhpalast Pinkus* (1916) and *Meyer aus Berlin* (1918)," *German Life and Letters* 59, no. 1 (2006), 111.
14. Kerry Wallach, *Passing Illusions: Jewish Visibility in Weimar Germany* (Ann Arbor: University of Michigan Press, 2017), 2.
15. Wallach, *Passing Illusions*, 21, 70–71.
16. Katrin Sieg, *Ethnic Drag: Performing Race, Nation, Sexuality in West Germany* (Ann Arbor: University of Michigan Press, 2002), 32, 40.
17. Wallach, *Passing Illusions*, 79–80.
18. Freund, "Behind My Camera," 511; Kracauer, *Theory of Film*, 100. In a review of the 1930 film *Der Liebling der Götter*, a critic noted that the Jewish actors in the minor roles, "gave a powerful example of their famous Jargon-art, so that even the patient West Berlin audience finally began to whistle loudly." Friedrich Brodnitz, "Politik auch im Film," *C.V. Zeitung* 42, 17 October 1930, 550.
19. See also Wallach's discussion of Wollenberg, Kolpenitzky, and other critics of the same period: Wallach, *Passing Illusions*, 78–81.
20. Hans Wollenberg, "Der Jude im Film," *C.V. Zeitung* 37, 16 September 1927, 523.
21. Wollenberg as translated in Wallach, *Passing Illusions*, 79.
22. Wollenberg, "Der Jude im Film," 523.
23. Max Kolpenitzky, "Der Jude im Film," *Israelitisches Familienblatt* 31, 4 August 1927, 10.
24. "Die Schlußpointe kann nur mit einem Juden besetzt werden." Rudolph Arnheim, Heinz Goldberg, and Fritz Grünbaum, "Selbstachtung oder Selbstverhöhnung: Der Jude als Typ im Film, Kabarett und auf der Bühne," *C.V. Zeitung* 49, 4 December 1931, 559.
25. Arnheim et al. "Selbstachtung oder Selbstverhöhnung," 558.
26. Arnheim et al. "Selbstachtung oder Selbstverhöhnung," 560.
27. Ella Shohat and Robert Stam, *Unthinking Eurocentrism: Multiculturalism and the Media* (London: Routledge, 1994), 183.
28. As Anton Kaes and other film scholars have pointed out, we can find in postwar German cinema images of the Jew as a dangerous parasite; these images correspond to the use of Jews as a scapegoat in the right-wing press, blaming Germany's military defeat in World War I on them. See Anton Kaes, *Shell Shock Cinema: Weimar Culture and the Wounds of War* (Princeton, NJ: Princeton University Press, 2009), 110–11.
29. Paul Wegener and Henrik Galeen, "Der Golem: Phantastisches Filmspiel in vier Akten," in *Henrik Galeen: Film—Materialien*, ed. Hans-Michael Bock and Wolfgang Jacobson (Hamburg: Cinegraph, 1992), 3.
30. Wegener and Galeen, "Der Golem," 4, 6, 9.
31. Wegener and Galeen, "Der Golem," 4.
32. See *Fragment des Spielfilms Der Golem: Phantastisches Spiel in vier Akten*, Paul Wegener and Henrik Galeen, (1915; Germany: absolut MEDIEN, 2007), DVD.
33. For a discussion of Paul Wegener's image as an actor, see Maya Barzilai, *Golem: Modern Wars and Their Monsters* (New York: New York University Press, 2016), 32–34.

34. For a detailed description of Granach's theatrical and filmic career, see also Margrit Frölich's essay in this volume.
35. Alexander Granach, *Da geht ein Mensch: Autobiographischer Roman* (Stockholm: Neuer Verlag, 1940), 423; Alexander Granach, *From the Shtetl to the Stage: The Odyssey of a Wandering Actor* (New Brunswick, NJ: Transaction, 2010), 276–77.
36. Granach, *Da geht*, 428; Granach, *Shtetl to the Stage*, 279; translation amended.
37. Arnheim et al. "Selbstachtung oder Selbstverhöhnung," 560.
38. Wallach discusses the character of the "shyster" Jewish lawyer in *Mensch ohne Namen* (1932), explaining that Grünbaum sought to make scene changes that might have "len[t] his character greater personal depth" but these scenes were not preserved and the actor's "ironic inflections" did not make it into the film. Wallach, *Passing Illusions*, 150, 154.
39. Kaes, *Shell Shock Cinema*, 112.
40. To complicate matters further, the character of Nosferatu is coded as Jewish itself. Eric Rentschler, for instance, has discussed the association of Nosferatu with Eastern Europe and contagious disease, claiming, "In Max Schreck's incarnation, the vampire bears a stunning similarity to National Socialist (Nazi) representations of degenerate Jewish physiognomies." Eric Rentschler, *The Ministry of Illusion: Nazi Cinema and Its Afterlife* (Cambridge, MA: Harvard University Press, 1996), 157.
41. Kaes, *Shell Shock Cinema*, 112.
42. "Die angstdurchbebte Stadt suchte ein Opfer: es war Knock." *Nosferatu*, directed by F.W. Murnau, (1922; Kino Lorber Films, 2013). DVD.
43. Kaes, *Shell Shock Cinema*, 112.
44. Uli Jung and Walter Schatzberg, *Beyond Caligari: The Films of Robert Wiene* (New York: Berghahn Books, 1999), 107–8.
45. Jung and Schatzberg, *Beyond Caligari*, 108.
46. Reinhold Zwick, "*Der Galiläer* (Express-Film, 1921) and *I.N.R.I.* (Neumann-Film, 1923): The Silence of Jesus in the German Cinema," in *The Silence of Jesus in the Cinema (1897–1927)*, ed. David J. Shepherd (New York: Routledge, 2016), 225.
47. This frame narrative is reconstructed in Jung and Schatzberg, *Beyond Caligari*, 109.
48. Hans Neumann's interview is quoted in Jung and Schatzberg, *Beyond Caligari*, 106.
49. The German review reads, "Alexander Granachs Judas gibt hier wieder ungehemmt seiner Neigung zu Unterstreichungen nach. Seine Gebärde bleibt dekorativ, weil sie nicht Selbstzweck ist, nicht Symbol eines inneren Zustandes, sein Mienenspiel Grimasse. Sein Judas wird nicht zum Typus, sondern bleibt Einzelindividuum, dem als solchem die innere Wahrheit fehlt." "I.N.R.I.," *Film-Kurier* 283, 27 December 1923.
50. Galili Shahar, "The Jewish Actor and the Theatre of Modernism in Germany," *Theatre Research International* 29, no. 3 (2004), 217.
51. Shahar, "The Jewish Actor," 221, 223.
52. Shahar, "The Jewish Actor," 223–24.

Bibliography

Arnheim, Rudolph, Heinz Goldberg, and Fritz Grünbaum. "Selbstachtung oder Selbstverhöhnung: Der Jude als Typ im Film, Kabarett und auf der Bühne." *C.V.-Zeitung* 49, 4 December 1931, 558-560.
Ashkenazi, Ofer. *Weimar Film and Modern Jewish Identity*. New York: Palgrave Macmillan, 2012.

Balázs, Béla. *Béla Balázs: Early Film Theory*, trans. Rodney Livingstone, ed. Erica Carter. New York: Berghahn Books, 2010.
Barzilai, Maya. *Golem: Modern Wars and Their Monsters*. New York: New York University Press, 2016.
Brodnitz, Friedrich. "Politik auch im Film." *C.V.-Zeitung* 42, 17 October 1930, 550.
Fragment des Spielfilms Der Golem: Phantastisches Spiel in vier Akten. Directed by Paul Wegener and Henrik Galeen. 1915; Germany: absolut MEDIEN, 2007. DVD.
Freund, Karl. "Behind My Camera: New Possibilities for Shooting Film." In *The Promise of Cinema: German Film Theory, 1907–1933*, ed. Anton Kaes, Nicholas Baer, and Michael J. Cowan, 509–11. Oakland: University of California Press, 2016.
Granach, Alexander. *Da geht ein Mensch: Autobiographischer Roman*. Stockholm: Neuer, 1940.
———. *From the Shtetl to the Stage: The Odyssey of a Wandering Actor*. New Brunswick, NJ: Transaction, 2010.
"I.N.R.I." *Film-Kurier* 283, 27 December 1923.
Jung, Uli, and Walter Schatzberg. *Beyond Caligari: The Films of Robert Wiene*. New York: Berghahn Books, 1999.
Kaes, Anton. *Shell Shock Cinema: Weimar Culture and the Wounds of War*. Princeton, NJ: Princeton University Press, 2009.
Kolpenitzky, Max, "Der Jude im Film." *Israelitisches Familienblatt* 29 no. 31, 4 August 1927, 10.
Kracauer, Siegfried. "Greta Garbo: A Study." In *The Promise of Cinema: German Film Theory, 1907–1933*, ed. Anton Kaes, Nicholas Baer and Michael J. Cowan, 144–46. Oakland: University of California Press, 2016.
———. *Theory of Film: The Redemption of Physical Reality*. Princeton, NJ: Princeton University Press, 1960.
Nosferatu. Directed by F. W. Murnau. 1922; Germany; Kino Lorber Films, 2013. DVD.
Rentschler, Eric. *The Ministry of Illusion: Nazi Cinema and its Afterlife*. Cambridge, MA: Harvard University Press, 1996.
Shahar, Galili. "The Jewish Actor and the Theatre of Modernism in Germany." *Theatre Research International* 29, no. 3 (2004): 216–31.
Shohat, Ella, and Robert Stam. *Unthinking Eurocentrism: Multiculturalism and the Media*. London: Routledge, 1994.
Sieg, Katrin. *Ethnic Drag: Performing Race, Nation, Sexuality in West Germany*. Ann Arbor: University of Michigan Press, 2002.
Wallach, Kerry. *Passing Illusions: Jewish Visibility in Weimar Germany*. Ann Arbor: University of Michigan Press, 2017.
Wegener, Paul, and Henrik Galeen. "Der Golem: Phantastisches Filmspiel in vier Akten." In *Henrik Galeen: Film—Materialien*, ed. Hans-Michael Bock and Wolfgang Jacobson, 3–16. Hamburg: CineGraph, 1992.
Weinstein, Valerie. "Anti-Semitism or Jewish 'Camp'? Ernst Lubitsch's *Schuhpalast Pinkus* (1916) and *Meyer aus Berlin* (1918)." *German Life and Letters* 59, no. 1 (2006): 101–21.
Wollenberg, Hans. "Der Jude im Film." *C.V.-Zeitung* 37, 16 September 1927, 523.
Zwick, Reinhold. "Der Galiläer (Express-Film, 1921) and *I.N.R.I.* (Neumann-Film, 1923): The Silence of Jesus in the German Cinema." In *The Silence of Jesus in the Cinema (1897–1927)*, ed. David J. Shepherd, 211–35. New York: Routledge, 2016.

Chapter 2

ENERGIZING THE DRAMATURGY

How Jewishness Shaped Alexander Granach's Performances in Weimar Cinema

Margrit Frölich

Dass ich einen wahnsinnigen Lebensdurst habe und dass ich einen Zentner Größenwahn besitze, darüber sind wir uns ja alle einig. [We all agree that I have an insane thirst for life and that I possess a hundredweight megalomania.]

—Alexander Granach, diary entry, circa January 1914

Hier freilich hat mich eine überaus traurige Nachricht erwartet: unser lieber Freund Alex Granach . . . ist plötzlich auf eine ganz sinnlose Art gestorben, Embolie nach einer Blinddarmoperation. Wir sind unbeschreiblich traurig darüber. [Here, admittedly, I was met by exceedingly sad news: our dear friend Alex Granach . . . died suddenly in a completely senseless fashion, an embolism following an appendix operation. We are indescribably sad about it.]

—Theodor W. Adorno, *Letters to his Parents 1939–1951*

In November 1925 Alexander Granach, a prominent eastern European Jewish actor in Berlin at the time, responded to a circular inquiry by the managing director of the Reform Jewish congregation in Berlin, in which he was asked to comment on the Jewish presence in the German theater.[1] Instead of paying tribute to the many Jewish talents in Weimar culture, Granach used the opportunity to express his disdain for antisemitic notions of race, rejecting with trenchant sarcasm the illusory concept of German national art based on the idea of racial purity. Insisting on both his Jewishness and his humanity, he repudiated antisemitic prejudice as anti-human. Furthermore, his response manifests his wishful optimism, since he anticipated a humanist society without antisemitic prejudice, just eight years before the National Socialists' (Nazis') rise to power forced him out of Germany:

> If I were not such a true *Ostjude* [eastern European Jew], in other words, if I were fair, blond, and German, I would be delighted that my fatherland, in this case, the arts of my fatherland, in particular the dramatic arts, were being plowed, fertilized, and supported by these *Fremdstämmigen* [members of a foreign race]. These artists, who with their eternally elastic Talmud-intellect incorporate their eastern Jewish *Vollblut* [pure blood] into German art, indeed even beget and fertilize it are being harassed instead by clueless so-called patriots . . . as members of a foreign race. But I do not believe that vital forces can be repressed or even held back. . . . Everyone who contributes to delight and enriches life on earth, be they who they are, they all must fulfill their mission and duty toward human kind.[2]

In this chapter I argue that Granach's sense of Jewishness was shaped by a set of distinct social, political, and cultural circumstances and concrete personal experiences resulting from a specific historical and geographical context: his eastern European Jewish roots; his proletarian background; and his experience as a soldier in World War I, who served in the Austrian army, and who witnessed the territorial upheavals following the collapse of the Habsburg Empire in the aftermath of the war and the ensuing pogroms against the Jewish population in the eastern territories. These experiences provided the base for his artistic sensibilities and came together in his acting, both on stage and on the screen.

I propose to view Granach as an example that the paradigm of passing—that is, to conceal one's Jewish identity and make oneself invisible as a Jew within mainstream German society—was not the only option for Jews in Weimar Germany. Granach pursued a different strategy to cross the minefield of marginalizing attributions. From the time that he returned to Germany after World War I, Granach did not camouflage his eastern European Jewishness. On the contrary, he marked his "otherness" as an integral part of Weimar culture. Drawing on the dramaturgical practices of the expressionist avant-garde, which was associated with Jewishness, and which he in turn contributed to shaping, allowed him to do so.[3]

Fritz Kortner, with whom Granach appeared on stage and in two noteworthy films—the expressionist film *Schatten* (1923, dir. Arthur Robison) and the period film *Danton* (1931, dir. Hans Behrendt)—makes reference to Granach's actual historical experiences in war-torn Galicia, when he describes his performances: "Then there was the black-eyed Alexander Granach, who fled from Polish antisemitism to the tolerant Berlin of the postwar period. A sturdy proletarian, he stood on the Berlin theater stages. Used to appealing to deaf ears, he screamed like somebody who doubts that he will ever be heard."[4] Kortner's sketch is insightful in that it relates Granach's otherness—that is, his overwhelming stage presence and impressive vitality as an actor, in equal measure to his concrete eastern European Jewish experience in postwar Galicia and his working-class background.

Particularly striking is the fact that Granach insisted on both his eastern European Jewishness and his self-conception as a proletarian with almost militant urgency. When, after serving in World War I, he returned to Germany to pursue his acting career, he used the unique character of his physiognomy and his vocal strength, as well as his cultural roots, to emphasize both his Jewishness and his self-concept as an antibourgeois artist with proletarian roots. His social background, that is to say his self-understanding as a proletarian, became as much an integral component of his Jewishness as his Galician origin.

From Baker's Apprentice in Galicia to Star Actor in Berlin

Granach's stellar ascent from baker's apprentice in Galicia to celebrated actor in Berlin during the Weimar Republic was an extraordinary accomplishment. Born into a poor Jewish family in rural eastern Galicia, Alexander Granach (born Jessaja Szajko Gronach) arrived in Berlin in 1906 as a sixteen-year-old runaway, with years of exploitation as a baker's apprentice behind him and the burning desire to become an actor. His fascination with the theater initially had been sparked through visits of performances at Jacob Ber-Gimpel's legendary Yiddish theater in Lemberg; these early impressions, along with the blend of superstition and religion in the pious *Chassidic* (Hassidic) environment in which he grew up in Galicia, shaped his imaginary.[5]

Granach was well aware of the antisemitic mindset in which "Galician" was a synonym for "Jewish": "None of the Germans I knew in Berlin had had a good word for Galicia," he recalls in his autobiographical novel. "Romania, Bulgaria, Hungary, Serbia, Montenegro—no one took offense when these Balkan countries were mentioned. But mention the word 'Galicia,' and everyone turned up his nose."[6]

In Berlin, Granach supported himself as a baker and by polishing coffins. He took inspirations from reading Maxim Gorki, who like him had started out as a baker, and he joined an anarchist theater group that performed ambitious plays in Yiddish in the *Scheunenviertel* (Berlin's eastern European Jewish immigrant quarter). Granach recalls his early steps into acting with a pinch of self-irony:

> Before I knew it, I was a member of an anarchist group. . . . All the members of the group were foreigners, and hence were not permitted to belong to any sort of political organization in the Berlin of that time. In order to reach a wider circle, to give these "world-shaking" ideas a broader base, we decided to found a "harmless" theatrical society. . . . On our cake-and-coffee evenings, when people would be chatting pleasantly and dancing, I would break in with one of these wild melodramatic poems. I bellowed them out with such vehemence that people put their fingers in their ears. I took it very seriously, and at certain moments in my performance I threw myself on the floor and writhed and shed tears and sobbed so desperately and so realistically that my audience felt with me and people said that I was an "artist." . . . The anarchist group that had thought to disguise itself as a group of actors became to me simply a disguise which gave me the opportunity to act.[7]

Six years later, Granach was accepted into Max Reinhardt's legendary acting school and landed a five-year contract at Deutsches Theater, where he found himself amid a group of aspiring actors, soon-to-be luminaries of Weimar cinema and theater, such as Ernst Lubitsch, Fritz Kortner, Conrad Veidt, Joseph Schildkraut, and Friedrich Wilhelm Murnau.

To be sure, Granach's career as an actor represented a significant break with his Galician Jewish family tradition and social background. It appears, however, that the theater and its magic became a substitute for the spiritual enchantment the Wonder Rabbis of his Galician childhood generated in their interactions with the *Chassidic* population:[8] "To stand on the stage was for me what serving God was for my father—except that it was more joyful!"[9] For Granach, experiencing the legendary theater director Max Reinhardt at Deutsches Theater equaled such a spiritual experience: "We listened to Reinhardt like young Chassidim listen to their Wonder Rabbi."[10] The theater, it seems, became Granach's temple.

Notwithstanding Granach's enormous efforts in the prewar years to transform himself into a German actor—he rigorously studied German and underwent risky surgery to have his knock-kneed legs corrected for the sake of his career[11]—in the end he did not renounce his background and defended himself when someone assaulted him with antisemitic prejudice.[12] Yet in the prewar years, when straight out of acting school, he had launched his first contract at the prestigious Deutsches

Theater in Berlin, he had been pressured to change his first name from Jessaja to Alexander by the theater administration, because "Jessaja ... sounds too Jewish for the German stage."[13] Irrespective of this name change, which did not reflect his own desire to conceal his Jewish origin, Granach openly identified as *Ostjude* (his friends called him "king of the *Ostjuden*"[14]). Even after he had become a star in Berlin's established theater world, he stayed connected, in the words of his son, with the "militant and self-confident" proletarian eastern European Jewry at the *Scheunenviertel*.[15] He also maintained a strong interest in Jewish artists and an attachment to the Yiddish theater, at the same time that he was fully immersed in German cultural production.[16] Granach's career and lifestyle in Berlin give evidence of the fact that in his particular case becoming a celebrated actor on the German theater stage, a prodigy whose bursting energy was legend, who succeeded in shaping his German linguistic and acting skills to perfection on the one hand, and the distinct assertion of his eastern European Jewishness on the other were in fact not mutually exclusive.

Granach's Acting Style

Granach came to fame through his performances in cutting-edge theater productions in the 1920s, ranging from the expressionist theater to Erwin Piscator's leftist avant-garde theater. His performance in the leading role in Piscator's production of Ernst Toller's *Hoppla, wir leben!* (1927), and his portrayal of Lenin in Piscator's monumental production of Tolstoy's drama on Rasputin (1927) were milestones in his career. Arnold Zweig saw the role of the young revolutionary, Karl Thomas, which Granach transformed from an intellectual into a worker, as a prime example of Granach's talent to create a particular type: "So goes and stands a worker. This is how his arms extend. This is how his head, with the pre-shorn hair, rests dead between the ungainly shoulders, like a tool that is difficult to move. His movements are fraught with the stiffness to which the straits of the working conditions and the monotony of their activities re-cultivates young people."[17] Zweig noted that Granach embodied this character persuasively "in an uncanny way, forceful, transparent, doom laden," while lending him a "calm and composed tone."[18]

One of the first significant character roles Granach played on stage was Shylock in a production of Shakespeare's *The Merchant of Venice* (1920; in Munich). It was a role Granach had long desired to play, and to which he would return at different stages of his career. It gave him the opportunity to express the humanity of the archetypical Jewish character in the theater and give voice to Jewish suffering.[19] One of the last significant theater roles Granach played in Germany, in 1933, before he had to escape imminent arrest by the Nazis, because he was a Jew and because of his political engagement, was the role of Mephisto, a role that according to Granach best corresponds to the *Urtrieb* (basic instinct) of acting.[20] As his son explained, Granach played Mephisto as an imp. Doing so, his performance differed vastly from the Gestapo-like demeanor that the renowned actor Gustav Gründgens, who eventually replaced Granach, brought to the same role.[21] Granach's performance of the two key characters, Shylock and Mephisto, marked the two opposite poles of his register.

With his hyperintensity and feverish energy, his extraordinary physical agility, and his artistic sensibilities, Granach was a unique phenomenon in Weimar culture. According to Arnold Zweig, he had "the strongest temperament of his generation."[22] Instead of seeking to blend in and tone down his otherness, Granach put every effort into achieving the contrary. Critics described his stage performances as "wild," his temper "volcanic" and "untamable." They not only saw him as an actor driven by fury who used a role to hurl out a "private ire,"[23] but they also emphasized Granach's ability for nuanced character portrayals. Other critics praised his talent to oscillate between opposite registers and switch from tragedy to comedy, from horror to the grotesque, blending comical or caricatured features with earnest drama. Paul Falkenberg, assistant director to G.W. Pabst and Fritz Lang, recalls the impression Granach made on him in the role of Franz Moor in the opening scene of a production of Schiller's *Die Räuber*: "I was particularly impressed with . . . the way he calmed down the father with his whiny voice . . . and how he burst into tears out of pity, and how this lachrymose voice of fake pity then transformed into a satanic laughter, after the father had disappeared, with such an intensity that a shudder would run down your spine."[24]

Granach's intense acting style touched on the nerves of his generation: "I cried out and shouted bloody murder together with the whole young generation who had come home. We found ourselves in a world that was fat and cowardly and wanted to be left in peace. We cried out our disillusionment, our despair, our protest in its face."[25] One of Granach's lauded performances was in Brecht's *Trommeln in der Nacht*, where he played the male lead, a soldier returning home after the war, who realizes that his fiancée has betrayed him with another man, a wartime profiteer. One critic wrote, "Alexander Granach is made for the crouching and then exploding figure of the soldier presumed dead, who experienced the tragedy of the homecoming. His scream of the tortured creature bursts from the core."[26] While Granach shared the sense of betrayal and devastation with the generation of German war participants, he had also gained first-hand experience of what it meant to be an impoverished underdog from Galicia subjected to the torment and antisemitism of his superiors in the Austrian army, only to find out after the war that, as a Galician, he was no longer entitled to Austrian citizenship, since the Austrian Empire had collapsed.[27] It was these distinct historical experiences as an eastern European Jew and war veteran exposed to social discrimination and antisemitic resentment that shaped his sensibilities as an actor.

Granach's Film Career

Granach also left a mark on Weimar cinema. Between 1921 and 1931 he acted in more than thirty German films, a fact that he himself understated in favor of his main passion, the theater. He was mostly cast in supporting roles, yet the characters he portrayed had a key function within the narrative of a film. The range of characters he performed was considerable, yet more often than not he played social outsiders, villains, or rebels. His roles included, among others, the real estate agent Knock in Friedrich Wilhelm Murnau's *Nosferatu* (1922), the dubious paternal figure Schigolch in Leopold Jessner's film debut, *Erdgeist* (1923),[28] an impish juggler in *Schatten* (1923), an honest shoemaker falsely accused of murder in Wilhelm Dieterle's *Der Mensch am Wege* (1923),[29] and the traitor Judas Iscariot in Robert Wiene's religious epic, *I.N.R.I.* (1923), who betrays Jesus when he fails to persuade him to rise against the Roman oppressors.[30] He played a hunchback violinist in *Svengali* (1927) and a sex-starved foreign legionary in Kurt Bernhardt's adventure film *Das letzte Fort* (1928), a performance that earned him critical appraisal: "Alexander Granach's treacherous and capricious goblin Gestino belongs to the film's most charming acting accomplishments. . . ."[31] He embodied a seedy scoundrel in Richard Eichberg's German-British film production *Großstadtschmetterling* (*Pavement Butterfly*; 1929), who implicates the Chinese dancer Mah (Anna May Wong) in a crime, when she does not reciprocate his love. He performed earnest characters in a number of historical films, such as the Prussian general Hans von Ziethen in

Sanssouci (1922) and in *Schicksalswende* (1923), and the French revolutionary Jean-Paul Marat in *Danton* (1931).

Granach's last film in Germany, before he escaped from being arrested by the Gestapo, was G.W. Pabst's coal-mining drama *Kameradschaft* (1931), one of the most significant early German sound films. In this film, Granach played a coal-miner named Kasper in a German-French border town. Together with two mining buddies, he tears down an underground border wall in the mineshaft in order to rescue a group of French miners trapped on the other side after a mining accident. Pabst's realist coal-mining drama, with scenes shot on location in the mining shaft, received strong attention both for its humanist message—namely, the appeal to Franco-German fraternization and friendship between the nations at a time when appeasement politics were under fierce attack by the Nazis and other right-wing groups pushing a nationalist agenda.[32] When the film was screened in Berlin, Nazis in the cinema unleashed torrents of hatred against the actors who played the film's two protagonists, Granach and Ernst Busch, both of whom were known for their leftist politics.[33]

Granach was at the height of his acting career when the Nazis came to power in Germany. In 1933 Granach fled from Germany via Warsaw to Moscow. In Warsaw, he played the title role in Friedrich Wolf's contemporaneous drama, *Professor Mamlock*, and performed mostly with Jewish theater groups. Speaking Russian, Polish, and Yiddish gave him opportunities to pursue his acting career in Moscow, Warsaw, and Kiev. Granach also participated in two Soviet films. He played the role of a Bulgarian journalist, a friend of the communist rebel Georgi Dimitroff, in Gustav von Wangenheim's exile film *Borzy* (1936). In *Poslednij Tabor* (1936, dir. Jewgenij Schneider and Moissej Goldblat), a popular film that addressed the relocation of Russian Roma in the context of Stalin's agricultural collectivization, Granach played the leader of a group of gypsies. In 1937, in the course of the Stalinist purges, Granach was arrested by the secret service. Upon the intervention of the writer Lion Feuchtwanger, he was released and allowed to leave the Soviet Union. In 1938, he immigrated to the United States. Granach participated in a number of Hollywood films, most notably Ernst Lubitsch's *Ninotschka* (1939), where he played, alongside Greta Garbo, a Russian communist agent in Paris.[34] He also played in Fred Zinnemann's *The Seventh Cross* (1944); he is probably best known for his role as Gestapo officer Gruber in Fritz Lang's anti-Nazi film *Hangmen Also Die* (1942).

Nosferatu—A Vampire's Liaison: Real Estate Agent Knock

Granach was highly perceptive of the dynamics of scapegoating, of social and economic difference, and antisemitic prejudice. He brought these sensibilities, which were shaped by the historical circumstances in which he grew up, to the role of the eerie real estate broker Knock, which he played in the legendary vampire film *Nosferatu* (1922) by Friedrich Wilhelm Murnau. This role was probably Granach's most memorable film role during the Weimar years. Contemporaneous Berlin audiences no doubt recognized the charismatic Jewish stage actor on the cinema screen, even when he was cast, as in *Nosferatu*, in a supporting role. In this role he could excel because of his talent at oscillating between opposite registers, and switching from tragedy to comedy, from horror to the grotesque, thereby blending exaggerated caricature or slapstick features with earnest drama.

Henrik Galeen (born Heinrich Weissenberg) wrote the script, loosely based on Bram Stoker's Gothic horror novel *Dracula*. Galeen, like Granach, had a Galician Jewish background, but, unlike Granach, he tried to camouflage it.[35] Granach's character, the real estate broker, is the influencing factor in the story. He sets the fateful events into motion when he sends his employee Hutter on a dangerous journey to Transylvania. A quirky gnome with a circle of thinning white hair garlanding his half-bald head, Knock is both an eerie and a grotesque figure, reminiscent of E.T.A. Hoffmann's Gothic horror universe and characters like Coppola in *The Sandman*, who epitomize phantasms and unconscious fears. The uncanny air that emanates from Knock unsettles the peaceful idyll of the northern German harbor town where the story is set. "All sorts of rumors circulated" about Knock, states an intertitle. "The only thing for certain was that he paid his people well." An alien to the local community, without familial ties or genealogical relationship to the place, but with a telepathic connection to the vampire from the faraway eastern European region, the character is a manifestation of fears that the town's comfortable idyll may not be sufficiently safeguarded from potential ruin looming outside, because Knock mischievously undermines the protective shield from within.

When we see the real estate broker for the first time, he is sitting at a high desk with distorted Kafkaesque dimensions, dressed in an elegant, disproportionally long tailcoat that overemphasizes his short stature. In a close-up, the camera focuses on his antic play of facial expressions as he closely studies a letter he holds in his hands, which is filled with strange hieroglyphs. We see a scary grin forming on his face, and watch him concoct a strategy to lure his naïve employee to leave his home and wife behind and embark on a dangerous journey to Transylvania, the land of phantoms, promising him monetary gain, though he ominously predicts that it will cost the young man "a little effort . . . some sweat . . . and perhaps . . . a little blood."[36] The way he lifts his thick dark eyebrow, which thanks to the close-up we are able to observe as if under a magnifying glass, says it all: he is scheming and knows of the danger to which Hutter will be exposed.

What reverberates in the figures of both the vampire, with his thirst for blood, and Knock, as the ultimate stranger who invades the national body and brings harm, are the standard set of antisemitic clichés. It is not surprising that the townspeople, afflicted by the plague pandemic and "panic-stricken," turn on Knock, who in the meantime has succumbed to raving madness, "for a victim."[37] In a slapstick scene that deflects the violent nature of the scapegoating assault, the townspeople chase after the impish madman, who escaped from his cell in the insane asylum, hopping swiftly from one place to another.[38] He laughingly bounces his head to and fro in reaction to the stones that the townspeople throw at his head while he is sitting on top of a roof. Granach's unique blend of comic and tragic talent comes to the fore and lends itself effectively to this scene. What is crucial here is the way this scene is directed and acted: it does not disseminate or reinforce antisemitic resentment, but instead points to its disturbing impact, and critically deflects it. In other words, by turning the scene into a grotesque, Murnau, Galeen, and Granach, through the latter's unique acting style, purposely undercut the horror of the persecution of an outcast by the townspeople without stripping the theme of its actual seriousness. The whimsical playfulness of Granach's character notwithstanding, his performance reverberates an acrid awareness of the dynamics of scapegoating and being an outsider.

Schatten—Granach Plays an Impish Juggler

Siegfried Kracauer notes that *Schatten* (1923) is one of "the masterpieces of the German screen" that "passed almost unnoticed."[39] Based on an idea by Albin Grau, the silent film was directed by the American-born film director Arthur Robison. In this visually and dramaturgically splendid film, which carried the subtitle *A Nocturnal Hallucination*, Granach plays an impish juggler who has white magic at his disposal. His performance appears to have been inspired by the popular imagination of the Yiddish theater and the Jewish environment in his native Galicia, including the Purim play with its folksy, satirical, and comic features. The carnivalesque sensibilities Granach brings to the role of the prankish yet benevolent traveling juggler resembles a figure like the ones one could find in a Purim play or in the Yiddish theater of eastern Europe (figure 2.1).

One evening the juggler shows up at a count's home, and is invited in to entertain the soiree guests with a shadow play. With the illusion of light and shadows, he confronts the host and his soiree guests with their unconscious repressed desires and jealous fantasies. When he realizes that the count, who is mad with jealousy, suspects his coquettish wife of dedicating herself to the erotic advances of one of the four gallants attending the dinner party, the juggler hypnotizes the soiree guests. Thereupon they act on their instincts and unleash their repressed desires. The nocturnal hallucination culminates in the four cavaliers throwing the count out of the window, thus divesting themselves of their host, who had goaded them on to stabbing his pinioned wife. However, at dawn the juggler reawakens all the protagonists from their trance, and their shadows realign with their bodies. The protagonists regain composure, and everything reverts back to normal, as though no chaos had ever been wreaked. They have been cured by the sobering shock of the juggler's white magic. The count and his wife are reunited in blissful harmony, while the four gallants leave the house, as does the juggler. As Kracauer writes, "Their metamorphosis at the very end of the film coincides with the beginning of a new day whose sober natural lighting splendidly symbolizes the light of reason."[40] Considering this outcome, Granach's character is a paradoxical figure: a playful imp in his manners and visual appearance. He is clearly aligned with the realm of enchantment, yet in applying white magic, similar to the effects of the psychoanalytic cure, he succeeds in restoring the faculty of reason and prudence in others.

With the light of the day, ordinary quotidian activities resume on the square in front of the count's house, where medieval merchants trade their goods. The last shot of this stunning and humorous film, however, evokes a disturbing association. Back on the square in front of the count's home, the prankish juggler waves good-bye to the villagers and the count, while he rides away with a wink on the back of a pig. To be sure, the film portrays the juggler benevolently as a playful wizard. However, regardless of how much this final shot was meant to be a playful banter, it draws on imagery connected with medieval Christian

Figure 2.1. Alexander Granach with Ruth Weyher in *Schatten* (1923, dir. Arthur Robison). Source: Deutsche Kinemathek.

anti-Judaism, which used the pig as a symbolic figure to insult Jews, because the pig was symbolically associated with the devil and with religious and moral impurity. This final shot indicates the thoughtless entry of a traditional anti-Jewish stereotype into a film that is highly reflective with regard to the unconscious and the imaginary. Notwithstanding the film's overall charm, the subliminal association with anti-Jewish stereotyping implied in this final shot is bewildering, especially in light of the fact that Granach's Jewishness was well known to his contemporaries. It is baffling that both the film's director and Granach, the actor performing in this scene, seem to have been oblivious to the symbolic association underlying the imagery.

The Scream of the Tortured Creature: *Svengali*'s Violinist

Svengali (1927) is a silent film that illustrates Granach's prowess to bring to the screen and to create a visual expression of "the scream of the tortured creature."[41] Granach plays the hunchback violinist Gecko, a significant supporting part. He uses his physiognomy and draws on exaggerated gestures and facial expressions familiar from the expressionist theater to translate the acoustic scream that was a hallmark of his stage performances into a visual sound image. Here again Granach's performance indicates how he boldly asserted his otherness, which was shaped by the set of social and historical experiences he had as an eastern European Jew from Galicia, while incorporating key elements from the expressionist avant-garde, and morphing all this into his artistic signature.

Svengali is based on the bestselling novel *Trilby* (1894), written by the English author and illustrator George du Maurier. The 1927 film is one of many film and theater adaptations that followed the sensationally successful publication of the novel. Directed by the Italian filmmaker Gennaro Righelli for the German production company Terra Film, *Svengali* tells the story of the demonic, yet irresistible hypnotizer Svengali (Paul Wegener), a virtuoso pianist, who subjects a young woman named Trilby to his will. The narrative is set in the bohemian world of Paris, but the film transfers the mid-nineteenth-century setting of the novel to the contemporaneous time of the 1920s. Trilby is a young laundress with artistic aspirations who is in love with a painter named Billy, a young English expatriate. On an evening out with Billy and his friends, Trilby encounters Svengali, who accompanies her at the piano. She falls under his hypnotic spell, and suddenly she can miraculously sing with a sublime voice, as long as she fixates on his eyes. Intuitively, Svengali recognizes Trilby's readiness to surrender her will under his command and lures her away from her love interest, the young painter. However, it is not sexual interest that motivates Svengali to entrap the young woman, but economic considerations. Determined to overcome his lack of money, Svengali uses Trilby as a tool to come to riches, transforming her into a famous concert singer. Yet the enslavement causes her physical and mental strain, and the more Svengali pressures Trilby to perform, the more exhausted she becomes.

Svengali is one of the manipulative tyrants that populated Weimar films, a fictional character akin to Caligari and Mabuse. Paul Wegener, famous for his performance as the Golem, persuasively plays this role of the sinister enchanter who infiltrates the soul of his victim. In the novel, George du Maurier portrays Svengali as a Jew, using prototypical late-nineteenth-century antisemitic stereotypes, when he introduces him with the following features: "of Jewish aspect, well-featured, but sinister."[42] The cultural historian David Pick comments, "As the quintessential dark hypnotist of turn-of-the-century culture, Svengali gave a very particular edge to familiar prejudices in which the Jews were routinely cast as financial wizards, omniscient seers or mysteriously omnipotent bankers."[43] The German film adaptation stripped the narrative of such stereotyping and avoided any features that would define the Svengali character overtly as Jewish. Paul Wegner's performance makes tangible the charismatic and diabolic dimension of Svengali, allowing the contemporaneous viewer to associate the character with a wider range of fears and fantasies. Overtones of the Jewishness of the hypnotist Svengali from the original literary source, however, echo in the film. Granach plays a hunchback violinist named Gecko. Although a supporting part, the film enlarges the significance of this character. The violinist belongs to Svengali's entourage. Gecko and Sascha, a woman who begs for Svengali's love, are the minions of the mysterious piano player. Both express their servility toward Svengali. Gecko accompanies him on the violin when Svengali is hired to play the piano in a dance bar. He also follows Svengali's orders and plays the violin on a street corner for a pittance. We do not know where Svengali and his entourage come from, or where they belong; their origin remains obscure. Their homelessness and indistinct origin evoke the association with the stereotype of the wandering Jew. It is not entirely clear what holds them together beyond bondage and economic dependence.

In the role of Gecko, Granach enacts the crooked body posture of the hunchback violinist, and in doing so poignantly epitomizes through his pantomime the submissive, dependent, and oppressed stooge. Wearing heavy white makeup to highlight his facial expressions, Granach's character radiates subjugation. In each of his physical postures and gestures, his fear of Svengali's unscrupulousness becomes tangible. For instance, when he ducks away from the imperious Svengali, we can sense the torment of the oppressed to an excruciating extent. However, although Gecko belongs to Svengali's orbit and submits to his will, he is a well-meaning character. Considering the erased Jewish subtext of this film, this makes him a virtuous Jew. Gecko genuinely cares for Trilby and warns her to beware of Svengali, although his efforts come to nothing as Trilby succumbs to Svengali's power of hypnosis. He has feelings for the young woman, as we see in one scene when his hands reach out, longing to caress Trilby's body, while she is asleep from exhaustion. However, Gecko keeps his desire to himself and never touches her. Granach's part differs from the novel and becomes significant for the outcome of the narrative. Gecko, the subjugated minion of Svengali, eventually revolts against the oppressor. In a crucial showdown, he stands up against his master, demanding that Svengali free Trilby, who has fallen into a helpless state of delirium. Ignoring his master's threats, admonishing him to keep quiet, Gecko insists, "No, I finally have to speak up. You have no right to destroy a human soul,"[44] and shouts, unperturbed, "I want to scream it out loud ... all the world must know who you are!"[45] Although the stout Svengali approaches the small violinist in a menacing gesture, Gecko shouts out loud, "Murderer, murderer!" The showdown between the master and his revolting minion culminates when Svengali violently presses his hand on Gecko's mouth and strangles him, seeking to silence his opponent by exerting physical force against him. In a close-up we see Granach's face contorted with pain, before he then pulls out a knife from his pocket and stabs it into Svengali's chest. Yet oddly, there is no blood. Although Svengali is not fatally wounded, he is physically weakened as a result of Gecko's assault, and dies hours later from heart failure, in the middle of Trilby's last concert. Once the hypnotic connection between her and Svengali is cut off, the young woman loses her enchanting voice and suffers a physical breakdown. Whereas in the novel Trilby dies, the film concludes with a happy ending. In the end, after Trilby has been successfully treated in the hospital, Billy and Trilby are reunited, when Trilby returns home. This final sequence is entitled "Homecoming." The scenery in Billy's painter studio radiates brightness as the couple takes a seat out on the balcony. Gecko, his dark suit replaced with a brighter outfit, is part of the setting, which signals that he has found a new place where he belongs, in a world rid of sinister, manipulating tyrants. However, although Gecko has found a new home and may consider himself no longer an outsider to mainstream society, in the final shot he still remains excluded to some degree, separated from the romantic couple by a windowpane. Whereas Trilby and Billy sit down on the balcony and have a romantic moment, Gecko stays on its other side, ultimately a bystander who rejoices at the romantic couple's bliss, of which he himself is deprived. The hunchback violinist Gecko, who successfully revolts against the oppression by his master and rescues Svengali's chief victim, Trilby, may well be rewarded for his virtuousness, yet he cannot overcome the opaqueness of his origin that associates the character loosely with the stereotype of the wandering Jew. Here, as with the whimsical real estate broker Knock in *Nosferatu*, or the prankish traveling juggler in *Svengali*, Granach plays characters that can never reconcile their status as outsiders to the respective social sphere in which they appear, and the otherness he asserted so boldly as an actor seems to lend itself to such roles.

An Unrealized Film Project: *The Wall*

To better understand how Granach's sense of eastern European Jewishness and artistic purpose was shaped by his immediate historical experiences, we will turn finally to a film manuscript that Granach wrote around 1930, when he was living in Berlin. It is entitled *The Wall: A Segment of Much Suffering in Five Acts*. This film project intended to address the pogroms inflicted on the Jewish population in the immediate aftermath of World War I. When Granach, still a soldier in the Austrian army who had escaped from an Italian prisoner of war camp, briefly returned to his war-torn home in eastern Galicia at the end of the war, he found his family home destroyed as a result of czarist Cossacks having incited the Galician population to commit pogroms against their Jewish neighbors. The film project sought to depict the complicated relationships between the Jewish and Ukrainian populations in rural Galicia in the immediate aftermath of World War I, which both sought to carve out a meager living through farming. In a film exposé Granach explains the idea on which his film project was based: "The Wall is the metaphor for the fate between partners who seek to understand one another, but cannot. This is where the tragedy sets in. This is what my film is about."[46] The theme and the idea of realizing this project stayed with him for the rest of his life. In May 1935 he wrote a letter from Moscow to his companion, Lotte Lieven, asking her to send the film manuscript to him, if possible: "If you could somewhere get a hold of my film manuscript 'The Wall,' I need it very urgently. Because my next goal is to make this film. Directing. You know that this is a desire of mine. The chances are here."[47] Although the material was never made into a film, Granach eventually incorporated some of it into his autobiographical novel, which was published shortly after his unexpected death in New York in March of 1945. Moreover, in 1940, Granach directed a theater play based on related historical facts, which was performed by a Jewish amateur theater group of workers in Los Angeles. The play centered on Scholem Schwarzbard, a Jewish watchmaker, poet, and anarchist, who had lost his entire family in the pogroms, and who in 1926 assassinated the former Ukrainian dictator Semjon Petljura (celebrated today as a Ukrainian national hero), who was responsible for the murder of approximately a quarter million Jews in the pogroms between 1917 and 1919.[48] It was not until the subsequent trial of Schwarzbard in October 1927, which ended with the acquittal of the defendant, that the global public became aware of the massive pogroms that had been perpetrated on the Jewish population in the former Galicia after the end of World War I. Granach commented in an article published in *Aufbau* in 1940, "The tragedy of the Jews and the disgrace of humanity," and described the shattering impact of the atrocities on the ethics and morale of a person like Schwarzbard, who had witnessed the pogroms: "The dignity of godlike nature has been violated. Human dignity, the spine of a people and an individual, has been broken."[49] After the theater production's premiere, Granach wrote to his companion Lotte Lieven, "Between us, I think it was the best theater work I ever did."[50]

Given the personal significance that this historical material held for Granach throughout his artistic career in Berlin up until his exile in Hollywood, where he wrote his autobiographical novel *Da geht ein Mensch*, we can infer the extent to which the concrete historical experiences, most notably the pogroms against the Jewish population that Granach witnessed in his native Galicia, shaped his sense of Jewishness and his sense of purpose as an actor, even in roles that were not explicitly Jewish. Granach's acting career in Berlin in the 1920s up until 1933, when he was forced to flee from Nazi Germany, clearly indicates how immersing himself as an actor into German theater and film culture did not mean for him that he would conceal his Jewishness. Passing as non-Jewish for him was not a strategy, neither on the stage, nor in the cinema, nor in real life. On the contrary, throughout his prolific acting career Granach remained affirmative and robustly self-confident of his proletarian Galician Jewish legacy that laid the foundation for his prodigy as an actor.

Margrit Frölich is a film scholar and a cultural historian. She specializes in Weimar cinema, exile studies, and European intellectual history. From 2012 to 2017 she was DAAD professor of history, culture, and media at the University of California, San Diego. She currently works as director of studies for film and transatlantic dialogue at the Protestant Academy in Frankfurt, Germany.

Notes

1. The epigraph is from Theodor W. Adorno, *Letters to his Parents 1939–1951*, ed. Christoph Gödde and Henri Lonitz, trans. Wieland Hoban (Cambridge, UK: Polity Press, 2006), 213–14. Originally published in German: Theodor W. Adorno, *Briefe an die Eltern 1939–1951*, Frankfurt am Main: Suhrkamp, 2003, 305. Theodor and Gretel Adorno met Alexander Granach in the 1940s in Los Angeles. Gretel organized "a large gathering" at their house, "to honour the actor Granach, who read excerpts from his extraordinarily significant autobiographical novel, which one could probably best compare to a modern Pojaz" (Adorno, *Letters to his Parents*, 125). In another letter to his parents, dated 23 April 1944, Adorno described Granach as "one of the dearest people we have met since emigrating." (Adorno, *Letters to his Parents*, 182).
2. Letter by Alexander Granach to Dr. Woyda, 5 November 1923, Alexander Granach Archive (Granach 9). "Wenn ich nicht ein so echter Ostjude wäre, d.h. wenn ich hell, blond und deutsch wäre, würde ich mich freuen, daß mein Vaterland, d.h. in diesem Falle die Kunst meines Vaterlandes, besonders die Theaterkunst von diesen Fremdstämmigen umgewühlt, befruchtet und mitgetragen wird. Statt dessen, lieber Herr, werden diese Künstler, die ihr ostjüdisches Vollblut und ihren ewig elastischen Talmudintellekt der deutschen Kunst einverleiben, ja sie begatten und befruchten, . . . von nichtsahnenden angeblichen Patrioten zumindest als Fremdstämmige drangsaliert. Ich glaube aber nicht, daß vitale Kräfte unterdrückt oder gar aufgehalten werden können, denn schließlich leben wir in der Zeit des Radios, in der Zeit des vorwärtswuchtenden Tempos, wo es nicht allzu lange dauern wird, daß die Bewohner dieser Erde, dieses kleinen Balles, bald, ja bald wie Erbsen in einem Sieb durchgeschüttelt werden. . . . Sei es Technik, Wissenschaft oder Kunst, sie gehören allen Menschen, und alle Menschen, so wie Moses, Christus, Mohammed, wie Shakespeare, Beethoven, Goethe, wie Dostojewski, Einstein, Lenin der Menschheit gehören, so gehören dazu—ja ich gehe weiter—der schwarze Sänger Hayes und der weiße Caruso, die Erfinder des Radios und die Erfinder der Flugzeuge, Alle, die dazu beitragen, das Erdendasein zu beglücken und zu bereichern, seien sie, wer sie wollen, sie müssen Alle ihre Mission und ihre Pflicht den Menschen gegenüber erfüllen." Unless otherwise noted, the translations are all by the author.
3. Jeannette R. Malkin, "Transforming in Public: Jewish Actors on the Expressionist Stage," in Jeanette R. Malkin and Freddie Rokem, eds. *Jews and the Making of the Modern German Theatre* (Iowa City: University of Iowa Press, 2010), 151–73.
4. Fritz Kortner, *Aller Tage Abend: Autobiographie* (Berlin: Alexander Verlag, 2005), 326–27. "Dann gab es den schwarzäugigen Alexander Granach, der vor dem polnischen Antisemitismus in das tolerante Berlin der Nachkriegszeit geflohen war. Ein stämmiger Proletarier, stand er auf den Berliner Bühnen. Gewöhnt, an taube Ohren zu appellieren, schrie er wie jemand, der zweifelt, je gehört zu werden."

5. *Alexander Granach und das jiddische Theater des Ostens* (Berlin: Akademie der Künste, 1971). Jacob Ber-Gimpel's theater in Lemberg, founded in 1898, was the first independent Yiddish theater in Europe. The writer Joseph Roth and the painter Marc Chagall, as well as Franz Kafka, who saw one of the theater's guest performances in Prague in 1910, were inspired by Gimpel's Yiddish theater from Lemberg.
6. Alexander Granach, *From the Shtetl to the Stage: The Odyssey of a Wandering Actor* (New Brunswick, NJ: Transaction, 2010), 190. This edition is based on the first English publication, which came out in 1945, and was entitled *There Goes an Actor*. Granach wrote his autobiographical novel in German while he was living in California in the 1940s. The German version was originally published in 1943 in Sweden and is available in a current edition (Alexander Granach, *Da geht ein Mensch: Autobiographischer Roman* (Augsburg: Ölbaum, 2003). Note the slight difference between the English version, emphasizing the "actor," and the German version, focusing on "Mensch," the humanity of the decent, likeable human being according to the meaning of the word in Yiddish. Granach, *Da geht ein Mensch*, 265. "Die Deutschen in Berlin hatte ich sehr hässlich über Galizien sprechen hören. Rumänien, Bulgarien, Ungarn, Serbien, Montenegro—kein Mensch nahm Anstoß, wenn man diese Balkanländer nannte. Aber wenn das Wort 'Galizien' fiel, rümpften nur alle die Nasen."
7. Granach, *Shtetl to the Stage*, 142–45. Granach, *Da geht ein Mensch*, 201–5. "Bevor ich mich umsah, gehörte ich einer anarchistischen Gruppe an. . . . Der ganze Kreis bestand aus Ausländern und durfte damals in Berlin keinerlei politischen Organisationen angehören. Um auf breitere Kreise zu wirken, um diesen 'weltumstürzenden' Plänen eine breitere Basis zu geben und die Ideen des Nichtjuden Rudolf Rocker unter das jüdische Volk zu bringen, wurde beschlossen, einen 'harmlosen' Theaterverein zu gründen. . . . Wir veranstalteten Vorträge, Unterhaltungsabende, gemütliches Beisammensein bei Kaffee und Kuchen, mit Tanz und Rezitationen. . . . Wenn die Leute auf so einem Abend bei Kuchen und Kaffee plauschten und tanzten, zerstörte ich ihnen ihren Spaß und ihre Gemütlichkeit mit diesen wilden Wein- und Lachgedichten. Ich brüllte diese Balladen mit einer Vehemenz, dass sie sich die Trommelfelle hielten. Ich nahm alles sehr ernst, und an gewissen Stellen des Vortrags warf ich mich auf den Boden und wälzte mich in Krämpfen und Tränen und schluchzte so verzweifelt und echt, dass die Leute mit mir Mitleid bekamen und sagten, ich sei ein 'Künstler.' . . . Die anarchistische Gruppe, die glaubte *mit* Theater spielen sich zu tarnen, wurde für mich eine Tarnung *fürs* Theater spielen."
8. Granach, *Shtetl to the Stage*, 121.
9. Granach, *Shtetl to the Stage*, 183. Granach, *Da geht ein Mensch*, 256. "Auf der Bühne stehen war für mich dasselbe, was für meinen Vater der Gottesdienst war,—nur noch freudiger!"
10. Granach, *Da geht ein Mensch*, 255. "Wir lauschten Reinhardt wie junge Chassidim ihrem Wunder-Rabbi lauschen." This sentence is missing from the English text version. Compare Granach, *Shtetl to the Stage*, 182.
11. The Israeli theater scholar Shelly Zer-Zion interprets Granach's operation "as a radical means of erasing the 'Jewishness' from his body and creating a physical encasement through which the new aesthetic being—the one slated to produce the spiritual text of the new theatre—could emerge." Shelly Zer-Zion, "The Shaping of the *Ostjude*: Alexander Granach and Shimon Finkel in Berlin," in Malkin and Rokem, *Jews and the Making of the Modern German Theatre*, 190. See, for a similar argument, Galili Shahar, *theatrum judaicum: Denkspiel im deutsch-jüdischen Diskurs der Moderne* (Bielefeld: Aisthesis, 2007), 197. Both Zer-Zion and Shahar convincingly show how misshapen legs had become a popular trope in the antisemitic discourse about the Jew-

ish body around 1900 that informed medical discourse. This analysis of Granach's risky physical transformation, however, downplays the fact that Granach desired to correct a physical disability he had acquired through extreme strain due to long years of physical labor as a baker from an early age.

12. Leopold Lindtberg, "Alexander Granach," in: *Alexander Granach und das jiddische Theater des Ostens* (Berlin: Akademie der Künste, 1971), 15.
13. Granach, *Shtetl to the Stage*, 168. *Da geht ein Mensch*, 236-37. "Für's deutsche Theater klingt es zu jüdisch."
14. Gad Granach, *Heimat los! Aus dem Leben eines jüdischen Emigranten* (Munich: btb, 2008), 30. "König der Ostjuden".
15. Granach, *Heimat los!*, 30. "Die Ostjuden im Scheunenviertel hatten etwas sehr Positives: Sie waren militant und selbstbewusst." We owe to Alexander Granach one of the most vivid descriptions of the hustle and bustle of street life as well as the rich diversity of Jewish culture in Berlin's *Scheunenviertel* before World War I. See Granach, *Shtetl to the Stage*, 139. See for a study about the *Scheunenviertel* as the center of eastern European Jewish immigration in the early twentieth century: Anne-Christin Saß, *Berliner Luftmenschen in der Weimarer Republik* (Göttingen: Wallstein, 2012); about Jewish immigrants from eastern Europe: Trude Maurer, *Ostjuden in Deutschland 1918–1933* (Hamburg: Christians, 1986); about the *Scheunenviertel* as the microcosm of eastern European Jewish culture: Michael Brenner, *The Renaissance of Jewish Culture in Weimar Germany* (New Haven, CT: Yale University Press, 1996), 185.
16. For example, Granach met with the actors from the Habima, the legendary Hebrew theater from Moscow, when the ensemble gave a guest performance in Germany in 1926. Albert Klein and Raya Kruk, *Alexander Granach: Fast verwehte Spuren* (Berlin: Edition Hentrich, 1994), 49.
17. Arnold Zweig, *Juden auf der deutschen Bühne* (Berlin: Der Heine-Bund, 1927), 153. "So geht und steht ein Arbeiter, so verlängern sich seine Arme, so sitzt sein Kopf dumpf mit den vorgeschorenen Haaren, ein schwer bewegliches Werkzeug, zwischen den plumpen Schultern. Seine Bewegungen sind belastet von der Ungelenkigkeit, zu der die Enge der Arbeitsbedingungen und die Monotonie des Tuns junge Menschen umzüchtet."
18. Zweig, *Juden auf der deutschen Bühne*, 154–55. "auf unheimliche Weise eindringlich, durchsichtig, schicksalsbeladen" (155), "den gedämpften, still gefassten Ton" (154).
19. Granach, *Shtetl to the Stage*, 273–79.
20. Alexander Granach Archive (Granach 472).
21. Statement by Gad Granach in a film by Angelika Wittlich: *Alexander Granach: Da geht ein Mensch*, DVD (Munich: Zorrofilm, 2012).
22. Zweig, *Juden auf der deutschen Bühne*, 152. "Wild, außer sich, das stärkste Temperament seiner Generation, stürzt er sich in seine Rollen."
23. Herbert Ihering, *Von Reinhardt bis Brecht*, vol. 1, 1909–23 (Berlin: Aufbau, 1958), 332. "Granach ist immer der verwandlungsbereite, der Rolle hingegebene, der schöpferische erregte Komödiant. Aber der Furor, mit dem er sich in die Gestalt stürzt, bleibt neben der Gestalt spürbar. . . . Granach gebraucht die dichterische Figur zum Herausschleudern privaten Ingrimms."
24. Paul Falkenberg interview with Albert Klein for ZDF, 1985 cited in Klein and Kruk, *Fast verwehte Spuren*, 27. "Besonders die Anfangsszene beeindruckte mich sehr: wie er zuerst den Vater mit weinerlicher Stimme—ja, Vater—beruhigte und vor Mitleid in Tränen ausbrach, wie sich dann aber nach dem Abgang des Vaters diese larmoyante Stimme falschen Mitleids in ein satanisches Gelächter verwandelte, mit einer Intensität, bei der einem nur so die Schauder über den Rücken rieselten."

25. Granach, *Shtetl to the Stage*, 273. Granach, *Da geht ein Mensch*, 371. "Ich schrie und brüllte wie am Spieß mit einer ganzen jungen, heimgekehrten Generation. Wir fanden eine Welt vor, die jetzt fett und feige ihre Ruhe haben wollte. Wir schrien ihr unsere Enttäuschung, unsere Verzweiflung, unseren Protest ins Gesicht."
26. Max Osborn, "Programmzettel 1922," cited in Klein and Kruk, *Fast verwehte Spuren*, 24. "Alexander Granach ist wie geschaffen für die geduckte und dann explodierende Gestalt des Verschollenen, der die Tragödie der Heimkehr erlebte. Aus Herz und Nieren ringt sich sein Schrei der gequälten Kreatur los."
27. Granach, *Shtetl to the Stage*, 205, 254, 271.
28. In his film review, critic Herbert Ihering raised the question, "What remains of this film? Granach's first appearance as Schigolch (whom to enhance he has no opportunity, however), and specific physical moments of Asta Nielsen...." ("Was bleibt von diesem Film? Der erste Auftritt von Granach als Schigolch (den er aber zu steigern keine Gelegenheit findet) und einzelne körperliche Momente von Asta Nielsen....") Herbert Ihering, "Erdgeist," in *Berliner Börsen-Courier*, 27 February 1923.
29. No copy of this film, which stars Marlene Dietrich in a supporting role, seems to have survived.
30. For a discussion, see Maya Barzilai's chapter in this volume.
31. *Lichtbild-Bühne*, No. 163, 10 July 1929. "Alexander Granachs tückischer und unberechenbarer Kobold von Gestino ist mit die schauspielerisch reizvollste Leistung des Films...."
32. Helga Belach and Hans-Michael Bock, *Kameradschaft. Drehbuch von Ladislaus Vajda, Karl Otten, Peter Martin Lampel zu G.W. Pabsts Film von 1931* (Munich: edition text & kritik, 1997).
33. Klein and Kruk, *Fast verwehte Spuren*, 94.
34. Alexander Granach participated in the following Hollywood films: *Ninotchka* (1939, dir. Ernst Lubitsch); *The Hunchback of Notre Dame* (1939, dir. Wilhelm Dieterle); *Foreign Correspondent* (uncredited; 1940, dir. Alfred Hitchcock); *So Ends Our Night* (1940–41, dir. John Cromwell); *A Man Betrayed* (1941, dir. John H. Auer); *It Started With Eve* (1941, dir. Henry Koster); *Marry the Boss's Daughter* (1941, dir. Thornton Freeland); *Joan of Paris* (1942, dir. Robert Stevenson); *Joan of Ozark* (1942, dir. Joseph Santley); *Half Way to Shanghai* (1942, dir. John Ravlini); *Northwest Rangers* (1942, dir. Joseph M. Newman); *Wrecking Crew* (1942, dir. Frank McDonald); *Hangmen Also Die* (1943, dir. Fritz Lang); *Mission to Moscow* (1943, dir. Michael Curtiz); *For Whom the Bell Tolls* (1943, dir. Sam Wood); *Three Russian Girls* (1943, dir. Henry S. Kesler); *Voice in the Wind* (1943–44, dir. Arthur Ripley); *The Hitler Gang* (1944, dir. John Farrow); *The Seventh Cross* (1944, dir. Fred Zinnemann); and *My Buddy* (1944, dir. István Székely).
35. Irene Stratenwerth and Hermann Simon, *Pioniere in Celluloid: Juden in der frühen Filmwelt* (Berlin: Henschel, 2004), 139–45.
36. The German intertitle reads: "... es kostet zwar ein wenig Mühe ... ein bißchen Schweiß und vielleicht .... ein wenig Blut..."
37. The German intertitle reads: "Die angstdurchbebte Stadt suchte ein Opfer: es war Knock."
38. See Anton Kaes's perceptive analysis of the slapstick scene. Anton Kaes, *Shell Shock Cinema: Weimar Culture and the Wounds of War* (Princeton, NJ: Princeton University Press, 2009), 112.
39. Siegfried Kracauer, *From Caligari to Hitler: A Psychological History of German Film* (Princeton, NJ: Princeton University Press, 1974; orig. 1947), 114.
40. Siegfried Kracauer, *From Caligari to Hitler*, 114.

41. Max Osborn, "Programmzettel 1922," cited in Klein and Kruk, *Fast verwehte Spuren*, 24. "Schrei der gequälten Kreatur".
42. George du Maurier, *Svengali*, cited in Edgar Rosenberg, *From Shylock to Svengali* (Palo Alto, CA: Stanford University Press, 1960), 242.
43. David Pick, *Svengali's Web: The Alien Enchanter in Modern Culture* (New Haven, CT: Yale University Press, 2000), 4.
44. The German intertitle reads, "Nein, ich muss endlich reden, Du hast kein Recht, eine Menschenseele zu zerstören!"
45. The German intertitle reads, "Ich will es herausschreien . . . alle Welt soll wissen, wer Du bist!"
46. Alexander Granach Archive (Granach 496). "Aber die Wand als Schicksal zwischen Partnern, die sich verstehen möchten und nicht können. Da setzt das Tragische ein. Darauf ist mein Film aufgebaut."
47. Alexander Granach, *Du mein liebes Stück Heimat: Briefe an Lotte Lieven* (Augsburg: Ölbaum Verlag, 2008), 114. "Solltest Du irgendwo mein Filmmanuskript 'Die Wand' auftreiben, ich brauche es sehr nötig. Denn das ist mein nächstes Ziel, diesen Film machen: Regie. Du weißt, eine Sehnsucht von mir. Die Chancen sind da."
48. Alexander Granach, "Jüdische Arbeiter spielen Theater: Die Geschichte eines Pogroms," in *Aufbau*, New York 1940, vol. 6, 29 November 1940, No. 48, 11; reprinted in Klein and Kruk, *Fast verwehte Spuren*, 196–98.
49. Granach, "Jüdische Arbeiter spielen Theater." "Die Tragödie der Juden und die Schande der Menschheit," 196. "Die Würde der Gottähnlichkeit ist verletzt. Die menschliche Würde, das Rückgrat eines Volkes und eines Einzelnen, ist gebrochen," 197.
50. Granach, *Du mein liebes Stück Heimat*, 302. "Unter uns gesagt, ich glaube, es war die beste Theaterarbeit meines Lebens."

Archival Sources

Alexander Granach Archive, Akademie der Künste (Academy of the Arts), Berlin.

Bibliography

Adorno, Theodor W. *Letters to his Parents 1939–1951*, trans. Wieland Hoban, ed. Christoph Gödde and Henri Lonitz. Cambridge, UK: Polity Press, 2006. Originally published in German: Theodor W. Adorno, *Briefe an die Eltern 1939–1951*, Frankfurt am Main: Suhrkamp, 2003.

Alexander Granach und das jiddische Theater des Ostens. Berlin: Akademie der Künste, 1971.

Belach, Helga, and Hans-Michael Bock. *Kameradschaft. Drehbuch von Ladislaus Vajda, Karl Otten, Peter Martin Lampel zu G.W. Pabsts Film von 1931*. Munich: Edition Text & Kritik, 1997.

Brenner, Michael. *The Renaissance of Jewish Culture in Weimar Germany*. New Haven, CT: Yale University Press, 1996.

du Maurier, George. *Trilby*. Oxford: Oxford University Press, 2009. (Originally published London: Osgood McIlvaine, 1894).

Granach, Alexander. *From the Shtetl to the Stage: The Odyssey of a Wandering Actor*. New Brunswick, NJ: Transaction, 2010.
———. *Da geht ein Mensch: Autobiographischer Roman*. Augsburg: Ölbaum, 2003.
———. *Du mein liebes Stück Heimat: Briefe an Lotte Lieven*. Augsburg: Ölbaum, 2008.
———. "Jüdische Arbeiter spielen Theater: Die Geschichte eines Pogroms." In *Aufbau*, New York 1940, vol. 6, 29 November 1940, no. 48.
Granach, Gad. *Heimat los! Aus dem Leben eines jüdischen Emigranten*. Munich: btb, 2008.
Ihering, Herbert. *Von Reinhardt bis Brecht*, vol. 1, 1909–23. Berlin: Aufbau, 1958.
Kaes, Anton. *Shell Shock Cinema: Weimar Culture and the Wounds of War*. Princeton, NJ: Princeton University Press, 2009.
Klein, Albert, and Raya Kruk. *Alexander Granach: Fast verwehte Spuren*. Berlin: Edition Hentrich, 1994.
Klein, Albert, and Raya Kruk. "Erdgeist." In *Berliner Börsen-Courier*, 27 February 1923.
Kortner, Fritz. *Aller Tage Abend: Autobiographie*. Berlin: Alexander, 2005.
Kracauer, Siegfried. *From Caligari to Hitler: A Psychological History of German Film*. Princeton, NJ: Princeton University Press, 1974. Originally published 1947.
Malkin, Jeannette R. "Transforming in Public: Jewish Actors on the Expressionist Stage." In Malkin and Rokem, *Jews and the Making of the Modern German Theatre*, 151–73.
Malkin, Jeanette R., and Freddie Rokem, eds. *Jews and the Making of the Modern German Theatre*. Iowa City: University of Iowa Press, 2010.
Maurer, Trude. *Ostjuden in Deutschland 1918–1933*. Hamburg: Christians, 1986.
Pick, David. *Svengali's Web: The Alien Enchanter in Modern Culture*. New Haven, CT: Yale University Press, 2000.
Rosenberg, Edgar. *From Shylock to Svengali*. Palo Alto, CA: Stanford University Press, 1960.
Saß, Anne-Christin. *Berliner Luftmenschen in der Weimarer Republik*. Göttingen: Wallstein, 2012.
Shahar, Galili. *theatrum judaicum: Denkspiel im deutsch-jüdischen Diskurs der Moderne*. Bielefeld: Aisthesis, 2007.
Stratenwerth, Irene, and Hermann Simon. *Pioniere in Celluloid: Juden in der frühen Filmwelt*. Berlin: Henschel, 2004.
Wittlich, Angelika. *Alexander Granach: Da geht ein Mensch*. DVD. Munich: Zorrofilm, 2012.
Zer-Zion, Shelly. "The Shaping of the *Ostjude*: Alexander Granach and Shimon Finkel in Berlin." In Malkin and Rokem, *Jews and the Making of the Modern German Theatre*, 174–96.
Zweig, Arnold. *Juden auf der deutschen Bühne*. Berlin: Der Heine-Bund, 1927.

Chapter 3

THE JEWISH VAMP OF BERLIN

Actress Maria Orska, Typecasting, and Jewish Women

Kerry Wallach

"Maria Orska, she is simply the actual embodiment of the human beast. . . . Here, again, she is the man-beguiling Lulu, so vivid in her performance that one can almost hear her words."[1] With these lines in his review of *Die Bestie im Menschen* (1920–21), critic Fritz Olimsky describes Orska as she was widely regarded: a femme fatale Lulu or vamp type known for her tragic, expressive performances, who was often cast in psychologically complex roles involving dramatic love affairs. Orska, like her Hollywood contemporary Theda Bara, rarely moved beyond her reputation for playing this type of character. In addition to exploring the largely overlooked work of Jewish theater and film actress Maria Orska (1893–1930), this chapter takes Orska as the basis for a broader discussion about casting, Jewishness, and gender. To what extent were known Jewish actresses cast in certain roles—including roles that were coded Jewish—in Weimar films? How did widespread perceptions of Jewish women affect the reception of the roles they played?

In early-twentieth-century Germany, the circulation of Jewish types and stereotypes extended beyond individual films to actors whose bodies and previous roles established a kind of intertextuality.[2] By studying these types and the actors who played them, we stand to gain a better understanding of how typecasting figured in the construction of images of Jews and other minorities associated with racial or ethnic difference. Gender, too, played a significant role when it came to the depiction of Jews on screen and the casting of Jewish parts. Maya Barzilai's chapter in this volume explores typecasting with respect to several Jewish male actors, including Henrik Galeen and Alexander Granach. Jewish women experienced typecasting somewhat differently from their male counterparts: notably, Jewish characters and roles that were coded Jewish did not always go to Jewish actresses. For example, although vamp characters were arguably coded Jewish, most of the dark-haired actresses who played these roles were not Jewish.[3] Instead, the actresses themselves were more likely to be taken for Jewish because of their roles, and Jewishness was constructed based on perceived differences. The casting of such roles demonstrates how typecasting relied on both physical profiling and gendered stereotypes.

Maria Orska represents one of only a few female actors in Weimar cinema who was regularly typecast in roles that, although not usually explicitly Jewish, still serve to some extent as ciphers for Jewish otherness. The otherness projected onto Maria Orska was an integral part of her public image, and many of her performances were coded Jewish due to her dark coloring and eastern European background. Orska's characters simultaneously invoke the orientalized beautiful Jewess figure of the nineteenth century, and the seductive, dark-haired vamp of the 1910s and 1920s.[4] Her so-called exotic and bestial presence represents a type that was feared, admired, and even renounced for its difference—and also for its connections to Jewishness.

Always a Lulu or a Salome: Orska's Life and Acting Career

Although Orska's biography was typical insofar as she first worked in Vienna and then in Berlin, Orska spent the first sixteen years of her life in Russia and thus possessed a stronger personal connection to eastern Europe than many of her contemporaries. She starred in fourteen films from the mid-1910s into the early 1920s, though she was better known as a theater actress. By her November 1916 performances of Lulu in Berlin, Orska was marked as a certain type: a vamp who preceded other non-Jewish actresses (Asta Nielsen, Louise Brooks) who later became better known for their vamp characters in German films. Orska stopped making films in 1923, and died in 1930 at age thirty-seven, which prevented her from having as great an impact on the Weimar film scene as others. Still, her legacy is deeply entangled with German performance culture and its many players, and hers is a lesser-known story worth telling.

By most accounts, Orska was born Rahel Blindermann in 1893 in Nikolaev in southern Russia (near Odessa; today Ukraine).[5] She was reportedly discovered by Ferdinand Gregori, who heard her doing a dramatic reading in Russian of Nikolai Gogol's *Diary of a Madman*. Due in part to political persecution in Russia, she made her way to Vienna in 1909. Several sources claim that when Blindermann arrived in Vienna she was especially wise for her years because she had already participated in such revolutionary activities as an assassination attempt against the governor of Kishinev.[6] In Vienna she studied German, acting, and philosophy. She adopted the stage name Daisy Maria Orska while training and performing in Vienna, Mannheim, and Hamburg. Her creativity also took other forms, and she even tried her hand at writing a short tragedy titled "The Astronomer."[7]

After her arrival in Berlin in 1914, Orska quickly made contacts in the Berlin theater and film worlds, and celebrity soon followed. She became known simply as Maria Orska, a name that did little to mask her well-known foreignness and Jewishness. Orska was a diva par excellence; she was known to be wild, fiery, passionate, and enchanting on stage, but especially difficult to work with backstage and when the cameras were not rolling. In Berlin she often performed at the theater in the Königgrätzer Straße (Hebbel-Theater), where she worked with directors Carl Meinhard and Rudolf Bernauer, and in Max Reinhardt productions. Orska often appeared in public wearing fur coats and wraps; she was known for her signature pearl necklace, which was rumored to have such illustrious yet improbable origins as Bismarck or Grand Duke Nikolai Nikolajewitsch of Russia. Like many other actresses, Orska occasionally appeared as a fashion model, as in one fashion show for the designers Herrmann Gerson, Regina Friedländer, and Schwabe & Meyer.[8] As her fame grew, she was often featured in such Berlin magazines as *Elegante Welt, Berliner Illustrirte Zeitung, Der Querschnitt*, and *Die Dame*. She was dubbed the "uncrowned queen of Berlin."[9] On several occasions, photo spreads of her elegant and extravagant apartment were included in these articles. A modern portrait from 1926–27 by the photographer Yva (Else Neuländer-Simon) shows Orska in three different powerful and even triumphant-looking roles (see figure 3.1).

Two of Orska's theatrical roles, as Lulu in Frank Wedekind's *Erdgeist* (*Earth Spirit*; 1895) and as the title role in Oscar Wilde's *Salome* (1891), remained the ones for which she was best known, though her repertoire also included Grillparzer and Ibsen, as well as numerous Strindberg plays. Lulu, an inscrutable and seductive creature who brings

Figure 3.1. Maria Orska. Portrait by Yva (Else Neuländer-Simon). Berlin, ca. 1926–27. Source: Author's private collection.

about the death of multiple husbands, is forebodingly characterized as a menacing animal, perhaps a murderous snake, in the prologue of Wedekind's play. Orska's performances of Lulu convinced audiences and critics that Orska was "truly authentic" and played Lulu "as no one else would be able to play her again."[10] One journalist argued that even while performing other roles, Orska remained the quintessential Lulu, Delilah, or Pandora-type, "the deliberate vampire, prompted by the inner demon to suck the blood of men."[11] In fact, Orska played Lulu on stage more than five hundred times. Prior to Orska's performance of Lulu, others' interpretations of the Lulu character supposedly closely resembled Salome. In Orska's rendering, Lulu became more reckless, belligerent, and sensual, but somehow more sophisticated in the end.[12]

But, for whatever reason, Orska did not star in any of the Lulu films made while she was still acting. The 1917 film *Lulu* starred Erna Morena, and several other non-Jewish actresses went on to become far more famous for their Lulu roles in Weimar films. These actresses also became iconic in part for cultivating dark images, though they were neither exoticized nor typecast in the same way. Danish-born Asta Nielsen (1881–1972), who played Lulu in the 1923 film version of *Erdgeist* (dir. Leopold Jessner), was cast in a wide range of roles and was associated not only with the vamp type but also with many others. Similarly, American actress Louise Brooks (1906–85), whose Lulu in *Die Büchse der Pandora* (*Pandora's Box*; 1929, dir. G.W. Pabst) made Brooks an instant sensation in Germany, played a number of vastly different roles and is known to have condemned typecasting because it did not work for her.[13] Ofer Ashkenazi has suggested that the Lulu of Weimar cinema can be read as an outsider who seeks to become part of a middle-class milieu, but ultimately remains too destructive to combine her distinctive background with a bourgeois identity.[14] If Lulu is at once vamp and outsider, it is not difficult to see how this type—and the women who played her—also stood in for aspects of Jewishness.

As Salome, one of Orska's few overtly Jewish theatrical roles, Orska enchanted audiences with her sinister, bestial demeanor. Oscar Wilde depicts his sought-after heroine as powerful and vengeful; following her performance of the dance of the seven veils at King Herod's request, Salome demands the head of Jokanaan (John the Baptist) in return. Artist Ottomar Starke remembered helping Orska rehearse her Salome role: "She jumped around evilly with my [the Baptist's] severed head."[15] One critic described Orska in an early performance of Salome in Hamburg: "Half-naked, animalistic, with those quiet screams, she made pathos seem melodramatic and emphasized the sense that the word pathos meant nothing other than deepest misery."[16] Repeatedly performing savage, untamable characters only exacerbated perceptions of Orska as the embodiment of a certain type. Even a portrait of Orska by Dietz Edzard immortalized Orska in what was described as an animalistic style.[17] Orska was not the only notable Jewish actress to play Salome, though Orska's Salome was considered the most bestial. Hollywood film legend Alla Nazimova (1879–1945), another Russian Jewish actress, famously produced and starred in a 1923 early art film version of Wilde's drama. Patricia White has suggested that Nazimova's Salome was decadent, American, and woman-made.[18] Orska's, in contrast, was menacing, inhuman, and evocative of women's presumed suffering and neuroses.

Many recollections of Orska suggest that the tumultuous, scandalous nature of her personal life mirrored and informed the roles she played on stage and screen.[19] Orska had several traumatic love affairs, including a troubled marriage to banker Baron Hans von Bleichröder (1888–1938) that ended in divorce in 1925. She was rumored to have behaved erratically and eccentrically, including breaking glass candlesticks on a Paris street, throwing tureens of hot soup onto waiters, throwing valuable jewelry out of cars, and hitting her chauffeur with the handle of her umbrella whenever he took a wrong turn.[20] Personal crises afflicted Orska throughout the 1920s, particularly when her sister, Gabriele Sera-Manischedda, hanged herself in a Berlin hotel in 1926, reportedly in part due to her addictions to morphine and cocaine.[21] Orska, too, notoriously suffered from a morphine addiction and spent considerable time intoxicated (*im Rausch*), including while performing. It is telling that a striking photograph of Orska with exaggeratedly black-rimmed eyes illustrates the section on cocaine in a 1927 book on the history of vice.[22] Like Anita Berber, a German actress and dancer who was also widely known for her substance abuse and vamp roles and who died in 1928, Orska's life was shortened significantly due to her addictions.

The final decade of Orska's life included many personal and health struggles that took place in the public eye, which only exacerbated associations of Jewish women with mental illness and suicide. She performed on stage only rarely after 1927.[23] In December 1929, Orska was admitted to a sanatorium near Vienna. Six months later, on 15 May 1930, she died from an overdose of veronal sleeping medicine. Veronal was a common method of suicide at the time, including among German-Jewish women, who had a disproportionately high suicide rate.[24] The medicine was also immortalized in Arthur Schnitzler's novella *Fräulein Else* (1924) in which a Jewish girl from Vienna takes her own life, and in the 1929 film version of *Fräulein Else*, which starred Elisabeth Bergner.[25] Director Carl Meinhard described Orska's death as a "terrible suicide that lasted ten years for all the world to see."[26] One obituary described her transformation from the "nameless, slender, dark-eyed Polish girl . . . to the actress Maria Orska," who enraptured the public with "a nervous temperament" and "dark timbered Slavic voice . . . which in the same breath whispered and screamed and chirped and wailed, never surrendering the charm of exotic articulation."[27] Even in death, Orska could not escape her image as foreign, exotic, dark, and seductive. She is supposed to have been buried next to her mother in the Jewish cemetery of Vienna.

Maria Orska as Jewish-Coded Silent Film Star

Performances in fourteen films between 1913 and 1923 established Maria Orska as a silent film actress of note, though it would be inaccurate to consider her mainly as an actress of the Weimar era. Rather, Orska's film career spanned the inflation period and overlapped with only the first few years of the Weimar Republic; nine of Orska's films were made in or before 1917. None of the characters that Orska played on screen were explicitly Jewish, though many emerged in Jewish or Jewish-coded contexts or were shaped by the work of Jewish filmmakers. This suggests that male filmmakers—both Jewish and non-Jewish—did not hesitate to cast a Jewish actress in roles that reproduced stereotypes about Jewish women. In many of Orska's films, and especially in the melodramas, she played characters reminiscent of Lulu or Salome on some level: an exotic dancer, a lusted-after woman who drives men crazy, a savage vamp who is sometimes also a murderess. Even when she did not play a femme fatale as in the comedy *Die Sektwette* (*The Champagne Bet*; 1916), she still played a mysterious dancer. While nothing about these types is distinctly Jewish, they nevertheless align with stereotypes about beautiful, dangerous, and foreign Jewish women.

Orska worked with a number of German-Jewish filmmakers, and at least ten of her films had Jewish directors. One of her earliest films, *Dämon und Mensch* (*Demon and Man*; 1915), costarred Rudolph Schildkraut and was adapted from Abraham Schomer's Yiddish play *The Inner Man* by director Richard Oswald and producer Jules Greenbaum.[28] In addition, half of Orska's films were directed by Jewish filmmaker Max Mack and were produced by Greenbaum-Film GmbH, including *Das tanzende Herz* (*The Dancing Heart*; 1916) and a six-film series released in 1916–17.[29] Max Mack (1884–1973), born Moritz Myrthenzweig as the son of a cantor in Halberstadt, was a prolific director who at times even drew on his Jewish background in his writing about film theory.[30] Orska was depicted in several photographic illustrations to Mack's 1916 edited book on screen culture, including in a photo of the diva who quarrels with the director and writer.[31] One early glowing review of Mack's Maria-Orska-Series noted that Orska was a "sensation" with a "decidedly distinctive individuality."[32]

Considered an identifiably Jewish actress mainly because of her striking dark looks, which were associated with Jewishness and eastern otherness, Orska's image was also shaped by body language, makeup, gestures, and temperament. Even though she played very few Jewish roles, she could not escape nominal Jewish associations. The right-wing nationalistic *Deutsche Zeitung* counted Orska among actors of Semitic origin (Jessner, Kortner, Bergner) whom it alleged should perform as such (i.e., as openly or obviously Jewish) rather than simply performing as German actors.[33] Countless critics reinforced Jewish stereotypes by relying on the same dubious adjectives to describe Orska's presence time and again: dark, exotic, and Russian or Slavic. Director Rudolf Bernauer deemed her especially capable of portraying "an exotic woman."[34] Critic Hanns Brodnitz described a vision of Orska playing Cleopatra (a role she never played) in part because Orska "was not of a Germanic temperament, she would have brought the whole world of Egypt."[35] Actor Hubert von Meyerinck, a friend of Orska's, described her as "a small, dark, very Slavic little person" with "night-black hair."[36] As a Russian-born actress, Orska was depicted as darker and more exotic than her contemporaries Elisabeth Bergner, Fritzi Massary, and Irene Triesch, who were also of Jewish descent and likewise lived in Vienna and later Berlin.[37] Journalist Doris Wittner suggested that Orska used her experience of being a foreign-born Jew to inspire her performance of exotic characters in Germany.[38] This sentiment was shared by other Jewish journalists, who focused on how Orska's intense empathy and the real tears she shed on stage were connected to the oppression she experienced as a Russian Jew.[39] It is worth noting that the terms "Russian" and "Slavic" were often code for "Jewish"; the fact that Orska was both only underscored her Jewishness.

Orska's performance in the title role of *Die schwarze Loo, oder Die Komposition des Anderen* (*The Black Dancer, or the Composition of the Other*; 1917), the last film in the series directed by Max Mack, offers an especially potent example of the exoticization of the Jewish-coded other, and of the transference of Jewishness onto otherness more generally. This is one of only a few Orska films that is not lost; in fact, it has been digitized and is available online. The film premiered on 6 September 1917, in the Marmorhaus Berlin.[40] The name "Loo" evokes Lulu on some level, and perhaps also Salome. Even Loo's epithet, "black," hints at her otherness and her eastern coloring. As a *temperamentvolle Zigeunerin* (temperamental gypsy) who dances in cellar bars, the "Black Loo" is subjected to the gaze and whims of rowdy drinkers. Loo's seductive dance moves with scarf and tambourine, paired with her heavily lined eyes and unruly black wavy hair, provide inspiration to Fredo (Bruno Ziener), a composer working on an operatic Hungarian dance scene, who discovers her in the bar. Loo moves in with Fredo and continues to dance for him at home; he credits Loo with a share of his future success. But Loo returns to the cellar bar to dance and, after a scuffle breaks out, is arrested and jailed. Thinking that she has left him, Fredo succumbs to his illness and dies. After Fredo's death, Loo charms her way into an upscale restaurant, where she dances to earn money for the burial. Here she meets another composer and conductor, Erwin Burchardt (Theodor Loos), and she achieves bourgeois respectability as his wife. When Erwin wants to publish Fredo's score as his own in order to be appointed to a professorship, Loo expressly forbids it, and Erwin attempts suicide. Erwin recovers and receives his position after all, and Loo is able to publish Fredo's papers.

The exotic gypsy character in *Die schwarze Loo* can be read as a cipher for eastern Jewish otherness. A short summary of the film in *Licht-Bild-Bühne* described Orska's dance in the cellar bar as "a free, unattached daughter of the vaste steppes."[41] The word "steppes" underscores the character's Russianness, which also stood in for Jewishness. In referencing gypsy otherness, the film also draws on stereotypes of exotic or transgressive femininity that extended beyond a strictly racialized group (Sinti and Roma). The category "gypsy" as it is used here includes those who embraced the fantasy of a Bohemian lifestyle (artists, prostitutes, beggars). This ambiguity leaves the character open to interpretation and circumvents accusations of antisemitic or Jewish-critical representation, while still situating Loo within this milieu. Hinting at sexual transgression and otherness evokes forms of difference ranging from gypsy to Jewish or Black; the erotic and exotic are closely intertwined. Indeed, Loo holds erotic power over men thanks in part to her connections to the exotic.

Furthermore, Loo's deeply expressive movements are exaggerated in the typical manner of expressionist silent film, which was often coded Jewish or conflated with Jewishness.[42] Both while dancing and in other scenes, such as her time in jail, Orska uses extreme facial expressions and flings her arms about wildly to conjure up a different type of creature. Yet unlike Lulu, Loo manages to suppress her urges to dance and become respectable. Her upward mobility points to the complex processes of acculturation and embourgeoisement of Jews in Germany and parallels the experience of many other Jewish-coded figures in Weimar cinema. As a femme fatale figure, Loo is more complicated in that she does not wish harm upon men who treat her well. Nevertheless, one could argue that Loo causes Fredo's death through her absence and insistence that she should be allowed to return to dancing, and that she nearly brings about Erwin's demise as well. Although she appears innocent enough, her unconventional and unruly acts serve her own agenda.

After 1917 Orska took a brief hiatus from film, possibly due to poor health, but she returned in 1920 and acted in five films during the early Weimar years (1920–23).[43] Her Weimar-era films included *Die letzte Stunde* (*The Last Hour*; 1920, dir. Dimitri Buchowetzki), *Die Bestie im Menschen* (*The Beast in Man*; 1920–21, dir. Ludwig Wolff), *Der Streik der Diebe* (*The Thieves' Strike*; 1920–21, dir. Alfred Abel), *Opfer der Leidenschaft* (*Victim of Passion*; 1922, dir. Paul Czinner), and *Sanssouci*, the third film of the four-part epic costume drama *Fridericus Rex* (1923, dir. Arsen von Cserépy). At least two of these films position Orska's character at the center of deathly love entanglements, and in her last film, she played the minor role of dancer Barbarina Campanini.[44] Reviews of Orska's performances in these films were generally favorable, though occasionally she disappointed. One typical complaint was that, like many other theater actors, she could not properly translate her acting skills to silent film.

As in *Die schwarze Loo*, Orska's Weimar film characters were often seductive, tempestuous, wicked, and/or exotic women who witness or bring about the deaths of their lovers. In *Die Bestie im Menschen*, the film referenced at the beginning of this chapter, which was based on a novel by Emile Zola, Orska played Severine, the wife of a train station manager, Roubaud (Eduard von Winterstein). After Roubaud kills Severine's first lover, she ultimately meets her death at the hands of another lover, Lantier (Josef Runitsch), whom she had seduced in an attempt to persuade him to kill Roubaud. The murderous intent of the vamp is again interwoven with the seductive powers of an emotional Orska character. But in the film it is Severine who, thanks to Orska, takes on bestial qualities; this stands in contrast to Zola's novel, where Lantier is depicted as the mentally ill human beast. In his review of this film, critic Hans Wollenberg commented on Orska's strange and paradoxical mix of attributes, from love and coquetry, to timidity and criminal instincts.[45]

In *Opfer der Leidenschaft*, Orska's character, Mia, indirectly brings about the death of her husband. Mia falls in love with Raolo Benghatti (Johannes Riemann), an artist who paints her likeness before ever meeting her—the painting is titled *Sehnsucht* (*Longing*). Devastated by losing Mia to the artist, her husband Alberto (Paul Bildt) kills himself. Mia and Raolo are wracked with guilt over the death of Alberto, and Raolo subsequently goes crazy and attempts to poison himself; Mia helps nurse him back to health. Here, as in many of director Paul Czinner's later films, two men desire the same woman, but in *Opfer der Leidenschaft* it is the men who fall victim. Later Czinner films starred not Orska but Elisabeth Bergner, who was far more likely to play tragic femme fragile types, who themselves died by suicide. In contrast to Bergner, Orska was cast as a femme fatale or vamp type that was bound up with her appearance, her Russian Jewish background and exotic appeal, and her wild personal life. Orska was not the only Jewish woman cast as a vamp or femme fatale, but she was the only major Jewish actress to play numerous roles of this type in German films of this era. A closer examination of the typecasting of Orska as well as two other actresses of the 1910s and 1920s sheds light on how gender and ethnicity worked together to determine potential roles.

Typecasting, Gender, and Racial/Ethnic Minorities

Film casting has always been dependent on the physicality of actors, and typecasting is to some degree unavoidable. Filmmakers use actors who can play certain types in order to help manage branding and minimize financial risk.[46] The use of types establishes a shorthand both for filmmakers and for viewers, who recognize character attributes more quickly when they have already seen an actor play similar roles. Some actors benefit from typecasting and get more work because they can play a type that is in demand, whereas others are denied parts because they do not meet the desired specifications. Jewish actors of the Weimar period fell into one or both of these categories. Although Jewish actresses were cast as different types (for example, Orska as a femme fatale and Bergner as a femme fragile), they were less likely than male actors to be cast as Jewish characters. In general, both male and female Jewish actors who fit stereotypes about Jewish appearance were at times typecast along ethnic lines, which included emphasizing anything that could be considered foreign or other. Gender also played a significant role in typecasting. Whereas perceptions of racialized or ethnic difference often resulted in the casting of Jewish male actors in stereotypically Jewish roles, the same traits led to the casting of certain Jewish actresses in sexualized and Jewish-coded roles that were not overtly Jewish.

A brief look at the origins of typecasting in early Hollywood—particularly when it came to minority parts—helps contextualize the kind of typecasting that took place in Weimar film. In 1910s Hollywood, typecasting originally took a more literal form, meaning that real people instead of actors were recruited to play parts that they somehow resembled. As psychologist Hugo Münsterberg put it in 1916, "If [the producer] needs the fat bartender with his smug smile, the humble Jewish peddler, or the Italian organ grinder, he does not rely on wigs and paint; he finds them all ready-made on the East Side."[47] With the emergence of the star system in the late 1910s, the focus turned to individual actors whose fame brought audiences to the theater time and again. Race played a major role in Hollywood casting, and in the 1910s and 1920s, Black actors were shut out of mainstream films and found work mainly through small, independent companies. For decades, Hollywood's avoidance of mixed-race love systematically excluded minority actors from lead roles; this exclusion was formalized with the strict enforcement of the Hays code (1934 to the 1950s), which prevented actors of color from playing characters in relationships with white actors. White actors, and especially white women, thus played minority parts in mainstream film with the help of makeup: blackface, brownface, and yellowface.[48] Jewish actors in Hollywood were far more privileged and avoided exclusion according to this racial divide, though they were at times cast in roles that highlighted Jewish or ethnic difference.

In German films in the late 1910s and in the Weimar Republic, a number of male Jewish actors were repeatedly cast in similar roles, including some roles as Jewish characters. Leading actors who were in this situation include Ernst Deutsch, Fritz Kortner, and Alexander Granach. Several others (Siegfried Arno, Fritz Grünbaum) worked as character actors and were often cast as Jewish-coded characters who were the subject of ridicule or mockery. In general, there were fewer films with Jewish women characters, and a number of non-Jewish actresses were profiled and cast in Jewish roles according to their background and appearance. Many hailed from eastern Europe or had dark coloring: Pola Negri (Lea in *Der gelbe Schein* [*The Yellow Ticket*], 1918), Lyda Salmonova (Miriam in *Der Golem*, 1920), and Elizza la Porta (Rahel Süß, the rabbi's daughter, in *Leichte Kavallerie* [*Light Cavalry*], 1927), to name a few. These and other non-Jewish actresses such as Lya de Putti were considered Jewish looking, and at times were presumed Jewish.[49] Only rarely did Jewish actresses perform Jewish characters in Weimar film, and in most of these instances their characters displayed Jewishness only in highly subtle ways, if at all.[50] One notable exception is Grete Berger's minor role as the rabbi's wife and mother of protagonist Baruch Mayer in *Das alte Gesetz* (*The Ancient Law*; 1923). It is also worth noting that a few other German-Jewish actresses played bold vamp-like or tyrannical characters that were coded Jewish on some levels: Betty Amman (in *Asphalt*, 1929) and Valeska Gert (especially in *Tagebuch einer Verlorenen* [*Diary of a Lost Girl*], 1929).[51]

More than other actresses, Maria Orska provides an important example of the typecasting of a Jewish woman according to a sense of racialized or ethnic Jewish difference. Orska was not only seen as dark-haired, foreign or Russian, and Jewish, but she was also notoriously wild. The combination of these characteristics resulted in the constant exoticization of Orska when it came to casting, which enables us to draw parallels between Orska and others who were perceived as ethnically exotic. Orska's dark coloring made her a natural fit for exotic eastern roles, from Salome to a gypsy dancer. On this level, Maria Orska can be understood as a German counterpart to Theda Bara, or as a Jewish counterpart to Anna May Wong. Like both Bara and Wong, Orska was considered exotically seductive; in several films, she, too, played a dancer. But as a white actress, Orska was cast in numerous lead roles. Still, it is likely that the roles for which she was considered were limited to some degree by how she was perceived. Although the vamp type for which Orska was known may have prevented her from being cast in different film roles, it presumably also helped her land some roles according to type, and thus was not necessarily detrimental to her career.

In many ways, Orska's career parallels that of her Hollywood contemporary Theda Bara (1885–1955), the very first actress to earn the vamp title thanks to her role as the vampire in *A Fool There Was* (1915). While Bara's vampire was more human and less otherworldly than other contemporary vampires (for example, Count Orlak in *Nosferatu*, 1922), representations of vampires have long been tied to antisemitic portrayals of Jews.[52] Theda Bara, a Jewish American actress, was born Theodosia Burr Goodman to parents from eastern Europe and Switzerland. Bara never managed to break away from this beautifully wicked type and was repeatedly cast as a vamp or villainess for the duration of her short film career, which fizzled after 1918–19 and ended completely in 1926. Like Orska, she, too, played exotic orientalized and sexualized characters, from Cleopatra to Salome. Thanks to the wide distribution of the (now lost) 1918 *Salome* film, Bara was possibly the best-known Salome actress of the 1910s in the United States.[53] Ronald Genini has suggested that Bara exemplified the psychic vampire—a human whose vampirism related to sexual conquest and did not include actual bloodsucking—which differed from the femme fatale only insofar as the vamp possessed a kind of extreme and quasi-supernatural exoticism. Bara achieved this image through hair dye and makeup that transformed her from a blonde to a brunette and emphasized the "dark and midnight beauty" associated with evil women. Dark eye makeup was used to make her look more exotic and sinful; dark blue costumes accentuated her ghostly whiteness.[54]

In part because Hollywood operated on a much larger scale, Bara was far more successful and better known than Orska—though Bara's stardom ended somewhat more abruptly. The *New York Times* estimated in 1916 that half a million people a day, or 182 million per year, watched Theda Bara films.[55] It is possible that Bara's Jewish background was not widely known until 1918, when an article critical of Bara suggested that her exotic persona was a cover for Jewishness. Some scholars have suggested that it was not a coincidence that Bara's image ceased to appeal once her Jewishness came under public scrutiny, whereas others argue it had more to do with production trends during and shortly after World War I.[56] Regardless of the extent to which Jewishness impacted the end of Bara's career, it is clear that her exotic appeal was part of what enabled her to achieve success as original vamp. But Jewishness was also associated with the "dangerous" influx of eastern European immigrants in both the United States and Germany, and exoticism linked to Jewishness was not always received positively. For Bara, being associated with the vamp type was the path to both celebrity and downfall.

Chinese American actor Anna May Wong (1905–61) offers another example of an actress who could not avoid being typecast—and racially profiled—in both Hollywood and Germany. In fact, it was partly due to Anna May Wong's exclusion from leading roles in Hollywood that she migrated to Germany in 1928. In leaving America for Europe, she joined other performers of color including Josephine Baker and Paul Robeson. Director Richard Eichberg quickly discovered and capitalized on Wong's talents, but perhaps because Wong represented an unknown kind of foreignness—there were not many people of Chinese descent in Weimar Germany—he helped create a "dangerous exotic quality that marginalized [her] characters and doomed their fates."[57] In her first four films in Germany, Wong was cast as a dancer, though unlike Orska's and Bara's femmes fatales, Wong's characters were more likely to perish or be exiled. For example, in her first German film, *Schmutziges Geld* (*Song*; 1928), Wong played Song, a rescued refugee who entrances audiences with her beauty and in one of the final scenes performs an exotic knife dance, ultimately dying after she falls on the knife. Cynthia Walk has argued that Song and other characters played by Wong posed a "multilayered sexual, racial, and colonial threat" that disappeared with their deaths.[58] Although race and racial profiling accompanied the casting of Wong and shaped the films in which she starred, Wong (like Orska and Bara) benefited to some extent from the stardom that came with repeat roles. Still, the fact that she was considered to be ethnically and racially different certainly prevented Wong from obtaining other roles.

Where typecasting becomes damaging is not at the level of the individual actor or filmmaker, for whom an actor's ability to deliver a certain type consistently has the potential to be advantageous, but rather when it creates and reinforces negative images that are projected onto minority cultures. Female characters coded as Jewish in German cinema were depicted as dangerous, dark, and foreign, which in turn might have reflected poorly on perceptions of Jews as a whole—a complaint that persisted also in Weimar Jewish film criticism with respect to male actors.[59] A Chinese actress whose characters were perceived as a threat was similarly not well positioned to advance the acceptance of Chinese and other East Asian actors in white-dominant contexts. The fact that numerous actresses of the 1910s and 1920s were time and again cast as exotic, sexualized characters only reinforced the exclusion of ethnic and racial or racialized minorities from both cinema and society. In recent years, both advocacy groups and scholars have drawn attention to the fact that twenty-first-century typecasting still disproportionately and adversely affects actors of color and other minorities. Sociologist Nancy Wang Yuen has pointed out that many Black actors have won awards for playing slaves, servants, and criminals, suggesting that stereotypes and racial bias still play a major role in how minority actors are cast, perceived, and valued.[60]

Already in the 1910s and 1920s, typecasting limited the range of parts offered to many actors, thereby preventing them from achieving their full potential. It was not only perceived ethnic difference or eastern heritage that led to the typecasting of such Jewish actresses as Maria Orska and Theda Bara, but these factors certainly played a role. With Anna May Wong, we see an even more extreme version of how typecasting led some minority actors to leave Hollywood in pursuit of lead roles abroad. In Germany in the early twentieth century, many Jewish actors inhabited an intermediate semi-ethnic category for which typecasting did not always apply. Jews were considered other, to be sure, but Jewish difference was not always obvious or known. Yet certain Jewish actors with dark coloring and eastern roots were highly susceptible to profiling and were especially likely to be typecast. In the case of Maria Orska, this took the form of repeatedly playing a femme fatale type who was equal parts Jewish-coded and evil.

Kerry Wallach is associate professor of German studies and an affiliate of the Jewish Studies Program at Gettysburg College. She is the author of *Passing Illusions: Jewish Visibility in Weimar Germany* (University of Michigan Press, 2017), as well as a number of articles on German-Jewish culture.

Notes

1. "Maria Orska, sie ist eben die gegebene Darstellung jener Verkörperung der menschlichen Bestie. . . . Auch hier ist sie die männerbetörende Lulu, so plastisch in ihrem Spiel, daß man fast ihre Worte zu hören glaubt." Fritz Olimsky, *Die Bestie im Menschen*, review dated 16 February 1921, folder F12086_OT, Stiftung Deutsche Kinemathek, Schriftgutarchiv, Berlin.
2. Amy Cook, *Building Character: The Art and Science of Casting* (Ann Arbor: University of Michigan Press, 2018), 13, 40.
3. Dark hair was less likely to appear in images of women in the early 1930s due in part to its associations with Jewishness. See Darcy Buerkle, "Gendered Spectatorship, Jewish Women and Psychological Advertising in Weimar Germany," *Women's History Review* 15, no. 4 (2006): 625–36.
4. S.S. Prawer briefly references the beautiful Jewess (*schöne Jüdin, belle Juive*) type in Weimar cinema. See S.S. Prawer, *Between Two Worlds: The Jewish Presence in German and Austrian Film, 1910–1933* (New York: Berghahn Books, 2005), 63, 198.
5. Conflicting versions of Orska's biography have been in circulation. For example, one Munich-based magazine reported that Orska was born Rachel Tobusch in Lodz, Poland. "Dämon Morphium (Leben und Sterben einer kranken Künstlerin)," *Illustrierter Sonntag, das Blatt des gesunden Menschenverstandes*, 27 July 1930.
6. "Daisy—Maria Orska," unidentified typed document, folder 7015, Stiftung Deutsche Kinemathek, Schriftgutarchiv, Berlin. On her revolutionary activities, see also "Tragödie einer Tragödin. Zum Tode von Maria Orska," *Israelitisches Familienblatt* 32, no. 21 (22 May 1930).
7. Hermann Sinsheimer, "Erinnerung an zwei Tote," *Berliner Tageblatt*, 20 May 1930.
8. Brunhilde Dähn, *Berlin Hausvogteiplatz: Über 100 Jahre am Laufsteg der Mode* (Göttingen: Musterschmidt-Verlag, 1968), 207.
9. "Ungekrönte Königin von Berlin." "Maria Orska und Hans Bleichröder: Tragödie einer großen Liebe." Gerson von Bleichroeder Family Collection. 1878–2002. Leo Baeck Institute, New York. AR 25234 1/6 (Folder 6) Hans von Bleichroeder, undated.
10. "Daß sie in ihrer Erscheinung und in allem, was sie dafür tut, eine ganz echte Lulu ist, versteht sich von selbst." F.E., "Theater in der Königgrätzerstraße. 'Erdgeist' von Frank Wedekind," *Berliner Tageblatt*, 5 November 1916, 3. "Maria Orska spielt die Lulu, wie sie ihr niemand nachspielen wird." Quote from review by Max Schievelkamp. "Maria Orska und Hans Bleichröder: Tragödie einer großen Liebe." Gerson von Bleichroeder Family Collection. 1878–2002. Leo Baeck Institute, New York. AR 25234 1/6 (Folder 6) Hans von Bleichroeder, undated.
11. "Der bewußte Vampyr, von dem inneren Dämon dazu bestimmt, den Männern das Blut auszusaugen." Gerd Stein, *Adolf Stein alias Rumpelstilzchen. "Hugenbergs Landsknecht"—einer der wirkungsmächtigsten deutschen Journalisten des 20. Jahrhunderts* (Berlin: LIT Verlag, 2014), 305.

12. Hans-Jochen Irmer, *Der Theaterdichter Frank Wedekind. Werk und Wirkung* (Berlin: Henschelverlag, 1975), 257–58.
13. Pamela Robertson Wojcik, ed., *Movie Acting, the Film Reader* (New York: Routledge, 2004), 165.
14. Ofer Ashkenazi, *Weimar Film and Modern Jewish Identity* (New York: Palgrave Macmillan, 2012), 72–74.
15. "Sie ist mit meinem abgeschlagenen Kopf bös umgesprungen." Ottomar Starke, "Die kleine Daisy Orska," *Der Querschnitt* 10, no. 6 (June 1926), 412–13; here 413.
16. "Halbnackt, animalisch, mit jenen leisen Schreien, die das Pathos pathetisch machen und fühlen lassen, daß dies Wort Pathos nichts bedeutet als tiefste Trauer." Wilfried Weinke, in *"Ich werde vielleicht später einmal Einfluß zu gewinnen suchen . . . ," Der Schriftsteller und Journalist Heinz Liepman (1905–1966)—Eine biografische Rekonstruktion* (Göttingen: Vandenhoeck & Ruprecht, 2017), 87.
17. Fritz Stahl, "Otto Müller—Dietz Edzard," *Berliner Tageblatt*, 5 March 1928, 2. Similarly, Oskar Kokoschka's more famous portrait of a smiling Orska emphasizes her wild hair and exaggerates her large eyes.
18. Patricia White, "Nazimova's Veils: Salome at the Intersection of Film Histories," in *A Feminist Reader in Early Cinema*, ed. Jennifer M. Bean and Diane Negra (Durham, NC: Duke University Press, 2002), 61.
19. See, e.g., [ro,] "Erinnerungen an die Orska," *Der Morgen* 13, no. 6 (September 1937), 265; and Ursula von Mangoldt, *Auf der Schwelle zwischen gestern und morgen. Begegnungen und Erlebnisse* (Weilheim: Otto Wilhelm Barth-Verlag, 1963). See also Jutta Dick and Marina Sassenberg, eds., *Jüdische Frauen im 19. und 20. Jahrhundert. Lexikon zu Leben und Werk* (Reinbek bei Hamburg: Rowohlt, 1993), 301–3.
20. See "Dämon Morphium"; and Hubert von Meyerinck, *Meine berühmten Freundinnen* (Düsseldorf and Vienna: Econ-Verlag, 1967), 104.
21. "Ein rätselhafter Selbstmord. Maria Orskas Schwester erhängt aufgefunden," *Berliner Tageblatt*, 11 February 1926, 5.
22. Leo Schidrowitz, ed., *Sittengeschichte des Lasters. Die Kulturepochen und ihre Leidenschaften* (Vienna: Verlag für Kulturforschung, 1927), 175.
23. Although some sources suggest Orska's last stage performance took place in 1927, she performed as Lulu in Paris in 1928, and in Barrie's *Medaillen einer alten Frau* in March 1929. See P.B., "Das deutsche Gastspiel in Paris. Urteile der französischen Kritik," *Berliner Tageblatt*, 20 June 1928, 3; and Alfred Kerr, "Orska. Lessing-Theater," *Berliner Tageblatt*, 9 March 1929, 4.
24. See Darcy C. Buerkle, *Nothing Happened: Charlotte Salomon and an Archive of Suicide* (Ann Arbor: University of Michigan Press, 2013), 163–72.
25. On Bergner and suicide, see Kerry Wallach, "Escape Artistry: Elisabeth Bergner and Jewish Disappearance in *Der träumende Mund* (Czinner, 1932)," *German Studies Review* 38.1 (2015): 17–34.
26. "Es war schrecklich, dieser zehn Jahre währende Selbstmord vor aller Welt." Carl Meinhard, "Maria Orska," *Berliner Tageblatt*, 16 May 1930.
27. "[V]on dem namenlosen, schmalen, dunkeläugigen Polenmädchen Rahel Blindermann zu der Schauspielerin Maria Orska führte. . . . ein nervöses Temperament auf der Klaviatur einer weichen, dunkel timbrierten slawischen Stimme spielte, einer Stimme, die im selben Atem flüsterte und schrie und zwitscherte und klagte, dabei nie den Reiz exotischer Artikulation preisgebend." A.M., "Maria Orska," *Vossische Zeitung*, 16 May 1930, 5.
28. Louis Lipsky, "'The Inner Man' by Abraham Schomer," *American Jewish Chronicle* 3, no. 15 (17 August 1917): 407.

29. The six films in the series directed by Max Mack were: *Das Geständnis der grünen Maske, Die Sektwette, Der Sumpf, Adamants letztes Rennen, Der lebende Tote,* and *Die schwarze Loo.*
30. Max Mack is discussed at length in Irene Stratenwerth and Hermann Simon, *Pioniere in Celluloid. Juden in der frühen Filmwelt* (Berlin: Henschel Verlag, 2004), 27–35. See also Michael Wedel, ed., *Max Mack: Showman im Glashaus* (Berlin: Freunde der deutschen Kinemathek, 1996). For a theoretical work that references Rabbi Akiva, see Max Mack, "The Conquest of the Third Dimension," in *The Promise of Cinema: German Film Theory, 1907–1933,* ed. Anton Kaes, Nicholas Baer, and Michael Cowan (Berkeley: University of California Press, 2016), 578–79.
31. Orska likely provided inspiration for the book's section on the *Kinodiva* with a demonic nature as well. See Rudolf Kurtz, "Der Herr Dramaturg" and "Filmweibchen," in *Die zappelnde Leinwand,* ed. Max Mack (Berlin: Eysler, 1916), 57–58, 67.
32. "Mit ihrer ausgesprochenen eigenen Individualität." "Die Maria-Orska-Serie," *Licht-Bild-Bühne* 9, no. 27 (8 July 1916), 58. Cited in Wedel, *Max Mack,* 197.
33. "Berliner Gastspiel eines palästinensischen Theaters," cited in *Der Querschnitt* 4, no. 4 (1924), 257.
34. "Eine Exotin." Rudolf Bernauer, *Das Theater meines Lebens. Erinnerungen* (Berlin: Lothar Blanvalet Verlag, 1955), 310–14, 323–24. See also Kerry Wallach, *Passing Illusions: Jewish Visibility in Weimar Germany* (Ann Arbor: University of Michigan Press, 2017), 47.
35. "Die Orska wäre nicht germanisches Temperament, sie brächte die ganze Welt Aegyptens." Hanns Brodnitz, "Schauspielerporträts. 2. Maria Orska," *Berliner Mittagszeitung,* no. 147 (30 June 1919). Cited in Hanns Brodnitz, *Kino intim. Eine vergessene Biographie,* ed. Gero Gandert and Wolfgang Jacobsen (Berlin: Hentrich & Hentrich, 2005), 176.
36. "Ein kleines, dunkles, sehr slawisches Persönchen." von Meyerinck, *Meine berühmten Freundinnen,* 100, 103.
37. As Arnold Zweig noted in *Juden auf der deutschen Bühne* (1928), many of the best-known Jewish actors in Germany—including Orska—were actually foreign-born *austro-jüdische Schauspieler.* Arnold Zweig, *Juden auf der deutschen Bühne* (Berlin: Welt-Verlag, 1928), 21–26, 137–42, 193–94. Julius Bab argued that a shared blood relationship of sorts was partly responsible for the success of the triumvirate of Jewish women actors—Maria Orska, Elisabeth Bergner, Fritzi Massary—whom he perceived as representative of the mastery of acting in general. Julius Bab, *Schauspieler und Schaukunst* (Berlin: Oesterheld & Co. Verlag, 1926), 121, 189–90. See also Wallach, *Passing Illusions,* 71.
38. Doris Wittner, "Maria Orska," *Jüdisch-liberale Zeitung* 10, no. 21 (21 May 1930), 2–3.
39. See "Tragödie einer Tragödin"; and Martha Wertheimer, "Seelentausch. Zur Begabung der Jüdin für die Schauspielkunst," *Frankfurter Israelitisches Gemeindeblatt* 12, no. 5 (January 1934), 211.
40. The Deutsche Kinemathek's three-act version of *Die schwarze Loo* is available online at www.europeanfilmgateway.eu. On the film's premiere, see "Der neueste hervorragende Sensationsschlager der Maria Orska-Serie 1917/18," *Licht-Bild-Bühne* 10, no. 36 (1917), 31, 80.
41. "Die Orska fühlte sich in der Kellerkneipe als freie, ungebundene Tochter der weiten Steppe." "Die schwarze Loo," *Licht-Bild-Bühne* 10, no. 36 (1917), 80.
42. See Maya Barzilai's chapter in this volume, and Jeanette Malkin, "Transforming in Public: Jewish Actors on the German Expressionist Stage," in *Jews and the Making of*

Modern German Theatre, ed. Jeanette R. Malkin and Freddie Rokem (Iowa City: University of Iowa Press, 2010), 151–73; here 165–66.
43. A letter from Maria Orska to Herr Direktor dated 11 May 1919 suggests she was ill and had canceled all performances at that time. Gerson von Bleichroeder Family Collection 1878–2002, Leo Baeck Institute, New York, AR 25234 1/6 (Folder 6) Hans von Bleichroeder, undated.
44. I was not able to view any of her Weimar-era films, though I did work with materials relating to these films. Of these five films, only one, *Fredericus Rex*, is listed as available at the Bundesarchiv-Filmarchiv in Berlin. With the exception of this film and *Die schwarze Loo*, all of Orska's other films have been lost.
45. Hans Wollenberg, "Zola im Film. Die Bestie im Menschen," *Licht-Bild-Bühne* 14, no. 8 (1921), 41.
46. Wojcik, *Movie Acting*, 166.
47. Hugo Münsterberg, *The Film, A Psychological Study, The Silent Photoplay* (1916; reprint, New York: Dover, 1971), 50. Cited in Elizabeth Ewen and Stuart Ewen, *Typecasting: On the Arts and Sciences of Human Inequality* (New York: Seven Stories Press, 2006), 8.
48. Nancy Wang Yuen, *Reel Inequality: Hollywood Actors and Racism* (New Brunswick, NJ: Rutgers University Press, 2017), 11–12.
49. See Wallach, *Passing Illusions*, 48.
50. Take, for example, the casting of Elisabeth Bergner as Fräulein Else and Grete Mosheim as Lucie Dreyfus. See Wallach, *Passing Illusions*, 93–94, 115.
51. See Prawer, *Between Two Worlds*, 91–93.
52. On vampire imagery in *Nosferatu*, see Ashkenazi, *Weimar Film*, 85–86.
53. Gaylyn Studlar, "Theda Bara: Orientalism, Sexual Anarchy, and the Jewish Star," in *Flickers of Desire: Movie Stars of the 1910s*, ed. Jennifer M. Bean (New Brunswick, NJ: Rutgers University Press, 2011), 113–36; here 131.
54. Ronald Genini, *Theda Bara: A Biography of the Silent Screen Vamp, with a Filmography* (Jefferson, NC: McFarland, 1996), 14, 58–59.
55. Genini, *Theda Bara*, 63.
56. See discussion in Studlar, "Theda Bara," 134–35.
57. Graham Russell Gao Hodges, *Anna May Wong: From Laundryman's Daughter to Hollywood Legend* (Hong Kong: Hong Kong University Press, 2012), 67.
58. Cynthia Walk, "Anna May Wong and Weimar Cinema: Orientalism in Postcolonial Germany," in *Beyond Alterity: German Encounters with Modern East Asia*, ed. Qinna Shen and Martin Rosenstock (New York: Berghahn, 2014), 137–67; here 144.
59. On concerns in the Weimar Jewish press about actors who played Jewish types, see Wallach, *Passing Illusions*, 77–81.
60. Yuen, *Reel Inequality*, 4, 69–78.

Bibliography

Ashkenazi, Ofer. *Weimar Film and Modern Jewish Identity*. New York: Palgrave Macmillan, 2012.
Bab, Julius. *Schauspieler und Schaukunst*. Berlin: Oesterheld, 1926.
Bernauer, Rudolf. *Das Theater meines Lebens. Erinnerungen*. Berlin: Lothar Blanvalet, 1955.
Brodnitz, Hanns. *Kino intim. Eine vergessene Biographie*, ed. Gero Gandert and Wolfgang Jacobsen. Berlin: Hentrich & Hentrich, 2005.

Buerkle, Darcy. "Gendered Spectatorship, Jewish Women and Psychological Advertising in Weimar Germany." *Women's History Review* 15 (4, 2006): 625–36.
———. *Nothing Happened: Charlotte Salomon and an Archive of Suicide*. Ann Arbor: University of Michigan Press, 2013.
Cook, Amy. *Building Character: The Art and Science of Casting*. Ann Arbor: University of Michigan Press, 2018.
Dähn, Brunhilde. *Berlin Hausvogteiplatz: Über 100 Jahre am Laufsteg der Mode*. Göttingen: Musterschmidt, 1968.
Dick, Jutta, and Marina Sassenberg, eds. *Jüdische Frauen im 19. und 20. Jahrhundert. Lexikon zu Leben und Werk*. Reinbek bei Hamburg: Rowohlt, 1993.
Ewen, Elizabeth, and Stuart Ewen. *Typecasting: On the Arts and Sciences of Human Inequality*. New York: Seven Stories Press, 2006.
Genini, Ronald. *Theda Bara: A Biography of the Silent Screen Vamp, with a Filmography*. Jefferson, NC: McFarland, 1996.
Hodges, Graham Russell Gao. *Anna May Wong: From Laundryman's Daughter to Hollywood Legend*. Hong Kong: Hong Kong University Press, 2012.
Irmer, Hans-Jochen. *Der Theaterdichter Frank Wedekind. Werk und Wirkung*. Berlin: Henschelverlag, 1975.
Kaes, Anton, Nicholas Baer, and Michael Cowan, eds. *The Promise of Cinema: German Film Theory, 1907–1933*. Berkeley: University of California Press, 2016.
Mack, Max, ed. *Die zappelnde Leinwand*. Berlin: Eysler, 1916.
Malkin, Jeanette R., and Freddie Rokem, eds. *Jews and the Making of Modern German Theatre*. Iowa City: University of Iowa Press, 2010.
Prawer, S.S. *Between Two Worlds: The Jewish Presence in German and Austrian Film, 1910–1933*. New York: Berghahn Books, 2005.
Schidrowitz, Leo, ed. *Sittengeschichte des Lasters. Die Kulturepochen und ihre Leidenschaften*. Vienna: Verlag für Kulturforschung, 1927.
Stein, Gerd. *Adolf Stein alias Rumpelstilzchen. "Hugenbergs Landsknecht"—einer der wirkungsmächtigsten deutschen Journalisten des 20. Jahrhunderts*. Berlin: LIT, 2014.
Stratenwerth, Irene, and Hermann Simon. *Pioniere in Celluloid. Juden in der frühen Filmwelt*. Berlin: Henschel, 2004.
Studlar, Gaylyn. "Theda Bara: Orientalism, Sexual Anarchy, and the Jewish Star." In *Flickers of Desire: Movie Stars of the 1910s*, ed. Jennifer M. Bean, 113–36. New Brunswick, NJ: Rutgers University Press, 2011.
von Mangoldt, Ursula. *Auf der Schwelle zwischen gestern und morgen. Begegnungen und Erlebnisse*. Weilheim: Otto Wilhelm Barth, 1963.
von Meyerinck, Hubert. *Meine berühmten Freundinnen*. Düsseldorf: Econ, 1967.
Wallach, Kerry. "Escape Artistry: Elisabeth Bergner and Jewish Disappearance in *Der träumende Mund* (Czinner, 1932)." *German Studies Review* 38.1 (2015): 17–34.
———. *Passing Illusions: Jewish Visibility in Weimar Germany*. Ann Arbor: University of Michigan Press, 2017.
Walk, Cynthia. "Anna May Wong and Weimar Cinema: Orientalism in Postcolonial Germany." In *Beyond Alterity: German Encounters with Modern East Asia*, ed. Qinna Shen and Martin Rosenstock, 137–67. New York: Berghahn Books, 2014.
Wedel, Michael, ed. *Max Mack: Showman im Glashaus*. Berlin: Freunde der deutschen Kinemathek, 1996.
Weinke, Wilfried. *"Ich werde vielleicht später einmal Einfluß zu gewinnen suchen . . . " Der Schriftsteller und Journalist Heinz Liepman (1905–1966)—Eine biografische Rekonstruktion*. Göttingen: Vandenhoeck & Ruprecht, 2017.

White, Patricia. "Nazimova's Veils: *Salome* at the Intersection of Film Histories." In *A Feminist Reader in Early Cinema*, ed. Jennifer M. Bean and Diane Negra, 60–87. Durham, NC: Duke University Press, 2002.
Wojcik, Pamela Robertson, ed. *Movie Acting, the Film Reader*. New York: Routledge, 2004.
Yuen, Nancy Wang. *Reel Inequality: Hollywood Actors and Racism*. New Brunswick, NJ: Rutgers University Press, 2017.
Zweig, Arnold. *Juden auf der deutschen Bühne*. Berlin: Welt, 1928.

Chapter 4

JEWISH COMEDIANS BEYOND LUBITSCH

Siegfried Arno in Film and Cabaret

Mila Ganeva

Traditionally, when it comes to Jewish comedy in Germany, the limelight has been on auteur Ernst Lubitsch (1892–1947), whose career in Germany takes off in the 1910s and lasts into the first years of the Weimar Republic. Characteristic for the Berlin period in Lubitsch's filmmaking, as Valerie Weinstein has emphasized, was his work as an actor in several highly popular milieu comedies, all set in and around the city's fashion district. These performances have shaped our longlasting notion of how Jewish stereotypes, realities, and questions of assimilation were perceived in early-twentieth-century Germany.[1] Lubitsch started out by playing Jewish apprentices in the garment industry, or rag trade (*Konfektion*), in *Die Firma heiratet* and *Der Stolz der Firma* (both 1914). Subsequently, he appeared in and directed a series of films set in Jewish commercial milieus including *Schuhpalast Pinkus* (1916) and *Der Blusenkönig* (1917). Lubitsch drew on the tradition of Jewish wit that had developed over the course of the nineteenth century—most famously, he brought onto the movie screen the stock figure of "the Jew." His performances portrayed the cunning lower-class Jewish character in an explicitly comic and at the same time sympathetic way that, according to Peter Jelavich, resonated strongly with both Jews and Gentiles in an audience that lacked the privileges of personal cultivation and education (*Bildung*).[2] This success was replicated in a number of other films that Lubitsch acted in and directed, such as *Das fidele Gefängnis* (1917), *Wenn vier dasselbe tun* (1917), *Meyer aus Berlin* (1918), and *Die Puppe* (1919), or those he only directed, such as *Die Austerprinzessin*

(1919). The last film in which Lubitsch performed, *Sumurun*, was made in 1920, and a few years later, in 1922, he left Berlin to continue his filmmaker career in Hollywood. What happened, however, after Lubitsch departed from Weimar Berlin, and from German cinema in particular? Was there anyone who picked up where he left off, especially in comedy and comic acting?

This chapter proposes a close look at the film career and stage presence of actor Siegfried Arno (1895–1975), who many—both among his contemporaries and in later scholarship—consider a true successor of Lubitsch's style as a comedian. Arno was one of the numerous entertainers of Jewish background—writers, directors, artists, actors, producers, composers, songwriters, and so on—who flocked to Berlin and worked with considerable success in the theater and film industry of the Weimar Republic. Especially in the final Weimar years some blockbusters were released that were shaped by a multitude of Jewish figures, who masterfully explored the cinematic potential of sound.[3] As a popular German-Jewish actor, Siegfried Arno stands at the intersection of three important cultural trends during this period and is therefore worthy of attention.

First, Arno exemplifies one of the most successful models of an actor combining his work on the cabaret stage (*Kabarett* or *Kleinkunstbühne*) with prolific work for films. In the Berlin cabaret, he was involved in comical sketches as well as musical and dancing performances for a live audience; on the silver screen, he became widely known for his humorous appearances in predominantly light comedies and farces. Second, the actor was equally skillful in the transition from supporting roles in silent film to a leading performer in sound productions (*Tonfilme*), since the medium embraced the possibilities of sound and changed considerably under its influence in the early 1930s. One could even argue that it was the experience of many German-Jewish performers like Arno in cabaret throughout the 1920s that significantly shaped the development of sound film genres in Germany after 1929. Finally, as an active participant in both the vibrant cabaret scene in Berlin and popular film comedies during the Weimar Republic, Siegfried Arno's career became the focal point of heated disputes about the appropriateness of Jewish jokes and the suitability of Jewish figures' representations within the context of Weimar Germany's mass culture. Like numerous other comedians of Jewish descent, Arno was both attacked and praised for the ways in which he concomitantly projects and suppresses his Jewishness on stage and on the silver screen.

To retrace Arno's remarkable ascent in the world of entertainment in the course of the Weimar Republic, I will address these three aspects of the performer's career. My explorations should be construed as an attempt to establish the comedic lineage linking Lubitsch to Arno and to shed light not only on the affinities between the two Jewish comedians, but also on the significant dissimilarities between both performers, especially with regards to their conception and presentation of Jewish identity.

Siegfried Arno's Early Career and Breakthrough in Film

The Jewish actor Siegfried Arno transitioned from the fashion business to theater and film in ways reminiscent of Lubitsch's early career. Born in an assimilated middle-class Jewish family in Hamburg in 1895 as Siegfried Aron, he later changed his last name to Arno, following what seems to be trend among Jewish actors who did not want to appear Jewish in public and who considered themselves primarily Germans who happened to be Jewish.[4] The future comedian Arno shared Lubitsch's familiarity with the fashion milieu, a traditional Jewish domain. After graduating from the Talmud-Tora Realschule in his hometown, Arno studied fashion drawing and design for three years at the School for Applied Arts in Hamburg. He started working in that capacity, as fashion illustrator (*Modezeichner*), in the prestigious Hamburger salon of Hirsch & Co., mostly following his parents' wishes to pursue a "respectable, solidly bourgeois career."[5]

Arno's interests, however, lay elsewhere (as did Lubitsch's). Almost immediately after taking the job at Hirsch's, he began to spend the nights at the theater, especially in the Thalia-Theater. Soon thereafter he started performing on the side, mostly small roles on various stages in and around Hamburg. During the decade 1912–22, Arno played and sang in a number of comedies and operettas around the country, establishing himself as an entertainer, a career that was not impeded even by his deployment to the western front during the war.[6]

Around 1922 the young comedian moved to Berlin, where his acting gigs in musical theater really took off. From 1923 till 1926 Arno was a member of the Metropol-Theater, where he continued to appear throughout the decade, while collaborating on at least three Eric Charell productions and costarring with celebrities such as Fritzi Massary and Max Hansen. Concurrently, he performed in variety shows and on the cabaret stage. In the mid-1920s Arno was discovered by the film industry and engaged in a number of supporting roles, in which he managed to im-press with his comedic talents. Within only four years—from early 1925 till the end of 1928—Arno played in more than fifty silent films. The critics singled him out immediately in their reviews. In discussing Richard Oswald's *Die Frau von vierzig Jahren* (1925), *Film-Kurier's* critic declares Siegfried Arno to be the true surprise of the film, "the German Chaplin," who has the potential to become "an autonomous, high-caliber comic actor in farces."[7] Such praise, especially of his exceptional comic talent, was shared across various publications by critics as diverse as Hans Feld, Herbert Ihering, Siegfried Kracauer, and H.G. Lustig. In reviews of films that were otherwise rather mediocre and disappointing, Kracauer, for example, called Arno "always good"[8] and "the only one who is truly delightful, a first-class cabaret comedian, who, luckily, has the opportunity to take on many roles."[9] Similarly, in his critical essay in the fan magazine *Der Film*, Hans Tasiemka praised Arno as the German Buster Keaton, an actor "who could not be pinned down in any way, who did not become a character actor despite many attempts at that, and who preserved his color and tempo in any scene, in any stupid film operetta."[10]

In fact, Siegfried Arno had already become somewhat of a character actor (*Chargenspieler*). Although initially he participated in a considerable variety of film genres, the Jewish actor was soon cast exclusively in light-fare comedies and later also in military farces (*Militärschwänke*), where his tall, thin, athletic figure and his big nose were immediately recognizable. Paired with his physical appearance was the role of Schlemihl, the archetypal Jewish figure of the guy with bad luck that he was playing again and again in diverse non-Jewish plots, and also in non-Jewish roles. Asked by *Film-Kurier* in 1928 what kind of roles he would like to be cast, Arno replied, "Always the *schlemiel*, who is never aware of the danger and always manages to avoid the fiasco at the last moment."[11] The critics perceived him in a similar way: "Arno, this is the pathetic Peter Schlemihl of our times," wrote Tasiemka, "the Schlemihl with a gorgeously tied cravat and a bleeding heart."[12] What Tasiemka saw in positive light, however, other critics—like *Film-Kurier's* Hans Feld—regarded as a possible risk. Feld published an open letter to the actor, acknowledging that Arno possesses the potential to become a great artist, but "only if he could grow out of his own type."[13] Warning him not to waste his unique comic talent, Feld pointed out how Arno could too easily slip into a routine, especially when misled by an inexperienced director: "Resist all attempts to be forced to play some kind of an Arno-type in every film."[14]

There are only few examples of Arno appearing on the silent film screen assuming the explicit role of a Jew. One such role is that of

Moritz Wasserstrahl, a general store owner in *Leichte Kavallerie* (1927, dir. Rolf Randolf), a film set in a village in Galicia at the beginning of World War I. While the film was not very warmly received by the critics, the casting of Arno in role of the merchant Jew was singled out and praised in the press: "The only ray of light in the dark Talmudic world is Siegfried Arno, who plays—with his eyes and hands—a Jewish junk dealer," wrote Kracauer in the *Frankfurter Zeitung*.[15] According to the review in the *Börsen-Zeitung*, the Jewish rural milieu "was depicted lovingly and with obvious expertise."[16] Two things are significant about Arno's performance in this film. First, in a slapstick male duo with Farkas (the military commander of the hussars, played by Fritz Kampers) he is part of a secondary, humorous plotline, which contributes considerably to the entertainment value of the film. In these specific parts, the film very much resembles the popular comedies of the time that were set in the military barracks. Farkas teases Wasserstrahl by constantly mispronouncing his name (Wasservogel, Wasserkopf, Wasserkrug), which further alludes to the character's Jewish identity that was often covered up by a changed name.[17] Second, Arno starts out in the film in the traditional garb of an orthodox Jew with sidelocks, but toward the end of the story his appearance has changed: he has joined in Farkas's unit as a volunteer and now wears the military uniform of the Austrian imperial army. This transformation is symptomatic of Arno's future performance of Jewishness on the Weimar screen, because it is exactly this—a performance, a superb impersonation, a skillful imitation, always with a wink, irony, and a touch of humor. At the end of *Leichte Kavallerie*, Arno's character reveals himself to have become an assimilated Jew, well-adjusted to his surroundings, and a secular bourgeois member of mainstream society, thus perhaps foreshadowing the actor's future performances in roles that are not encoded as stereotypically and explicitly Jewish.

    The other notable casting of Arno as a Jew is in the film *Familientag im Hause Prellstein* (1927, dir. Hans Steinhoff), a work that is not only an important milestone, but also a true outlier in his filmic career. Conceived by Universum Film Aktiengesellschaft (UFA) as a low-budget comedy and assigned to the production company Rex-Film, led by Lupu Pick, *Familientag im Hause Prellstein* was filmed in early 1927, but the release was constantly postponed by UFA and delayed until the very slow week before Christmas. The premiere was relegated to a peripheral UFA-Theater, Königstadt in Prenzlauer Berg.[18] After a two-week run, the film was not picked up by any other venue, and, due to the timing, only three reviews appeared, all of them in the trade press; no daily newspaper reviewed the film.[19]

The obvious Jewishness of the film was definitely a factor in the circumstances of its release. *Familientag im Hause Prellstein* had its cast recruited almost entirely from the Jewish-dominated Berlin cabaret scene: from Paul Morgan and Szöke Szakall, to Ilka Grüning and Max Ehrlich. The cabaret stage not only provided all the actors for the characters that are unambiguously linked to the Jewish milieu, but also influenced the structure of the film: it opened with a prologue delivered as if from the cabaret stage and its plotline was built from a loose sequence of sketches. Siegfried Arno, who at that time was very much part of that thriving cabaret scene, played the central title figure of Prellstein, a cunning family friend who detects the opportunity for enrichment, starts an affair with Sami Bambus's wife, and schemes to deceive all of the alleged heirs of the Bambus family. Sami Bambus, for his part, has faked his death in order to avoid paying back an enormous debt from reckless gambling. As many commentators of the film have noticed, Arno's character seems the most complex one and contributed considerably to the Jewish image of events in the film. With his big nose and gaunt body, he is not only typecast as "the typical Jew"[20] (reminding us of the roles Lubitsch played in his early comedies), but he is also marked by a certain urban sophistication, "cosmopolitan charm," "airiness," and a "mixture of melancholy and cheekiness"—qualifications that Siegfried Kracauer uses often in his reviews of Arno's performances.[21] Ofer Ashkenazi emphasizes this duality between typical Jewishness and assimilated, middle-class urbanity in both the film's narrative and in Arno's performance (figure 4.1).[22] This duality would be the lenses through which his future performances in Weimar cinema would be seen.

Figure 4.1. Siegfried Arno, publicity postcard, no date. Courtesy of Theaterwissenschaftliche Sammlung, Universität zu Köln.

Arno, Antisemitism, and the Tradition of Jewish Popular Theater

One of the very few reviews that appeared in the press characterized *Familientag im Hause Prellstein* as a film featuring only two female characters but "very many sons of Israel who talk, curse, cheat and are in turn duped, and then talk again."²³ Overall, the critic Georg Herzberg conceded, this was "clean film, at which one can laugh heartily and which the audience—with the exception of the incorrigible antisemites—will certainly perceive as a welcome relief from operettas and comedies set on the Rhein or in Heidelberg."²⁴

Herzberg's reference to the film audience's possible antisemitic sentiments hints at the widespread attitudes toward Jewish themes and the reception of Jewish comedy within the popular culture of the Weimar Republic. Producing and showing a film on an exclusively Jewish topic with a predominantly Jewish cast of performers gave rise to a certain apprehension, as became apparent from UFA's tactics for a delayed and limited distribution. After all, the film was based directly on the eponymous 1905 play by the brothers Herrnfeld and this may have been a reason for UFA's reservations. From around 1890 till the end of World War I, the Gebrüder Herrnfeld Theater had been one of the most popular entertainment venues in Berlin, devoted to ethnic comedies written, directed, performed, and taken on tours all around Germany by two Jewish brothers, Anton and Donat Herrnfeld.²⁵ Donat Herrnfeld passed away in 1916, but Anton Herrnfeld continued performing and was cast in the role of Jaromir Schestak in the 1927 movie *Familientag im Hause Prellstein*.²⁶

The Herrnfeld Company, a family enterprise, was a prime example of what was called *Jargon*-Theater (slang theater), since Donat spoke an artificial dialect that was the conventional marker of Jewishness on stage: German, liberally peppered with some well-known Yiddish and Hebrew words. In Berlin the Jewish Herrnfeld Theater was most popular in the two decades before the end of World War I and had a lasting impact on different forms of mass entertainment—especially on the revues and cabarets, but also on early film. For example, the first comedies that Ernst Lubitsch acted in and later also directed (*Die Firma heiratet, Der Stolz der Firma, Schuhpalast Pinkus,* and *Der Blusenkönig*) presented pioneering cinematic versions of the humorous characters and sympathetic characters of Jewish popular theater; in a way, these films were the silent-film equivalent to the Herrnfeld brothers' skits.²⁷ From this point of view, casting the Hamburg-born Jew Arno in the title role of the 1927 filmic version of the Herrnfeld play signals the passing of the comedian's baton from Lubitsch to Siegfried Arno, who was capable of "ironic, confident, and skillful representation of Jewish stereotypes tinted by antisemitism."[28]

In their heyday before the war, the Herrnfelds made benign fun not only of Jews, but also of Bavarians, Bohemians, Berliners, Saxons and other ethnic groups, and their sketches always ended with some kind of harmonious resolution of the differences, especially between Jews and Gentiles. Nevertheless, the common perception was that their skits were obsessed with exaggerated representations of some of the most egregious stereotypes regarding Jewish looks and traits. Many Jews, too, especially those who embraced Zionism, opposed assimilationist plots and the self-deprecatory humor of the Herrnfeld Theater and accused it of stoking antisemitism among the Gentiles in the audience.[29]

During the war and in the early years of Weimar Republic, antisemitism among German Gentiles intensified and radicalized. *Jargon* theater, as Marline Otte wrote, began to decline in a society riddled by inflation, unemployment, and racial discrimination.[30] Jewish humor, whose most-visible domain used to be the Herrnfeld stage, found an exclusive home in cabaret. Jewish jokes and skits were performed by German-Jewish actors on numerous live-entertainment venues in Berlin in the course of the 1920s and into the early 1930s: Metropol-Theater, Schall und Rauch, Künstler-Kabarett, Das Kabarett der Komiker (KadeKo), Charlott-Casino, Femina, and many others. Explicit onscreen representations of Jews such as in the film *Familientag im Hause Prellstein*, on the other hand, remained a rather rare occurrence.[31]

As antisemitism was on the steep rise among nationalists and as National Socialist (Nazi) ideas began to spread in Germany, the Jewish jokes told by Jewish performers from the cabaret stage increasingly disturbed the Centralverein deutscher Staatsbürger jüdischen Glaubens (Central Association of German Citizens of Jewish Faith). It saw them as feeding into anti-Jewish agitation. Centralverein represented the community of middle-class, assimilated Jews, decidedly non-Zionists, who—as the name implies—considered Germany their homeland. In the course of the 1920s, the Centralverein and its press organ, the weekly *C.V.-Zeitung*, engaged in a campaign against the Berlin cabarets ("unser Kampf gegen das mauschelnde Kabarett") disputing the appropriateness of the humor that permeated indignant jokes, satiric sketches, and songs performed by Jewish actors on various stages.[32]

Because of his prolific work in both cabaret and film, Siegfried Arno, along with other Jewish comedians, found himself often at the center of the Centralverein's attacks. The campaign against the satirical representations of Jews by Jews on the cabaret stage started on the pages of the *C.V.-Zeitung* in fall 1925 and culminated in two public protest meetings on 22 April 1926 in Berlin, a sensational event widely covered in the daily press.[33] Both meetings released a common resolution, published in the *C.V.-Zeitung* under the title "Against the Distortion of Jewishness" ("Gegen die Verzerrung des jüdischen Wesens").[34] The brunt of the criticism fell on KadeKo, its founders Kurt Robitschek and Paul Morgan, prominent Jewish artists (Willy Prager, Kurt Gerron, and Siegfried Arno) who performed frequently there, as well as songwriters (Friedrich Holländer) and some female comedians (Annemarie Haase and Ilse Bois).[35] Centralverein claimed to have received complaints from members who had visited cabarets in Berlin and elsewhere in the country and were indignant about what was seen as *Jüdeln* (performing like a Jew) and *Mauscheln* (mumbling).[36] This self-deprecating humor was done, supposedly, for cheap laughs, without respecting the sensibilities of the Jewish patronage, which formed about half of the audience, and unwittingly playing into the hands of antisemites.

The actions taken by Centralverein were relentless—official inquiries and letters were sent to the owners of the venues, sometimes threatening them with legal action. In 1927, although conceding there were some "corrections" made on the Berlin stages, *C.V.-Zeitung* followed up with new accusations against several venues and actors and concluded that there were "lapses back into indignity" on the cabaret stage.[37] KadeKo and most of its Jewish performers were chastised again, especially after Robitschek declared defiantly in the magazine *Die Frechheit*, that his establishment could be considered a "synagogue of the muses" (*Musensynagoge*).[38]

In 1927 the campaign against the cabarets expanded to include film, reflecting Centralverein's awareness of the exponentially rising popularity of the medium. In his article "Der Jude im Film," Hans Wollenberg, a critic for *Lichtbild-Bühne*, discussed Paul Morgan, Szöke Szakall, and Siegfried Arno. He considered them representative of those Jewish actors, who through their performances in the roles of "attorneys, pawnbrokers, black-marketers, and garment store employees" almost always emboldened the antisemitic tendencies in the audience.[39] Arno, specifically, was singled out for appearing frequently in supporting roles in military farces, such as *Die dritte Eskadron* (1926, dir. Carl Wilhelm), where he, the Jew, is cast as the irreverent, lazy, or cowardly soldier, and never as a heroic figure. Arno was not supposed to take the sole blame for this: according to Wollenberg, Jewish directors, Jewish scriptwriters, and other Jewish filmmakers (*Filmfabrikanten*) facilitated the circulation of such antisemitic, self-hating images on the silver screen.[40]

Arno in Cabaret and Sound Film

The Centralverein sustained the cabaret campaign, albeit in a more subdued format, throughout the remaining years of the decade. At the same time, Siegfried Arno continued with prolific work for both cabaret and film, exemplifying what Kerry Wallach defines as the strong "trend in Weimar Germany toward displaying Jewishness" mostly without playing explicitly Jewish roles.[41] Undoubtedly Arno belonged, to use Wallach's formulation, to this widespread "web of theatrical, cinematic and everyday performances of Jewishness that enabled Jews to be recognizable to each other."[42] In every moment of his numerous screen and live performances, Arno was identifiable for his contemporaneous audience as a Jewish actor, with his dark eyes and hair, big nose, and lithe acrobatic body with swift and smooth movements. Some of his cabaret appearances, especially his monologues, still drew ire, because he imitated eastern Jews (*Ostjuden*) and their specific way of talking or mumbling (*Mauscheln*), and because he continued to tell Jewish jokes. This is well documented by the Centralverein, for example, in a letter to the director of the Boulevard-Theater in Berlin, where Arno had performed the title role of Otto Kollmann in a skit entitled "Der Herr Unteroffizier:" "We have received several dozen complaints about Mr. Siegfried Arno's appearance on your stage. "He plays a corporal. Because of the mumbling [*Mauscheln*], his appearance is simply disgusting," writes a gentleman from Berlin. "We presume that you are not aware of the fact that the majority of Jews in Berlin find such mumbling and disgrace unacceptable."[43] Upon repeated visits to the theater, audience members sent reports to the Centralverein confirming that Arno was mumbling in another one-act farce within the same program as well, "Heringsdorf," and that no other actors mumbled or told Jewish jokes on those nights.[44] Despite various protests initiated by the Centralverein, however, Arno continued to appear on the cabaret stage, especially in the KaDeKo, where he became one of the most sought-after members of the troupe and participated regularly in the annual benefit events "Die Nacht der Prominenten" or "Die Nacht der Komiker" that raised funds to support struggling actors.[45]

Like most of his colleagues, Siegfried Arno worked at an extraordinary level of commitment for both cabaret and film throughout the final years of the Weimar Republic. As he was performing night after night in KadeKo as well as on other stages in Berlin, he also managed to appear in more than twenty sound films that were released between 1929 and his exile in 1933, including several films in which he was the male lead and often the star. For him and many of his colleagues, the work in the film studios took place during the day, while cabaret rehearsals were in the late afternoon in preparation for the night shows that started after eight. To be sure, this arrangement resulted often in a grueling daily schedule. Kurt Robitschek describes a typical situation at the KadeKo: "Every afternoon the actors arrive for the rehearsal of their skits [before the evening performance]. Cabaret is their second job. They are a dead tired, exhausted from filming during the day. They assure each other and the director that they have never played in such a crap film [*Dreck*] before."[46]

Yet there were notable exceptions to the proliferating lightweight and thoroughly forgettable film comedies before the advance of sound technology. One of the signature films with two of KadeKo's most prominent regulars, Kurt Gerron and Siegfried Arno, was *Aufruhr im Junggesellenheim* (1929, dir. Manfred Noa). The critics saw this work as a rather ambitious project. It had its origins in the Herrnfeld skit and the early Lubitsch films. At the same time, the film aimed to detach Gerron and Arno from any associations with Jewish humor and establish them as a filmic comedian duo in the popular American slapstick tradition of Laurel and Hardy or the Danes known in Germany as Pat and Patachon.[47] Arno and Gerron certainly had the contrasting physical characteristics and the talent to form that comedian pair—Gerron was stout and burly, Arno was thin and nimble. In addition, they were given English nicknames Beef (Arno) and Steak (Gerron) in the hope that the trademark "Beef & Steak" would establish itself as a novel, modern form of a German film farce (*Filmgroteske*) with a possible international reach.[48] Overall, *Aufruhr* disappointed the critics despite the film's ambition, its emphasis on situational and physical comedy, and the bold performances from the "two extraordinarily talented and courageous actors Gerron and Arno."[49] According to some more benevolent reviews, there was some hope that the sequel might be better. Yet when Gerron and Arno followed up the same year with the second installment in their Beef & Steak series, *Wir halten fest und treu zusammen* (1929, dir. Herbert Nossen), the reception was devastating, mostly due to the weak work of the director.[50] The actors' attempts to create a German film farce that would resemble the popular American "Fix- und Fax-Lustspiele" (imported by UFA in 1924) apparently failed.[51]

After the fiasco, the comedian duo Beef & Steak was discontinued, but both actors kept appearing in different comedies with considerable success. It was the advance of sound technology that opened new possibilities for film as well as cabaret. The intensive parallel toil of performers in film and cabaret gave rise to strong mutual influence and fortuitous stylistic cross-pollination between the two popular media, especially in the early 1930s, as sound films became the norm and cabaret sought to reach a broader and more diverse audience.

With the spread of sound technology in production and distribution, cabaret as a form of popular entertainment ventured, literally, into the world of film. Although KadeKo's director Kurt Robitschek vehemently rejected the idea of broadcasting cabaret performances over the radio in 1930, in the same issue of the magazine *Die Frechheit* he announced that his cabaret is planning its "own sound film productions, shot in the new Theater am Reichskanzlerplatz," with the ambition "to spread our tradition of laughter to the most faraway corners of the world: Guben, Gleiwitz, Tutzing, and Bebra."[52] The plan was to produce six cabaret films (*Kabarett-Film*) with UFA, all of them with a different cast but directed by Kurt Gerron and produced by Bruno Duday.[53] The first one premiered in May 1931, a twenty-four-minute short film in which Siegfried Arno sang and step-danced with the rising star from musical theater, Trude Berliner, in a six-minute number called "Es muss Abend sein."[54] Despite worries that cabaret more than any other performance art would need a live audience for maximum effect, the first cabaret film enjoyed, according to critics, "an unbelievable success" and was applauded everywhere where it was shown as part of the complementary film program (*Beiprogramm*).[55] Watching the first *Kabarett-Film*, the audience could recognize all familiar faces from the cabaret stage: not only Siegfried Arno, but also Otto Wallburg, Willi Schaeffers, Max Ehrlich, Maria Ney, and many others. Yet these short films reproduce the Weimar cabaret culture on the big screen only in a limited way. The irreverence of Jewish humor, the sharp edge, aggression, and the improvisational sparkle of the live performance were missing in the sleek UFA-production, as it sought to please, in the most conformist way, the widest audience possible.[56]

While cabaret sought collaboration with UFA in order to reach a broader public through the film industry's distribution network, full-feature sound comedies that borrowed heavily from the structure and aesthetics of live cabaret performances proliferated. This was visible already in one of the first sound films produced in early 1930 and preceded by an intensive publicity campaign in *Film-Kurier: Wien, du Stadt der Lieder* (1930, dir. Richard Oswald). *Wien, du Stadt der Lieder* not only used the entire star ensemble of KadeKo for its cast, but also built its narrative loosely out of short skits that demonstrated the singing and dancing talents of the various comedians (Paul Morgan, Max Ehrlich, Max Hansen, Paul Graez, Sigi Hofer, and Siegfried Arno). Witty dialogue, slapstick comedy, and musical brilliance are definitely privileged at the expense of a tight and logical plot.[57]

It was during these first years of the rise of the talkies that Siegfried Arno—straddling both worlds, of cabaret performance and film—transitioned from supporting roles to a lead actor and a real movie star. His physical agility and his voice made possible the musical performances that launched his rapid ascent. During the years 1930 and 1931 Arno reached the highest point in his cinematic career. He starred in nearly twenty movies and those in which he played the lead male role were advertised in the press as "Siegfried Arno films." These films put on display the full spectrum of Arno's comical talent and are not limited to him being typecast as a Jew. In *Die von Rummelplatz* (1930, dir. Carl Lamač) and *Die große Attraktion* (1931, dir. Max Reichmann) Arno played a performer in a circus/variety show and sang and danced alongside female stars such as Anny Ondra and Margo Lion, respectively. In *Moritz macht sein Glück* (1931, dir Jaap Speyer) and *Ein ausgekochter Junge* (1931, dir. Erich Schönfelder), Arno returned as the stereotypical lower-level clerk in a fictional Jewish garment store (Meyer & Co.) and got entangled in a complicated comedy of errors and mistaken identities. In *Moritz macht sein Glück* Arno was cast in a role similar to that of Lubitsch in his early comedies—shrewd salesman falling in love with the top model in a fashion salon. Indeed, this is Arno's most Lubitsch-like appearance as he, too, is falling off ladders, plotting against and deceiving his bosses as well as his customers, gagging and mugging for the camera.[58] His performance and his physical appearance are clearly stylized to resemble the early Lubitsch. The departure from Lubitsch's milieu comedies is determined to a large extent by the role of sound. Arno delivers smooth singing and dancing performances alongside the respective female leads such as Irene Ambrus (1904–90). He also seeks to follow—in a satirical way—the examples set by American film and American popular culture rather than early German comedy. In a central sequence in the film involving a fashion show, for example, Arno's character Moritz Meyer lip-synchs and dances in blackface with a gramophone attached to his back explicitly mimicking Al Jolson in American film *The Jazz Singer* (1927, dir. Alan

Crosland). While contemporary scholarship views the unambiguous references to *The Jazz Singer* and the use of blackface as contributing to the coding of Moritz as Jewish, I would interpret this more as Weimar's widespread infatuation with exotic forms of contemporary American, often racialized entertainment affecting Jews and non-Jews alike;[59] after all, blackface was not uncommon in live entertainment in Berlin as well as in film: The movie *Die große Attraktion* (1931, dir. Max Reichmann) opens with the female protagonist Kitty, played by 21-year-old non-Jewish dancer Marianne Winkelstern, performing in blackface.[60] Also famous was a program called *Varieté! Varieté!* at the Kadeko in 1927, with which the German-Jewish comedienne Ilse Bois made a big splash as she appeared in blackface and Afro-styled hair and presented the banana skirt dance, spoofing Josephine Baker's performance in Paris and Berlin.[61]

In *Ein ausgekochter Junge* and the other successful sound films of the period, mostly comedies of error—*Um eine Nasenlänge* (1931, dir. Johannes Guter), *Der Storch streikt. Siegfried, der Matrose* (1931, dir. E.W. Emo), *Die Nacht ohne Pause* (1931, dir. Franz Wezler and Andrew Marton), *Keine Feier ohne Meyer* (1931, dir. Carl Boese), and the last one, *Der schönste Mann im Staate* (1932, dir. Carl Boese)—Arno plays the lead and is not cast in explicitly Jewish roles.[62] Although the narratives—often interrupted by songs and dance and mostly consisting of a string of comical skits—are undoubtedly influenced by Berlin cabaret culture, there is no controversial mumbling (*Mauscheln*), no imitation of talking in Yiddish (*Jüdeln*), and no Jewish jokes as were so common on stage. In his films as well as off screen, Arno, now a star, sustained a reputation of being always stylishly dressed, dapper, modern. Fan magazines publicized his elegance as well as his habit of driving his car everywhere in Berlin.[63] Yet at the same time, his Jewishness—like his long nose—could not be concealed; it is referred to rather indirectly through his film characters' assignment to lower-middle-class professions in a clear urban context (marriage broker, shop assistant, municipal clerk, newspaper deliverer). In two of the films—*Um eine Nasenlänge* and the military farce *Der schönste Mann im Staate*, the long nose is an important element of the plot, contributing significantly to the protagonist's success in winning, for example a competitive bike race by the length of a nose. The various protagonists embodied by Arno in the comedies of the sound period follow a tendency that, as Ofer Ashkenazi has pointed out, was established in earlier, explicitly Jewish comedies such as *Familientag im Hause Prellstein*: the bourgeois protagonist is equated with the

Jewish protagonist, who has already assimilated and is defined primarily by his adaptability, his social flexibility, and his new urban, very much middle-class experiences.[64]

Coda

Within his cohort of Jewish cabaret performers and film actors, Siegfried Arno was among the lucky ones who managed to escape Germany in 1933 and resume his career as a cabaret comedian in exile, initially in the Netherlands, and later in other European countries. Unlike Lubitsch, he was never tempted by the opportunity to direct or write for the movies. He remained faithful to the cabaret performance and toured as tirelessly as ever.[65] The Dutch press reported that Arno, who had left his homeland after posters with his name had been smeared with antisemitic slurs, demonstrated a remarkable natural ability to learn new languages and adapt quickly.[66] Around 1939 the actor emigrated to the United States and continued to have success on the big screen as well as on Broadway under the name Sig Arno. Yet the peak of his career remained those final years of the Weimar Republic, when during a time of mass unemployment, economic instability, political unrest, and existential disquiet, he contributed to light and escapist sound comedies, where the singing, dancing, and physical agility of this "cabaret artist of the highest caliber" deservedly earned him qualifications such as "the best comedian since Lubitsch" and "better than all of his rivals, at least by a nose length," or in other words the best Jewish comedian.[67]

Mila Ganeva is professor of German and film studies at Miami University in Ohio. She is author of *Women in Weimar Fashion: Discourses and Displays in German Culture, 1918–1933* (Camden House, 2008) and, more recently, of *Film and Fashion Amidst the Ruins of Berlin: Between Nazism and Cold War, 1939–1953* (Camden House, 2018). Her publications focus on fashion journalism, fashion photography, early German film comedies, the history of modeling, beauty pageants, and Berlin in film. She edited a volume of collected articles by Helen Hessel: *Ich schreibe aus Paris. Über die Mode, das Leben und die Liebe* (Nimbus, 2014).

Notes

I am grateful to Ofer Ashkenazi for generously sharing with me numerous scans of letters to and from Centralverein. These provided an invaluable sense of context for the role of Jewish presence in cabaret in Weimar Berlin.

1. See Valerie Weinstein, "Anti-Semitism or Jewish 'Camp'? Ernst Lubitsch's *Schuhpalast Pinkus* (1916) and *Meyer from Berlin* (1918)." *German Life and Letters* 59.1 (January 2006a): 101–21; and her lecture, Valerie Weinstein, "Performing Jewishness. Ernst Lubitschs frühe Milieukomödien," available at https://www.filmportal.de/node/195049/video/1377175.
2. See Peter Jelavich, "Popular Entertainment and Mass Media: The Central Arenas of German-Jewish Cultural Engagement," in *The German Jewish Experience Revisited*, ed. Steven E. Ashheim and Vivian Liska (Berlin, 2015) 103–16, here 107.
3. See Ofer Ashkenazi, *Weimar Film and Modern Jewish Identity* (New York, 2012), 4–5.
4. Max Reinhardt was originally Max Goldmann, Otto Brahm was Otto Abrahamsohn, Elizabeth Bergner was Ella Bergner, Fritz Kortner was Nathan Kohn, and Paul Morgan was Paul Morgenstern. See Marline Otte, *Jewish Identities in German Popular Entertainment, 1890–1933* (New York, 2006), 146.
5. Klaus Gille, "Siegfried Arno," in *Hamburgische Biografie*, ed. Franklin Kopitzsch and Dirk Brietzke (Göttingen, 2010), 26–27.
6. The biographical exposition follows the account by Jörg Schöning, "Biografie" in *Siegfried Arno*, ed. Hans-Michael Bock (Hamburg, 1995) 11–15; and Siegfried Arno, "Ich über mich," in *Filmkünstler: Wir über uns selbst*, ed. Hermann Treuner (Berlin: Sibyllen, 1928) n.p. See also Edith Hamann, "Das Interview der Filmwoche: Siegfried Arno," *Die Filmwoche*, No. 15, 1931, 453–56.
7. "[Arno ist] ein ganz selbständiger Groteskkomiker großen Formats," M-s. "Die Frau von vierzig Jahren," *Film-Kurier*, 15 April 1925.
8. Siegfried Kracauer, "Moderne Piraten," review of *Moderne Piraten. Ein Südseeabenteuer* (1928, dir. Manfred Noa), *Frankfurter Zeitung*, 8 November 1928. Reprinted in Siegfried Kracauer, *Kleine Schriften zum Film*, vol. 6.2., ed. Inka Mülder-Bach (Frankfurt am Main, 2004), 137–38.
9. "Ein reines Vergnügen bereitet einzig Siegfried Arno, ein Kabarettkomiker ersten Ranges, der zum Glück Gelegenheit hat, sich ausgiebig zu produzieren." Siegfried Kracauer, "Der Schuß in der großen Oper," Review of *Das letzte Souper* (1928, dir. Mario Bonnard), *Frankfurter Zeitung*, 3 November 1928. Reprinted in Kracauer, *Kleine Schriften zum Film*, 139–40.
10. "Der durch nichts festgelegt werden konnte, der trotz vieler Versuche nicht Chargenspieler wurde" and "der in jeder Passage, in jedem noch so blöden Operettenschmarren der Leinwand Farbe und Tempo gehalten hat." Hans Tasiemka, "Siegfried Arno: Kritischer Essay," *Der Film*, 19, 15 October 1928.
11. "Was sie spielen:'Siggi' ist meine Marke," *Film-Kurier*, 6 October 1928.
12. "Arno, das wäre der pathetische Peter Schlemihl unserer Zeit, der Peter Schlemihl mit der herrlich gebundenen Krawatte und dem blutenden Herzen." Tasiemka, "Siegfried Arno."
13. Hans Feld, "Kleine Epistel an Siegfried Arno," *Film-Kurier*, 5 February 1927. Feld's criticism is triggered, most likely, by a recent genre film in which Arno appeared: *Wenn der junge Wein blüht* (1927, dir. Carl Wilhelm). According to Feld, the film had received terrible reviews and Carl Wilhelm (the director) and Hanni Weisse (the female lead) stormed Feld's offices to protest.

14. "Lassen Sie sich nicht in jedem Film einen Typ aufzwingen, der nur ein unkonstruierter Pseudo-Arno ist." Feld, "Kleine Epistel."
15. "Der einzige Lichtstrahl aus dem Talmud ist Siegfried Arno, der mit Augen und Händen einen jüdischen Trödler mimt," Kracauer, "Der Krieg als Milieu," *Frankfurer Zeitung*, (107–8). See also E.Cz.: "Leichte Kavallerie," *Vossische Zeitung*, 16 October 1927; and Hans Sahl, "Leichte Kavallerie," *Berliner Börsen-Courier*, 16 October 1927.
16. Oly [Fritz Olimsky], "Leichte Kavallerie," *Berliner Börsen-Zeitung*, 16 October 1927.
17. Philipp Stiasny, "Blind Spots and Jewish Heroines: Refashioning the Galician War Experience in 1920s Hollywood and Berlin," in *Beyond Inclusion and Exclusion: Jewish Experiences of the First World War*, ed. Jason Crouthamel, Michael Geheran, Tim Grady, and Julia Barbara Köhne (New York, 2019): 257–85. On representation of Jewishness in the film, see Kerry Wallach, *Passing Illusions: Jewish Visibility in Weimar Germany* (Ann Arbor, 2017), 89–92.
18. See the meticulously researched account of the production and release circumstances and of UFA's delaying maneuvers in Horst Claus, *Filmen für Hitler: Die Karriere des NS-Starregisseurs Hans Steinhoff* (Vienna, 2013), 128–35.
19. Horst Claus speculates that the film *Familientag im Hause Prellstein* may have been intended primarily for export to the United States; with this film UFA hoped to replicate the enormous success of the American comedy *Potash and Perlmutter* (1923, dir. Clarence Badger), also a film situated in a Jewish milieu and based on a popular play, an imported production that was shown in UFA theaters in 1924–25. See Claus, *Filmen für Hitler*, 128–29.
20. "Siegfried Arno als ein echter jüdischer Typ," in Felix Henseleit, "Familientag im Hause Prellstein," *Reichsfilmblatt*, 27 December 1927.
21. "Ein Weltstädter, dem niemand etwas weiß machen kann; eine Vereinigung von Wehmut und Impertinenz; eine durchtriebene Schmachtgestalt, der man trotz mancher anrüchigern Handlung jede Anständigkeit vertraut," writes Siegfried Kracauer in "Siegfried Arno als Komiker," *Frankfurter Zeitung*, 12 December 1929; "Ein glänzender Komiker, der durch seine Großstadtgesten erheitert," writes Siegfried Kracauer, "Gaunerliebchen: Ein Kriminalfilm," *Frankfurter Zeitung*, 27 February 1930. Reprinted in Kracauer, *Kleine Schriften zum Film* 306, 343.
22. See Ashkenazi, *Weimar Film* 39–40.
23. Georg Herzberg, "Familientag im Hause Prellstein," *Film-Kurier*, 17 December 1927.
24. Herzberg, "Familientag."
25. For a detailed account on the history of the Herrnfeld Company, see Otte, *Jewish Identities* 146–59.
26. The only film in which both brothers appeared (alongside Hanni Weisse) is *Endlich allein* (1913, dir. Max Mack), a screen adaptation of an 1895 Herrnfeld play known also as *Isidors Brautfahrt*.
27. See Peter Jelavich, "When Are Jewish Jokes no Longer Funny? Ethnic Humour in Imperial and Republican Berlin," *The Politics of Humour: Laughter, Inclusion, and Exclusion in the Twentieth Century*, ed. Martina Kessel and Patrick Merziger (Toronto, 2012) 22–51. On the relationship between Lubitsch and the Herrnfelds, see Irene Stratenwerth, "Vorspiel auf dem Theater: Vom Possenspiel der Brüder Herrnfeld zu den Lubitsch-Komödien im Kino," *Pioniere in Celluloid: Juden in der frühen Filmwelt*, ed. Irene Stratenwerth and Hermann Simon (Berlin, 2004), 147–65.
28. Ronny Loewy, "Ist ein Komiker jüdisch-komisch oder, wie ein exzellenter jüdischer Geiger, schier ein exzellenter Komiker," *Spaß beiseite, Film ab. Jüdischer Humor und verdrängendes Lachen in der Filmkomödie bis 1945*, ed. Jan Distelmeyr (Frankfurt a.M., 2004), 19. The same point about the affinity between Lubitsch and Arno is made by Alfred

Stalzer, "Jüdische Bühnenkünstler im deutschen und österreichischen Film," *Der jüdische Witz. Zur unabgegoltenen Problematik einer alten Kategorie* (Paderborn, 2015), 228–29.

29. See N.N. "Die antisemitischen Gebrüder Herrnfeld," *Jüdische Rundschau*, 28 August 1908.
30. In 1923 anti-Jewish sentiments culminated in mob violence and pogroms against *Ostjuden* in Berlin's Scheunenviertel. See Otte, *Jewish Identities* 172–73.
31. On the same page of *Film-Kurier*, next to the review of *Familientag im Hause Prellstein*, there was a review of another film with Siegfried Arno, *Eine kleine Freundin braucht jeder Mann* (1927, dir. Paul Heidemann). It premiered in the central Tauentzienpalast (Tauentzien palace), had a much longer run, and was an example of the numerous entertaining comedies with Arno, in which Jewish themes were not present at all. Here one encounters "the trio Arno-Morgan-Falkenstein" and "all props, situations, figures of the popular film farce that are put together in order to give the audience a piece of sophisticated entertainment." See Ernst Jäger, "Eine kleine Freundin braucht jeder Mann," *Film-Kurier*, 17 December 1927.
32. The formulation comes from N.N., "Eine letzte Mahnung—immer noch Würdelosigkeiten in Berlins Kabaretts," *C.V. Zeitung*, 31 December 1926. See also Heidelore Riss, *Ansätze zu einer Geschichte des jüdischen Theaters in Berlin 1889–1936* (Frankfurt am Main, 2000).
33. For a sympathetic coverage of the cabaret-campaign, see "Juden gegen das jüdische Kabarett: eine Protestkundgebung," *Tägliche Rundschau*, 24 April 1926; Siegmund Feldmann, "Jeder Jude sein eigner Antisemit," *Die Weltbühne*, 12 December 1926; Emil Faktor, "Das Mauscheln," *Berliner Börsen-Courier*, 23 April 1926; "Der Jargon im Kabarett," *Berliner Lokal-Anzeiger*, 24 April 1926; "Protest gegen das Jargon-Kabarett," *Berliner Tageblatt*, 23 April 1926; "Kundgebung gegen das 'mauschelde Kabarett,'" *Deutsche Allgemeine Zeitung*, 23 April 1926; For dissenting opinions, see Hans Tasiemka, "Der jüdische Antisemit," *Die literarische Welt*, 7 May 1926 and Kurt Robitschek, "Der Standpunkt der Künstler," *C.V.-Zeitung*, 30 April 1926.
34. L.H., "Gegen die Verzerrung des jüdischen Wesens," *C.V.-Zeitung*, 30 April 1926.
35. Other venues that featured Jewish artists with allegedly offensive material against Jews were Künstlerkabarett, Charlott-Casino, Femina, Alhambra and others. Kurt Robitschek, Kurt Gerron, and the director of the Charlott-Casino attended the April meeting of the Centralverein representing the cabarets. For more on the prominence and stature of KadeKo, see Volker Kühn, "Die Großstadt schreit: Keine Zeit, keine Zeit! Deutsches Kabarett zwischen den Kriegen," in *Alle Meschugge? Jüdischer Witz und Humor*, ed. Marcus G. Patka and Alfred Stalzer (Vienna, 2013), 73–83; and Klaus Völker, *Kabarett der Komiker: Berlin 1924–1950* (Munich, 2010). Völker, however, does not address the accusations of antisemitism hurled at KadeKo.
36. The archives of the Centralverein contain dozens of letters from members and readers of the *C.V. Zeitung* who complained after attending various performances and letters documenting subsequent actions taken by the Centralverein.
37. Singled out were Paul O'Montis, Willy Prager, Willy Rosen, Charlott-Casino, Alhambra-Lichtspiele, and Künstler-Kabarett. See Artur Schweriner, "Rückfälle ins Unwürdige in Berliner Kabaretts," *C.V.-Zeitung*, 9 December 1927.
38. *Die Frechheit* (with a subtitle *Ein Magazin des Humors*) was a monthly publication of the KadeKo, advertising the upcoming program and featuring stories about individual comedians. See Schweriner, "Rückfälle ins Unwürdige."
39. Hans Wollenberg, "Der Jude im Film," *C.V.-Zeitung*, 16 September 1927.
40. A subsequent issue of *C.V. Zeitung* published another article by Wollenberg arguing that claims about the strong Jewish influence within the German film industry are

exaggerated. See Hans Wollenberg, "Die Fabel vom 'verjudeten' Film: eine sachliche Widerlegung," *C.V. Zeitung*, 26 September 1927.
41. Wallach, *Passing Illusions*, 72.
42. Wallach, *Passing Illusions*, 73.
43. Letter to the director of Boulevard-Theater, (Tauentzienstr. 19 in Berlin W.) from 29 March 1928.
44. Letter from Moritz Licht (5 March 1928) to the Centralverein.
45. See "Die Nacht der Komiker," *Die Frechheit*, No. 1, January 1930, 5–7.
46. Kurt Robitschek, "Vom Ersten zum Letzten," *Die Frechheit*, No. 4, April 1929, 3–4.
47. See "Beef und Steak," *Die Rote Fahne*, 6 July 1929; Walter Kaul, "Beef und Steak," *Berliner Börsen-Courier*, 7 July 1929; Leo Hirsch, "Deutsche Lustspiele: Aufruhr im Juggesellenheim," *Berliner Tageblatt*, 7 July 1929; raca. [Siegfried Kracauer], "Ein 'Großlustspiel'" *Frankfurter Zeitung*, 11 October 1929. All reprinted in *Der Film der Weimarer Republik: ein Handbuch der zeitgenössischen Kritik*, ed. Gero Gandert (Berlin, 1997) 59–61.
48. The film exists only as an inaccessible archival copy in Deutsche Kinemathek Berlin. My discussion is entirely based on the reviews that appeared at the time. See Heinrich Braune, "Versuch einer deutschen Filmgroteske," *Hamburger Echo*, 24 August 1929; Ernst Jäger, "Beef & Steak: Aufruhr im Junggesellenheim," *Film-Kurier*, 7 July 1929.
49. Braune, "Versuch einer deutschen Filmgroteske."
50. The scriptwriter Hans Kahan, who had supposedly consulted Paul Morgan and Max Ehrlich and gotten their enthusiastic approval, blamed the failure on the incompetence of the inexperienced director Nossen. See Hans Kahan, "Der 'leere und alberne' Autor bittet ums Wort," *Film-Kurier*, 28 September 1929.
51. "Fix- und Fax-Lustspiele" were twenty-six two-act American farces produced by Harry and Jack Cohn featuring Sid Smith and Harry McCoy. They played in German theaters in 1924. See F.S. [Felix Scherret], "Eine deutsche Groteske," *Der Abend*, 15 September 1929. Reprinted in *Der Film der Weimarer Republik*, 722.
52. Kurt Robitschek, "Eigene Tonfilmproduktion der Kabarett der Komiker," and Kurt Robitschek, "Kabarett im Rundfunk," *Die Frechheit*, No. 5, May 1930. Kurt Gerron, a popular comedian and actor in KadeKo, had little experience as director. Prior to this assignment he had only directed another UFA short comedy (*Tonfilmlustspiel*), *Der Stumme von Portici* (1931, 28 minutes), also intended to be shown as a short sound feature before the main film. Gerron cast Siegfried Arno and other colleagues from KadeKo in the main roles. See "Der Stumme von Portici," *Filmwelt*, no. 19, 10 May 1931; and Lotte H. Eisner, "Der Stumme von Portici," *Film-Kurier*, 15 May 1931.
53. "1. Kabarett-Film," *Film-Kurier*, 6 June 1931; "Weitere Kabarett-Filme der Ufa," *Film-Kurier*, 6 June 1924; "Dritter Ufa-Kabarettfilm," *Film-Kurier*, 10 September 1931.
54. This segment is available on YouTube: https://www.youtube.com/watch?v=fPvU2cQZM74. Trude Berliner (1903–77) was a popular German-Jewish entertainer, who like Arno was forced to leave Germany in 1933 and continue her career in the movies first in France and then in Hollywood.
55. "Eine unerwartete Sensation: Die ersten 6 Kabarett-Filme der UFA, Beifall überall und in jeder Vorstellung," *Film-Kurier*, 11 August 1931. Only the first cabaret short film has been preserved in the National Film Archive (Bundesarchiv); the second through sixth films were in preparation throughout 1931 and some of them premiered in theaters. Some stills were published in fan magazines, but I have not been able to locate any copies of the cabaret films themselves except for the first one. See "Tonfilm-Kabarett," *Filmwelt*, No. 27, 5 July 1931. See also www.filmportal.de.

56. See Karl Prümm, "Arrangeur des Gefälligen," in *Kurt Gerron—gefeiert und gejagt, 1897–1944*, ed. Barbara Felsmann and Karl Prümm (Berlin, 1992) 208–10.
57. This pioneering musical sound film proved to be a huge success in Berlin, Vienna, and in a number of cities throughout Germany as it was in distribution for over six weeks. See Michael Wedel, "Richard Oswald und der Tonfilm," in *Richard Oswald: Kino zwischen Spektakel, Aufklärung und Unterhaltung*, ed. Jürgen Kasten and Armin Loacker (Vienna, 2005), 323–24. See also "Oswalds Sprechfilm der sechs Komiker," *Film-Kurier*, 12 February 1930, and "Oswalds Tonposse zum zweiten Mal prologiert!," *Film-Kurier*, 14 April 1930. One of the funniest and most memorable scenes in the film is a grotesque dance duet in drag with Arno and Max Hansen.
58. The cast features a number of prominent Jewish filmmakers: Irene Ambrus was Arno's costar, Willy Prager contributed to the script and is also performing, and Heinz Letton (Heinz Lewin) composed the music.
59. Wallach, *Passing Illusions*, 84.
60. See Jonathan O. Wipplinger, *The Jazz Republic: Music, Race, and Weimar Germany* (Ann Arbor, 2017), 131–32. Marianne Winkelstern (1910–66) had a brief but glamorous career in dancing and in the movies. She was a star dancer in Eric Charell revues in Wintergarten and in Schauspielhaus.
61. Christine Naumann, "African American Performers and Culture in Weimar Germany," in *Crosscurrents: African Americans, Africa, and Germany in the Modern World*, ed. David McBride, Leroy Hopkins, Carol Blackshire-Belay (Columbia, SC, 1998) 103. Ilse Bois was a star performer at KadeKo between 1926 and 1933.
62. Only some of these titles have survived: *Moritz macht sein Glück, Die Nacht ohne Pause*, and *Die große Attraktion* can be viewed at the Bundesarchiv-Filmarchiv in Berlin; *Keine Feier ohne Meyer* and *Ein ausgekochter Junge* are available on YouTube. I could not locate any copies of *Um eine Nasenlänge, Der Storch streikt*, and *Der schönste Mann im Staate*—they are presumed lost. Because the latter three films are not accessible, it is hard to determine to what extent Jewishness, the Jewish nose, and Jewish facial features have been directly thematized by the plot.
63. See Hamann, "Das Interview."
64. See Ashkenazi, *Weimar Film and Modern Jewish Identity*, 40.
65. See Katja B. Zaich, *"Ich bitte dringend um ein Happyend." Deutsche Bühnenkünstler im niederländischen Exil 1933–1945* (Frankfurt am Main, 2001), 43–44.
66. Quoted in Zaich, *"Ich bitte dringend um ein Happyend,"* 44.
67. See Kracauer, "Moderne Piraten," and e., "Um eine Nasenlänge," *Film-Kurier*, 28 August 1931.

Bibliography

"1. Kabarett-Film." *Film-Kurier*, 6 June 1931.
Arno, Siegfried. "Ich über mich." In *Filmkünstler: Wir über uns selbst*, ed. Hermann Treuner, n.p. Berlin: Sibyllen, 1928.
Ashkenazi, Ofer. *Weimar Film and Modern Jewish Identity*. New York: Palgrave Macmillan, 2012.
"Beef und Steak." *Die Rote Fahne*, 6 July 1929.
Braune, Heinrich. "Versuch einer deutschen Filmgroteske." *Hamburger Echo*, 24 August 1929.

Claus, Horst. *Filmen für Hitler: Die Karriere des NS-Starregisseurs Hans Steinhoff*. Vienna: Filmarchiv Austria, 2013.
"Der Jargon im Kabarett." *Berliner Lokal-Anzeiger*, 24 April 1926.
"Der Stumme von Portici." *Filmwelt* (19, 10 May 1931).
"Die Nacht der Komiker." *Die Frechheit* (1, January 1930): 5–7.
"Dritter Ufa-Kabarettfilm." *Film-Kurier*, 10 September 1931.
e., "Um eine Nasenlänge." *Film-Kurier*, 28 August 1931.
E.Cz. "Leichte Kavallerie." *Vossische Zeitung*, 16 October 1927.
"Eine unerwartete Sensation: Die ersten 6 Kabarett-Filme der Ufa, Beifall überall und in jeder Vorstellung." *Film-Kurier*, 11 August 1931.
Eisner, Lotte H. "Der Stumme von Portici." *Film-Kurier*, 15 May 1931.
Faktor, Emil. "Das Mauscheln." *Berliner Börsen-Courier*, 23 April 1926.
Feld, Hans. "Kleine Epistel an Siegfried Arno." *Film-Kurier*, 5 February 1927.
Feldmann, Siegmund. "Jeder Jude sein eigner Antisemit." *Die Weltbühne*, 12 December 1926.
F.S. [Felix Scherret]. "Eine deutsche Groteske." *Der Abend*, 15 September 1929.
Gandert, Gero, ed. *Der Film der Weimarer Republik: ein Handbuch der Zeitgenössischen Kritik*. Berlin: de Gruyter, 1997.
Gille, Klaus. "Siegfried Arno." In *Hamburgische Biografie*, ed. Franklin Kopitzsch and Dirk Brietzke, 26–27. Göttingen: Wallstein, 2010.
Hamann, Edith. "Das Interview der Filmwoche: Siegfried Arno." *Die Filmwoche* (15, 1931): 453–56.
Henseleit, Felix. "Familientag im Hause Prellstein." *Reichsfilmblatt*, 27 December 1927.
Herzberg, Georg. "Familientag im Hause Prellstein." *Film-Kurier*, 17 December 1927.
Hirsch, Leo. "Deutsche Lustspiele: Aufruhr im Juggesellenheim." *Berliner Tageblatt*, 7 July 1929.
Jäger, Ernst. "Eine kleine Freundin braucht jeder Mann." *Film-Kurier*, 17 December 1927.
———. "Beef & Steak: Aufruhr im Junggesellenheim." *Film-Kurier*, 7 July 1929.
Jelavich, Peter. "Popular Entertainment and Mass Media: The Central Arenas of German-Jewish Cultural Engagement." In *The German Jewish Experience Revisited*, ed. Steven E. Ashheim and Vivian Liska, 103–16. Berlin: De Gruyter, 2015.
———. "When Are Jewish Jokes no Longer Funny? Ethnic Humour in Imperial and Republican Berlin." In *The Politics of Humour: Laughter, Inclusion, and Exclusion in the Twentieth Century*, ed. Martina Kessel and Patrick Merziger, 22–51. Toronto: University of Toronto Press, 2012.
"Juden gegen das jüdische Kabarett: eine Protestkundgebung." *Tägliche Rundschau*, 24 April 1926.
Kahan, Hans. "Der 'leere und alberne' Autor bittet ums Wort." *Film-Kurier*, 28 September 1929.
Kaul, Walter. "Beef und Steak." *Berliner Börsen-Courier*, 7 July 1929.
Kracauer, Siegfried. "Der Krieg als Milieu." *Frankfurter Zeitung*, 2 August 1928.
———. "Der Schuß in der großen Oper." *Frankfurter Zeitung*, 3 November 1928.
———. "Gaunerliebchen: Ein Kriminalfilm." *Frankfurter Zeitung*, 27 February 1930.
———. "Moderne Piraten." *Frankfurter Zeitung*, 8 November 1928.
———. "Siegfried Arno als Komiker." *Frankfurter Zeitung*, 12 December 1929.
———. *Kleine Schriften zum Film*, vol. 6.2, ed. Inka Mülder-Bach. Frankfurt am Main: Suhrkamp, 2004.
Kühn, Volker. "Die Großstadt schreit: Keine Zeit, keine Zeit! Deutsches Kabarett zwischen den Kriegen." In *Alle Meschugge? Jüdischer Witz und Humor*, ed. Marcus G. Patka and Alfred Stalzer, 73–83. Vienna: Jüdisches Museum Wien, 2013.

"Kundgebung gegen das 'mauschelnde Kabarett.'" *Deutsche Allgemeine Zeitung*, 23 April 1926.
L.H. "Gegen die Verzerrung des jüdischen Wesens." *C.V.-Zeitung*, 30 April 1926.
Loewy, Ronny. "Ist ein Komiker jüdisch-komisch oder, wie ein exzellenter jüdischer Geiger, schier ein exzellenter Komiker." In *Spaß beiseite, Film ab. Jüdischer Humor und verdrängendes Lachen in der Filmkomödie bis 1945*, ed. Jan Distelmeyer, 13–20. Munich: Edition Text & Kritik, 2010.
M-s. "Die Frau von vierzig Jahren." *Film-Kurier*, 15 April 1925.
Naumann, Christine: "African American Performers and Culture in Weimar Germany." In *Crosscurrents: African Americans, Africa, and Germany in the Modern World*, ed. David McBride, Leroy Hopkins, Carol Blackshire-Belay, 96-114. Columbia, SC: Camden House, 1998.
Oly. [Fritz Olimsky]. "Leichte Kavallerie." *Berliner Börsen-Zeitung*, 16 October 1927.
"Oswalds Sprechfilm der sechs Komiker." *Film-Kurier*, 12 February 1930.
"Oswalds Tonposse zum zweiten Mal prologiert!" *Film-Kurier*, 14 April 1930.
Otte, Marline. *Jewish Identities in German Popular Entertainment, 1890–1933*. New York: Cambridge University Press, 2006.
"Protest gegen das Jargon-Kabarett." *Berliner Tageblatt*, 23 April 1926.
Prümm, Karl. "Arrangeur des Gefälligen." In *Kurt Gerron—gefeiert und gejagt, 1897–1944*, ed. Barbara Felsmann und Karl Prümm, 208–10. Berlin: Edition Hentrich, 1992.
raca. [Siegfried Kracauer], "Ein 'Großlustspiel.'" *Frankfurter Zeitung*, 11 October 1929.
Riss, Heidelore. *Ansätze zu einer Geschichte des jüdischen Theaters in Berlin 1889–1936*. Frankfurt am Main: Peter Lang, 2000.
Robitschek, Kurt. "Der Standpunkt der Künstler." *C.V.-Zeitung*, 30 April 1926.
———. "Eigene Tonfilmproduktion der Kabarett der Komiker." *Die Frechheit* (5, May 1930): 10.
———. "Kabarett im Rundfunk." *Die Frechheit* (5, May 1930): 10.
———. "Vom Ersten zum Letzten." *Die Frechheit* (4, April 1929): 3–4.
Sahl, Hans. "Leichte Kavallerie." *Berliner Börsen-Courier*, 16 October 1927.
Schöning, Jörg. "Biografie." In *Siegfried Arno*, ed. Hans-Michael Bock, 11–15. Hamburg: CineGraph, 1995.
Schweriner, Artur. "Rückfälle ins Unwürdige in Berliner Kabaretts." *C.V.-Zeitung*, 9 December 1927.
Stalzer, Alfred. "Jüdische Bühnenkünstler im deutschen und österreichischen Film." In *Der jüdische Witz. Zur unabgegoltenen Problematik einer alten Kategorie*, ed. Burkhard Meyer-Sickendiek and Gunnar Och, 225–35. Paderborn: Wilhelm Fink, 2015.
Stiasny, Philipp. "Blind Spots and Jewish Heroines: Refashioning the Galician War Experience in 1920s Hollywood and Berlin." In *Beyond Inclusion and Exclusion: Jewish Experiences of the First World War*, ed. Jason Crouthamel, Michael Geheran, Tim Grady, and Julia Barbara Köhne, 257–85. New York: Berghahn Books, 2019.
Stratenwerth, Irene. "Vorspiel auf dem Theater: Vom Possenspielder Brüder Herrnfeld zu den Lubitsch-Komödien im Kino." In *Pioniere in Celluloid: Juden in der frühen Filmwelt*, ed. Irene Stratenwerth and Hermann Simon, 147–65. Berlin: Henschel, 2004.
Tasiemka, Hans. "Der jüdische Antisemit." *Die literarische Welt*, 7 May 1926.
———. "Siegfried Arno: Kritischer Essay." *Der Film* (19, 15 October 1928).
"Tonfilm-Kabarett." *Filmwelt* (27, 5 July 1931).
Völker, Klaus. *Kabarett der Komiker: Berlin 1924–1950*. Munich: Edition Text & Kritik, 2010.
Wallach, Kerry. *Passing Illusions: Jewish Visibility in Weimar Germany*. Ann Arbor: University of Michigan Press, 2017.
"Was sie spielen: 'Siggi' ist meine Marke." *Film-Kurier*, 6 October 1928.

Wedel, Michael. "Richard Oswald und der Tonfilm." In *Richard Oswald: Kino zwischen Spektakel, Aufklärung und Unterhaltung*, ed. Jürgen Kasten and Armin Loacker, 323–24. Vienna: Filmarchiv Austria, 2005.

"Weitere Kabarett-Filme der Ufa." *Film-Kurier*, 6 June 1931.

Weinstein, Valerie. "Anti-Semitism or Jewish 'Camp'? Ernst Lubitsch's *Schuhpalast Pinkus* (1916) and *Meyer from Berlin* (1918)." *German Life and Letters* 59 (1, January 2006): 101–21.

———. "Performing Jewishness. Ernst Lubitschs frühe Milieukomödien." Retrieved 14 August 2018 from https://www.filmportal.de/node/195049/video/1377175.

Wipplinger, Jonathan O. *The Jazz Republic: Music, Race, and Weimar Germany*. Ann Arbor: University of Michigan Press, 2017.

Wollenberg, Hans. "Der Jude im Film." *C.V.-Zeitung*, 16 September 1927.

Wollenberg, Hans. "Die Fabel vom 'verjudeten' Film: eine sachliche Widerlegung." *C.V. Zeitung*, 26 September 1927.

———. "Die Fabel vom 'verjudeten' Film: eine sachliche Widerlegung." *C.V.-Zeitung*, 9 December 1927.

Zaich, Katja B. *"Ich bitte dringend um ein Happyend." Deutsche Bühnenkünsler im niederländischen Exil 1933–1945*. Frankfurt am Main: Peter Lang, 2001.

Chapter 5

ALFRED ROSENTHAL'S RHETORIC OF COLLABORATION, THE POLITICS OF JEWISH VISIBILITY, AND JEWISH WEIMAR FILM PRINT CULTURE

Ervin Malakaj

By 1922, when Alfred Rosenthal (1888–1942) became editor-in-chief of Weimar Germany's leading film trade publication, *Der Kinematograph*, he had proven himself worthy of stature among the key figures in Wilhelmine and Weimar film criticism in particular and the film industry in general. Throughout the 1910s, he wrote for the film magazine *Bild und Film*, where he worked alongside Emilie Altenloh.[1] In 1919 Rosenthal took on the title of founding editor for two film magazines, *Der schwarze Bär* and *Film und Brettl*, while serving as regular contributing editor to *Der Kinematograph*.[2] Moreover, he established professional organs designed to institutionalize and advance film. For instance, he helped found and preside over the Provinzialverband Rheinland-Westphalen des Verbandes zur Wahrung gemeinsamer Interessen der Kinematographie und verwandter Branchen zu Berlin e.V. [Provincial association Rheinland-Westphalia of the association for the protection of the common interests of cinematography and related industries in Berlin].[3] Under the auspices of the organization, he had been a vocal opponent in the public discussion about the institution of a local censorship board in Düsseldorf during World War I while maintaining professional ties to Berlin.[4] Through his connections, Rosenthal secured a position as public relations director for Bioscop from 1918 onward, which also led him to form his own production company, Die

Radio-Film AG, in 1920.[5] However, his work as editor-in-chief of *Der Kinematograph* remains one of his more prominent professional positions, one that he acquired as a result of his respected work for the periodical under the leadership of Emil Perlmann, who had edited the trade journal until his death in 1922.[6] Rosenthal's ties to the Scherl Verlag, the media corporation that published *Der Kinematograph*, helped secure him an influential position from which he was also able to conceptualize new film magazines (including the popular *Film-Magazin* that later became *Film Welt*) and publish a series of short mass-market monographs about star personas of the 1920s.

Despite his extensive contributions, Rosenthal was visible in different ways to different audiences. For key players of the Weimar culture industry he was a fixture in the field. As Christian Dirks has shown, Rosenthal was a regular "at banquets, premieres, and receptions of the film industry, the associations, and advocacy groups for film."[7] His speaking engagements at such functions repeatedly fed his stature among industry professionals, who came to know him as a powerful cultural contributor with extensive reach, which included audiences among experts in the industry as well as refined readers of his work in trade journals and popular magazines. For popular audiences, which included the general readership of his articles, the situation was different, largely as a result of his use of a pseudonym. Rosenthal's writings in trade journals, magazines, and newspapers appeared predominantly under the pen name "Aros." That is, his personal identity remained discursively veiled behind the secondary persona produced by the use of an alias.[8] And yet the pseudonym also came to be a recognizable brand in its own right—a standard feature for audiences reading film reviews and trade articles alike. Rosenthal was one of the earliest journalists to enjoy widespread reach of his work through newspapers, even if through a pseudonym. For instance, he wrote, "Film-Echo," the first film column that appeared in a daily newspaper—the highly circulated *Berlin Lokal-Anzeiger*—and commenced cultivating a broad readership in ways few other journalists could during his time.[9] To this end, the *Film-Kurier* does not name Alfred Rosenthal but rather names Aros among the top twenty film critics in 1931—the only critic to be listed under their pseudonym.[10]

Such varied tiers of visibility—in face-to-face interactions among key players of the film industry and in semi-veiled fashion through the use of the pseudonym with audiences who may or may not have known his full name and field of influence—troubled the historical record and likely contributed to Rosenthal's minimal recognition in writing on German film history. Unlike Rudolf Arnheim, Béla Balázs, Willy Haas, Siegfried Kracauer, Kurt Tucholsky, or other prominent Jewish critics of his time, Rosenthal does not enjoy a canonical standing in academic writing on Wilhelmine and Weimar film today. Notwithstanding his sparse mention in scholarly writing, Rosenthal's influence on film writing is undeniable. He wrote leading articles on the state of cinema and thereby used the largest Weimar film trade publication along with other contributions to film periodicals during the 1920s to steer what Sabine Hake calls the "consciousness industry" of film.[11] Moreover, Rosenthal's extensive work in the context of different publishing venues made him into a key player in the "institutionalization of cinema and the institution of criticism."[12] In this light, he took on the role of what Robert Darnton has called cultural middlemen—namely, those cultural practitioners who served as mediators between the production and the consumption of cultural texts and who exhibited great impact on the development of cultural taste.[13]

In this chapter I seek to foreground Rosenthal as an important figure in the Weimar film industry by considering the politics informing his navigating public life as a Jew in Weimar Germany. Although Rosenthal refrained from self-identifying as a Jew in his print publications, he was not exempt from the politics of Jewish visibility dictating Jewish public life in the 1920s. To this end, the chapter unveils a profile of a prolific German-Jewish publishing expert, whose work as editor and film critic sheds light onto the professional life of a German Jew as media culture expert. One focus of the chapter will be to examine Rosenthal's work in the context of his relationship to the Scherl media conglomerate, which cultural pundits throughout the 1920s criticized for its lack of journalistic objectivity in light of its increasingly growing nationalist-conservative bent. This affiliation becomes a central means by which Rosenthal's Jewishness enters public discourse. Critics of his work for Scherl repeatedly foregrounded the paradox of a Jewish cultural critic working for a nationalist-conservative publisher. By analyzing Rosenthal's work in *Der Kinematograph*, the chapter unveils how Rosenthal repeatedly occupied a rhetorical position from which he advocated for a stronger sense of collaboration among the disparate sectors of German film criticism in particular and the German film industry more broadly. This rhetorical stance in his writing, as I will examine below, is a method of discursively navigating public life as a Jew in a prominent position in Weimar film print culture.

German–Jewish Cooperation, the Politics of Passing, and Precarity of Jewish Film Print Culture

Scholarship examining the Jewish influence on Weimar cinema describes a collaborative spirit between Jews and non-Jews fueling the formation of film cultures during the 1920s.[14] S.S. Prawer's work, for instance, notes that the Weimar film industry exhibited a "harmonious cooperation between Jewish and non-Jewish men and women . . . which produced the distinctive forms German and Austrian cinema took" and for which Weimar cinema in particular is celebrated and remembered today.[15] In a similar vein, Ofer Ashkenazi's work on Weimar film and Jewish identity explains that the cultural realities of capitalist modernity turned the Weimar film industry into a "unique sphere in which Jewish 'outsiders' could influence the shaping of mainstream bourgeois culture."[16] Ashkenazi identifies Ernst Lubitsch, Richard Oswald, and Reinhold Schünzel, among other Jewish filmmakers, as key players in the Weimar German film industry, who were able to connect to cultural pundits and shape the Weimar public sphere. "Observing the collapse of the traditional social and political institutions and the plethora of novel experiences during the Great War and its aftermath," Ashkenazi writes, "[Jews] played a crucial part in the attempt to reconsider the values, desires, and anxieties of the urban middle class."[17] Jewish life, if at times only marginally recognizable as distinctly Jewish for non-Jews, came to shape Weimar popular culture through cinema by virtue of the Jewishness of its key cultural producers.

Acquiring the cultural codes that signal belonging to German middle classes of the 1920s defined the processes of assimilation for Jews and were requisites for any collaboration in the Weimar public sphere in which Jews connected to non-Jews. That is, cultural figures in the film industry (and those navigating Weimar daily life in general) explicitly or implicitly came to exhibit certain practices in order to acculturate into the context from which they could exhibit influence and forge connections.[18] As Kerry Wallach's work on the politics of Weimar Jewish visibility has shown, the process of assimilation, which she discusses through the analytic category of Jewish passing, was neither simple nor harmless. Wallach defines such passing "as an act in which a self-identified Jew: (1) deliberately presents as non-Jewish; (2) omits information or avoids offering a corrective when taken for non-Jewish; (3) takes advantage of privileges that result from being perceived as a member of the dominant culture."[19] A driving force for Jewish passing—its reason for existing—was antisemitism. Although Weimar Germany was a period of "a newly discovered sense of Jewish identity and pride" as a result of great cultural productivity and civic protections among Jews, the period is also characterized by "a deep-seated fear of antisemitic attacks" among the Jewish communities.[20] Jewish passing thus became a social strategy of navigating threatening scenarios ranging from quotidian interactions to public appearances. However, because Weimar era Berlin was, as Wallach has shown, not only "a thriving cultural center that attracted residents and visitors from all over the world," but also housed "the largest Jewish community in Germany," it facilitated a number of sites in which Jews could be visibly Jewish as well.[21] Thus, "for Weimar Jews, passing figured as a means toward achieving a type of dual legibility, of appearing simultaneously non-Jewish and Jewish, depending on the viewer."[22] In traversing the sites in which their Jewishness could be recognized by other Jews and public sites of the dominant culture, passing became a central mode for public life.

For the cultural pundits shaping the Weimar film print culture industry—a network of Jewish publishers, editors, and critics to which Rosenthal belonged—passing became a central category for professional success. That is, although a significant number of magazine editors (e.g., Willy Haas, Hans Feld) and film critics (e.g., Hans Sahl, Rudolf Arnheim) were Jewish, they refrained from foregrounding their Jewishness in their writing and in their self-presentation to their reading public.[23] Such examples of Jewish passing, at least in part, were an extension of the ongoing discussions about the professionalization of film criticism throughout the 1920s. Essayists debated the nature of film criticism—a still emerging genre of writing about a relatively new medium—by considering the parameters of film criticism, who should engage in it, and in which capacities it should reach readers. The disputes about film criticism regularly concerned questions of authenticity and objectivity. A predominant topic was the threat of bias. Pundits scrutinized that, for example, a publisher could benefit from favorable reviews of films produced by a production company that owned the magazine in which the review was published (e.g., the Scherl publishing house had strong connections to Universum Film Aktiengesellschaft [UFA] while it published *Der Kinematograph*, which regularly published reviews of UFA films). Or, for instance, when film periodicals blurred the line between advertisement space and critical reviews. E.A. Dupont critiqued this practice when he wrote in 1919, "In Germany, there are no other trade journals where the boundaries between journalism and advertisement have disappeared so completely as in the film trade press. In these journals, almost every single line is for sale."[24] Editors and critics were thus particularly keen on upholding an objectivism—even if only in gesture and not in reality—in order to preserve some respectability among readership and ward off accusations of competing publications.

In the case of Rosenthal, as well as other Jewish editors and critics, being a contributor to the field of film criticism meant not just managing what Hake calls the conflicting roles of film trade press—namely, that writing "had to create a positive image of the industry in which artistic considerations were primary and economic considerations secondary, and, at the same time, it had to evaluate its own products from the perspective of cultural consumers"[25]—but having to manage the added factor of Jewish visibility. The rhetoric of collaboration at the core of Rosenthal's writing, examined below, thus not only serves the professional endeavors of the publication by securing it a level of objective respectability regularly expected by professional and lay readers, but also becomes a tool for passing.

Rosenthal's Media Context: Film Periodical Culture and Hugenberg's Scherl Verlag

The medial context in which Rosenthal worked is marked by a strong symbiotic relationship between print media and cinema. That is, Weimar film audiences were, in addition to being prolific consumers of visual culture, voracious readers of newspapers, magazines, and other periodical and print enterprises. As Bernhard Fulda has shown, although cinema and radio featured prominently in the Weimar popular culture industry, "the 1920s were undoubtedly the decade of the press" with "twenty times as many newspaper copies" and magazines being consumed than cinema tickets sold in 1929.[26] The print media market was thus saturated in different ways. In the realm of film periodicals, Hake's work shows that "in 1919 alone, seventeen new journals appeared," a number that would expand throughout the 1920s and would feature the daily film magazine *Film-Kurier* and the monthly *Film-Magazin*, which had a run of more than 100,000 copies.[27] Such sizeable venues with high circulation runs and different strategies to engage different kinds of readership, all of them eager to connect to the cinema culture of their time through print, point to a centrality of print media in understanding the broader medial context in which Weimar cinema culture came into its own.[28] Print media agents were certainly aware of their significance, as this Rosenthal statement from his *Der*

Kinematograph column on 27 May 1923 suggests: "The newspaper and the magazine are just as necessary for film and the film industry as the raw material."[29]

Precisely because Weimar print culture played such a central role for the cultivation of various film audiences, it came to the attention of the nationalist-conservative Alfred Hugenberg, whose longstanding interest in controlling and shaping media discourse in the 1920s led to his standing as one of the most powerful media moguls of the 1920s. Hugenberg, who served as head of Krupp and leader of the Deutschnationale Volkspartei, sought to expand his commercial and ideological interests.[30] He purchased small and medium-sized newspapers throughout the Weimar era before acquiring a significant holding in the film industry: the Scherl publishing house, which published widely circulated newspapers (e.g., *Berliner Lokal-Anzeiger*), film periodicals (e.g., *Der Kinematograph, Film-Magazin*) and owned large shares of UFA in addition to the Deulig film newsreel company.[31] That is, he effectively established a protocol for controlling film production, trade publications, film criticism, and advertising at the same time, a media system which later served as blueprint for National Socialist (Nazi) propaganda networks.[32]

Hugenberg's media empire was criticized already during the 1920s, most prominently by the editor of *Der Film*, Max Feige, and the former editor of *Lichtbild-Bühne*, Kurt Mühsam. Mühsam sued *Der Kinematograph* for libel, accusing Rosenthal, among others, of abusing the publication to favor film productions tied to the Hugenberg media empire.[33] The trade journal came to be read by a handful of critics as unreliable and ideologically tarnished to serve the film industry objectively because, as intimated above with regard to the broader film periodical industry, it blurred the lines between criticism and advertisement.

Stylizing Rosenthal as Expert and the Rhetoric of Collaboration in *Der Kinematograph*

The precarious perception of a trade journal walking the fine line of presenting critical perspectives on the film industry and profiting from those perspectives—a process that Thomas J. Saunders correctly describes as directed by people "who mixed critical functions with personal enrichment from the industry"—made Rosenthal's editorial work in *Der Kinematograph* regularly vulnerable to criticism.[34] Cultivating a rhetorical stance from which to write columns while appearing less biased than the critique warrants was essential for his sustained contribution to the field. One means by which he secured a standing among industry professionals and readers was through his rhetorical position of collaboration in weekly columns on the state of the film industry. These columns, written from the perspective of a figure interested in forming a unified front to rebuild the German film industry and position it as a major competitor on the international film market, functioned to ward off criticism (even if they did not successfully create a fully impervious defense) of a practice effectively carried out by *Der Kinematograph* under Rosenthal's supervision.

A 1923 editorial announcing Rosenthal's appointment as editor-in-chief of the journal lays the foundation for the rhetoric of collaboration. The masthead of *Der Kinematograph* stylized the periodical as "the oldest film trade paper" and its columns regularly evoked and celebrated its traditions.[35] The editorial announcement about Rosenthal's takeover foregrounds his extensive credentials and, by doing so, aligns them with the narrative stylizing the journal as the oldest and most widely respected German trade journal. "The fact that Mr. Alfred Rosenthal—Aros—was entrusted with the spiritual guidance and mentoring of *Der Kinematograph*, a man who fought for his film-journalistic spurs at *Der Kinematograph* years ago and who was able to gain rich experience working for our paper, has made it much easier for the periodical to be transplanted to Berlin."[36]

Notably, Rosenthal's appointment coincides with the move of the magazine from Düsseldorf to Berlin, a move that marks a closer alignment of *Der Kinematograph* with the key functionaries of the Weimar film industry, who had been increasingly (although not exclusively) clustering in Berlin since the end of the war. The move for the periodical meant signaling to its reading public that it was very close to the centers of influence about which it hoped to inform its readers. Rosenthal's appointment fits into this narrative of rejuvenation for the trade journal because of the heavy credentials he brings not only as a figure familiar with the periodical for which he served as contributing editor, but also as experienced critic with extensive Berlin-based connections in the film industry.

The initial editorial narrative establishing Rosenthal as part of a long tradition of quality affiliated with the periodical would not die with the initial announcement and be buried as new issues of the periodical appeared. Rather, the narrative introduced in the editorial would serve as groundwork for Rosenthal's writing. In his columns, Rosenthal repeatedly evokes the language from the initial announcement about his promotion and continues to stylize himself in every piece as an integral purveyor of objective approaches, which he intends to defend and to see used in the periodical. In his first column as editor-in-chief on 6 May 1923, Rosenthal proclaims that *Der Kinematograph* will continue to play a central role in the discussion and promotion of the German film industry: "*Der Kinematograph* was the first to bring the word of German film into the world. It wrapped the first threads between Germany and overseas and has always been a fighter for film, as promoter and admonisher, high above the individual parties who have to navigate the whole structure of the industry following fights with one another."[37]

Beyond its evocation of tradition, the editorial establishes the magazine as the central mediator among the brawling critics of the film industry, who in the past created a discord the magazine could help remedy through its committed editorial work. To this end, Rosenthal notes, "We will remain true to this principle of absolute impartiality in the future. We will neither serve parties nor persons, but we will take the position on big and small issues that we consider to be the only correct and righteous position."[38] Such rhetorical gesture assures the readers that the editorial approach for the magazine is one of elusive objective authenticity. Because the magazine saw itself as purveyor of critical debates on the nature of the industry, the rhetoric of Rosenthal's inaugural editorial as editor-in-chief had to assure readership of such a depoliticized approach if it were to stay in business.

Importantly, Rosenthal remarks in the column not only that he will approach the curation of discussions and debates with an eye to high quality, but also that his work is not one of a lone practitioner. As a final request, Rosenthal's inaugural editorial issues an open invitation for contributions to the critical discussion in the pages of the publication: "We call on all our friends throughout the world, all those who have something meaningful to say on film matters, to collaborate. We know that we can accomplish very little on our own if we lack the support of professionals."[39] What could strike readers at first sight as a contradiction—only a couple of paragraphs earlier, Rosenthal assures readers that the periodical has all it needs to continue serving the public as it did earlier—it actually serves the same function that the evocation of quality and tradition served before—namely, through an evocation of the magazine as a communal or collaborative venture among different agents, and not only those sanctioned by the publisher, Rosenthal seeks to preemptively defend the journal of accusations about industry bias. That is, Rosenthal's inaugural editorial as head of *Der Kinematograph* fashions the journal—if only discursively—as a space of intellectual collaboration and fair exchange.

One gesture frequently visible in Rosenthal's writing, which expanded the rhetoric of collaboration, was to discuss in which ways the German film industry is and can be positioned on the international market. *Der Kinematograph* regularly printed international reports on the film industries in the Balkans (where Rosenthal had been foreign correspondent for a time), Japan, the United States, France, and other countries. Rosenthal's colleague Max Albert, for instance, was sent to Montevideo to generate a special feature on the South American film market.[40] On 10 June 1923 Rosenthal, in one of his numerous pieces on the international film market, warns that German production has to become aware that it has serious competition and that it has to improve if it is to stay viable: "Our industrialists have to recognize that the fight for stature in our own country already started."[41] Referencing the extensive presence of U.S. films on the German film market and anticipating the Parufamet Agreement, Rosenthal discursively unites the German film industry in casting it a victim of an global threat.[42] He speaks of "our industrialists" and juxtaposes them with an "other," thereby forming a simple rhetorical union of what, although seen as one industry, in reality were frequently disparate institutions of production, distribution, and exhibition. Rosenthal regularly explicitly named culprits in what he saw as industry fragmentation, insisting that the miscommunication among industry sectors and discord among functionaries not only damages national interests but also renders the industry as a whole vulnerable in light of international competition. To this end, in a column on 5 August 1923, which was an open letter to Wilhelm Graf (a key figure in the film distribution sector) and Ludwig Scheer (the president of the Reichsverband Deutscher Lichtspieltheater-Besitzer [Reich Association of German Movie Theater Owners]) who could not reach an agreement about distribution prices, he issues a call for collaboration: "You have to sit down together and consider if there are not mutually beneficial points of contact."[43] Not only does this open letter critique an inability of two major figures to come together, but it also positions Rosenthal as mediator with a vested interest in unifying and thus strengthening the German film industry.

Rosenthal likewise advocated for an apolitical cinema that, according to him, the German film industry should strive toward. In a column dated 10 May 1925 he sees in apolitical cinema a method for unification of the film industry: "German cinema is apolitical and must be apolitical because it reflects on visitors from all party camps."[44] In such columns, Rosenthal manipulated a particular topic (e.g., apolitical cinema, disagreements among industry functionaries, internationalization of German cinema) in the spirit of a rhetoric of collaboration. As a result, Rosenthal frequently appears to walk the path of a moderate cultural critic even while working for a conservative publication.[45] One reason for such center politics was to foster a rhetorical venue capable of serving as many ideological tendencies as possible in order to appease a pluralistic readership. Another reason was, as the following section explores, Rosenthal's politics of visibility as a prominent film critic and editor and Jewish man.

Rosenthal's Politics of Jewish Visibility and Passing

The rhetoric of collaboration and the political middle ground that it fostered served as a major strategy to preemptively manage and subsequently to navigate politics of Jewish visibility for Rosenthal. Most prominently, the rhetoric of collaboration emerges as a necessary technology of passing when Rosenthal's passing in public had failed—or, rather, when his Jewishness had been discovered. Take for instance the manner in which the Nazi newspaper *Der Angriff*, under the editorial leadership of Joseph Goebbels, criticized the Scherl media conglomerate in 1932 for harboring a Jewish editor. The editorial criticized Scherl for employing Rosenthal, who was hiding behind a pseudonym that disguised "in truth only the superficial Nordic impostor son of a rabbi."[46] Here the mention of Rosenthal's Jewishness serves the function of critiquing the Scherl publishing house: that is, the antisemitic stance presumes that the act of hiding Rosenthal behind his pseudonym points to a broader problem of a misalignment between the Scherl publishing conglomerate and Nazi endeavors. This rhetoric would eventually lead to Rosenthal's dismissal from his post and is part of a rhetoric ultimately responsible for his murder in a concentration camp. In 1932, however, the rhetoric of outing underscores the fact that up until the moment of publication—in this case in *Der Angriff*—Rosenthal's Jewishness had been "hidden," insofar as the authors of the editorial perceived his Jewishness not to have been part of the public narrative of the Scherl publishers previously.

In fact, other pundits established a similar scenario of discovery in their critical writing about Rosenthal, in that their mention of Rosenthal's Jewishness presumably serves a dramatic effect of revelation of a secret. Carl von Ossietzky, for instance, referred to Aros as "the Jewish head of cinema press affairs for the Teutonic Hugenberg."[47] This articulation of Rosenthal's relationship to Hugenberg seeks to garner a shock-effect in readers who would be presumably discomforted by the articulation of a Jew working for an ethnonationalist conservative. Unlike the editorial in *Der Angriff*, von Ossietzky's language does not suggest Rosenthal's background to be new information for him, but rather presents the information of his Jewishness as potentially shocking to readers who would not have known of this association. The von Ossietzky article points out that, in addition to explicit antisemitic criticism by the Nazi press, not only by authors in *Der Angriff* but also by those writing for the *Völkische Beobachter*, Rosenthal was attacked by the left for serving nationalist-conservative ideals. The left certainly saw Rosenthal's Jewishness as serving no small part in the rhetoric it deployed in its critiques, underscoring a notion that Rosenthal had been in various capacities concerned about concealing his Jewish background.

Still other critics, such as Kurt Tucholsky, painted the Rosenthal and Hugenberg collaboration as a mutually beneficial endeavor, leaving no room to read Rosenthal as merely a middleman in a broader system of power manipulated by influential figures but rather painting him as agent in control of a powerful field of influence. Tucholsky famously refers to Rosenthal as "Aros Hugenberg."[48] The critique foregrounds Rosenthal's mixed ideological and economic commitments and rhetorically fuses what are two people into one, suggesting that there was no distinction between Rosenthal and Hugenberg. Each depended on the other in the orchestration of a nationalist conservative print industry through the Scherl publishing conglomerate.

Conclusion

The last *Kinematograph* to be edited by Rosenthal appeared 31 March 1933, before he was officially fired from the post.[49] After a difficult stay in Vienna, where he was supposedly arrested for trying to pay a hotel bill with an uncovered check, he sought refuge in Prague.[50] There, he is said to have established the weekly periodical *Prag sieht und hört* [Prague sees and listens], according to Paul Marcus's exile newsletter *Pem's Privat-Berichte*.[51] Thereafter, Rosenthal was deported to a concentration camp in Riga, where he was murdered.[52] Even though Rosenthal refrained from publicly acknowledging his Jewish background in his writings, and carefully nurtured the rhetoric of collaboration in *Der Kinematograph* to preemptively ward off any critiques, his critics frequently drew on his Jewishness to condemn his contribution to the Scherl media conglomerate. Because critics foreground his Jewishness, they suggest that it had not been part of the public discourse previously in extensive ways. Rosenthal, following the notion of the management of Jewish visibility through passing, effectively stayed in the public discourse but veiled his identity partially through the use of a pseudonym and also through a rhetorical position intended to focus on uniting the German film industry.

Rosenthal was a tastemaker in various capacities as editor and contributor to film print culture. As a Jew, he was able to contribute to popular culture and aim to harness it, because, as Marline Otte has shown, "popular entertainment contributed to a redefined public sphere in the first decade of the twentieth century" in which marginalized peoples saw opportunity for contribution, even as collaborators with a conservative ethnonationalist such as Hugenberg.[53] Moreover, despite (or perhaps because of) his management of the politics of Jewish visibility in Weimar Germany, Rosenthal effectively contributed to public life. As Ofer Ashkenazi writes, Jewish cultural production in the Weimar era positioned Jewish Germans to produce "vocabulary that enabled the integration of [German Jews'] particular experiences, hopes and fears into the cultural discourse of the bourgeoisie."[54] It is in this light that even the work of a problematic cultural pundit such as Rosenthal helped shape film print culture of the Weimar era. This cultural work is immediately tied to Rosenthal's extensive navigation of professional life as a key figure in the media industry who was not exempt from the politics of Jewish visibility dictating Jewish public life in the 1920s.

Ervin Malakaj is assistant professor of German studies and affiliate faculty in the Institute for European Studies at the University of British Columbia. His research focuses on German media history, nineteenth-century literary cultures, early film studies, and queer theory. In addition to articles on German literature and film studies, his publications include the two coedited volumes: *Market Strategies and German Literature of the Nineteenth Century* (de Gruyter, 2020) and *Diversity and Decolonization in German Studies* (Palgrave, 2020).

Notes

1. The most extensive biography of Alfred Rosenthal was written by Christian Dirks for a short essay in a volume accompanying a prominent exhibit at the Centrum Judaicum Berlin, February–May 2004. The present chapter draws extensively from Dirks's work. Christian Dirks, "Alfred Rosenthal 1888–1942: Filmjournalist und Filmlobbyist," *Pioniere in Celluloid: Juden in der Frühen Filmwelt*, ed. Irene Stratenwerth and Hermann Simon (Berlin: Henschel, 2004).
2. Sabine Hake, *The Cinema's Third Machine: Writing on Film in Germany 1907–1933* (Lincoln: University of Nebraska Press, 1993), 113.
3. Dirks, "Alfred Rosenthal," 82–83. Unless otherwise noted, the translations are all by author.
4. See Sabine Lenk, "Censoring Films in Düsseldorf during the First World War," *Film History* 22.4 (2010): 426–39.
5. Dirks, "Alfred Rosenthal," 83.
6. Dirks, "Alfred Rosenthal," 84. See Kay Weniger, *"Es wird im Leben dir mehr genommen als gegeben . . . " Lexikon der aus Deutschland und Österreich emigrierten Filmschaffenden 1933–1945—Eine Gesamtübersicht* (Hamburg: Acabus Verlag, 2011), 604.
7. "Auf den Banketten, Premieren und Empfängen der Filmwirtschaft, der Verbände und Interessensvertretungen des Films." Dirks, "Alfred Rosenthal," 84.
8. Most readers of Aros's work could not know that it stood for Alfred Rosenthal, even if the initial article announcing Rosenthal as new editor of *Der Kinematograph* made this relationship between pseudonym and real name explicit. A small-print editorial contact address in the large format *Film-Magazin* lists Aros and Rosenthal's full name as a contact. The majority of his reviews in *Der Kinematograph* and other newspapers and magazines do not list his full name.
9. Dirks, "Alfred Rosenthal," 84.
10. Redaktion, "Welche Zeitung bringt die besten Filmkritiken?," *Film-Kurier* Vol. 119, 23 May 1931.
11. Hake, *Cinema's Third Machine*, xii.
12. Hake, *Cinema's Third Machine*, ix.
13. Robert Darnton, *The Kiss of Lamourette: Reflections in Cultural History* (New York: Norton, 1990), 120, 111. See also Pierre Bourdieu, *The Field of Cultural Production: Essays on Art and Literature*, ed. Randal Johnson (New York: Columbia University Press, 1993), 76. Bourdieu's notion of the cultural businessmen refers primarily to art dealers, but could be extended to address Rosenthal's extensive impact on cultural production.
14. For a discussion of the contributions of German Jews to the broader social, economic, cultural aspects of Weimar Germany, see Anthony Kauders, "Weimar Jewry," in *The Short Oxford History of Germany: Weimar Germany*, ed. Anthony McElligott (Oxford: Oxford University Press, 2009), 234–57. To this end, Amos Elon pronounces Weimar Germany as an era in which "Jews were finally equal not only in theory but in practice." Amos Elon, *The Pity of It All: A Portrait of the German-Jewish Epoch, 1743–1933* (New York: Picador, 2002), 358.
15. S.S. Prawer, *Between Two Worlds: Jewish Presence in German and Austrian Film, 1910–1933* (New York: Berghahn, 2005), viii.
16. Ofer Ashkenazi, *Weimar Film and Modern Jewish Identity* (New York: Palgrave Macmillan, 2012), 3.
17. Ashkenazi, *Weimar Film*, 3.

18. For a study of quotidian life of Jews in Weimar Germany, see Trude Maurer, "From Everyday Life to a State of Emergency: Jews in Weimar Germany and Nazi Germany," in *Jewish Daily Life in Germany, 1618–1945*, ed. Marion A. Kaplan (Oxford: Oxford University Press, 2005), 271–374.
19. Kerry Wallach, *Passing Illusions: Jewish Visibility in Weimar Germany* (Ann Arbor: University of Michigan Press, 2017), 5.
20. Wallach, *Passing Illusions*, 10.
21. Wallach, *Passing Illusions*, 4.
22. Wallach, *Passing Illusions*, 21.
23. For a longer list of not only Jewish critics and editors, but also other figures in the broader German film industry of the 1920s, see Prawer, *Between Two Worlds*, 211–14.
24. E.A. Dupont, "Filmkritik und Filmreklame." *Film-Kurier*, 24 August 1919. Quoted in Hake, *Cinema's Third Machine*, 120. Hake's book provides an extensive overview of the film print culture of the 1920s and the debates I mention in my chapter.
25. Hake, *Cinema's Third Machine*, 115.
26. See Bernhard Fulda, *Press and Politics in the Weimar Republic* (Oxford: Oxford University Press, 2009), 3.
27. Hake, *Cinema's Third Machine*, 114.
28. For Weimar print periodical engagement strategies and the shaping of early cinephiles, see Michael Cowan, "Learning to Love the Movies: Puzzles, Participation, and Cinephilia in Interwar European Magazines," *Film History* 27.4 (2015): 1–45.
29. "Die Zeitung und die Zeitschrift ist für den Film und für die Filmindustrie genauso notwendig wie das Rohmaterial." Aros, "Das Problem der Filmkritik," *Der Kinematograph* Vol. 849, 27 May 1923, 5.
30. For the most comprehensive contemporary account of the expansion of the Hugenberg media empire, see Ludwig Bernhard, *Der Hugenberg-Konzern: Psychologie und Technik einer Großorganisation der Presse* (Berlin: Julius Springer, 1928).
31. Fulda, *Press and Politics*, 2.
32. Hilmar Hoffmann, *The Triumph of Propaganda: Film and National Socialism, 1933–1945*, tranls. John A. Broadwin and V.R. Berghahn (Providence, RI: Berghahn, 1996), 82. See also Corey Ross, *Media and the Making of Modern Germany: Mass Communications, Society, and Politics from the Empire to the Third Reich* (Oxford: Oxford University Press, 2008), 176–78.
33. Thomas J. Saunders, *Hollywood in Berlin: American Cinema and Weimar Germany* (Berkeley: University of California Press, 1994), 44–45.
34. "Daß im neuen Verlag die geistige Führung und Ueberwachung des 'Kinematograph' in Herrn Alfred Rosenthal—Aros—einem Manne anvertraut ist, der seine filmjournalistischen Sporen vor Jahren beim 'Kinematograph' sich erkämpfte und auch im geschäftlichen Dienste unseres Blattes seine reichen Erfahrungen sammeln konnte, hat dem bisherigen Verlag die Uebertragung und Verpflanzung des Blattes nach Berlin wesentlich erleichtert." Saunders, *Hollywood in Berlin*, 44.
35. "Das älteste Film-Fach-Blatt."
36. A.Z., "'Der Kinematograph' und sein Verlag," *Der Kinematograph* Vol. 844–45, 22 and 29 April 1923, 6.
37. Aros, "Neue Wege zum alten Ziel," *Der Kinematograph* Vol. 846, 6 May 1923, 7.
38. Aros, "Neue Wege zum alten Ziel," 7.
39. "Wir rufen alle unsere Freunde, alle diejenigen, die in Filmfragen etwas Belangvolles zu sagen haben, in der ganzen Welt zur Mitarbeit auf. Wir wissen, daß wir selbst nur wenig erreichen können, wenn uns die Unterstützung der Berufenden fehlt." Aros, "Neue Wege zum alten Ziel," 7.

40. Max Albert, "Montevidianische Kino-Variétés," *Der Kinematograph* Vol. 834, 11 February 1923, 6.
41. "Unsere Fabrikanten müssen klar erkennen, daß der Kampf um die Position im eigenen Lande schon begonnen hat." Aros, "Die Eroberung Deutschlands," *Der Kinematograph* Vol. 851, 10 June 1923, 5.
42. Compare with Klaus Kreimeier, *The Ufa Story: A History of Germany's Greatest Film Company, 1918–1945*, transl. Robert Kimber and Rita Kimber (Berkeley: The University of California Press, 1999), 127. Sabine Hake, *German National Cinema* (New York: Routledge, 2002), 34–35. Thomas Elsaesser, *Weimar Cinema and After: Germany's Historical Imaginary* (New York: Routledge, 2000), 117.
43. "Sie müssen sich einmal zusammensetzen und gemeinsam überlegen, ob es nicht doch wieder gemeinsame Berührungspunkte gibt." Aros, "Ruf zur Verständigung," *Der Kinematograph*, Vol. 859, 5 August 1923.
44. "Das deutsche Kino ist unpolitisch und muß unpolitisch sein, weil es auf Besucher aus allen Parteilagern reflektiert." Aros, "Politisches Kino," *Der Kinematograph*, Vol. 951, 10 May 1925.
45. Notably, Rosenthal's critics who leaned left ideologically in the years 1928–31 would see in the call for apolitical filmmaking a silent support for conservative ideological cinema while the right-wing critique regularly saw in the rhetoric a support of the left and increasingly grew suspicious of his commitment to Scherl because of his Jewishness. Throughout the 1920s, however, Rosenthal steadfastly believed the rhetoric of collaboration as grounded in apolitical ideology would unite pundits occupying various positions on the political spectrum.
46. "In Wahrheit de[n] nur oberflächlich aufgenordete[n] Sohn eines Rabbiners." Quoted in Hans-Albert Walter, *Deutsche Exilliteratur 1933–1950* Vol. 1 (Stuttgart: Metzler, 2003), 262.
47. "Des Teutonen Hugenberg semitischer Kinopressechef." Carl von Ossietzky, "Attentat and die Filmkritik," *Die Weltbühne*, 4 November 1930.
48. Peter Panter, "Auf dem Nachttisch," *Die Weltbühne* 2 February 1929, 337. Peter Panter was one of Kurt Tucholsky's pseudonyms. See Nele Lenze, ed. *Tucholsky in Berlin: Gesammelte Feuilletons 1912–1930* (Berlin: Berlin Story Verlag, 2012).
49. Dirks, "Alfred Rosenthal," 87.
50. Dirks, "Alfred Rosenthal," 88–89.
51. Pem, *Pem's Privat-Berichte*, January 5, 1938.
52. Dirks, "Alfred Rosenthal," 89.
53. Marline Otte, *Jewish Identities in German Popular Entertainment, 1890–1933* (Cambridge: Cambridge University Press, 2006), 13.
54. Ashkenazi, *Weimar Film*, 3.

Bibliography

Albert, Max. "Montevidianische Kino-Variétés." *Der Kinematograph* (834, 11 February 1923).

Aros. "Das Problem der Filmkritik." *Der Kinematograph* (849, 27 May 1923).

———. "Die Eroberung Deutschlands." *Der Kinematograph* (851, 10 June 1923).

———. "Neue Wege zum alten Ziel." *Der Kinematograph* (846, 6 May 1923).

———. "Politisches Kino." *Der Kinematograph* (951, 10 May 1925).

———. "Ruf zur Verständigung." *Der Kinematograph* (859, 5 August 1923).

Ashkenazi, Ofer. *Weimar Film and Modern Jewish Identity*. New York: Palgrave Macmillan, 2012.
A.Z. "'Der Kinematograph' und sein Verlag." *Der Kinematograph* (844-45, 22 and 29 April 1923).
Bernhard, Ludwig. *Der Hugenberg-Konzern: Psychologie und Technik einer Großorganisation der Presse*. Berlin: Julius Springer, 1928.
Bourdieu, Pierre. *The Field of Cultural Production: Essays on Art and Literature*, ed. Randal Johnson. New York: Columbia University Press, 1993.
Cowan, Michael. "Learning to Love the Movies: Puzzles, Participation, and Cinephilia in Interwar European Magazines." *Film History* 27 (4, 2015): 1–45.
Darnton, Robert. *The Kiss of Lamourette: Reflections in Cultural History*. New York: Norton, 1990.
Dirks, Christian. "Alfred Rosenthal 1888–1942: Filmjournalist und Filmlobbyist." *Pioniere in Celluloid: Juden in der Frühen Filmwelt*, ed. Irene Stratenwerth and Hermann Simon, 81–91. Berlin: Henschel, 2004.
Dupont, E.A. "Filmkritik und Filmreklame." *Film-Kurier*, 24 August 1919.
Elon, Amos. *The Pity of It All: A Portrait of the German-Jewish Epoch 1743–1933*. New York: Picador, 2002.
Elsaesser, Thomas. *Weimar Cinema and After: Germany's Historical Imaginary*. New York: Routledge, 2000.
Fulda, Bernhard. *Press and Politics in the Weimar Republic*. Oxford: Oxford University Press, 2009.
Hake, Sabine. *The Cinema's Third Machine: Writing on Film in Germany 1907–1933*. Lincoln: University of Nebraska Press, 1993.
———. *German National Cinema*. New York: Routledge, 2002.
Hoffmann, Hilmar. *The Triumph of Propaganda: Film and National Socialism, 1933–1945*. trans. John A. Broadwin and V.R. Berghahn. Providence, RI: Berghahn Books, 1996.
Kauders, Anthony. "Weimar Jewry." In *The Short Oxford History of Germany: Weimar Germany*, ed. Anthony McElligott, 234–57. Oxford: Oxford University Press, 2009.
Kreimeier, Klaus. *The Ufa Story: A History of Germany's Greatest Film Company, 1918–1945*. transl. Robert Kimber and Rita Kimber. Berkeley: University of California Press, 1999.
Lenk, Sabine. "Censoring Films in Düsseldorf during the First World War." *Film History* 22 (4, 2010): 426–39.
Lenze, Nele, ed. *Tucholsky in Berlin: Gesammelte Feuilletons 1912–1930*. Berlin: Berlin Story, 2012.
Maurer, Trude. "From Everyday Life to a State of Emergency: Jews in Weimar Germany and Nazi Germany." In *Jewish Daily Life in Germany, 1618–1945*, ed. Marion A. Kaplan, 271–374. Oxford: Oxford University Press, 2005.
Otte, Marline. *Jewish Identities in German Popular Entertainment, 1890–1933*. Cambridge: Cambridge University Press, 2006.
Panter, Peter. "Auf dem Nachttisch." *Die Weltbühne*, 2 February 1929.
Pem. *Pem's Privat-Berichte*, 5 January 1938.
Prawer, S.S. *Between Two Worlds: Jewish Presence in German and Austrian Film, 1910–1933*. New York: Berghahn Books, 2005.
Redaktion. "Welche Zeitung bringt die besten Filmkritiken?" *Film-Kurier*, 23 May 1931.
Ross, Corey. *Media and the Making of Modern Germany: Mass Communications, Society, and Politics from the Empire to the Third Reich*. Oxford: Oxford University Press, 2008.
Saunders, Thomas J. *Hollywood in Berlin: American Cinema and Weimar Germany*. Berkeley: University of California Press, 1994.
von Ossietzky, Carl. "Attentat and die Filmkritik." *Die Weltbühne*, 4 November 1930.

Wallach, Kerry. *Passing Illusions: Jewish Visibility in Weimar Germany*. Ann Arbor: University of Michigan Press, 2017.
Walter, Hans-Albert. *Deutsche Exilliteratur 1933–1950*, vol. 1. Stuttgart: Metzler, 2003.
Weniger, Kay. *"Es wird im Leben dir mehr genommen als gegeben . . ." Lexikon der aus Deutschland und Österreich emigrierten Filmschaffenden 1933–1945—Eine Gesamtübersicht*. Hamburg: Acabus, 2011.

PART II

CODING AND DECODING JEWISH DIFFERENCE

Chapter 6

Two Worlds, Three Friends, and the Mysterious Seven-Branched Candelabrum

Jewish Filmmaking in Weimar Germany

Philipp Stiasny

On 15 and 16 September 1930 two feature films premiered in Berlin that are both bound up, though in entirely different ways, with the work of Jewish filmmakers and the depiction of Jewishness in Weimar cinema. The first, *Die Drei von der Tankstelle* (*The Three from the Filling Station*; 1930, dir. Wilhelm Thiele), has become a German classic and part of the nation's cultural memory. It was the most popular movie of the season in 1930–31 and there were times when everybody in Germany knew its songs by heart. Jewish filmmakers largely were responsible for this success—as they were for the international success of Weimar cinema in general. The second movie was *Zwei Welten* (*Two Worlds*) by E. A. Dupont. It is mostly forgotten today and virtually invisible due to a problematic archival situation. The story takes place during World War I in a Jewish town in Galicia, where the Jews literally are caught between the fronts and are mistreated and discriminated against. *Two Worlds* sheds light on the endangered world of eastern European Jews and makes the case for sympathy and understanding.[1]

The theatrical release of these two films coincided with the Reichstag elections of 14 September 1930, which had a catastrophic outcome for German Jews. Under the headline "6,400,000 National Socialist voters," the *Jüdische Rundschau*, the journal of the German Zionists, commented on the result and its effects: "Approximately 560,000 Jewish souls live in Germany. For every Jewish soul there are 11 adult non-Jews who have agreed to a radical antisemitic policy and are prepared to harm the Jews by all legal and illegal means. This is a fact that characterizes the situation of German Jewry in the most blatant way." The newspaper complained that, although the electoral success of the Nazis "represents a terrible threat to Jewry in Germany," this was perceived by the other parties only as a secondary issue. The Jews were abandoned. The struggle against Nazism, especially on the Jewish side, had been "useless in the face of the prevailing sentiment generated by antisemitic agitation in large sections of the German people." The verdict of the *Jüdische Rundschau* would prove prescient: "Like a deluge, a wave of reckless hostility closes in on the German Jews."[2]

In the context of September 1930, *Two Worlds* appears as an example of a Jewish-themed film that is set in the past, but clearly connects to a present-day problem. *Two Worlds*, one might argue, took part in the fight against antisemitism or even Nazism. In the medium of film, this fight was almost exclusively taken up by Jewish filmmakers, in this case the director E. A. Dupont, who had already made an important Jewish-themed film, and the producer Hermann Millakowsky.

One could not say the same of *The Three from the Filling Station*. The story has—with the exception of a few allusions—no obvious connection to Judaism. On the other hand, the producer Erich Pommer, the scriptwriter Franz Schulz (who also wrote the script of *Two Worlds*), the director Wilhelm Thiele, the composer Werner Richard Heymann, and the librettist Robert Gilbert were Jews. But did they see themselves as Jewish filmmakers at the time the film was made? Or were they transformed into this only when, in 1933, the Nazis took away their livelihoods and expelled them from Germany on the grounds that they were Jews and thus forbidden to continue working in the film industry? If we retroactively identify Pommer, Schulz, Thiele, and the others as Jewish filmmakers, are we not reproducing the same essentialism that the Nazis practiced in the name of *Volk* —the people—and race? Or are such scruples incompatible with the historical situation? Would the common experience of discrimination and persecution not inevitably lead filmmakers to see themselves as part of a group in which members' unifying element was their Jewish heritage—whether that heritage was embraced, externally attributed, or considered unimportant by the individual?

Forms of Jewish Presence and Identity in Weimar Cinema

In their pioneering studies, Siegfried Kracauer and Lotte H. Eisner, who both had to emigrate from Germany because they were considered Jewish and whose work shaped the discourse on Weimar cinema for decades, rarely directly address the question of a specifically Jewish filmmaking and of the presence of Jewish filmmakers.[3] Jewishness, in these books, is the elephant in the room. It was not until 2005 that Siegbert Prawer presented the first comprehensive documentation of the Jewish presence in German and Austrian film before 1933 in his book *Between Two Worlds*. In it, he identifies Jewish individuals in the industry, discusses individual films with Jewish themes, and examines many films on which Jews collaborated, but which—like *The Three from the Filling Station*—would be labeled inadequately, if not incorrectly, with the term "Jewish filmmaking." Prawer's book has provided many starting points for further research.[4] By looking at both Germany and Austria, Prawer was also able to show what was acceptable in Viennese cinema at that time, but not in Berlin, such as the positive and delightful portrayal of Jewish immigrants from eastern Europe and their Yiddish culture in movies that obviously addressed a Yiddish-speaking audience.[5]

In Germany at the time, the closest connection between a Jewish filmmaker and Jewish subject matter could be found in the early work of Ernst Lubitsch, which is discussed in some detail by Prawer. Lubitsch made a name for himself as a comedian during World War I with bawdy comedies set in a Jewish milieu. The fact that he drew on and simultaneously parodied common clichés and prejudices met with displeasure among emancipated bourgeois German Jews, as the snide remarks of Lotte H. Eisner (who was raised Protestant) would show even decades later.[6] Around 1918, when his film projects became larger and more expensive and when he began to focus on film direction, Lubitsch seems to have lost his former interest in Jewish stories. Nevertheless, his work continued to reflect the conditions of his Jewish identity, as Richard McCormick has pointed out. McCormick uses Lubitsch's *Madame Dubarry* (1919), the first international success of Weimar cinema, as his example. The film describes the social ascent of a young woman shortly before the French Revolution: She starts off working in a hat shop, only later to become the lover of the French king and the most powerful woman in the country. She owes this to her looks, her charm, and her open-mindedness in questions of sex and morality. In the end, she has to pay for it all on the scaffold. According to McCormick, one can interpret this ambivalent female figure (played by Pola Negri) as the alter ego of the director, who in his "Jewish films"—like the Pola Negri character in *Madame Dubarry*—had often played the smart, up-and-coming apprentice in the clothing industry. The story of Madame Dubarry then appears as a metaphor for the joys and perils of the rise of a Jew from the margins of society to the center. The film clearly sympathizes with the female heroine, who reverses social and gender hierarchies and thus acts like a revolutionary herself, making her desire for social advancement quite understandable. For McCormick, the fact that this figure is finally executed by the revolutionaries illustrates Lubitsch's skepticism: He promoted liberality and tolerance, but, as a former outsider, always mistrusted the masses that could so easily be manipulated and turned into a violent mob.[7]

Ofer Ashkenazi's study *Weimar Film and Modern Jewish Identity* (2012) ascribes a special position to Lubitsch's early work, as well.[8] Ashkenazi argues that Jewish filmmakers were negotiating their own German-Jewish identity and their position in Weimar society in genre films that made no explicit reference to Judaism—for example, popular comedies, adventure films, and melodramas. In effect, they reflected their status as Jews indirectly on a metaphorical level. Ashkenazi's thesis suggests a need to reconsider Weimar genre cinema and the investment of Jewish filmmakers in shaping it. In this revision, it appears as a cinema whose stories speak to the same ambitions and fears that drove a bourgeois, liberal, and acculturated urban Jewish community. From this perspective, the modern German-Jewish identity probed in the films encompassed not only the experience of hostility and the fear of discovery, but also a playful and performative approach to identity, as well as an optimism toward the future and the chance for social acceptance and integration.[9]

In addition to the ambiguous and fluid Jewish identities on the screen, there was also a critical response in German-Jewish journalism to the portrayal of Jewishness in films, as Kerry Wallach has shown.[10] In Berlin, several Jewish newspapers represented different branches of Judaism, among them the *C.V.-Zeitung* (the newspaper of the Centralverein deutscher Staatsbürger jüdischen Glaubens [Central Association of German Citizens of Jewish Faith], which claimed to represent 60 percent of the German Jews), the *Jüdische Rundschau* (the newspaper of the Zionist Association for Germany, with 20,000 members) and the *Jüdisch-liberale Zeitung* (the newspaper of the Union for Liberal Judaism, with 10,000 members).[11] Film and cinema were of minor interest to these papers. The rare reports on such topics deal, for example, with documentary films produced by Jewish organizations to provide information about Jewish welfare and reconstruction work in Palestine.[12] The papers also commented on a number of positive Jewish-themed feature films, including American imports like *His People* (*Seine Söhne*; 1925, dir. Edward Sloman), starring the Jewish stage actor Rudolf Schildkraut, and *The Jazz Singer* (*Der Jazzsänger*; 1927, dir. Alan Crosland), which were released in Germany. The Jewish press paid attention to the representation of Jews on stage and on screen, and strongly criticized what they saw as a generally stereotypical filmic representation of Jews. For example, Wallach refers to the important film journalist Hans Wollenberg, who opposed the spread of stereotypical images of Jews and vigorously attacked both "Jewish self-mockery in film" and the "disgusting antisemitism as business [*Geschäftsantisemitismus*]," namely Jewish film actors, directors, and producers who trafficked in antisemitic stereotypes as sources of amusement.[13]

The production of Yiddish-language films in Vienna suggests that there was some sort of visible Jewish film and cinema culture. With the exception of Lubitsch's Jewish comedies and a few other films, this cannot be said of Berlin or other major German cities where the Jewish population was significant, but small. Although many Jews were involved in film production, the subject matter generally aimed at a broad and often international audience, that is, not primarily a Jewish audience. The same was true for the sector of film exhibition, although most advertisements in Jewish newspapers were clearly tailored to a Jewish audience. The issue of a specifically Jewish audience, and indeed Jewish film reception, is one that bears further research.

The question I am concerned with here is how Jewishness was staged in Weimar cinema in the context of what Jewish filmmaking meant at the time. I approach this question from two vantage points. First, with *Two Worlds* as my reference, I consider Jewish-themed films that address antisemitic prejudice. Yet while a small group of Jews were prominent in the film business, Jewish-themed films actually played only a marginal role among hundreds of films produced each year. So, with *The Three from the Filling Station* as my reference, I address those other works with narratives that had no obvious connection to the Jewishness of their creators.

The Advent of Modern Antisemitism and the Response by Jewish Filmmakers

In the history of the Jews in Germany, World War I was a watershed. Until then, since the middle of the nineteenth century, their history was essentially a success story. According to Reinhard Rürup, it represented "one of the most spectacular leaps of a minority into the social history of Europe."[14] During the war, however, antisemitic polemics increased sharply, partly in connection with the war-related westward migration of eastern European Jews. The number of these *Ostjuden* (eastern Jews) was greatly exaggerated in public discourse during and after the war, not least because they often were outwardly recognizable as "representatives of an orthodox ghetto culture" due to their dress and language.[15] In the course of Germany's military defeat, the revolution, the founding of the republic, and the end of the monarchy, an "antisemitic storm surge" of millions of pamphlets, leaflets, and brochures flooded Germany.[16]

In those years, the antisemitic movement changed profoundly: The religiously, economically, and socially motivated antisemitism of earlier decades turned into a racial ideology, "modern racial antisemitism." Groups and associations with a *völkisch* (ethno-populist) and racist agenda developed a strong following. In addition to antisemitic texts and speeches, there were now antisemitic campaigns and violent attacks on Jewish people and institutions.

At the center of antisemitic discourse was the stereotype of the eastern European Jew. According to Moshe Zimmermann, this stereotype referred to "the exact opposite of the German or the assimilated Jew: lazy and unproductive, polluted and carriers of disease, criminals from birth, Asian and revolutionary."[17] With regard to the so-called *Ostjudenfrage* (the question of the eastern European Jews), politicians demanded immigration bans and deportations, sometimes directed against refugees from Russia and Ukraine who had fled anti-Jewish pogroms at home.[18] During the postwar years, violent riots and attacks on eastern Jews occurred in several German cities.[19] The liberal-bourgeois, orthodox, and Zionist German Jews responded very differently to these events and developments. Their reactions ranged from distancing themselves from the eastern Jews, whose immigration was sometimes seen as the source of increasing antisemitism, to the call for assimilation or acculturation, to the idealization of a putative "authentic Judaism" represented by the refugees.

Jewish associations, communities, and individuals faced antisemitic hostilities on multiple fronts.[20] While most non-Jewish Germans saw antisemitism primarily as an insignificant problem for a fringe group, Jewish filmmakers actively struggled against antisemitism and carried this struggle into the movies, too.

The director and producer Richard Oswald is an example of this struggle. In 1920, he announced a film project entitled *Antisemiten* (Antisemites). "Antisemitism is—perhaps more so than capitalism or communism—the problem of this day and this hour, the question that most urgently needs resolution," Oswald proclaimed.[21] He had already experienced an antisemitic campaign himself in response to his 1919 feature film *Anders als die Andern* (*Different from the Others*), a taboo-breaking film that advocated tolerance of homosexuals. The film caused a sensation and conservative and nationalist groups fiercely attacked it. Referring to the Jewish descent of Oswald and his scientific adviser, Magnus Hirschfeld, they accused the film of representing a "Jewish-homosexual 'contamination' of *Volk* and race."[22] In fact, the scandal surrounding *Different from the Others* served mainly to express and build public support for aggressively antisemitic sentiments.

In his 1920 film against antisemitism, Oswald wanted to collaborate with individuals from all political camps on "a work of education and enlightenment on the grandest scale."[23] However, his film project *Antisemites* was never realized. Oswald spoke to representatives of the government and campaigned for his idea of a film that sought reconciliation and "by no means want[ed] to glorify the Jews." But the Foreign Office was not interested. On the contrary, they advised Oswald not to pursue his project any further.[24] While he adhered to this advice, Jewish-themed stories and the struggle against antisemitism ran like a common thread through Oswald's work. His 1915 film *The Schlemihl* was set in Jewish Galicia and starred Rudolf Schildkraut; in 1918 he adapted a novel about bourgeois Jewish family life, *Jettchen Gebert*, by Georg Hermann, for the screen. In 1927 *Dr. Bessel's Transformation* criticized discrimination against Jewish immigrants from eastern Europe, when the non-Jewish hero openly professes his solidarity with the persecuted.[25] The same year Oswald's *Feme* from a novel by Vicki Baum depicted a plot of right-wing terrorists against a liberal politician; the story was loosely based on the 1922 assassination of Walther Rathenau, the minister of foreign affairs and probably the most famous German Jew in these years. Most prominent among Oswald's Jewish-themed films is *Dreyfus*, a dramatization of the notorious Dreyfus affair in late-nineteenth-century France; in September 1930, when *Two Worlds* premiered, *Dreyfus* had been in cinemas for weeks and had proven to be a great success.[26]

The failure of Oswald's film project *Antisemites* can be attributed to a lack of interest on the part of authorities, in this case the Foreign Office. Nevertheless, in the early 1920s a series of ambitious films of epic scale telling instructive stories about Jews that articulate a stance against antisemitism were made by other directors. In these films—from which *Two Worlds* effectively descended—we hear the echo of Oswald's demand that a "work of education and enlightenment of the largest scale" had to be attempted.[27]

From *Pogrom* (1919) to *Two Worlds* (1930)

As early as 1919 three large-scale productions about eastern Jews beset by antisemitic agitation were released. These films dealt with Jews in the antiquated czarist empire of the prewar era, with the legal and social discrimination against them, with life in the ghetto, the notorious rumors about Jewish ritual murder, and anti-Jewish pogroms. Today, all of these films are considered lost.[28] Only the thematically related, but somewhat later film *Die Gezeichneten* (1922) by Carl Theodor Dreyer has survived, which, in impressive detail, describes the origins of a pogrom. It depicts how—for selfish reasons—an agitator spreads hatred of the Jews and eventually sparks murder and expulsion.[29] There were also several films in the postwar period dealing with Jewish subjects in biblical times. However, they are lost, too.[30] The most important and most famous surviving Jewish-themed film from that era is Paul Wegener's *Der Golem. Wie er in die Welt kam* (*The Golem: How He Came into the World*; 1920). It relates the legend of Rabbi Loew who—with the help of a superhuman creature—saves the Jews of Prague, when they are threatened with expulsion from the German Empire. Whether the film reproduces antisemitic imagery or, on the contrary, sides with the oppressed, is still the subject of debate.[31]

People who aimed to shed light on the injustice to which the Jews were subjected and who campaigned for understanding and sympathy, faced fierce opposition in the ideologically polarized climate of the Weimar Republic. Thus, when Lessing's *Nathan der Weise* (*Nathan the Wise*), adapted for the screen by Jewish director Manfred Noa, was about to be released in Munich in 1922–23, local Nazis created a scandal and threatened cinema owners, so that the film ultimately was not shown there. While antisemitic polemics in the case of *Different from the Others* were aimed at the Jewish producer and scientific adviser, Oswald and Hirschfeld respectively, *Nathan the Wise* was accused of being a pro-

Jewish propaganda film by the Nazis.[32] After that, aggressive antisemitic scandals and disturbances were used repeatedly as a means of banning a film or preventing it from being shown.[33]

Ewald André Dupont's 1923 film *Das alte Gesetz* (*The Ancient Law*) deserves special mention in this context. Here the audience encountered a Jewish protagonist who was self-confident, talented, and, not least, sexually desirable. Although he initially experiences some harassment, he gains the support of a powerful patron who actively promotes his acting career. *The Ancient Law* tells a success story of social recognition. Set in Austria in the mid-nineteenth century, a young Jew (Ernst Deutsch) leaves the shtetl in Galicia against the wishes of his father and makes a name for himself as an actor at the Burgtheater in Vienna. The film focuses on the conflict between tradition, assimilation, and the quest for identity.[34] The film's German release in November 1923 coincided with hyperinflation, Hitler's putsch against the republic in Munich, and a violent pogrom in Berlin. When it was shown in Vienna a little later, the Jewish *Wiener Morgenzeitung* praised films "showing the traditional customs and practices of the Jews" in general and this film's "pro-Jewish tendencies" in particular. In a climate of heated political and religious agitation the film was supposed to foster understanding among non-Jews who previously held misconceptions regarding Judaism. Well-made films like *The Ancient Law* should "do good service in contributing to the education of the populace when presented in the cinema in civilized countries."[35]

Antisemitic agitation reached new heights in 1930, at the time when Dupont released his second large-scale Jewish-themed film, *Two Worlds* (of which German, French, and English-language versions were shot). In this German-British coproduction set in World War I, an Austrian officer (Peter Voss) overcomes the arrogance and prejudice of his class against the Jews and finally is even willing to give up his military career for the love of a Jewish woman (Helene Sieburg). He rescues her during a pogrom and she, in turn, saves and shelters him later on. But this Jewish-Christian romance is thwarted by the woman's orthodox Jewish father (Hermann Vallentin) and the officer's father (Friedrich Kayßler), who is also his military superior. The two fathers represent the two separate, irreconcilably opposed worlds of the title, which the younger generation tries to overcome. At the end, the lovers must resign themselves to their tragic failure.

Two Worlds presents us with multiple confrontations and contrasts, as Siegbert Prawer has shown (figure 6.1). There is the confrontation between Christian and Jewish religions and rites; between power and

Figure 6.1. Hermann Vallentin and Helene Sieburg in *Zwei Welten* (1930), dir. E.A. Dupont). Production still. Source: DFF-Deutsches Filminstitut & Filmmuseum.

powerlessness; between the generation of the sons and daughters and their fathers, who are unwilling to accept their children's new ways.[36] Confrontations and contrasts can be found on various levels of the film: in the narrative construction; in camera work and lighting; in casting, clothing, and makeup; and in the use of parallel editing and songs.[37] The mise-en-scène is telling: again and again, the spectator's view of the protagonists is blocked or framed through doors, window frames, and furniture, suggesting the characters' feelings of entrapment and their limited mobility. With its low ceilings, big staircase, narrow spaces, and meaningful shadows, the house of the Jewish father, in which much of the action takes place and that serves as the young officer's hide-out during the Russian occupation of the town, resembles an ancient castle and a prison at the same time.

Compared with Georg Wilhelm Pabst's *Westfront 1918* (*Western Front 1918*), the first major German sound film set in World War I, which premiered a few months earlier in May 1930, *Two Worlds* marks the end of an era and an outdated aesthetic in the war film genre. In Dupont's film, the war experience is still narrated as a melodrama, focused on individual suffering and tragic mistakes, with elements of a spy thriller. In no way does it engage with the anonymous mass killing of a whole generation as it is portrayed in *Westfront 1918*. The critic Ernst Jäger pointed to a "philosemitic essence of the story" and noted the great distance between the two films, "*Ostfront 1917*" (as he called *Two Worlds*) and *Westfront 1918*. For him, the script of *Two Worlds* appealed to popular tastes for "Austro-Schnitzlerian flirtation," "Hungarian sensations," and "the strong tradition of Jewish theater." But that script completely ignored the present: "The curtain has fallen over these fairy tale worlds. We are standing in front of an entirely different set of still smoking ruins. Six million Hitler voters: we cannot ignore them (and with epic adventure movies, this German labyrinth will not be pacified)." For Jäger, the final weakness of *Two Worlds* was that it entered the battle of public opinion without a clear political stance: "Whoever fights for two worlds must step in in favor of *one* world. From the bird's-eye view of a neutral bystander, it is impossible to give shape to confessions and passions in a film."[38]

Two Worlds generally received poor reviews. Critics lamented a clichéd depiction of the characters and milieus and a tendency toward kitsch and false melodrama. The *Jüdisch-liberale Zeitung* spoke of a "demagogic experiment that is more inappropriate today than ever" and accused the film of "rehashing the old fairy tale of the incompatibility of the two races."[39]

Despite all its anachronisms and inadequacies, the love story between Jews and Austrians that *Two Worlds* tells is clearly based on romantic and humanistic motives and was intended as a parable that reached beyond the war years into the present of 1930. In retrospect, *Two Worlds* appears as a film against antisemitism, which joined the struggle against Nazism. In Thuringia, the film was banned by the minister of the interior, Nazi party official Wilhelm Frick. However, the Berlin-based board of censorship did not support Frick's request to ban *Two Worlds* nationwide. Frick had argued that it was a "rabble-rousing film" because it denigrated the Austrian officers allied with the Germans during the war and gave the impression that "the Jews are better people than the officers."[40]

In the case of *Two Worlds*, the Nazis did not succeed. But they did succeed a little later, when in December 1930 they staged a scandal on the occasion of the Berlin premiere of *All Quiet on the Western Front*, the American film adaptation of Erich Maria Remarque's antiwar novel. With demonstrations and violence, the street became a new battlefield for antisemitic and antidemocratic agitation. The film served as an excuse to attack the much-despised Weimar Republic loudly, violently, and publicly. In the end, the supposedly anti-German movie was banned, if only temporarily. Still, for Joseph Goebbels, the mastermind behind the scandal, it was a triumph: "With this, in every respect the National Socialist movement has won the fight against this Jewish trickery."[41]

The Mysterious Seven-Branched Candelabrum

While the pogrom in *Two Worlds* takes place on the street, we see the Jewish father and his daughter in their house, terrified by the events. In the room is a menorah. A Jewish cultural object as part of the mise-en-scène here is hardly unusual, since the film is set in a Jewish milieu. But what does it mean if a menorah appears in the home of characters whose religious affiliation is not disclosed? What conclusions can be drawn from this? What questions surface about the representation of Jewishness in film, Jewish filmmaking, or Jewish filmmakers?

In a scene in G.W. Pabst's *Die Büchse der Pandora* (*Pandora's Box*), which premiered some twenty months before *Two Worlds* in 1929, Dr. Schön, the protagonist played by Fritz Kortner, stands with his back to the camera; in front of him we see a divan, on which Louise Brooks lolls in the role of young playful Lulu, the mistress of Dr. Schön. Behind her on the wall there is a large painting, a portrait of Lulu in the costume of a harlequin. And to the left of the painting a menorah stands on a shelf.

Clearly visible in the mise-en-scène, is there a hidden relationship between the painting and the seven-branched candelabrum? Does the presence of the menorah suggest that Lulu, the resident of the apartment, or Dr. Schön, the owner, is Jewish?[42] And what is more interesting: that there is a menorah or that, in the course of the film, a search for further clues of an affiliation between Lulu or Schön with Judaism goes nowhere?

If a Jewish presence were to be evoked or smuggled in, it seems to be irrelevant in what follows. This Jewish moment would appear to be incidental, negligible, perhaps even a false clue—a red herring—that the spectator might register, to which the film however does not attach any deeper meaning. But is it conceivable that in the age of antisemitic parties, loud agitation, and prejudice, the artistic decision to place a menorah in the scene has no significance? Did the visible menorah not increase the likelihood that a figure, a milieu, and a story about power and sexuality were coded in a particular way?

Regarding context, one might point out that the actor Fritz Kortner was Jewish with a distinguished career playing the role of Shylock on the Berlin stage. He was perceived as a Jew, at least in parts of the public, including some Jewish journals.[43] If audiences drew a connection between the role of Dr. Schön and his impersonator Fritz Kortner (who later played the main role in Oswald's *Dreyfus*), then Dr. Schön could also be considered a Jew. Several other actors involved in the film, such as Franz Lederer and Siegfried Arno, were Jewish, as was the producer Seymour Nebenzahl.

Pandora's Box illustrates the conundrum of how Jewishness was negotiated, if only marginally, in one of the biggest productions of the 1928–29 season. One might argue that the film suggests the affiliation of one or more protagonists to Judaism as a possibility, but one could also state that these protagonists are interesting in the film and its story only because they are interesting characters and not because they are interesting *Jewish* characters. That is, the film avoids taking one particular trait of these characters as the whole.

Indisputably, Jewish filmmakers played a significant role in the film. But whether these filmmakers were already perceived as *Jewish* filmmakers by the industry, by the general public, or by the Jewish public when the film was made in 1928–29, and whether this was important for its reception, is much more difficult to figure out. Any attempt to identify, reconstruct, or memorialize an explicitly Jewish presence in filmmaking at that time moves on somewhat precarious ground, because the decision about what and who is and should be considered Jewish depends on many, often contradictory, factors and is possibly based on essentialist assumptions as well.[44] Such considerations also apply to *The Three from the Filling Station*.

When the Whole World Falls Apart

"A friend, a good friend, that's the most beautiful thing in the world." Right at the beginning of *The Three from the Filling Station*, Willy Fritsch, Heinz Rühmann, and Oskar Karlweis perform that hit song and conjure a friendship that survives all hardships. With its stars, jolly songs, and self-reflexive mixture of comedy of crisis and musical, *The Three from the Filling Station* appears as an ideal of Weimar cinema as a whole (figure 6.2). Here, commercial and artistic ambitions, genre cinema, and avant-garde aesthetics do not contradict each other, but rather merge into a popular form.

Figure 6.2. Oskar Karlweis, Willy Fritsch, and Heinz Rühmann in *Die Drei von der Tankstelle* (1930, dir. Wilhelm Thiele). Production still. Source: DFF-Deutsches Filminstitut & Filmmuseum.

In *The Three from the Filling Station*, evidence of the Jewish presence in Germany can hardly be found in the plot, in the dialogues, or the sets. If at all, it appears random and hidden. At one point, Kurt, one of the three friends, calls a stingy customer a nebbish. This Yiddish expression could point to Kurt's never-discussed Jewish heritage.[45] No doubt the filmmakers had often encountered prejudice, harassment, and hostility toward Jews—if not personally, then in the news. But since they were not making a documentary to raise awareness about the plight of a minority, but rather a light entertainment film, it may have seemed advisable to avoid further characterization of any figure as Jewish.[46]

At the same time, it must have become increasingly difficult to neglect both the predicament of Jews in general and their own as Jewish filmmakers. When the new government under Hitler forbade Jews to work in the film industry in 1933, a large group was forced into exile, among them the creators of *The Three from the Filling Station*. Creatives from *The Three from the Filling Station* who went into exile included Pommer, Schulz, Thiele, Heymann, Gilbert, Viktor Gertler (the editor), and

Franz Planer (the cinematographer), whose spouse was Jewish. Of approximately 10,000 employees in the German film industry, 2,000 were expelled by the Nazis, most of them Jews. The German film career of Oskar Karlweis, who plays Kurt and sings and dances so wonderfully with Lilian Harvey and says "nebbish" at one time, abruptly ended in 1933 because he was a Jew. He survived the Holocaust in American exile. Kurt Gerron, who played the Jewish lawyer of the three friends, emigrated, too, but was tracked down by Nazi henchmen in Holland in 1943 and murdered in Auschwitz in 1944.

While *Two Worlds* made a politically valuable statement in choosing a Jewish story, *The Three from the Filling Station* took a different path. At the very moment when the Nazis became the second-strongest party in the Reichstag, *The Three from the Filling Station* staged its own utopia in a lighthearted way, as a sort of message in the bottle. If it was possible in the most popular film of the season that one could nonchalantly and incidentally refer to the Jewish heritage of a character (who was also played by a Jew), what did that mean? It meant that it did not matter in the friendship if someone was Jewish. Kurt is not in any way represented as "other," as an outsider or a member of a minority; he is socially emancipated and fully integrated. Following Kerry Wallach's reflections on the sociological phenomenon of "passing," one could say that Kurt, played by the Jewish actor Oskar Karlweis, passes as a non-Jew in the film. Instead of his Jewish identity, he "performs" his identity as a bachelor in love as part a trio of bon vivants or playboys who embody the cosmopolitan lifestyle and liberalism of Berlin and Weimar culture during the Roaring Twenties.[47]

Two Worlds presented the opposite of *The Three from the Filling Station* in depictions of Jewish identity. In *Two Worlds*, the Jewish minority threatened by war and violence is ruled by patriarchs with traditional values; here the Jews use Hebrew letters and, because of their distinctive clothing, language, and habitus, appear as different and other, eternal victims of violence and discrimination. And yet both *Two Worlds* and *The Three from the Filling Station* address the larger question of how Jewish identity can be imagined in a modern age in which there is not one notion of Jewishness but several. Is Jewishness defined by religious and cultural differentiation, the quest for national autonomy (as postulated by the Zionists), or integration into a mainly non-Jewish society? *Two Worlds* and *The Three from the Filling Station* offer different answers with their stories. Both films tell of love and friendship. One invokes love and friendship in the face of failure, the other resists crisis and skepticism with laughter and joy. While the Germans continued to love the eternal optimists from the filling station, sadly enough for one of them, the wish never to be abandoned expressed in their jolly song remained unfulfilled: "A friend always stays a friend, even if the whole world falls apart."

Philipp Stiasny is a freelance film historian and worked at Potsdam Film Museum for several years. He is a researcher in the Franco-German ERC project "BodyCapital" at Max Planck Institute for Human Development, editor of the film historical journal *Filmblatt*, an associate at the research center CineGraph Babelsberg, and a curator of film series. His publications include *Das Kino und der Krieg: Deutschland 1914–1929* (Edition Text & Kritik, 2009) and numerous articles. With Jürgen Kasten and Frederik Lang he is editor of *Ufa international. Ein deutscher Filmkonzern mit globalen Ambitionen* (Edition Text & Kritik, 2020).

Notes

My greatest thanks go to Ariane Kwasigroch and Jacob Klingner.
Many thanks also to Anjeana Hans (Wellesley College) and Cynthia Walk (University of California, San Diego) for revision and help. Many thanks to Christian Rogowski (Amherst College) and Mila Ganeva (Miami University) for commenting on an earlier version of this article, too.

1. An earlier version of this chapter appeared under the title "Ein Freund, ein guter Freund, das wär das Schönste, was es gibt auf der Welt. Jüdisches Filmschaffen in der Weimarer Republik." *Aus Politik und Zeitgeschichte* 68: 18–20 (30 April 2018), 46–52.
2. j.r., "6.400.000 nationalsozialistische Wähler. Niederlage der bürgerlichen Demokratie," *Jüdische Rundschau*, no. 73, 16 September 1930. The translations are all by the author.
3. Siegfried Kracauer, *From Caligari to Hitler. A Psychological History of The German Film* (Princeton, NJ: Princeton University Press, 1947); Lotte H. Eisner, *The Haunted Screen: Expressionism in the German Cinema and the Influence of Max Reinhardt* (London: Secker & Warburg, 1973).
4. Siegbert Salomon Prawer, *Between Two Worlds: The Jewish Presence in German and Austrian Film, 1910–1933* (New York: Berghahn, 2005). For a brief overview, see also Irene Stratenwerth and Hermann Simon (eds.), *Pioniere in Celluloid: Juden in der frühen Filmwelt* (Berlin: Henschel, 2004).
5. Prawer, *Between Two Worlds*, 63–71; James Hoberman, *Bridge of Light: Yiddish Film Between Two Worlds* (New York: Museum of Modern Art, 1991). A biopic of Theodor Herzl, cofounder of Zionism, was shot in Austria, too. See, e.g., Nicholas Baer, "The Rebirth of a Nation: Cinema, Herzlian Zionism, and Emotion in Jewish History," *Leo Baeck Institute Year Book*, vol. 59 (2014), 233–48.
6. See Eisner, *The Haunted Screen*, 79.
7. See Richard McCormick, "Sex, History, and Upward Mobility: Ernst Lubitsch's *Madame Dubarry / Passion*, 1919," *German Studies Review* 33:3 (2010), 603–17. Several

monographs have been written on Lubitsch and other important film people like Joe May, Erich Pommer, Kurt Bernhardt, and Robert Siodmak who were Jews but in whose films Jewishness does not figure in the center. Together with Lubitsch and Dupont, one might regard Richard Oswald as an exception to the rule.

8. See Ofer Ashkenazi, *Weimar Film and Modern Jewish Identity* (New York: Palgrave Macmillan, 2012).
9. While Ashkenazi points to Jewish filmmakers who were interested in the fluidity of identities, one might add that Jewish filmmakers were also prominently involved in the production of films that—in terms of story, mise-en-scène, and acting—were regarded as particularly national. This goes, for example, for *Die letzte Kompagnie* (1930), *Das Flötenkonzert von Sanssouci* (1930), *Theodor Körner* (1932), and *Der Rebell* (1932)—and also for the racist, anti-French propaganda film *Die schwarze Schmach* (1921).
10. See Kerry Wallach, *Passing Illusions: Jewish Visibility in Weimar Germany* (Ann Arbor: University of Michigan Press, 2017), 75–95.
11. All the journals are accessible online at http://sammlungen.ub.uni-frankfurt.de/cm/nav/index/title. For information on Jewish associations and newspapers see Avraham Barkai, "Die Organisation der jüdischen Gemeinschaft," *Deutsch-Jüdische Geschichte in der Neuzeit*, ed. Michael A. Meyer on behalf of the Leo Baeck Institute. Vol. 4: Aufbruch und Zerstörung 1918–45, by A. Barkai and Paul Mendes-Flohr (Munich: C.H. Beck, 1997), 74–102.
12. See Ronny Loewy, "Bilder vom Aufbau der Jüdischen Heimstätte. Zionistische Propagandafilme," *Filmblatt* 7:18 (2002), 12–16; Jeanpaul Goergen and Ronny Loewy, "Filme von und über jüdische Organisationen und die jüdische Besiedlung von Palästina," *Filmblatt* 7:18, 17–23; Wallach, *Passing Illusions*, 86–88.
13. See Hans Wollenberg, "Der Jude im Film," *C.V.-Zeitung*, no. 37, 16 September 1927; Wallach, *Passing Illusions*, 79–80.
14. Reinhard Rürup, "Jüdische Geschichte in Deutschland. Von der Emanzipation bis zur nationalsozialistischen Gewaltherrschaft," in *Zerbrochene Geschichte: Leben und Selbstverständnis der Juden in Deutschland*, ed. Dirk Blasius and Dan Diner, (Frankfurt am Main: Fischer, 1991), 79–102, quote on 95.
15. Werner Bergmann, *Geschichte des Antisemitismus* (Munich: C.H. Beck, 2002), 76. In the following I am mainly referring to Bergmann and to Moshe Zimmermann, *Die deutschen Juden 1914–1945* (Munich: Oldenbourg, 1997).
16. Bergmann, *Geschichte des Antisemitismus*, 74.
17. Zimmermann, *Die deutschen Juden*, 23. On the stereotype of the "eastern Jew" see, e.g., Ludger Heid, "Der Ostjude," in *Antisemitismus: Vorurteile und Mythen*, ed. Julius H. Schoeps and Joachim Schlör (Munich: Piper, 1995), 241–51.
18. On the transit of eastern European Jews and pogrom refugees, see Jochen Oltmer, *Migration und Politik in der Weimarer Republik* (Göttingen: Vandenhoeck & Ruprecht, 2005), 219–61.
19. Dirk Walter, *Antisemitische Kriminalität und Gewalt: Judenfeindschaft in der Weimarer Republik* (Bonn: Dietz, 1999); Cornelia Hecht, *Deutsche Juden und Antisemitismus in der Weimarer Republik* (Bonn: Dietz, 2003).
20. On the struggle against antisemitism, see Zimmermann, *Die deutschen Juden*, 44–46.
21. L.F.K. [Lothar Knud Fredrik], "Antisemiten—das Problem der Stunde. Ein neues Wagnis Richard Oswalds," *Film-Kurier*, no. 173, 7 August 1920. The quotes that follow are from there. On Oswald in general see Jürgen Kasten and Armin Loacker (eds.), *Richard Oswald: Kino zwischen Spektakel, Aufklärung und Unterhaltung* (Wien: Filmarchiv Austria, 2005).

22. Kai Nowak, *Projektionen der Moral: Filmskandale in der Weimarer Republik* (Göttingen: Wallstein, 2015), 115. See also: Valerie Weinstein, "Homosexual Emancipation, Queer Masculinity, and Jewish Difference in *Anders als die Andern* (1919)" in this volume; James Steakley, *"Anders als die Andern": Ein Film und seine Geschichte* (Hamburg: Männerschwarm Verlag, 2007), 76–85.
23. L.F.K., "Antisemiten—das Problem der Stunde."
24. On Oswald's attempt to win government officials for his project see, see Akten der Filmstelle des Auswärtigen Amtes von August 1920, Bundesarchiv Berlin, R 901/72192, Blatt 1–5.
25. On *Dr. Bessels Verwandlung* see Ashkenazi, *Weimar Film*, 134–42; Philipp Stiasny, "'Überall das gleiche, wie bei uns': Der deutsch-französische Doppelgänger in 'Dr. Bessels Verwandlung' (1927) und die Figur des Heimkehrers im Weimarer Kino," *Zeitschrift für Germanistik*, Neue Folge 24 (3, 2014): 582–96.
26. On *Dreyfus* see, e.g., Prawer, *Between Two Worlds*, 149–59; Wallach, *Passing Illusions*, 92–95.
27. L.F.K. [Lothar Knud Fredrik], "Antisemiten—das Problem der Stunde. Ein neues Wagnis Richard Oswalds," *Film-Kurier*, no. 173, 7 August 1920.
28. See *Die Geächteten (Der Ritualmord)* (1919, dir. Joseph Delmont), *Pogrom* (1919, dir. H. Fredall = Alfred Halm), *Der gelbe Tod* (1919, dir. Carl Wilhelm). See contemporary reviews reprinted in Stratenwerth and Simon, *Pioniere in Celluloid*, 234–37. On the theme of ritual murder, see also *Kaddisch* (1924, dir. A.E. Licho).
29. See Prawer, *Between Two Worlds*, 29–33.
30. See *Das Buch Esther* (1919, dir. Uwe Jens Krafft and Ernst Reicher), *Gerechtigkeit* (1920, dir. Stefan Lux), *Jeremias* (1922, dir. Eugen Illés).
31. See, e.g., the different perspectives and interpretations in Noah Isenberg, "Of Monsters and Magicians: Paul Wegener's *The Golem: How He Came into the World* (1920)," Isenberg (ed.), *Weimar Cinema: An Essential Guide to Classic Films of the Era* (New York: Columbia University Press, 2009), 33–54; Nicholas Baer, "Messianic Musclemen: *Homunculus* (1916) and *Der Golem* (1920) as Zionist Allegories," Martin Blumenthal-Barby (ed.), *The Place of Politics in German Film* (Bielefeld: Aisthesis, 2014), 35–52; Maya Barzilai, *Golem: Modern Wars and Their Monsters* (New York: New York University Press, 2016), 45–68, 87–94.
32. See Martin Loiperdinger, "'Nathan der Weise': Faschistische Filmzensur, Antisemitismus und Gewalt anno 1923," *Lessing Yearbook* 14 (1982), 61–69; Stefan Drößler: "'Nathan der Weise': Ein klassisches Drama und die öffentliche Gewalt," Stratenwerth and Simon, *Pioniere in Celluloid*, 215–19.
33. The events at the German premiere of the Austrian film *Die Stadt ohne Juden* (1924) may serve as an example. See Guntram Geser and Armin Loacker (eds.), *Die Stadt ohne Juden* (Wien: Filmarchiv Austria, 2000).
34. See, e.g., Prawer, *Between Two Worlds*, 21–28; Cynthia Walk, "Romeo with Sidelocks: Jewish-Gentile Romance in E.A. Dupont's *Das alte Gesetz* (1923) and Other Early Weimar Assimilation Films," Christian Rogowski (ed.), *The Many Faces of Weimar Cinema: Rediscovering Germany's Filmic Legacy* (Rochester, NY: Camden House, 2010), 84–101.
35. Felix Brasch, "'Das alte Gesetz,'" *Wiener Morgenzeitung*, no. 1810, 29 February 1924.
36. See Prawer, *Between Two Worlds*, 140 ff.
37. For instance, the popular song "Rosa, wir fahr'n nach Lodz" (1915) by Fritz Löhner-Beda (lyrics) and Artur M. Werau (music) is juxtaposed later in the film with a Yiddish song.
38. E.J. [Ernst Jäger], "Zwei Welten," *Film-Kurier*, no. 220, 17 September 1930.

39. Doris Wittner, "Zwei Welten," *Jüdisch-liberale Zeitung*, no. 39, 25 September 1930.
40. Quoted from the record of Film-Oberprüfstelle, no. 952, 16 October 1930, accessible at https://www.filmportal.de/sites/default/files/Zwei%20Welten_O.00952_1930.pdf. On *Two Worlds* see also Prawer, *Between Two Worlds*, 141–49.
41. Joseph Goebbels, "In die Knie gezwungen," *Der Angriff*, 12 December 1930, reprinted in Schrader, *Der Fall Remarque*, 161–65, quote 161.
42. "Is the director of that film, G.W. Pabst, hinting that he thinks of Kortner's character as Jewish when he has a ritual candelabrum, a *menorah*, appear in the background?" Prawer, *Between Two Worlds*, 84.
43. For example, Kortner is mentioned as the leading Jewish actor in Germany in addition to Alexander Granach in Hugo Lachmanski, "Wer entsittlicht das deutsche Volk? Eine Antwort an den 'Völkischen Beobachter.'" *C.V.-Zeitung*, 10 October 1930, 72.
44. For a more pragmatic approach, one might suggest that whoever was listed in the Jewish directory at that time was Jewish and—to whatever degree—felt affiliated to the Jewish community. In the case of *Pandora's Box* this goes for Fritz Kortner, Siegfried Arno (Aron) and Seymour Nebenzahl, the assistant director Paul Falkenberg and the bit player and still photographer Hans G. Casparius. See the entries in *Jüdisches Adressbuch für Gross-Berlin* (Berlin: Goedega Verlag, 1929 ff.).
45. For this and other examples, see Prawer, *Between Two Worlds*, 167–73, esp. 168.
46. An important factor was that UFA, the production company of *The Three from the Filling Station*, was part of the Hugenberg company, headed by Alfred Hugenberg, chief of Deutschnationale Volkspartei. Deutschnationale Volkspartei, which had a strong antisemitic section, was partly a rival of the Nazis but had been cooperating with them in 1929.
47. See Wallach, *Passing Illusions*. A similar idea is presented by Christian Rogowski, "Strange Bedfellows: The Politics of Sound in Ludwig Berger's *Ich bei Tag und du bei Nacht* (1932)," *Colloquia Germanica* 44 (3, 2011): 331–48.

Bibliography

Ashkenazi, Ofer. *Weimar Film and Modern Jewish Identity*. New York: Palgrave Macmillan, 2012.
Baer, Nicholas. "Messianic Musclemen: *Homunculus* (1916) and *Der Golem* (1920) as Zionist Allegories." In *The Place of Politics in German Film*, ed. Martin Blumenthal-Barby, 35–52. Bielefeld: Aisthesis, 2014.
———. "The Rebirth of a Nation: Cinema, Herzlian Zionism, and Emotion in Jewish History." *Leo Baeck Institute Year Book* 59 (2014): 233–48.
Barkai, Avraham. "Die Organisation der jüdischen Gemeinschaft." In *Deutsch-Jüdische Geschichte in der Neuzeit*, ed. Michael A. Meyer on behalf of the Leo Baeck Institute, vol. 4: Aufbruch und Zerstörung 1918–1945. By A. Barkai and Paul Mendes-Flohr. Munich: C.H. Beck, 1997, 74–102.
Barzilai, Maya. *Golem: Modern Wars and Their Monsters*. New York: New York University Press, 2016.
Bergmann, Werner. *Geschichte des Antisemitismus*. Munich: C.H. Beck, 2002.
Brasch, Felix. "'Das alte Gesetz.'" *Wiener Morgenzeitung*, 29 February 1924.
"Die Schicksalsstunde des deutschen Judentums." *Jüdische Rundschau*, 9 November 1923.
Drößler, Stefan. "'Nathan der Weise': Ein klassisches Drama und die öffentliche Gewalt." In Stratenwerth and Simon, *Pioniere in Celluloid*, 215–19.

Eisner, Lotte H. *The Haunted Screen: Expressionism in the German Cinema and the Influence of Max Reinhardt*. London: Secker & Warburg, 1973.
E.J. (Ernst Jäger). "Zwei Welten." *Film-Kurier*, 17 September 1930.
Geser, Guntram, and Armin Loacker, eds. *Die Stadt ohne Juden*. Wien: Filmarchiv Austria, 2000.
Goebbels, Joseph. "In die Knie gezwungen." *Der Angriff*, 12 December 1930. Reprint Schrader, *Der Fall Remarque*, 161–65.
Goergen, Jeanpaul, and Ronny Loewy. "Filme von und über jüdische Organisationen und die jüdische Besiedlung von Palästina." *Filmblatt* 7 (18, 2002): 17–23.
Hecht, Cornelia. *Deutsche Juden und Antisemitismus in der Weimarer Republik*. Bonn: Dietz, 2003.
Heid, Ludger. "Der Ostjude." *Antisemitismus: Vorurteile und Mythen*, ed. Julius H. Schoeps, Joachim Schlör, 241–51. Munich: Piper, 1995.
Hoberman, James. *Bridge of Light: Yiddish Film Between Two Worlds*. New York: Museum of Modern Art, 1991.
Isenberg, Noah. "Of Monsters and Magicians: Paul Wegener's *The Golem: How He Came into the World* (1920)." In *Weimar Cinema: An Essential Guide to Classic Films of the Era*, ed. Noah Isenbert, 33–54. New York: Columbia University Press, 2009.
j.r. "6.400.000 nationalsozialistische Wähler. Niederlage der bürgerlichen Demokratie." *Jüdische Rundschau*, 16 September 1930.
Jüdisches Adressbuch für Gross-Berlin. Berlin: Goedega, 1929.
Kasten, Jürgen, and Armin Loacker (eds.). *Richard Oswald: Kino zwischen Spektakel, Aufklärung und Unterhaltung*. Wien: Filmarchiv Austria, 2005.
Kracauer, Siegfried. *From Caligari to Hitler: A Psychological History of The German Film*. Princeton, NJ: Princeton University Press, 1947.
Lachmanski, Hugo. "Wer entsittlicht das deutsche Volk? Eine Antwort an den 'Völkischen Beobachter.'" *C.V.-Zeitung*, 10 October 1930.
L.F.K. [Lothar Knud Fredrik]. "Antisemiten—das Problem der Stunde: Ein neues Wagnis Richard Oswalds." *Film-Kurier*, 7 August 1920.
Loewy, Ronny. "Bilder vom Aufbau der Jüdischen Heimstätte: Zionistische Propagandafilme." *Filmblatt* 7 (18, 2002): 12–16.
Loiperdinger, Martin. "'Nathan der Weise': Faschistische Filmzensur, Antisemitismus und Gewalt anno 1923." *Lessing Yearbook* 14 (1982): 61–69.
McCormick, Richard. "Sex, History, and Upward Mobility: Ernst Lubitsch's *Madame Dubarry / Passion*, 1919." *German Studies Review* 33 (3, 2010): 603–17.
Nowak, Kai. *Projektionen der Moral: Filmskandale in der Weimarer Republik*. Göttingen: Wallstein, 2015.
Oltmer, Jochen. *Migration und Politik in der Weimarer Republik*. Göttingen: Vandenhoeck & Ruprecht, 2005.
Prawer, Siegbert Salomon. *Between Two Worlds: The Jewish Presence in German and Austrian Film, 1910–1933*. New York: Berghahn Books, 2005.
Rogowski, Christian. "Strange Bedfellows: The Politics of Sound in Ludwig Berger's *Ich bei Tag und du bei Nacht* (1932)." *Colloquia Germanica* 44 (3, 2011): 331–48.
Rürup, Reinhard. "Jüdische Geschichte in Deutschland: Von der Emanzipation bis zur nationalsozialistischen Gewaltherrschaft." In *Zerbrochene Geschichte: Leben und Selbstverständnis der Juden in Deutschland*, ed. Dirk Blasius and Dan Diner, 79–102. Frankfurt am Main: Fischer, 1991.
Schrader, Bärbel, ed. *Der Fall Remarque: "Im Westen nichts Neues." Eine Dokumentation*. Leipzig: Reclam, 1992.

Steakley, James. *"Anders als die Andern": Ein Film und seine Geschichte*. Hamburg: Männerschwarm, 2007.

Stiasny, Philipp. "'Überall das gleiche, wie bei uns': Der deutsch-französische Doppelgänger in Bessels Verwandlung' (1927) und die Figur des Heimkehrers im Weimarer Kino." *Zeitschrift für Germanistik* Neue Folge 24 (3, 2014): 582–96.

Stratenwerth, Irene, and Hermann Simon, eds. *Pioniere in Celluloid: Juden in der frühen Filmwelt*. Berlin: Henschel, 2004.

Walk, Cynthia. "Romeo with Sidelocks: Jewish-Gentile Romance in E. A. Dupont's *Das alte Gesetz* (1923) and Other Early Weimar Assimilation Films." In *The Many Faces of Weimar Cinema: Rediscovering Germany's Filmic Legacy*, ed. Christian Rogowski, 84–101. Rochester, NY: Camden House, 2010.

Wallach, Kerry. *Passing Illusions: Jewish Visibility in Weimar Germany*. Ann Arbor: University of Michigan Press, 2017.

Walter, Dirk. *Antisemitische Kriminalität und Gewalt: Judenfeindschaft in der Weimarer Republik*. Bonn: Dietz, 1999.

Wittner, Doris. "Zwei Welten." *Jüdisch-liberale Zeitung*, 25 September 1930.

Wollenberg, Hans. "Der Jude im Film. " *C.V.-Zeitung*, 16 September 1927.

Zimmermann, Moshe. *Die deutschen Juden 1914–1945*. Munich: Oldenbourg, 1997.

Chapter 7

HOMOSEXUAL EMANCIPATION, QUEER MASCULINITY, AND JEWISH DIFFERENCE IN *ANDERS ALS DIE ANDERN* (1919)

Valerie Weinstein

The interarticulation of discourses of Jewishness, male homosexuality, and masculinity in late nineteenth- and early twentieth-century central Europe is well documented.[1] Antisemites and homophobes disparaged both gay and Jewish men as effeminate and sexually deviant, as infamously illustrated by Otto Weininger's bestselling *Geschlecht und Charakter: Eine prinzipielle Untersuchung* (*Sex and Character*).[2] Male effeminacy, inversion, intermediary, and third sex models of gender and sexuality were coded as "Jewish," in contrast to a Greek model of love between manly men, cultivated by masculinist subcultures in German right-wing circles.[3] Because of the problematic connections drawn between Jewishness and nonnormative gender and sexuality in the late-nineteenth and early-twentieth centuries, it is difficult to address the queerness of Jewish texts or the Jewishness of queer texts from the Weimar period without invoking that era's antisemitism and homophobia. And yet, as part of the project of rethinking Jewishness in Weimar cinema, a topic that postwar scholars long avoided, this chapter revisits an encounter between the Jewish and the queer, whose Jewishness was emphasized primarily by antisemites and thus has been avoided by other critics. Seeking to reassesses the relationship between queer and Jewish visibility in Weimar cinema while resisting antisemitic and homophobic frameworks, I turn to a film that reactionaries attacked as both too gay and too Jewish, Richard Oswald's *Anders als die Andern* (*Different from the Others*; 1919).

Anders occupies an important place in history as the first known feature film to promote gay rights. *Anders*, a didactic melodrama about gay life, love, and blackmail, was made to educate the public about homosexuality and to argue against Paragraph 175 of the German legal code, which criminalized same-sex sex acts between men. Historical and contemporary audiences, critics, and scholars receive *Anders* primarily as a gay rights film, as was intended. Additionally, in the early twentieth century, antisemites perceived it as a Jewish film. Director Richard Oswald made *Anders* in cooperation with Magnus Hirschfeld, renowned sexologist and leader of the Scientific Humanitarian Committee, an organization that fought for the rights of sexual and gender minorities, and *Anders*'s release coincided with Hirschfeld's founding of the Institut für Sexualwissenchaft (Institute for Sexual Research), which opened 6 July 1919. Both Oswald and Hirschfeld were Jewish, a fact seized on by the historical right wing.[4] Because antisemites framed *Anders* as a Jewish film, anti-antisemitic scholars have hesitated to focus on possible encodings of Jewish difference in *Anders*.[5] Resisting the defensive impulse, this chapter deepens our understanding of *Anders* and of the nexus between the Jewish and the queer in Weimar cinema by examining the sometimes overlapping and sometimes competing discourses of sexuality, gender, and Jewish difference in and around *Anders*.

Queerness and Jewishness are both forms of difference whose visibility is situational, recognized differently by insiders and outsiders, and controlled only partially by those marked by them. Theorists have written about parallels between queer and Jewish visibility since the beginning of what we call "queer theory," for example, Eve Kosofky Sedgwick in her foundational *Epistemology of the Closet*.[6] Queer theory also informs Jewish cultural studies, an intellectual movement that "emerged since the 1990s to analyze the co-construction of Jewishness, race, gender, sexuality, class, nation, and diaspora" and that has emphasized the modern "co-construction" of Jewish and queer identities and stereotypes.[7] Current scholarship on Jewishness in Weimar cinema draws on both these traditions, analyzing Jewish difference as social construct and emphasizing mechanisms of representation, visibility, closeting, and recognition.

Building on developments in Weimar film studies, German-Jewish cultural studies, and queer studies, this chapter will show that in making male homosexuality visible, *Anders* also exposed the Jewish. The first section will explain how politicized homophobia and antisemitism in the historical reaction to *Anders* built on preexisting associations between Jewishness and queerness and discouraged potential alliances between the Jewish community and the homosexual emancipation movement. The second part of this chapter investigates the dynamic between queer and Jewish visibility in *Anders*. The Jewishness I refer to here is a socially constructed conceptual category that sometimes overlaps with but is not coextensive with religious practice or ethnic identity. It is part of a larger system of Jewish difference, which coded not only people, but also places, objects, and ideas as "Jewish" or "not Jewish," and which Lisa Silverman has shown to have been particularly powerful in interwar Germany and Austria.[8] Attention to *Anders*'s liberal humanist agenda and Jewish subtext reveals how the film connects the political projects of homosexual and Jewish emancipation and codes the actors' performances of masculinity as both Jewish and queer.

Politicized Homophobia and Antisemitism in the Historical Reception of *Anders als die Andern*

Anders, which survives only in truncated, restored form, is a silent film that blends expository educational segments with melodrama to argue that homosexuality is normal and natural, to show the harm Paragraph 175 inflicts on gay men, and to inspire political solidarity with them.[9] The plot centers on a concert violinist, Paul Körner (Conrad Veidt), who must contend with a world in which his same-sex desires are shameful and same-sex sex acts illegal. Paul becomes the victim of a blackmailer, Franz Bollek (Reinhold Schünzel), who threatens to expose him as gay and ruin his relationships and career. The blackmail escalates and Paul decides to press charges. A court convicts not only the blackmailer but also Paul under Paragraph 175. The resulting professional and personal ostracism drives Paul to commit suicide.[10] Hirschfeld appears in several scenes in *Anders*, explaining that homosexuality is biologically determined and that homosexuals play a productive role in society. He asks the audience to help end legal persecution of people who love according to their natural inclinations. Finally, Hirschfeld encourages Kurt Sivers (Fritz Schulz), Paul's beloved former student, who is devastated by his death, to fight against Paragraph 175.[11]

Anders belongs to a spate of social hygiene films, or *Aufklärungsfilme* (enlightenment films), made and shown in Germany between 1918 and 1920, when Germany had repealed its film censorship laws in the wake of World War I.[12] Some *Aufklärungsfilme* promoted public health education and political reform, whereas others made spurious educational claims as an excuse to show titillating subject matter. This made *Aufklärungsfilme* and Richard Oswald, the genre's most prominent director, the target of cinema reformers and other citizen groups keen to police sexual morality and reestablish film censorship. Critics of *Aufklärungsfilme* "soon noticed that Oswald and many of his collaborators were Jewish, and some of the other directors and authors of films in the 'enlightenment' mode were Jewish too."[13] Rhetoric about morals, sex, and money around *Anders* and other *Aufklärungsfilme* coded the genre as "Jewish." Accusations of "speculation," "exploitation," and *Wucherei* (usury) invoked discourses of Jewish war profiteering and older antisemitic tropes.[14] Detractors accused makers of *Aufklärungsfilme* of not only moral corruption but also *Geschäftemacherei* (promoting lurid content to make a profit).[15] Oswald, an extraordinarily prolific filmmaker, was dogged by criticisms of his films' commercialism throughout his career. In context of widespread antisemitic stereotypes of Jews as greedy capitalists and of Jewish profit-mongering tainting German and international film industries, such pecuniary criticisms of Oswald and other makers of *Aufklärungsfilme* deployed codes of Jewish difference and functioned as inferential antisemitism.[16] Other attacks on *Aufklärungsfilme* were overtly antisemitic. For example, at his cinema reform meetings Karl Brunner, former censorship officer with the Berlin police, launched "anti-Semitic tirades" against *Aufklärungsfilme* and attendees proudly proclaimed themselves antisemites.[17]

Anders's focus on homosexuality and gay rights was unique among late-Wilhelmine and early-Weimar *Aufklärungsfilme* and therefore faced particular hostility that was not only antisemitic but also homophobic. Overall, reviews were mixed, and the film did quite well at the box office.[18] Yet, it elicited powerful objections from "German nationalist and populist groups, church representatives, cinema reformers, and activists from the [anti-] smut and trash movement."[19] Drawing on biopolitical discourses of degeneracy and eugenics, homophobic critics accused *Anders* of infecting the moral and physical health of the nation by spreading homosexuality.[20] Antisemitic critics blamed Hirschfeld's Jewishness for *Anders*'s "pseudoscience," moral corruption, and challenges to heteronormativity.[21] Radical antisemite and future National Socialist (Nazi) war criminal Alfred Rosenberg accused Oswald and Hirschfeld of conspiring to inhibit the growth of the German population with their "prostitution and pederasty films."[22] Johann Ude, writing for the *Christliche Volkswacht*, characterized *Anders* as a product of Hirschfeld's Jewish self-promotion and lack of sympathy with the German people's current plight. Conceding that the film is technically brilliant and that Paragraph 175 probably should be revised, Ude nevertheless argues that by depathologizing homosexuality, the *Assimilationsjude* (assimilated Jew) Hirschfeld attacks German morals at a vulnerable time, and that *Anders* and other films like it should be banned.[23]

Screenings of *Anders* were sites of both antisemitic and homophobic activism. Summer 1919 was a period of "comprehensive antisemitic agitation" in Germany, of "wild antisemitic rabble rousing" that was part of the right-wing reaction to the German defeat in World War I and the creation of the Weimar Republic.[24] *Anders*, which premiered at the end of May, was sucked into that whirlwind. In July of that year right-wing groups protested the film and the press reported both homophobic and antisemitic heckling.[25] On 10 July 1919 protesters disrupted a screening in Berlin, shouting "Should we Germans allow ourselves to be contaminated by the Jews?"[26] It is helpful to understand the reaction against *Anders* not only as a part of broader postwar eruptions of antisemitic furor but also as instances of politicized homophobia. Ashley Currier defines politicized homophobia as a strategy "that turns homophobia from an interpersonal phenomenon into a wider set of antihomosexual discourses and practices that saturate political rhetoric."[27] Currier's study of politicized homophobia in contemporary Malawi shows how its deployment "ensnares not only gender and sexual minorities but also different social movements," and can discourage members of those other social movements from supporting gender and sexual minorities.[28] Below I explain how debates around *Anders* reveal a similar phenomenon: Weimar reactionaries mobilized personal prejudices toward political ends, and, in doing so, ensnared multiple minority groups. My analyses illustrate how politicized homophobia and antisemitism ensnared both the Jewish community and the homosexual emancipation movement and effectively discouraged alliances between the two.

Some German-Jewish journalists responded to accusations that Jews promoted homosexuality by distancing themselves from it. In the *Film-Kurier* on 13 July 1919, Walther Friedmann accused the right wing of politicizing homophobia to tarnish the Jews and using antisemitism to mobilize the public in favor of censorship. He described the antisemitic attacks against *Anders* as a reactionary tactic to force the reinstatement of censorship laws and he encouraged Social Democrats and Democrats to avoid cooperating with such "abhorrent, ludicrous, and dirty company."[29] For Friedmann, "what is significant about the whole affair is simply the almost unbelievable fact that the blame for homosexuality is now also placed on the Jews."[30] He uses logic, a tone that shifts from disgust to sarcasm, and multiple other rhetorical strategies to distance himself and other Jews from homosexuality. Friedmann first characterizes homosexuality as an "extremely regrettable ... repulsive degeneration of the sex drive," and then argues that it "occurs in all social classes, independent of nation, race, and denomination."[31] After seeming to acknowledge that homosexuality can be found among Jews and non-Jews, Friedman then suggests that, if anything, it is more common among non-Jews. He notes that the most famous homosexuals ("We'll mention only Frederick the Great, Plato, Oscar Wilde, even Schiller!") were Gentile.[32] By contrast, he claims, Jews are known for large families, early marriage, and their survival despite generations of persecution and oppression. Such fecundity, Friedmann argues, which so annoys antisemites, is "counterevidence to Jews' alleged homosexuality," unless Jews "have secretly devised a way of reproducing themselves through homosexual means as well."[33]

Contrary to Friedmann's professed indignation and snarky disbelief, neither the right-wing tactic of co-politicizing homophobia and antisemitism nor his arguments against such coupling were new. Since the late nineteenth century, social and behavioral scientists had posited a Jewish predisposition to homosexuality.[34] At the same time, Jews were overrepresented in branches of medicine associated with sexuality, criminality, and mental illness, because of antisemitic barriers in more prestigious specialties.[35] Concurrently right-wing critics identified "sexuality reform, progressive science, and sensationalism" as Jewish.[36] The trope of Jews promoting homosexuality gained additional traction around the 1907 Harden-Eulenburg affair, a scandal that outed elite members of the German military, nobility, and government and resulted in a series of libel trials. Friedmann cites this scandal as proof that there are prominent non-Jewish homosexuals.[37] The men around Eulenburg accused of having violated Paragraph 175 were not Jewish. Journalist Maximilian Harden, however, who broke the story, as well as one of the defense attorneys were converts from Judaism to Protestantism. Antisemites considered both men to be Jewish.[38] Hirschfeld testified as an expert witness and, believing that exposing same-sex practices among the elite would help his cause, used the opportunity to voice his objections to paragraph 175. The antisemitic press fixated on Hirschfeld and ranted that "the Jews wanted to contaminate the German people with oriental, Caananite vices."[39] In an argument that Friedmann would later echo, the *Allgemeine Zeitung des Judentums* countered that Jews reject homosexuality culturally and religiously; modernity, not the Jews, is responsible for its spread; and the actions and opinions of a few black sheep should not reflect on the entire Jewish community.[40]

The German-Jewish press remained largely silent about the antisemitic outcry against *Anders*. This silence is consistent with both the heteronormativity of traditional Judaism and the immediate postwar German context, in which discussing homosexuality in public was "completely taboo."[41] Yet antisemites' focus on *Anders* captured the attention of Jakob Scherek of *Im Deutschen Reich*, a monthly publication of the Centralverein deutscher Staatsbürger jüdischen Glaubens (Central Association of German Citizens of Jewish Faith) and a predecessor of the weekly *C.-V. Zeitung*, founded in 1922.[42] Scherek does not mention *Anders* but intervenes directly in the *Anders* debate by refuting an article about the film in the antisemitic *Deutschvölkische Blätter*. The author of that article, "Kramer," argued that Jews used cinema to promote sodomy and pederasty because the Jews themselves are "anders als die andern" (different from the others).[43] Unlike Friedmann, who responded to the politicized homophobia and antisemitism around *Anders* by emphasizing Jews' lack of affinity for homosexuality, Scherek erases homosexuality from the conversation altogether.

Scherek's article criticizes both the *Deutschvölkische Blätter*'s misassessment of "cinema as a weapon of Jewry" and a teacher cited by Kramer who had written in the *Israelitischen Familienblatt* that film and theater should be used to teach pupils to "love thy neighbor as thyself."[44] The teacher wanted to promote "religious enlightenment films" but Scherek believes the risk of slippage between *Aufklärung* (enlightenment) and *Tendenz* (tendentiousness) is too great and too dangerous for Jews to risk.[45] The distinction between enlightenment and tendentiousness was an important one in legal, scientific, and aesthetic debates around *Anders*.[46] It differentiates between art and politics, education and activism. Ultimately, assessment of *Anders* as a *Tendenzfilm* rather than an *Aufklärungsfilm* became part of the newly restored Berlin Censorship Office's 16 October 1920 justification for banning *Anders* for all but scientific and educational use.[47] Scherek argues that, although loving thy neighbor is a worthy goal, it is one thing when glorified with the artistic quality of Gotthold Ephraim Lessing's *Nathan der Weise* (*Nathan the Wise*, 1779), a parable about religious tolerance considered a classic of German literature. It is another matter when productions offer "tendentious assistance. As soon as the public learns that such welcome performances were launched by Jews, their efficacy crashes to the ground."[48] Scherek seems to critique unnamed, tendentious "love thy neighbor" religious-tolerance films but implicitly refers to *Anders*, its political advocacy against Paragraph 175, and the damage done to both that advocacy and Jewish bystanders by antisemitic outrage. He hides

Anders's explicit plea to eliminate Paragraph 175 behind the broader edict to "love thy neighbor," cites a religious educator interested in interfaith tolerance rather than a voice for homosexual emancipation, and contrasts *Nathan the Wise* to an unnamed tendentious film.[49] In doing so, Scherek renders homosexuality, homophobia, and homosexual emancipation invisible and substitutes Jewishness, antisemitism, and religious tolerance for them, creating a relationship in which Jewishness displaces rather than intersects with homosexuality.

Scherek's failure to mention homosexuality, a topic otherwise implied by the rebuttal of Kramer's article, recalls Sigmund Freud's textual "repression of homoerotic desire," his failure to see or cite it when its presence is obvious, which Daniel Boyarin attributes to Freud's anxieties around masculinity, assimilation, and the interarticulation of antisemitism and homophobia.[50] Boyarin interprets Freud's textual repression of homosexuality as a panicked response to "the discursive configuration imposed on him by three deeply intertwined cultural events: the racialization/gendering of antisemitism, the fin de siècle production of sexualities, including the 'homosexual,' and the sharp increase in contemporary Christian homophobic discourse."[51] The right wing's copoliticization of homophobia and antisemitism in the debates around *Anders* was a direct descendant of this discursive configuration. So too were Scherek's and Friedmann's responses. Boyarin writes, "Assimilation for these Jews [Sigmund Freud, Theodor Herzl, and their contemporaries] was a sexual and gendered enterprise, an overcoming of the political and cultural characteristics that marked Jewish men as a 'third sex,' as queer in their world. . . . It is impossible to separate the question of Jewishness from the question of homosexuality in Freud's symbolic, textual world. In that world, passing, for Jews, entailed homosexual panic, internalized homophobia, and, ultimately, aggression.[52]

To distance Jewishness from queerness, Scherek does not deride homosexuality, as Friedmann did. Instead, he separates the two by not mentioning *Anders*, homosexuality, or Paragraph 175 when responding to Kramer. This erasure of homosexuality and gay rights from a debate in which they were central is analogous to Freud's repression of homosexuality from his writing. Such erasure dodges the joint thrust of politicized homophobia and antisemitism and it excludes possible overlaps or alliances between the projects of homosexual and Jewish emancipation.

In response to the toxic mixture of politicized homophobia and antisemitism, not only Jewish journalists but also homosexual rights activists resisted associations between homosexuality and Jewishness. For example, the *Jahrbuch für sexuelle Zwischenstufen mit besonderer Be-*

rücksichtigung der Homosexualität, a publication of Hirschfeld's Scientific Humanitarian Committee, rejected the notion that homosexuality was particularly Jewish when it reported on a right-wing flyer in the form of a wanted poster. In describing the flyer, which accused Hirschfeld "of importing oriental morals into Germany," the reporter for the *Jahrbuch* quipped, "as if there had never been a round table in Liebenberg," a snide reference to the Harden-Eulenburg affair.[53] This reference to Prince Eulenburg and his companions highlighted the irony that antisemites accused Jews of importing homosexuality when it was already present among the German nobility. By citing the Harden-Eulenburg affair to refute the coding of homosexuality as Jewish, the *Jahrbuch* deploys one of the same rhetorical strategies as Friedmann did in the *Film-Kurier*.

Attempts by some leaders of the homosexual emancipation movement outside Hirschfeld's circle to separate homosexuality from Jewishness were more serious and more sustained. Disagreement over tactics and a combination of antisemitism and misogyny fractured the homosexual emancipation movement from within. Masculinist and nationalist leaders emphasized their distance from the presumptive Jewishness of Hirschfeld and the nonbinary approach to gender inherent in his *sexualle Zwischenstufenlehre* (theory of sexual intermediacy), a theory that encompassed an assortment of what we now call queer identities, and that posited that some people are a blend of male and female. In the Wilhelmine era, Benedict Friedländer had theorized a masculinist, nationalist version of male Eros "in constitutive opposition to a homosexuality [Hirschfeld's model of sexual intermediacy] that could be read only as always already Jewish."[54] Friedländer's ideas were consonant with others', like Hans Blüher's, whose explicitly nationalist, antisemitic and antifeminist writings theorized homoeroticism, homosociality, and scouting as forms of male bonding and leadership.[55] Such polarization of the movement into a masculinist, nationalist wing and a Jewish-coded wing, which construed gay people as sexual intermediaries or representatives of a third sex, accelerated around the "homosexual panic" and antisemitism of the Harden-Eulenburg affair and persisted into the 1930s.[56]

Adolf Brand, leader of the *Gemeinschaft der Eigenen* (community of the special) characterized the distinction between masculinist approaches like his own and Hirschfeld's version of homosexuality as sexual intermediacy as differences between "Nordic" and "Oriental," and asserted in 1925 that "as a Jew" Hirschfeld was unsuitable to lead the fight against Paragraph 175.[57] In that same year, an article by Karl Heimsoth in Brand's journal, *Der Eigene*, contended,

Otto Weininger's characterization of mental Semitism applies to the executive circle of the WhK [Scientific Humanitarian Committee]. Word for word: Jewish, commercial (not cultural!), feminine, racial (understood in terms of inversion, not personality), worldly oriented (not metaphysically!). Of the worth of a total lack of values, I hold my tongue.

Here lies the root of the problem presented in this article—here lies the basis of the differing conceptions: physically, constitutionally grounded "homosexuality," or "friend-love" with the complete benefits of male-masculine [*mann-männlichen*] eros.[58]

Friedrich Radszuweit, founder of the Bund für Menschenrecht (League for Human Rights), criticized *Anders* on the grounds that "everything that can do harm to homosexuals [should] be censured, and foremost here belongs the presenting of films which always show only the effeminates among the homosexuals. Similarly, such scenes must also be suppressed where the great masses are made aware of older men who only lure youth into homosexual acts."[59] By 1931 Radszuweit would argue that Hirschfeld's Jewishness hurt the cause of homosexual emancipation because antisemitic publications like the Nazi newspaper *Der völkischer Beobachter* were not hostile to homosexuals per se; they were simply hostile to crass, "Jewish" representations of human sexuality.[60]

Anders als die Andern promoted gay rights by making gay men and their persecution under Paragraph 175 visible. The right-wing reaction to the film politicized homophobia and antisemitism in support of film censorship and rendered not only the homosexual emancipation movement but also Jewish-coded components of that movement visible. In response to politicized homophobia and antisemitism around *Anders*, journalists and activists sought to disentangle Jewishness from the film's overt gay advocacy. The historical impulse to resist coding *Anders* as Jewish laid the foundation for later scholarship, which also deemphasizes *Anders*'s Jewishness. Yet, both the antisemitic historical reception and the minimal postwar attention to Jewishness in *Anders* make a reconsideration of Jewish difference in that film a critical component of rethinking Weimar cinema's Jewishness overall.

Decoding Jewish Difference in *Anders als die Andern*

Historical clues can help us decode layers of implicit meanings and explain the relationships between queer and Jewish visibility in *Anders*. Homosexuality and homosexual emancipation are unspoken referents for Scherek's argument about Jewish filmmaking and religious tolerance. Analogously, Jewish emancipation invisibly underpins *Anders*'s advocacy against paragraph 175.[61] Whereas *Anders* represents gay men and demands justice for them overtly, subtle references code the pursuit of justice and gay rights as "Jewish." Historically, the actors' performances of queer masculinity could be read as Jewish also. Decoding *Anders*'s references to Jewish difference reveals that a politics of enlightenment and visibility connect the Jewish and the queer in this film; how *Anders* makes the queer visible also exposes Jewishness.

In *Weimar Film and Modern Jewish Identity*, Ofer Ashkenazi locates Weimar cinema's Jewishness in its Enlightenment ideals and its advocacy for a cosmopolitan society that would welcome Jews. His analyses of representative genre films, including works by Oswald, illustrate how they promoted cosmopolitanism using double-coded narratives, which both spoke to general audiences and addressed Jewish difference beneath the surface. Audiences that recognize subtle markers of Jewishness and scholars who reconstruct how they resonated in their historical context are able to crack such codes. Like other examples of Jewish Weimar film highlighted by Ashkenazi, *Anders* promotes liberal, cosmopolitan views and is similarly double coded. Taken at face value, *Anders* enlightens the general public about homosexuality and the fatal effects of Paragraph 175. Secondarily, it construes Jewish emancipation as a model for homosexual emancipation. Moreover, viewers familiar with Weimar-era discourses of Jewish difference can interpret *Anders*'s central characters as not only queer but also Jewish. The film's central argument, that the law should not discriminate against people who are born different, applies to both queers and Jews.

Enlightenment principles drive both *Anders*'s melodramatic narrative, which illuminates how Paragraph 175 destroys gay men, and Hirschfeld's expository scenes. In one scene, Hirschfeld lectures on sexual intermediacy and explains homosexuality in a dry technical style that references well-known scholars like Eugen Steinach and Richard von Krafft-Ebing. Hirschfeld shows photos of lesbian, gay, intersex, and transgender people and compares their persecution to the burning of heretics and witches. He then cites France as a just model for legal reform, which was precipitated by the Enlightenment and the subsequent Declaration of the Rights of Man: "It was not until the French Revolution that a transformation came about. Everywhere that the Napoleonic Code was introduced, the laws against homosexuality fell, because they were seen as a violation of the fundamental rights of the individual." By not repealing Paragraph 175, Germany remains in the dark, ignorant of scientific discoveries and behind on human rights. Hirschfeld proclaims, "May justice soon prevail over this grave injustice, science conquer superstition, love achieve victory over hatred!"

Weimar viewers easily could have understood *Anders*'s reliance on Enlightenment discourse as Jewish. Hirschfeld's reference to the French Revolution and Napoleonic Code invokes Frenchness and Enlightenment on behalf of homosexual emancipation. In a Weimar context, this constellation was coded Jewish. Negative associations between liberal Enlightenment thought, Jewishness, and Frenchness were standard antisemitic fare.[62] Kerry Wallach notes that Frenchness also could serve as cover or code for Jewishness.[63] It plays a similar role in Ashkenazi's reading of Oswald's 1927 film *Dr. Bessels Verwandlung* (*The Transformation of Dr. Bessel*).[64] The German Enlightenment and *Haskalah* (Jewish Enlightenment) were closely related and the German-Jewish thinker Moses Mendelssohn was central to both. Adam Sutcliffe argues that Jewishness occupied an ambivalent and overdetermined space in Enlightenment philosophy and the effects of Enlightenment on modern Jewish life were equally overdetermined and ambivalent. On the one hand, traditional religious Judaism symbolized an intractable and irrational Other for many Enlightenment thinkers. On the other hand, the Enlightenment motivated Jewish legal emancipation, dissolved boundaries between Jewish and Gentile communities, and shaped both modern Jewish thought and modern antisemitism.[65]

The influence of the Enlightenment on Hirschfeld's experience of Jewishness is evident in his personal views and his work as a scientist and activist. Raised in a Jewish home, the adult Hirschfeld dissented from religious Judaism without converting to another faith.[66] Elena Mancini writes that Hirschfeld embraced "the secular and humanistic aspects of [Jewishness]. He identified with the nomadic history of the Jews, and he read into the condition of the wanderer a pretext for a cosmopolitan outlook and a natural drive for freedom."[67] His work for social justice is consistent with both the Enlightenment and Jewish philosophical traditions.[68] James Steakley notes that Enlightenment philosophy was pivotal for Hirschfeld, as evidenced across his scholarship, activism, and this film.[69] Similarly, S.S. Prawer identifies the "sense of social justice" and "dedicat[ion] to the eradication of legal and moral inequities" in *Anders* and Oswald's other *Aufklärungsfilme* as Jewish.[70]

Hirschfeld's final words to the bereaved Kurt summarize the film's Enlightenment philosophy, invoke Frenchness, and draw an analogy between homosexual and Jewish emancipation. "This is the life task I assign to you. Just as Zola struggled on behalf of one man who innocently languished in prison, what matters now is to restore honor and justice to the many thousands before us, with us, and after us. Through knowledge to justice!" The final exclamation encapsulates this *Aufklärungsfilm*'s main impulse, which reflects fundamental principles of Enlightenment thought: more knowledge and better understanding of homosexuality will lead to justice and the elimination of Paragraph 175.

Hirschfeld's comparison to Zola invokes Jewishness because it is a reference to the Dreyfus affair, a case that revealed the limits antisemitism placed on Jewish emancipation, and which captured the attention of Jewish intellectuals in the German-speaking world and beyond.[71] Alfred Dreyfus was a French military officer whose false conviction for espionage and treason in 1894 and resulting events polarized the French elite. One of the most famous moments of this affair was the 1898 publication of Émile Zola's open letter, "J'Accuse . . . " (I accuse), which refutes the case against Dreyfus and accused French officials of injustice and antisemitism. Zola's subsequent conviction for libel drove him into exile. Steakley correctly notes, "Hirschfeld's allusion to the Dreyfus affair draws a noteworthy parallel between anti-Semitism and homophobia."[72] It also calls for activism and solidarity. Although addressed to Kurt, the use of the second- and first-person plural in this intertitle hails the spectator as part of a community that seeks honor and justice. "You" must take on this task, and you are one of "us," whether or not you are different. Just as the Gentile Zola risked himself to oppose antisemitism, Kurt and the audience should make sacrifices to win justice and freedom for gay men, whether or not they themselves are gay.

To advance its Enlightenment agenda, *Anders* made gay men visible to audiences composed predominantly of people who did not identify as gay. Its visibility strategies blend narrative cinema with the show-stopping techniques of the cinema of attractions, rejecting the comfort created by seamless narrative.[73] Ervin Malakaj argues that *Anders*'s narrative brings gay men's lives and loves out of the shadows and invites viewers to envision a better world, using melodramatic conventions to engage spectators' affect and imagination.[74] Several arresting spectacles display homosexuality as an attraction, halting the narrative and challenging comfortable conceptual frameworks. In the version restored by the Munich Filmmuseum, a production still replaces missing footage of Paul's vision of "an endless procession of [gay men], from all times and countries." The intertitles describe the procession as "including such luminaries as Peter Tchaikovsky, Leonardo da Vinci, Oscar Wilde, King

Friedrich II of Prussia, and King Ludwig II of Bavaria." The production still—which shows a diagonal line of men vanishing into darkness at the back of the screen, the men's extravagant European costumes, and the lineage of "extraordinary and productive" homosexuals from different periods—suggest that this spectacle was a kind of fantasized pride parade *avant la lettre*, as Ina Linge has argued, attempting to counter gay shame by constructing an affirmative ancestry.[75] The procession depicts gay men as ubiquitous, powerful, visible, and glorious, even with Paragraph 175 hanging like a sword of Damocles over their heads.

Hirschfeld's slide show during his lecture turns the bodies of sexual intermediaries into a spectacle as well. Framed as showing that nature is boundless in its creations, these images of queer people transgress the cultural norms of their target audience in a variety of ways: partial nudity, cross dressing, intersex bodies, nonbinary gender presentation, gender nonconforming behaviors, and same-sex affection. For mainstream German audiences in 1919, such images must have been both titillating and conceptually challenging. The slides assert that the era's cultural norms and categories fail to account for bodies and desires that nevertheless exist. The narrative interruption caused by the spectacle highlights this failure of dominant narratives. Intertitles refer to Steinach's work with hormones to explain the biological origins of sexual intermediacy. The emphasis on the natural, biologically determined nature of sexual intermediacy insists that it is the hegemonic norms and narratives, not people's bodies and desires, that are unnatural. The effect of this spectacle is to show that Paragraph 175 is out of alignment with nature and science and, like persecution of witches and heretics, a superstition that should be discarded.

Although Hirschfeld acknowledges in this scene that "there are feminine men who are not homosexual, and homosexuals who make little or no female impression," *Anders* makes homosexuality visible primarily through gender inversion.[76] Hirschfeld's slides only show people presenting as cisgender when accompanied by images of them presenting as the opposite gender too. The ornate costumes of the men in Paul's procession code them as effeminate, with frippery like wigs, hose, and heels, which by the early twentieth century signified femininity rather than male class privilege. A scene at a ball with queer folks dancing is where "sexual intermediacy is portrayed most vividly."[77] Linge describes it as follows: "Various figures appear deliberately androgynous or cannot be read as clearly male or female. The lush costumes worn by the dancers make elaborate pageantry a key feature of queer experience."[78] The spectacle of sexual intermediates at a ball was so particularly arresting and transgressive that it "precipitated a riot in one Berlin cinema in 1919."[79] *Anders*'s spectacles of homosexuality as gender inversion and narrative disruption reinforce Hirschfeld's scientific and political positions. They also dovetail with stereotypes of both queer and Jewish masculinities.

Anders's actors' performances of queer masculinity echo Hirschfeld's concept of sexual intermediacy, a gender presentation construed as Jewish. As Shane Brown elaborates, Paul's sensitive emotional reactions, his anguished sighs, his exotic appearance, and weak, almost lethargic, physical movements all depict him as effeminate and show how he "conforms to Hirschfeld's theory of the third sex."[80] Klaus Kreimeier interprets Veidt's "neurasthenic" performance in this role as a reminder of the failure of German masculinity after World War I.[81] Richard Dyer highlights the resonances of Veidt's and Schünzel's performances with the *Tante* (auntie) and *Bube* (boy) styles of the Weimar gay scene.[82] The setting where Paul and Franz meet—the ball described above with androgynous, cross-dressed, and same-sex couples dancing in the background—provides the context to interpret the characters as such. Veidt's slender physique, his kohl-rimmed eyes, and the uncanny quality of his gaunt face and spidery movements, which landed him roles in *Das Cabinet des Dr. Caligari* (*The Cabinet of Dr. Caligari*; 1919–20) and other horror films, suited the "effeminized male look" of the *Tante* style.[83] His "loose satin robe with a hood" in the dance scene and the kimono-style dressing gown he wears at home accentuate his androgyny.[84] Franz Bollek (Paul's seducer and eventual blackmailer) looks like the *Bube* with the "broad, crude features [of] . . . the working class lad," whose lipstick is nevertheless visible in this introductory scene.[85] Wolfgang Theis reads Bollek, as performed by Schünzel, as "the really queer character" in *Anders*.[86] According to Theis, Schünzel's sartorial elegance, physiognomic brutality, and realistic performance style blend feminine and masculine traits and embody Hirschfeld's theory of sexual intermediacy.[87] Steakley summarizes: "Both characters—villain and victim alike—may be seen as sexual intermediates, whose contrary temperaments serve precisely to confound unitary notions of 'the' homosexual."[88]

As explained above, not only antisemites and homophobes, but also gay thinker-activists like Blüher, Brand, and Friedländer understood sexual intermediacy as Jewish. Their writings and other widespread late-nineteenth- and early-twentieth-century discourses that construed Jewish masculinity as effeminate make it possible to interpret the actors' performances of queer masculinity in *Anders* also as Jewish.[89] Schulz's performance of Kurt too is feminized. His and Paul's gender presentation injects Jewish difference into their relationship, even as that relationship recalls non-Jewish factions of the homosexual emancipation movement. Dyer interprets Paul and Kurt's romance as a chaste example of the pedagogic Eros and the male identified, Greek homosexuality favored by the homosexual emancipation movement's masculinist, nationalist wing. *Anders* depicts pedagogic Eros favorably in comparison with the sexualized and criminalized *Tante/Bube* configuration that it associates with a gay underworld.[90] Decoded in racialized terms, the German male-male love and artistic collaboration between Paul and Kurt are pure while the sexual-pecuniary relationship between Paul and Franz begun in the Jewish milieu of the gay ball is dirty. Yet, in effect, the two historically competing, racialized models of homosexual identity coexist in the film and, indeed, are both lived by Paul.[91] Paul's and Kurt's effeminacy indicates that the split between German and Jewish homosexuality is a false binary. Schulz's subtle makeup and his dapper suit with an open white-collared shirt and pocket square make him look much younger and prettier than Veidt, although the actors were only three years apart in age and Veidt, in his day, was known as handsome.[92] The affective register of melodrama and Schulz's sentimental performance, like Veidt's, are culturally coded as feminine. For example, the final shot of Kurt, kneeling and sobbing over Paul's body, displays feminine emotionalism rather than masculine constraint. By feminizing both Kurt and Paul, *Anders* makes pedagogic Eros, which some gay rights activists framed as hyper-masculine, Greek, or German, also look effeminate, queer, and, by extension, Jewish.

Veidt's, Schünzel's, and Schulz's exaggerated, feminine performances of queer masculinity can be attributed partially to Hirschfeld's theories, partially to melodramatic conventions, and partially to the exigencies of silent film, in which exaggerated performances frequently compensated for the missing communicative possibilities of synchronized sound. Normative masculinity is less immediately accessible to straight audiences as a mode of queer self-presentation and more commonly associated with passing and closeting. Male femininity communicates queerness more efficiently because it resonates with stereotypes about gay men. In this instance, male femininity and histrionics function as shorthand for queer. These exaggerated performances also embody an important intersection between queerness and Jewishness.

In 1919 the exaggerated performances of queer masculinity in *Anders* could be and were decoded as Jewish, as was support for *Anders*. We see this in K's report about a disrupted Berlin screening of *Anders* in the *Deutsche Zeitung*, a conservative, nationalist paper. K.'s article attributes *Anders* to a spreading "un-German spirit" and along the way labels some characters and audience members as "Jewish."[93] Summarizing *Anders*'s plot, K. describes Kurt as "a truly glorious example of the Jewish race" and Bollek as "a Jewish pimp."[94] K. writes about the tumult created as antisemites and homophobes interrupted the screening: "At times it appeared really threatening, especially when a number of Jew-boys had recovered from the initial shock and then spoke about enlightenment and science with wild enthusiasm."[95] Actors Fritz Schulz and Reinhold Schünzel both had Jewish ancestry but K. may or may not have been aware of that and does not make that point. Instead, K. uses the word "Jewish" to describe the characters, does not name the actors at all, and could not have known the religious or ethnic background of the "Jew-boys" in the audience. Rather than identifying individuals' religious or ethnic backgrounds, K. deploys antisemitism here as what Shulamit Volkov calls a "cultural code," which members of the German right wing used as shorthand for their own identifications with a slew of anti-modern, conservative, nationalist views including antisemitism, homophobia, and more.[96] By referring to Kurt, Bollek, and *Anders*'s defenders as "Jews," K. instructs like-minded readers to disapprove of them. At the same time, K. participates in the coding and decoding of Jewish difference, informing readers of *Deutsche Zeitung* which people and characters they should understand as "Jewish." By calling Kurt, Bollek, and supportive audience members Jewish when they did not identify themselves as such, K. implies that queerness and support for gay rights are inherently Jewish. Such coding was consistent with decades of scientific, philosophical, and cultural discourse in which Jewish and queer masculinities were symbolically intertwined. *Anders*'s politics and performances brought this connection to the surface.

Conclusion

The entanglement between Jewishness and queerness in and around *Anders* was both productive and treacherous. The film promotes sexual and political enlightenment, notes parallels between homosexual and Jewish emancipation, and displays queer masculinities that historically could be decoded also as Jewish. Despite the promise of Jewish-queer alliance invoked by *Anders*'s final analogy and call to action, the homophobic and antisemitic responses to the film reveal the limits of its strategies of visibility, enlightenment, and analogy and the risks of alliance between different marginal groups. Wallach's study of Jewish passing in Weimar Germany shows that Jewish visibility was a complex and vexed issue and that decisions to display or conceal Jewishness had psychological and material consequences. By making homosexuality visible through stylized, effeminate performances and construing Jews as allies, *Anders* also exposed Jewishness to a hostile gaze. Politicized homophobia and antisemitism directed at the film and its makers became tools to promote cinema censorship and tested the potential alliances that *Anders* made visible.

Much work remains to be done at the intersection of the Jewish and the queer in Weimar cinema. Historical discourses around these two forms of difference were neither fully separable nor fully interchangeable. My focus on *Anders* does not address encounters between Jewishness, gender, and lesbian representation in Weimar cinema or ways in which Jewish women might have been read as queer. It also leaves other important questions unanswered: How is Jewish difference encoded in other Weimar films about same-sex desire or gender transgression, films like *Geschlecht in Fesseln* (*Sex in Chains*; 1928, dir. Wilhelm Dieterle), *Mädchen in Uniform* (*Girls in Uniform*; 1931, dir. Leontine Sagan), *Ich möchte kein Mann sein* (*I Don't Want to Be a Man*; 1918, dir. Ernst Lubitsch), or *Der Fürst von Pappenheim* (*The Prince of Pappenheim*; 1927, dir. Richard Eichberg)? And vice-versa, how might we read some of the films with overtly Jewish characters and narratives also as queer? When we consider characters' passing or narratives' double coding, how might we account for additional layers of difference and visibility and theorize how Jewishness and queerness are co-, inter-, or differently articulated? Do the absences, silences, and codes that mask them coincide or take different forms? How do films negotiate the complex mixture of hope and vulnerability experienced by folks who identified as queer and/or Jewish in the Weimar Republic, which is particularly visible in *Anders* and its reception?

Valerie Weinstein is Professor of Women's, Gender, and Sexuality Studies, Niehoff Professor in Film and Media Studies, and affiliate faculty in German Studies and Judaic Studies at the University of Cincinnati. She is the author of *Antisemitism in Film Comedy in Nazi Germany* (Indiana University Press, 2019) and numerous articles on Weimar and Nazi cinema. She is co-editor, with Barbara Hales and Mihaela Petrescu, of *Continuity and Crisis in German Cinema 1928-1936* (Camden House, 2016).

Notes

Many thanks to Nicholas Baer, Barbara Hales, Gergana Ivanova, Ervin Malakaj, Deborah Meem, Sunnie Rucker-Chang, and Kerry Wallach for their very generous help and feedback on this chapter.
1. Daniel Boyarin, Daniel Itzkovitz, and Ann Pellegrini, "Strange Bedfellows: An Introduction," in *Queer Theory and the Jewish Question*, ed. Daniel Boyarin, Daniel Itzkovitz, and Ann Pellegrini (New York: Columbia University Press, 2003), 1–4; Daniel Boyarin, *Unheroic Conduct: The Rise of Heterosexuality and the Invention of the Jewish Man* (Berkeley: University of California Press, 1997); Sander Gilman, *Difference and Pathology: Stereotypes of Sexuality, Race, and Madness* (Ithaca, NY: Cornell University Press, 1985); Sander Gilman, *The Jew's Body* (New York: Routledge, 1991); George Mosse, *Nationalism and Sexuality: Middle-Class Morality and Sexual Norms in Modern Europe* (Madison: University of Wisconsin Press, 1985); Scott Spector, *Violent Sensations: Sex, Crime, and Utopia in Vienna and Berlin 1860–1914* (Chicago: University of Chicago Press, 2017); Robert Deam Tobin, *Peripheral Desires: The German Discovery of Sex* (Philadelphia: University of Pennsylvania Press, 2015), 83–110; Matti Bunzl, *Symptoms of Modernity: Jews and Queers in Late Twentieth-Century Vienna* (Berkeley: University of California Press, 2004), 12–18.
2. Otto Weininger, *Geschlecht und Charakter: Eine prinzipielle Untersuchung* (Vienna: Wilhelm Braumüller, 1903).
3. Tobin, *Peripheral Desires*, 83–110.
4. Kai Nowak, *Projektionen der Moral: Filmskandale in der Weimarer Republik* (Göttingen: Wallstein Verlag, 2015), 113–17; S.S. Prawer, *Between Two Worlds: The Jewish Presence in German and Austrian Film 1910–1933* (New York: Berghahn Books, 2005), 73–74; James D. Steakley, *"Anders als die Andern": Ein Film und seine Geschichte* (Hamburg: Männerschwarm Verlag, 2007), 76–85; James D. Steakley, "Cinema and Censorship in the Weimar Republic: The Case of *Anders als Die Andern*." *Film History* 11.2 (1999): 191.
5. One scholar who centers *Anders*'s Jewishness is Nicholas Baer. Baer describes the interarticulation of homosexuality and Jewishness in *Anders* and its reception in two short publications: Nicholas Baer, "The Dialectic of the *Aufklärungsfilm*: Essentialism and Nominalism in Richard Oswald's *Anders als die Andern* (1919)," [Hebrew language], *Slil: Online Journal for History, Film and Television*, Issue 5, Winter 201, https://en.slil.huji.ac.il/book/issue-5-winter-2011; Nicholas Baer, "*Different from the Others: Anders als die Andern*," in *Directory of World Cinema: Germany*, ed. Michelle Langford (Chicago: Intellect, 2012), 172–73.
6. Eve Kosofsky Sedgwick, *Epistemology of the Closet* (Berkeley: University of California Press, 1990), 75–82. See also Boyarin, Itzkovitz, and Pellegrini, *Queer Theory*; Jonathan Branfman, "Failed Fatherhood and the 'Trap of Ambivalence': Assimilation, Homonormativity, and Effeminophobia in *The New Normal*," *Journal of Homosexuality* 66.12 (2019): 1671–92; Kerry Wallach, *Passing Illusions: Jewish Visibility in Weimar Cinema* (Ann Arbor: University of Michigan Press, 2017), 168–73.
7. Branfman, "Failed Fatherhood," 1673. See also Matti Bunzl, "Jews, Queers, and Other Symptoms: Recent Work in Jewish Cultural Studies," *GLQ: A Journal of Lesbian and Gay Studies* 6.2 (2000): 321–41.
8. Lisa Silverman, *Becoming Austrians: Jews and Culture Between the World Wars* (Oxford: Oxford University Press, 2012); Lisa Silverman, "Beyond Antisemitism: A Critical Approach to German Jewish Cultural History," in *Nexus 1: Essays in German Jewish*

Studies (Rochester, NY: Camden House, 2011), 27–45; Lisa Silverman, "Reconsidering the Margins: Jewishness as an Analytical Framework," *Journal of Modern Jewish Studies* 8.1 (March 2009): 103–20.

9. For in-depth analysis of how melodrama works in *Anders*, its strengths, and its limitations, see Ervin Malakaj, "Richard Oswald, Magnus Hirschfeld and the Possible Impossibility of Hygienic Melodrama," *Studies in European Cinema* 14.3 (2017): 216–30.
10. Suicide is a repeated, problematic motif in gay literature and film in the early twentieth century. Paul's suicide can also be linked to perceptions, discourses, and the rising rates of "reported suicides among Jews, women, and Jewish women in particular" in Weimar Germany, as analyzed by Darcy Buerkle. Buerkle, *Nothing Happened: Charlotte Solomon and an Archive of Suicide* (Ann Arbor: University of Michigan Press, 2013), 167.
11. James Steakley rightly cautions that it is impossible to interpret *Anders* as its original audiences did, because more than half the original film footage and the original score are missing (Steakley, *Anders*, 49). The excellent restoration by the Filmmuseum München, however, which carefully reconstructs the narrative and intertitles based on censorship records and inserts still images to represent lost footage, makes it possible to analyze the plot, dialogue, and surviving footage.
12. See Steakley, "Cinema and Censorship," 189–92.
13. Prawer, *Between Two Worlds*, 74.
14. Laurie Marhoefer, *Sex and the Weimar Republic: German Homosexual Emancipation and the Rise of the Nazis* (Toronto: University of Toronto Press, 2015), 38.
15. Nowak, *Projektionen der Moral*, 112.
16. Valerie Weinstein, *Antisemitism in Film Comedy in Nazi Germany* (Bloomington: Indiana University Press, 2019), 37, 70–71.
17. Steakley, "Cinema and Censorship," 191, 201, n60; Thomas Schorr, "Die Film-und Kinoreformbewegung und die deutsche Filmwirtschaft. Eine Analyse des Fachblatts 'Der Kinematograph' (1907–1935) unter pädagogischen und publizistischen Aspekten," Dissertation, Submitted to the Universität der Bundeswehr, Munich, Department of Pedagogy, Institute of Media Pedagogy, 13 November 1989, 173–74.
18. Steakley, *Anders*, 69.
19. "Deutschnationale und völkische Gruppierungen, Kirchenvertreter, Kinoreformer sowie Aktivisten der Schmutz- und Schundbewegung." Nowak, *Projektionen der Moral*, 111. Unless otherwise noted, translations are all by the author.
20. Nowak, *Projektionen der Moral*, 112–13.
21. Nowak, *Projektionen der Moral*, 113–14. See also Manfred Herzer, *Magnus Hirschfeld und seine Zeit* (Berlin: Walter de Gruyter, 2017), 328–29.
22. "Prostitutions- und Päderastenfilms" [sic]. Alfred Rosenberg, "Juden, Judentzer und Deutsche," *Auf gut Deutsch: Wochenschrift für Ordnung und Recht* 1.40–41 (December 1919): 634.
23. Johann Ude, "Wissenschaftlicher Kinoschund," *Christliche Volkswacht: Monatschrift des Volkswachtbundes* 1.10 (1919): 12. Ude is not alone among critics in praising *Anders*'s technical proficiency, despite other reservations. See, for example, Ludwig Marcuse, cited in Steakley, *Anders*, 62.
24. "Umfassende antisemitische Agitation"; "einer wilden antisemitischen Hetze." Star, "Jüdischer Film," *Jüdische Korrespondenz* 5.31 (22 August 1919): 2–3.
25. Steakley, *Anders*, 79–81.
26. "Sollen wir Deutschen uns denn von den Juden verseuchen lassen?"; K., "Ein Skandal!" *Deutsche Zeitung* 24.318 (11 July 1919, evening edition): 3.

27. Ashley Currier, *Politicizing Sex in Contemporary Africa: Homophobia in Malawi* (Cambridge, UK: Cambridge University Press, 2018), 1.
28. Currier, *Politicizing Sex*, 2.
29. Walther Friedmann, "Homosexuality and Jewishness: The Latest Method of Agitation Against 'Aufklärungsfilme,'" *Film Kurier*, 13 July 1919, trans. Nicholas Baer, in *The Promise of Cinema: German Film Theory, 1907–1933*, ed. Anton Kaes, Nicholas Baer, and Michael Cowan (Oakland: University of California Press, 2016), 242.
30. Friedmann, "Homosexuality and Jewishness," 241.
31. Friedmann, "Homosexuality and Jewishness," 241.
32. Friedmann, "Homosexuality and Jewishness," 241.
33. Friedmann, "Homosexuality and Jewishness," 241.
34. Steakley, *Anders*, 83; Nowak, *Projektionen der Moral*, 114.
35. Katie Sutton, *Sex between Body and Mind: Psychoanalysis and Sexology in the German-Speaking World, 1890s–1930s* (Ann Arbor: University of Michigan Press, 2019), 22.
36. Spector, *Violent Sensations*, 164.
37. Friedmann, "Homosexuality and Jewishness," 241. For more on the Harden-Eulenburg affair, see Clayton J. Whisnant, *Queer Identities and Politics in Germany: A History 1880–1945* (New York: Harrington Park Press, 2016), 48–59; Spector, *Violent Sensations*, 161–65.
38. "Noch eine Lektion," *Allgemeine Zeitung des Judentums* 71.51 (20 December 1907): 601–2, http://sammlungen.ub.uni-frankfurt.de/cm/periodical/titleinfo/3224737.
39. "Die Juden wollten das deutsche Volk mit orientalischen, mit Caananitischen Lastern verseuchen." "Noch eine Lektion," 601–2. See also Herzer, *Magnus Hirschfeld*, 167.
40. "Die Lehren eines Prozesses," *Allgemeine Zeitung des Judentums* 71.45 (8 November 1907): 529–30, http://sammlungen.ub.uni-frankfurt.de/cm/periodical/titleinfo/3224737.
41. "Völlig tabuisiert." Jürgen Kasten, "Dramatische Instinkte und das Spektakel der Aufklärung: Richard Oswalds Filme der 10er-Jahre," in *Richard Oswald: Kino zwischen Spektakel, Aufklärung und Unterhaltung*, ed. Jürgen Kasten and Armin Loacker (Vienna: Verlag Filmarchiv Austria, 2005), 102.
42. Donald L. Niewyk identifies the byline "J. Sch." for the "Umschau" in *Im deutschen Reich* in 1919 as a pseudonym for Jakob Scherek; Niewyk, "The German Jews in Revolution and Revolt 1918–19," in *Studies in Contemporary Jewry Volume IV: The Jews and the European Crisis, 1914–1921*, ed. Jonathan Frankel, Peter Y. Medding, and Ezra Mendelsohn (Oxford: Oxford University Press, 1988), 60. See also Avraham Barkai, *"Wehr Dich!": der Centralverein deutscher Staatsbürger jüdischen Glaubens (C.V.) 1893–1938* (Munich: Beck, 2002), 404, n11.
43. Kramer, "Unerhörter Mißbrauch des Kinos," *Deutschvölkische Blätter* 34.31 (22 August 1919): 1, cited by Steakley in *Anders*, 83.
44. "Das Kino als Kampfmittel des Judentums." J. Sch., "Umschau," 367–68; http://sammlungen.ub.uni-frankfurt.de/cm/periodical/pageview/2356341?query=film.
45. "Konfessionelle Aufklärungsstücke." J. Sch. "Umschau," 367.
46. Steakley, *Anders*, 109.
47. Steakley, *Anders*, 125.
48. "Tendenziöses Nachhelfen. Sobald die Oeffentlichkeit erfährt, daß derartige begrüßenswerte Aufführungen durch Juden lanciert werden, fällt auch ihre Wirkung zu Boden." J. Sch. "Umschau," 368.
49. The analogy to Lessing also posits classic German literature as superior to film.
50. Boyarin, *Unheroic Conduct*, 208.

51. Boyarin, *Unheroic Conduct*, 208. Jay Geller makes a related argument "that the changes in Freud's depiction of homosexuality in his accounts of social origins ["his corpus from *Totem and Taboo* to *Moses and Monotheism*"]—the increasingly sharp distinction between homosociality and homosexuality that ultimately culminated in the foreclosure of homosexuality from Freud's narrative—may be connected with the antisemitic, *Völkisch* turn of *Männerbund* theories as well as the racialization of homosexual identities." Jay Geller, "Freud, Blüher, and the *Secessio Inversa*: *Männerbünde*, Homosexuality, and Freud's Theory of Cultural Formation," in Boyarin, Itzkovitz, and Pellegrini, *Queer Theory*, 90–91. In sum, Boyarin and Geller show that the historic interarticulation of antisemitism and homophobia led Freud to dismiss homosexuality in his writings. I argue that the politicized homophobia and antisemitism around *Anders* had similar effects on other Jewish writers.
52. Boyarin, *Unheroic Conduct*, 222.
53. "'Wegen Einführung orientalischer Sitten in Deutschland,' als ob es niemals eine Tafelrunde in Liebenberg gegeben hätte." "Aus der Bewegung," *Jahrbuch für sexuelle Zwischenstufen mit besonderer Berücksichtigung der Homosexualität* 19.3–4 (1919–1920): 121.
54. Bunzl, "Jews, Queers, and Other Symptoms," 339. See also Mosse, *Nationalism and Sexuality*, 41; Robert Beachy, *Gay Berlin: Birthplace of a Modern Identity* (New York: Alfred A. Knopf, 2014), 117.
55. Geller, "Freud, Blüher, and the *Secessio Inversa*," 90–120; Beachy, *Gay Berlin*, xviii, 140–59; Whisnant, *Queer Identities*, 190–91; Herzer, *Magnus Hirschfeld*, 227–33.
56. Whisnant, *Queer Identities and Politics in Germany*, 59.
57. Steakley, *Anders*, 35. On Brand's and his organization's antisemitism, see Herzer, *Magnus Hirschfeld*, 238; and Beachy, *Gay Berlin*, xix, 117, 228. On the proximity of Brand and his circle to fascism, see Marhoefer, *Sex and the Weimar Republic*, 152–53.
58. Karl Heimsoth, "Freundesliebe oder Homosexualität," *Der Eigene* 10.9 (1925): 415–25. Cited in Glenn Ramsey, "The Rites of Artgenossen: Contesting Homosexual Political Culture in Weimar Germany," *Journal of the History of Sexuality* 17.1 (January 2008): 105.
59. Friedrich Radszuweit, "Falsche Wege: Männliche Kultur oder medizinische Wissenschaft?" *Blätter für Menschenrecht* 3.11 (November 1925): 17–18. Cited in: Ramsey, "The Rites of Artgenossen," 85.
60. Radszuweit cited in Steakley, *Anders*, 123. See also Marhoefer, *Sex and the Weimar Republic*, 171.
61. *Anders*'s embedded references to Jewish emancipation are consistent with Scott Spector's observation that Jewish emancipation was "very much present in the minds of homosexual activists in the generations following Ulrichs." Spector, *Violent Sensations*, 91.
62. Scott Spector, "Modernism Without Jews: A Counter-Historical Argument," *Modernism/Modernity* 13.4 (November 2006): 615.
63. Wallach, *Passing Illusions*, 165, 171. See also Silverman, *Becoming Austrians*, 75, 86.
64. Ashkenazi, *Weimar Film and Modern Jewish Identity*. New York: Palgrave Macmillan, 2012, xiii–xvi, 133–47.
65. Adam Sutcliffe, "Judaism and the Politics of Enlightenment," *The American Behavioral Scientist* 49.5 (January 2006): 702–15.
66. Ralf Dose, *Magnus Hirschfeld: The Origins of the Gay Liberation Movement*, trans. Edward H. Willis (New York: Monthly Review Press, 2014), 32–33.
67. Elena Mancini, *Magnus Hirschfeld and the Quest for Sexual Freedom: A History of the First International Sexual Freedom Movement* (New York: Palgrave Macmillan, 2010), 137.

68. Dose, *Magnus Hirschfeld*, 37.
69. Steakley, *Anders*, 31.
70. Prawer, *Between Two Worlds*, 81.
71. In 1930 Richard Oswald directed a film about the Dreyfus affair, *Dreyfus*, which promoted sympathy with the Jewish protagonist. See Prawer, *Between Two Worlds*, 149–59; Wallach, *Passing Illusions*, 82–95.
72. Steakley, "Cinema and Censorship," 187.
73. See Tom Gunning, "The Cinema of Attractions: Early Film, its Spectator, and the Avant Garde," in *Early Cinema: Space, Frame, Narrative*, ed. Thomas Elsaesser and Adam Barker (London: British Film Institute, 1990), 56–62.
74. Malakaj, "Richard Oswald."
75. Ina Linge, "Sexology, Popular Science and Queer History in *Anders als die Andern (Different from the Others)*," *Gender and History*, 30.3 (October 2018), 604.
76. Cf. Richard Dyer, "Less and More than Women and Men: Lesbian and Gay Cinema in Weimar Germany," *New German Critique* 51 (August 1990): 19–31. Dyer argues that *Anders* shows elements of both sexual intermediacy and male identification.
77. Steakley, "Cinema and Censorship," 195.
78. Linge, "Sexology, Popular Science," 600.
79. Steakley, "Cinema and Censorship," 195.
80. Shane Brown, *Queer Sexualities in Early Film: Cinema and Male-Male Intimacy* (London: I.B. Tauris, 2016), 26.
81. Klaus Kreimeier, "Aufklärung, Kommerzialismus und Demokratie, oder: der Bankrott des deutschen Mannes," in *Richard Oswald: Regisseur und Produzent*, ed. Helga Balach and Wolfgang Jacobsen (Munich: Edition Text + Kritik, 1990), 17.
82. Dyer, "Less and More," 21–23.
83. Dyer, "Less and More," 23.
84. Dyer, "Less and More," 23. See also: Brown, *Queer Sexualities in Early Film*, 32.
85. Dyer, "Less and More," 23.
86. Wolfgang Theis, "Schünzels Requisiten. Zum Beispiel: die Handschuhe," in *Reinhold Schünzel: Schauspieler und Regisseur (revisited)*, ed. Jörg Schöning and Erika Wottrich (Munich: Edition Text + Kritik, 2009), 33.
87. Theis, "Schünzels Requisiten," 33.
88. Steakley, "Cinema and Censorship," 195.
89. Boyarin, *Unheroic Conduct*; Gilman, *Difference and Pathology*; Mosse, *Nationalism and Sexuality*; Spector, *Violent Sensations*; Tobin, *Peripheral Desires*, 83–110; Bunzl, *Symptoms of Modernity*, 12–18.
90. Dyer, "Less and More," 24–29.
91. Dyer, "Less and More," 30; Brown, *Queer Sexualities in Early Film*, 31.
92. Brown, *Queer Sexualities in Early Film*, 32.
93. "Undeutschen Geist." K. "Ein Skandal!" 3.
94. "Einem wahren Prachtexemplar der jüdischen Rasse"; "ein jüdischer Zuhälter." K., "Ein Skandal!," 3.
95. "Zeitweise sah es echt drohend aus, besonders als sich eine Anzahl von Judenjungens von dem ersten Schreck erholt hatten und nun mit wilder Begeisterung von Aufklärung und Wissenschaftlichkeit redeten." K. "Ein Skandal!" 3.
96. Shulamit Volkov, "Antisemitism as a Cultural Code—Reflections on the History and Historiography of Antisemitism in Imperial Germany," *Leo Baeck Yearbook* 23 (1978): 25–46.

Bibliography

Anders als die Andern. Dir. Richard Oswald. Perfs. Conrad Veidt, Reinhold Schünzel, Fritz Schulz, 1919. DVD. Filmmuseum München/Goethe-Institut München, 2006.
Ashkenazi, Ofer. *Weimar Film and Modern Jewish Identity.* New York: Palgrave Macmillan, 2012.
"Aus der Bewegung." *Jahrbuch für sexuelle Zwischenstufen mit besonderer Berücksichtigung der Homosexualität* 19 (3–4, 1919–20): 111–33.
Baer, Nicholas. "*Different from the Others: Anders als die Andern.*" In *Directory of World Cinema: Germany,* vol. 9, ed. Michelle Langford, 172–73. Chicago: Intellect, 2012.
———. "The Dialectic of the *Aufklärungsfilm*: Essentialism and Nominalism in Richard Oswald's *Anders als die Andern* (1919)" [Article in Hebrew]. *Slil: Online Journal for History, Film and Television* 5 (Winter 2011). https://en.slil.huji.ac.il/book/issue-5-winter-2011
Barkai, Avraham. "*Wehr Dich!*": *der Centralverein deutscher Staatsbürger jüdischen Glaubens (C.V.) 1893–1938.* Munich: Beck, 2002.
Beachy, Robert. *Gay Berlin: Birthplace of a Modern Identity.* New York: Alfred A. Knopf, 2014.
Boyarin, Daniel. *Unheroic Conduct: The Rise of Heterosexuality and the Invention of the Jewish Man.* Berkeley: University of California Press, 1997.
Boyarin, Daniel, Daniel Itzkovitz, and Ann Pellegrini, eds. *Queer Theory and the Jewish Question.* New York: Columbia University Press, 2003.
Boyarin, Daniel, Daniel Itzkovitz, and Ann Pellegrini. "Strange Bedfellows: An Introduction." In Boyarin, Itzkovitz, and Pellegrini, *Queer Theory,* 1–4.
Branfman, Jonathan. "Failed Fatherhood and the 'Trap of Ambivalence': Assimilation, Homonormativity, and Effeminophobia in *The New Normal.*" *Journal of Homosexuality* 66 (12, 2019): 1671–92.
Brown, Shane. *Queer Sexualities in Early Film: Cinema and Male–Male Intimacy.* London: I.B. Tauris, 2016.
Buerkle, Darcy. *Nothing Happened: Charlotte Solomon and an Archive of Suicide.* Ann Arbor: University of Michigan Press, 2013.
Bunzl, Matti. "Jews, Queers, and Other Symptoms: Recent Work in Jewish Cultural Studies." *GLQ: A Journal of Lesbian and Gay Studies* 6 (2, 2000): 321–41.
———. *Symptoms of Modernity: Jews and Queers in Late Twentieth-Century Vienna.* Berkeley: University of California Press, 2004.
Currier, Ashley. *Politicizing Sex in Contemporary Africa: Homophobia in Malawi.* Cambridge: Cambridge University Press, 2018.
"Die Lehren eines Prozesses." *Allgemeine Zeitung des Judentums* 71 (45, 8 November 1907): 529–30. http://sammlungen.ub.uni-frankfurt.de/cm/periodical/titleinfo/3224737
Dose, Ralf. *Magnus Hirschfeld: The Origins of the Gay Liberation Movement,* trans. Edward H. Willis. New York: Monthly Review Press, 2014.
Dyer, Richard. "Less and More than Women and Men: Lesbian and Gay Cinema in Weimar Germany." *New German Critique* 51 (August 1990): 5–60.
Friedman, Sara. "Projecting Fears and Hopes: Gay Rights on the German Screen After World War I." *Journal of the History of Ideas Blog.* https://jhiblog.org/2019/05/28/projecting-fears-and-hopes-the-1919-anders-als-die-andern-controversy/
Friedmann, Walther. "Homosexuality and Jewishness: The Latest Method of Agitation against 'Aufklärungsfilme.'" *Film-Kurier,* 13 July 1919, trans. Nicholas Baer. In *The*

Promise of Cinema: German Film Theory, 1907–1933, ed. Anton Kaes, Nicholas Baer, and Michael Cowan, 240–42. Oakland: University of California Press, 2016.

Gilman, Sander. *Difference and Pathology: Stereotypes of Sexuality, Race, and Madness*. Ithaca, NY: Cornell University Press, 1985.

———. *The Jew's Body*. New York: Routledge, 1991.

Gunning, Tom. "The Cinema of Attractions: Early Film, its Spectator, and the Avant Garde." In *Early Cinema: Space, Frame, Narrative*, ed. Thomas Elsaesser and Adam Barker, 56–62. London: British Film Institute, 1990.

Herzer, Manfred. *Magnus Hirschfeld und seine Zeit*. Berlin: Walter de Gruyter, 2017.

J. Sch. "Umschau: 'Unerhörter Mißbrauch des Kinos.'" *Im Deutschen Reich: Zeitschrift des Zentralvereins deutscher Staatsbürger jüdischen Glaubens* 25 (9, September 1919): 367–68. http://sammlungen.ub.uni-frankfurt.de/cm/periodical/titleinfo/2316602

K. "Ein Skandal!" *Deutsche Zeitung* 24.318, 11 July 1919.

Kasten, Jürgen. "Dramatische Instinkte und das Spektakel der Aufklärung: Richard Oswalds Filme der 10er-Jahre." In *Richard Oswald: Kino zwischen Spektakel, Aufklärung und Unterhaltung*, ed. Jürgen Kasten and Armin Loacker. Vienna: Filmarchiv Austria, 2005.

Kreimeier, Klaus. "Aufklärung, Kommerzialismus und Demokratie, oder: der Bankrott des deutschen Mannes." In *Richard Oswald: Regisseur und Produzent*, ed. Helga Balach and Wolfgang Jacobsen, 9–18. Munich: Edition Text & Kritik, 1990.

Linge, Ina. "Sexology, Popular Science and Queer History in *Anders als die Andern* (Different from the Others)." *Gender and History* 30 (3, October 2018): 595–610.

Malakaj, Ervin. "Richard Oswald, Magnus Hirschfeld and the Possible Impossibility of Hygienic Melodrama." *Studies in European Cinema* 14 (3, 2017): 216–30.

Mancini, Elena. *Magnus Hirschfeld and the Quest for Sexual Freedom: A History of the First International Sexual Freedom Movement*. New York: Palgrave Macmillan, 2010.

Marhoefer, Laurie. *Sex and the Weimar Republic: German Homosexual Emancipation and the Rise of the Nazis*. Toronto: University of Toronto Press, 2015.

Mosse, George. *Nationalism and Sexuality: Middle-Class Morality and Sexual Norms in Modern Europe*. Madison: University of Wisconsin Press, 1985.

Niewyk, Donald L. "The German Jews in Revolution and Revolt 1918–19." In *Studies in Contemporary Jewry*, vol. 4, *The Jews and the European Crisis, 1914–1921*, ed. Jonathan Frankel, Peter Y. Medding, and Ezra Mendelsohn, 41–66. Oxford: Oxford University Press, 1988.

"Noch eine Lektion." *Allgemeine Zeitung des Judentums* 71.51 (20 December 1907): 601–2. http://sammlungen.ub.uni-frankfurt.de/cm/periodical/titleinfo/3224737.

Nowak, Kai. *Projektionen der Moral: Filmskandale in der Weimarer Republik*. Göttingen: Wallstein, 2015. bookcentral.proquest.com/lib/uc/reader.action?docID=4341022&ppg=519

Prawer, S.S. *Between Two Worlds: The Jewish Presence in German and Austrian Film 1910–1933*. New York: Berghahn Books, 2005.

Ramsey, Glenn. "The Rites of Artgenossen: Contesting Homosexual Political Culture in Weimar Germany." *Journal of the History of Sexuality* 17 (1, January 2008): 85–109.

Rosenberg, Alfred. "Juden, Judentzer und Deutsche." *Auf gut Deutsch: Wochenschrift für Ordnung und Recht* 1 (40–41, December 1919): 634–43. http://sammlungen.ub.uni-frankfurt.de/cm/periodical/titleinfo/9443879

Schorr, Thomas. "Die Film-und Kinoreformbewegung und die deutsche Filmwirtschaft. Eine Analyse des Fachblatts ‚Der Kinematograph' (1907–1935) unter pädagogischen und publizistischen Aspekten." Dissertation. Submitted to the Universität der Bundeswehr, Munich, Department of Pedagogy, Institute of Media Pedagogy, 13 November 1989.

Sedgwick, Eve Kosofsky. *Epistemology of the Closet*. Berkeley: University of California Press, 1990.

Silverman, Lisa. *Becoming Austrians: Jews and Culture between the World Wars*. Oxford: Oxford University Press, 2012.

———. "Beyond Antisemitism: A Critical Approach to German Jewish Cultural History." In *Nexus 1: Essays in German Jewish Studies*, 27–45. Rochester, NY: Camden House, 2011.

———. "Reconsidering the Margins: Jewishness as an Analytical Framework." *Journal of Modern Jewish Studies* 8 (1, March 2009): 103–20.

Smith, Jill Suzanne. "Richard Oswald and the Social Hygiene Film: Promoting Public Health or Promiscuity?" In *The Many Faces of Weimar Cinema: Rediscovering Germany's Filmic Legacy*, ed. Christian Rogowski, 13–30. Rochester, NY: Camden House, 2010.

Spector, Scott. "Modernism Without Jews: A Counter-Historical Argument." *Modernism/Modernity* 13 (4, November 2006): 615–33.

———. *Violent Sensations: Sex, Crime, and Utopia in Vienna and Berlin 1860–1914*. Chicago: University of Chicago Press, 2017.

Star. "Jüdischer Film." *Jüdische Korrespondenz: Wochenblatt für jüdische Interessen*. 5 (25, 18 July 1919): 2–3. http://sammlungen.ub.uni-frankfurt.de/cm/periodical/titleinfo/3495418

———. "Jüdischer Film." *Jüdische Korrespondenz* 5 (31, 22 August 1919): 2–3. http://sammlungen.ub.uni-frankfurt.de/cm/periodical/titleinfo/3495418

Steakley, James D. *"Anders als die Andern": Ein Film und seine Geschichte*. Hamburg: Männerschwarm, 2007.

———. "Cinema and Censorship in the Weimar Republic: The Case of *Anders als Die Andern*." *Film History* 11 (2, 1999): 181–203.

Sutcliffe, Adam. "Judaism and the Politics of Enlightenment." *The American Behavioral Scientist* 49 (5, January 2006): 702–15.

Sutton, Katie. *Sex between Body and Mind: Psychoanalysis and Sexology in the German-speaking World, 1890s–1930s*. Ann Arbor: University of Michigan Press, 2019.

Theis, Wolfgang. "Schünzels Requisiten. Zum Beispiel: die Handschuhe." In *Reinhold Schünzel: Schauspieler und Regisseur (revisited)*, ed. Jörg Schöning and Erika Wottrich, 33–36. Munich: Edition Text & Kritik, 2009.

Tobin, Robert Deam. *Peripheral Desires: The German Discovery of Sex*. Philadelphia: University of Pennsylvania Press, 2015.

Volkov, Shulamit. "Antisemitism as a Cultural Code—Reflections on the History and Historiography of Antisemitism in Imperial Germany." *Leo Baeck Yearbook* 23 (1978): 25–46.

Wallach, Kerry. *Passing Illusions: Jewish Visibility in Weimar Cinema*. Ann Arbor: University of Michigan Press, 2017.

Weininger, Otto. *Geschlecht und Charakter: Eine prinzipielle Untersuchung*. Vienna: Wilhelm Braumüller, 1903.

Weinstein, Valerie. *Antisemitism in Film Comedy in Nazi Germany*. Bloomington: Indiana University Press, 2019.

Whisnant, Clayton J. *Queer Identities and Politics in Germany: A History 1880–1945*. New York: Harrington Park Press, 2016.

Chapter 8

DER FILM OHNE JUDEN: G.W. PABST'S *DIE FREUDLOSE GASSE* (1925)

Lisa Silverman

> And there is the very brief shot of two coats hanging on neighbouring pegs—the one poor and threadbare, the other a dainty grey fur which will have to be paid for in kind.
> —Lotte H. Eisner, *The Haunted Screen*

The scene that film critic Lotte H. Eisner describes above appears in one of the most celebrated films of Weimar cinema: G.W. Pabst's *Die freudlose Gasse* (1925, dir. G.W. Pabst) (figure 8.1).[1] Highly regarded for its originality, artistic merit, and biting social commentary on class and gender, the film focuses on the struggles of several women as they attempt to feed their families, navigate rigid social orders, and maintain their dignity in the midst of economic crisis and misogynist objectification. In this scene, the coats symbolize the limited choices faced by one of those women, the film's protagonist Grete Rumfort (played by Greta Garbo), the impoverished daughter of an Austrian civil servant whose family is facing starvation. Choosing the threadbare coat will allow her to remain morally pure, while opting for the luxurious fur coat comes at the price of turning her body into a commodity in order to feed her family. Although she dons the fur coat and takes the first step on the path to prostitution, at the end of the film a brave, handsome American army lieutenant wraps the coat tenderly around her shoulders, signaling that he has saved her from the debauched life it symbolizes, enabling her to escape from prostitution and uphold her virtue.

As a critic, Eisner had little patience with what she viewed as Pabst's simplistic use of expressionist symbolism. But the reception of this melo-

Der Film ohne Juden: G.W. Pabst's Die freudlose Gasse *(1925)* 179

Figure 8.1. Screenshot from *Die freudlose Gasse* (1925, dir. G.W. Pabst).

drama as a masterpiece of Weimar cinema suggests that such stark juxtapositions helped the film transmit its critique of greed, misogyny, and general cold-heartedness to broad audiences. In this context, Grete's fur bears even more of a symbolic burden. In an era when women strove to have "at least a touch of fur" on their clothes, a fur coat was an expensive luxury item and fashion signifier that lay beyond the grasp of many who desired it.[2] Moreover, as a literary device, fur had long served to evoke erotic appeal, as in Austrian author Leopold Sacher-Masoch's *Venus im Pelz* (*Venus in Furs*), first published in 1869, which explicitly describes the ability of fur to spur arousal.[3] Assistant director Marc Sorkin recalls that it was Maurice Stiller, the Swedish-Jewish director who mentored Greta Garbo, who suggested to Pabst that the coat should be made of fur.[4] Stiller himself was known for wearing an ankle-length, yellow fur coat trimmed with a black collar and belt, along with gold and pearl tie pins and other precious accoutrements as part of his own, unconventional self-stylization.[5]

Yet this chapter argues that the full rhetorical force of fur as a symbol of wealth and seduction in *Die freudlose Gasse* hinges in particular on its association with women who are coded as Jewish.[6] By the time Grete is first coaxed into trying on that fur, the audience has already seen three women in fur coats: Frau Rosenow, the wife of a wealthy banker who has earned his money at the expense of poor Austrians; their daughter Regina Rosenow, who is looking for an equally wealthy husband; and Lia Leid, who has risen from the working class to marry a rich lawyer and is now eager to seduce Egon Stirner, a clerk employed by Rosenow. Unlike the book on which it is based, the film never explicitly states that these women are Jewish, but their Jewish-sounding names (Lia is akin to Leah, and audiences would have recognized Rosenow as a Jewish name), dark and curly hair, interest in money and jewelry, conniving spirits, and their furs are enough to subtly code them as such. In one of the film's first scenes, set in a fancy hotel, all three women arrive wearing fur coats. There, both Regina and Lia attempt to seduce Stirner, finally striking something of an "erotic deal," according to which Lia will have an affair with him while also giving him the money he needs to be maritally palatable to Regina.[7]

In this context, the fur coats serve as important markers not only of status but also of these women's seductive, materialistic, and cold-hearted goals—Lia and Regina pursue exploitative relationships and all three women are recipients of unearned or ill-gotten wealth—which in turn reflect common stereotypes of Jewish women that were often used as rhetorical devices in European culture.[8] The symbolic weight of fur is furthered by its long association with Jews, who played a major role in the European fur trade for centuries.[9] In early twentieth-century Austria, 67 percent of furriers were Jews, as were 70 percent of those who worked in the clothing industry as a whole, resulting in not just fur but all luxury and fashionable items of apparel being coded as Jewish.[10] Jewish women thus often bore the brunt of responsibility for the marketing *and* consumption of luxury items in twentieth-century central Europe.

The fur coats are just one example of how *Die freudlose Gasse* relies on unarticulated codes of Jewish difference to strengthen the explicit critique of gender and class norms for which it is so celebrated. On the surface, the film has nothing to do with Jews or Jewish topics. But linking luxury, materialism, fashion, and prostitution with Jewish-coded women helped ensure its success in powerfully criticizing oppressive social norms, economic strife, and urban corruption. Such negative codings of the "Jewish" as inferior to the "non-Jewish" were commonplace in interwar central Europe, characterizing not only overtly antisemitic acts but also much culture created by both Jews and non-Jews, often in collaboration. It was not unusual for Jews in the film industry to dismiss or downplay Jewishness in their films, if they mentioned it at all.[11] Examining how this particular film's subtle codings of Jewish difference emerged from more-explicit manifestations in the novel and screenplay on which it was based allows us to see how eliminating the explicit Jewishness of characters in the film did not lessen the powerful role Jewish difference played in its critiques of class, economics, and gender. At the same time, suppressing the novel's and screenplay's explicit Jewish characters—particularly, its Jewish women—perpetuated their scapegoating as receptacles for society's fears.

However, while explicitly Jewish characters and antisemitism play a central role in Jewish-born Viennese writer Hugo Bettauer's 1924 novel *Die freudlose Gasse. Ein Wiener Roman aus unseren Tagen*, Willy Haas, the film's Prague-born Jewish screenwriter, suppressed some of the novel's specifically Jewish characters and themes. (He embellished others, but his additions did not make it into the final film.)[12] As many scholars have noted, both Jewish and non-Jewish writers and filmmakers of this era deployed stereotypes about Jews for a variety of reasons, whether to make sure their points resonated with broad audiences or to criticize the society that created them. Examining how Bettauer and Haas used positive and negative stereotypes about Jews in their respective versions of this narrative will help us better understand the implications of the absence of explicitly Jewish characters from Pabst's film, as well as their subtle yet unarticulated presence.

This examination rests on the ways that interwar central European culture, regardless of whether it was created or consumed by Jews or non-Jews, relied on constructed categories of Jewish difference—according to which the "Jewish" is subordinate to the "non-Jewish"—as a powerful framework to buttress arguments, attitudes, and anxieties about class and gender. Using the term "Jewish difference" as an analytical category, as I do here, calls for exploring how a text engages all of these constructed categories, which themselves are constantly evolving and overlapping depending on time and place. Even though there are—and were—no fixed definitions of the "Jewish" and "non-Jewish," we simply cannot overlook the fact that central Europeans relied on and clung to an often unspoken belief in the existence of these binary essences as tightly as they clung to the nonexistent and yet nevertheless inescapable ideals of the "masculine" and "feminine."[13]

Because the film *Die freudlose Gasse* does not name any Jewish characters or themes, we cannot determine how it uses the Jewish/not-Jewish binary on the basis of explicitly visible Jews and Jewish content. However, when we examine how the novel and screenplay deployed or repressed explicitly Jewish characters, we can see that Jewish difference still played an important role in boosting the film's critique of unscrupulous speculation, social decay, and the paucity of choices for women, albeit by subtly hinting at negative stereotypes about Jews without explicitly referencing either antisemitism or its particular effects on Jewish women. By removing Jews but keeping Jewish difference, the film transforms a novel that offers a sympathetic view regarding the plight of Jewish women into a narrative that further demonizes them.

Darcy Buerkle's scholarship highlights the significant role of Jewish visibility—and invisibility—in a number of central European films from the 1920s that focus on Jewish secular life and assimilation. Using the 1923 film *Das Alte Gesetz* as an example, she argues that Weimar cinema served as an important venue for the visualization of unspoken emotions that are palpable yet unarticulated in texts by German Jews. Buerkle, Cynthia Walk, Valerie Weinstein, and Ofer Ashkenazi have traced how German Jews used film to transform their concerns about assimilation, authenticity, and self-identification into powerful narratives that resonated with audiences far beyond the relative tiny percentage of Jews in the population.[14] Building on this scholarship, I suggest that this film's suppression of explicit Jewish characters and subtle engagement with the codes of Jewish difference arose from a combination of concerns about Jews—and Jewish women in particular—shared by the Jewish and non-Jewish men who contributed to the film's production, as well as the novel and screenplay on which it was based. Examining all three—the novel, the screenplay, and the film—illuminates how Jewish difference served as a crucial framework for conveying messages that would resonate forcefully with broad audiences, even when its presence was not explicit.

The Novel

Most scholars echo screenwriter Willy Haas's low opinion of the literary merits of Bettauer's novel, preferring what they consider the artistic genius of Pabst's film, which they see as less melodramatic, sensationalist, and narrow, and more sharply critical of societal ills.[15] But these evaluations overlook the way Jewish characters and antisemitism are important to the novel's plot. Bettauer sets his story in Vienna's seventh district during the interwar period, when the area was known for its mix of Jewish and non-Jewish residents. The action takes place on a fictional street, the Melchiorgasse, where the lives of several men and women of various classes intersect. The plot hinges on Otto Demel, a journalist and newspaper editor, as he investigates the murder of Lia Leid, who grew up in a poor Jewish family but married a wealthy lawyer. Demel's profession and his reputation for caustic wit correspond to Bettauer's own personal history, suggesting that he is something of an autobiographical character, and thus has some degree of Jewish origin (Bettauer converted to Protestantism in 1890).[16]

In the course of his reporting, Demel rents a room in the Melchiorgasse from Grete Rumfort, the daughter of an Austrian civil servant, whose family, like many in the city, is now in dire financial circumstances. Down the street, a fashion boutique run by Frau Greifer serves as a front to a boozy nightclub/bordello, for which Greifer serves as the madam. Although the book never mentions Greifer's religion, Jewish women were associated with both fashion and brothels.[17] Other characters include the impoverished Marie Lechner, daughter of an abusive working-class father, and Mr. Rosenow, a wealthy eastern European Jewish bank director, and his wife. Egon Stirner, Rosenow's clerk, openly courts his daughter Regina while secretly carrying on affairs with both Lia and Marie. When Lia is murdered, Egon is falsely accused of committing the crime, but Regina stands by her lover. We eventually learn that Marie murdered Lia in an act of jealous, antisemitic rage. Marie dies from illness and drug addiction soon after her confession, while Demel rescues Grete from work as a prostitute for Greifer. In the final pages, the two move away from the Melchiorgasse to one of Vienna's outer districts.

The novel caused a sensation when it first appeared as a serial in the Viennese newspaper *Der Tag* between October and December 1923. At a time of deep economic crisis, audiences were eager for a story that highlighted the difficulties of the middle and working classes, the problems caused by financial corruption, and the particular disadvantages of the circumstances for women. The serial became the talk of the town, and when the book was published in its entirety, it sold 30,000 copies.[18]

It was no accident that Bettauer chose a mix of Jewish and non-Jewish characters to drive his narrative of urban greed, corruption, and crime. As noted above, Jews, and in particular Jewish women, occupied a special place in the central European cultural imagination. Beginning in the 1920s, linking the New Woman to sexuality, consumerism, and greed via Jewishness underscored claims that she was a danger to society.[19] This sense of danger could be deployed for or against Jewish women—and sometimes even both at once. Weimar-era articles and advertisements often featured positive representations of independent women who, as Darcy Buerkle notes, were often coded as just Jewish enough (for instance, with dark or curly hair) to stimulate consumer desire.[20] These images flipped the generally negative casting of Jewish women as the ultimate consumers both to please Jewish women, who positively identified with them, and to attract non-Jewish women, who embraced the Jewish woman's consumer savvy, even if they scorned Jewish qualities in other situations.

To some extent, these attitudes toward Jewish women echoed the general misogyny of and fears within Austrian society as the emergence of the New Woman pushed gender boundaries. However, Jewish women served as particularly powerful receptacles for these anxieties, having been associated with conspicuous consumption since around 1900, when Jewish and non-Jewish men began to blame them for fulfilling popular antisemitic stereotypes of Jewish materialism, cosmopolitanism, and superficiality. Along with his even more popular 1922 novel *Die Stadt ohne Juden,* which I have discussed elsewhere, the characterizations and plot of *Die freudlose Gasse* indicate that Bettauer was well aware of the way Jewish women provoked this fear in the cultural imagination and was prepared to deploy its consequences in his narratives.[21] Indeed, the openly Jewish characters Regina and Lia dominate the first chapter of *Die freudlose Gasse* as seductive and dangerous objects of men's anxieties who are attractive, wealthy, and morally questionable. Meanwhile, although Frau Rosenow, Regina's mother, is unattractive and loyal to her husband, she is still overly concerned with society and etiquette and becomes embarrassing in her failed efforts to gain social status.

Bettauer briefly describes Rosenow as a nouveau riche Jew from Bielitz (Poland), who changes his name from Rosenstrauch after the war and becomes a wealthy real estate magnate and banker. Rosenow barely hides his Jewish roots and sometimes speaks Yiddish. However, Bettauer devotes significantly more narrative space to Regina, who conforms to society's stereotypes about wealthy, assimilated Jewish woman in many ways, including her management of the family's social engagements: "And now, at the instigation of his daughter Regina, who quite lately had been singing Leopoldi and Wiesenthal's latest hit, 'Yes, We Have No Bananas,' to the gentlemen who sat round her in in the little bourgeois drawing-room, he was giving his first big party. The slim vivacious girl, who excelled her parents in stature as much as in education and intellect, had in inviting the guests, cleverly scattered a dozen authors, painters, musicians, and even a journalist among the eminences of the banking and financial world."[22]

While Regina's social and musical know-how would not have been taken seriously at the time as evidence of either intellect or stature, scholars have subsequently argued that the Jewish women who organized informal salons like Regina's actually did much more than provide mere social backdrops for others. They helped foster original intellectual ideas, artistic movements, and women's political, social, and, intellectual engagement.[23] Bettauer, however, would have known that the contemporary negative stereotype of the Jewish woman as a superficial, if cunning, salon host figured prominently in the public imagination.

Lia Holzer, by contrast, is "a poor typist of obscure Jewish family,"[24] who lacks Regina's advantages of inherited wealth, education, and intellect. Lia is even more superficial than Regina and an inattentive wife with no maternal instinct to boot: "But Lia had no children and did not want any. . . . [She] flung herself into social life, dances when he's at work, yawns with boredom when he comes home tired, and does not read the books he leaves her. . . . [She] had nothing in her pretty little head but clothes, tea-parties, motor-drives, theaters and balls."[25] Lia is, if anything, even less sympathetic than Regina, suggesting that class has its rewards, even for Jews.

Some see Bettauer's representations as mere repetitions of negative Jewish stereotypes.[26] But while Bettauer was not exactly a feminist writer, in the novel's final scenes, he expresses sympathy for the plight of these women and thus highlights how misogyny and antisemitism place the blame for greed, corruption and morality squarely on Jewish women. One crucial scene reveals that for Demel, "Lia Leid and Regina Rosenow were, for him, the typical modern married woman and the typical modern girl" in that they had abandoned old-fashioned ideas of morality and paired with men into unhappy unions. In contrast, Grete Rumfort, is "cut from other wood."[27]

The novel's engagement with Jewish difference—which posits the "Jewish" as negative and the "non-Jewish" as positive—could not be clearer in this juxtaposition. But Bettauer also uses these remarks to critique Demel's fears. Even as Demel pities the poor, non-Jewish women who have little financial choice but to become prostitutes, his interactions with modern Jewish women make him afraid of intimate unions and eager to blame them for their failure. Later in the novel, however, Demel revises his original attitudes toward Jewish women in the face of Regina's reaction to the jailing of her lover Egon. When, instead of reacting angrily and petulantly, Regina stands by Egon out of love, despite the protests of her parents, Demel realizes that his perception of the radical differences between girls who are modern, overly cultivated, and immoral (i.e., Jewish) and girls with old-fashioned values (that is, non-Jewish) is in fact a misperception.

While Grete serves as Regina's non-Jewish, bourgeois counterpart, Lia's alter ego is the working-class Marie, a "perfect example of the Viennese slum girl who has had the fortune or misfortune to be beautiful" and whose father is an "honest laborer."[28] At the end of the novel, Marie, severely ill and coughing up blood, confesses at trial to having murdered Lia. Marie has always been jealous of Lia's finer clothing, and hated her for her condescending and humiliating manner—and her Jewishness. Indeed, her illness and poverty combined with her depiction of Lia as a "schönes, kokettes Judenmädel" (beautiful, coquette Jewish girl) who had insulted her as a common working-class girl, garners sympathy from the jury—and, perhaps, from some readers—and leads to her acquittal.[29] But for some readers, Marie's antisemitism makes her less sympathetic and serves to temper the otherwise wholly negative depiction of Lia, suggesting a critique of antisemitism.

Before his untimely death in 1925, Hugo Bettauer was one of the few men in Vienna who made a point of publicly opposing misogyny and championing the rights of women, as well as openly opposing antisemitism. In *Die Stadt ohne Juden*, Bettauer uses stereotypes about Jews to explicitly criticize antisemitism, for the novel's glaring lack of Jewish women characters serves as a means to critique Jewish and non-Jewish men who blame Jewish women for the ills of modern society and for antisemitism.[30] *Die freudlose Gasse* deliberately places Jewish women in prominent roles. Although Bettauer deploys negative stereotypes in their characterizations, their prominence and the critical moments when they belie those stereotypes suggest that Bettauer sees through those who view Jewish women as receptacles for their own anxieties about gender, marriage, and money, rather than as complex individuals in their own right.[31]

The Screenplay

Prague-born screenwriter, journalist, and editor Willy Haas claimed that his goal in adapting Bettauer's novel was to replace the overly romantic plot with factual and objective reporting about real life.[32] Given this statement, it is curious to note that his adaptation eliminates Lia's explicit Jewishness (and downplays her role altogether), while embellishing the Rosenows'. Haas's descriptions of Jews are in many ways as stereotypical as Bettauer's. Whereas in the novel Mrs. Rosenow is a "small, fat lady with a round, friendly face," Haas's screenplay describes her as a "small, fat, very pleasant Jewess," indicating that he thought it important for the audience to recognize her Jewishness.[33] Haas also adds a scene in which the wealthy Mr. Rosenow offers starving children cash and sweets, after which a flashback shows him *jüdelnd* (haggling "like a Jew") with a farmer for clothing at a cold winter market while his wife and little Regina try to stay warm.[34] These scenes complicate the Rosenows and their Jewishness, depicting a common negative stereotype about haggling Jews from eastern Europe, while also humanizing them by revealing Rosenow's generosity and the family's humble origins.

At other points, however, Haas's depiction of Rosenow is hardly as forgiving. For example, he elaborates on the magnate's connections to Frau Greifer, both as a client of her bordello and as a former clothing salesman, that is, through prostitution and the textile industry, both of which had strong negative associations with Jews.[35] Other versions of Haas's screenplay also mock Rosenow as having a "goldenes jüdisches Herz" (golden Jewish heart) that sentimentally breaks when he discovers Grete is in dire need of money.[36] This quickly repairs itself into "jüdischer Skepsis" (Jewish skepticism) when he realizes she nevertheless has no intention of becoming his lover.[37] Rosenow subsequently jokes "Jewishly," ("jüdische Witzelei") that if Grete wants a starring role in a film, he will discuss it with Ernst Lubitsch—surely a dig at the well-known Jewish director.[38]

At the same time that Haas underscored and extended some of the novel's Jewish elements, he eliminated others. For example, he replaced Otto Demel, the Jewish-coded journalist at the novel's core, with Lieutenant Davy, an American officer and Red Cross worker who, unlike Demel, focuses only on Grete. Davy is strong, neutral, and, most importantly, not coded as Jewish, which further links him to Grete and distances him from the novel's Jewish characters. Haas also moved Melchiorgasse, the street where the story takes place, from Vienna's seventh district (Neubau), a mixed residential area inhabited by Jews, non-Jews, the petit bourgeois, and the working class, to the sixteenth district (Ottakring), a more homogenous and proletarian residential area. This change serves to intensify the contrast between Melchiorgasse and the wealthy, Jewish-coded first district, where the women arrive at the luxury hotel in their furs, among other such scenes.[39] He also downplays Regina and Lia's roles in the narrative, omitting an entire chapter about Regina, and not only erasing Lia's Jewishness, but also practically eliminating her character; she appears only briefly in the screenplay. Meanwhile, Grete Rumfort and the working-class Marie take center stage, joined by major new non-Jewish characters, such as the butcher Geiringer and the working-class Else. One newspaper speculated that Haas replaced Demel with Davy to avoid the implications of the common stereotype of effete Jewish men or to appeal to American audiences.[40] But whatever his rationale, his adaptation abandoned the novel's explicit engagement with misogyny and antisemitism, largely experienced and voiced by Demel.

Haas's other writings suggests that his decision to downplay Demel's Jewishness and emphasize the Rosenows' may have had deeper roots. When Haas contributed a chapter on writer Hugo von Hofmannsthal (whose grandfather was a prominent Jew, though he was raised Catholic by his converted parents) to Gustav Krojanker's 1922 volume *Juden in der deutschen Literatur*, Hofmannsthal apparently objected strongly to its depiction of the Jewish elements in his writing. After it was published, Hofmannsthal wrote to Haas, declaring that their friendship was over and urging him to give up his profession as a literary critic. Haas said it was the "most horrible" letter he had ever received, and turned to screenwriting and *Die freudlose Gasse*.[41]

As this incident suggests, Haas was well aware of the stigma associated with labeling a person or text as Jewish, and his screenplay reflected his engagement with that very issue. In his memoirs, Haas claims to understand what led some Jewish writers to antisemitism. In an appropriately lightly ironic tone, he suggests that there is no finer, more complicated, and more interesting topic for Jewish irony than Jewish irony itself, which leads to Jews' adoption of antisemitism.[42] This statement, like his experience with Hofmannsthal, indicates that Haas understood the complexities of Jews writing about Jews. Labeling the inclusion of negative stereotypes about Jews in his own writing as outright antisemitism thus overlooks his—and other Jewish writers of his era's—more nuanced engagement with Jewish difference. But it was his efforts to downplay, rather than augment, Jewishness that would prove crucial to the final cut of the film.

The Film

Haas's amplifications of the Rosenows' Jewishness never made it into the final film of *Die freudlose Gasse*, though his downplaying of Regina and Lia and suppression of their explicit Jewishness remained on the screen. Despite his efforts, however, Regina and Lia's dark hair, conniving spirits, anxieties about social status, and interest in money, furs, and jewelry still coded them as Jews for the film's audience, and thus boosted the film's criticism of greed, consumption, and corruption. As noted above, coding Frau Rosenow, Regina, and Lia as Jewish activates the binary of Jewish difference (negative "Jewish" and positive "non-Jewish"), which in turn generates sympathy for the non-Jewish women who come into contact with them in the film. Unlike the novel, then, the film perpetuates the scapegoating of Jewish women as receptacles for society's fears, rather than critiquing their vilification.

Lia's status in the film is particularly significant to this shift. Besides removing Lia's Jewishness and marginalizing her role, the film renames the novel's character Marie, her impoverished proletarian rival, Maria, rendering her conspicuously Christian. Because Lia is not explicitly Jewish, however, Maria's antisemitism is submerged as a motive for her rage.[43] According to Patrice Petro, the film portrays Maria's murder as an act of rebellion against the instrumentalization of women. Petro lauds the film for addressing female audiences directly as it works to expose the social order that harms them.[44] However, the film's rejection of the novel's Jewishness and antisemitism lets viewers sympathize with Maria's hatred of Lia without being complicit in her antisemitic prejudices. In effect, it allows Jewish difference to do its work behind the scenes, underscoring the roles of Maria as victim and Lia as femme fatale, without exposing the antisemitism—individual and societal—of Maria's act of murder. This in turn forecloses any real engagement with the film's negative codings of Jews, and Jewish women, even in her confession.

It remains unclear who made the decision to scrub Jewishness from the final film, although it is likely that Haas and Pabst worked together to downplay the Jewish elements of the novel. Pabst had acquired the rights to a film based on S. Ansky's Yiddish play *Der Dybuk*, but he scrapped those plans to make *Die freudlose Gasse*. According to Mark Sorkin, the film's Russian Jewish editor, Pabst believed that a less explicitly Jewish film would be more lucrative and thus more desirable to his Russian Jewish investors.[45] This observation suggests that Pabst may have planned to eliminate the novel's Jewishness even before he commissioned the screenplay. Pabst also expressed interest in turning Arnold Zweig's 1912 play "Die Sendung Semaels," which was based on the false accusation of blood libel of Hungarian Jews in Tisza-Eszlar, into a film, suggesting his preference for philosemitic portrayals of Jews.[46] But regardless of who made those specific decisions, *Die freudlose Gasse* indicates that, in the Weimar era, the narrative power of encoding a character or theme as Jewish did not require overt representation. Rather, the association of Jews with parvenus, speculators, clothing marketers, pimps, and madams allowed such characters to figure as Jewish regardless of their explicit Jewishness, as they do in the novel, screenplay, and film discussed here. *Die freudlose Gasse* exemplifies how unarticulated tropes of Jewish difference enabled messages about unscrupulous speculation, social decay, and moral and spiritual decline to resonate forcefully with audiences.

Valerie Weinstein has argued that Jewish film directors such as Ernst Lubitsch often deployed antisemitic stereotypes as a means of exaggerating, mocking, and critiquing them, while Ofer Ashkenazi suggests that Lubitsch used stereotypes of Jews as a broad metaphor to critique the conservative middle class.[47] In many ways, Bettauer's novel *Die freudlose Gasse* echoed these aims, deploying negative stereotypes about Jews at least in part to critique how society scapegoated Jewish women. In downplaying the Jewishness of Lia and Regina, Haas's screenplay echoed most films of Weimar Germany, in which, as Kerry Wallach notes, "the most desirable Jewish female characters either were not coded as particularly Jewish or were barely visible at all."[48] However, it also removed Bettauer's critique, even as his embellishment of Mr. and Mrs. Rosenow's Jewishness helped to humanize Jews. While the portrayal of these characters in the novel and screenplay was not particularly positive, their overt Jewishness highlighted how antisemitism functioned to support society's fears about finance, gender, and modernity. By only subtly hinting at Jewishness, the film could use the narrative boost of Jewish difference to support its critique of oppressive social norms, economic strife, and urban corruption, without having to engage directly with that society's antisemitism. Viewers of the film would understand that materialism and excess consumption were bad because they were associated with Jews, but they would not have to question the social systems that scapegoated Jews in the first place. Once we see how Jewishness was scrubbed from the film, we can begin to understand how the powerful effects of Jewish difference continue to operate, even when they are hidden.

Lisa Silverman is associate professor of history and Jewish studies at the University of Wisconsin-Milwaukee. She serves as contributing editor for the *Leo Baeck Institute Year-Book* for German-Jewish history. She is author of *Becoming Austrians: Jews and Culture between the World Wars* (Oxford, 2012) and coauthor with Daniel H. Magilow of *Holocaust*

Representations in History an Introduction (Bloomsbury, 2015/2019). Her coedited volumes include *Austrian Studies 24: Jews, Jewish Difference and Austrian Culture: Literary and Historical Perspectives* (2016); *Making Place: Space and Embodiment in the City* (Indiana, 2014) and *Interwar Vienna: Culture between Tradition and Modernity* (Camden House, 2009).

Notes

1. Sabine Hake, *German National Cinema* (London, 1993), 39; Patrice Petro, *Aftershocks of the New: Feminism and Film History* (New Brunswick, NJ, 2002), 98–99.
2. Jenna Weissman Joselit, *A Perfect Fit: Clothes, Character, and the Promise of America* (New York, 2001), 149.
3. Sacher-Masoch may have been inspired by Peter Paul Rubens's portrait of his second wife Helene Fourment at Vienna's Kunsthistorisches Museum, "Het Pelsken" (The Little Fur; 1630s) in which she appears wearing a black fur that only partially covers her naked body. See Elana Shapira, "Gaze and Spectacle in the Calibration of Class and Gender: Visual Culture in Vienna 1900," in *A History of Visual Culture: Western Civilization from the 18th to the 21st Century*, ed. Jane Kromm and Susan Benforado Bakewell (Oxford, 2010), 159–60.
4. Gideon Bachman, "Interview with Marc Sorkin," *Cinemages* (1955), 29.
5. John Bainbridge, "Greta's Haunted Path to Stardom: A Hypnotic Director Made Over Even 'Her Very Soul,'" *Life*, 17 January 1955: 78.
6. For a discussion about the use of fur as a code for Jewish women's conspicuous consumption in popular culture, see Kerry Wallach, "Buy Me a Mink: Jews, Fur, and Conspicuous Consumption," in *Jewish Consumer Cultures in Nineteenth- and Twentieth-Century Europe and North America*, ed. Paul Lerner, Anne Schenderlein, and Uwe Spiekermann (New York, forthcoming.).
7. Alexandra Seibel, "Vienna, Girls, and Jewish Authorship: Topographies of a Cinematic City, 1920–40," PhD. Diss., New York University, 2009, 199–200.
8. See, e.g., Andrea Freud Loewenstein, *Loathsome Jews and Engulfing Women: Metaphors of Projection in the Works of Wyndham Lewis, Charles Williams, and Graham Greene* (New York, 1993); Nadia Valman, *The Jewess in Nineteenth-Century British Literary Culture* (Cambridge, UK, 2007); Florian Krobb, *Die schöne Jüdin: Jüdische Frauengestalten in der deutschsprachigen Erzählliteratur vom 17. Jahrhundert bis zum Ersten Weltkrieg* (Tübingen, 1993).
9. Mark Wischnitzer, "Origins of the Jewish Artisan Class in Bohemia and Moravia, 1500–1648," *Jewish Social Studies* 16, no. 4 (1954): 344. See also Wilhelm Harmelin, "Jews in the Leipzig Fur Industry," *Leo Baeck Institute Year Book* 9, no. 1 (1964).
10. Egon Schwarz, *Wien und die Juden: Essays zum Fin de Siècle* (Munich, 2014), 19.
11. Ofer Ashkenazi, *Weimar Film and Modern Jewish Identity* (New York, 2012), 4, 6. On the collaboration of Jews with non-Jews in Weimar cinema, see also S.S. Prawer, *Between Two Worlds: The Jewish Presence in German and Austrian Film, 1910–1933* (New York, 2005).
12. Of course, many scholars have pointed out that the film was heavily censored, making it difficult to thoroughly assess the actual content of the original version. See Jan-Christopher Horak, "Film History and Film Preservation: Reconstructing the Text of *The Joyless Street* (1925)," in *Screening the Past* 5, ed. Ina Bertrand (Melbourne, 1998).

See also Hugo Bettauer's novel, *Die freudlose Gasse* (Leipzig, 1924). The novel appeared in English translation as *Viennese Love* in 1929.
13. See Lisa Silverman, *Becoming Austrians: Jews and Culture between the World Wars* (New York, 2012).
14. See Darcy Buerkle, "Caught in the Act: Norbert Elias, Emotion, and *The Ancient Law*," *Journal of Modern Jewish Studies* 8, no. 1 (2009); Cynthia Walk, "Romeo with Sidelocks: Jewish-Gentile Romance in E.A. Dupont's *Das Alte Gesetz* (1923) and Other Early Weimar Assimilation Films," in *The Many Faces of Weimar Cinema: Rediscovering Germany's Filmic Legacy*, ed. Christian Rogowski (Rochester, 2010); Valerie Weinstein, "Dissolving Boundaries: Assimilation and Allosemitism in E.A. Dupont's *Das alte Gesetz* (1923) and Veit Harlan's *Jud Süss* (1940)," *German Quarterly* 78, no. 4 (2005); Ashkenazi, *Weimar Film*.
15. Sara Hall notes that changes were made to the film in order make it more appealing to broad, international audiences. Sara Hall, "Inflation and Devaluation: Gender, Space, and Economics in G.W. Pabst's The Joyless Street (1925)," in *Weimar Cinema: An Essential Guide to Classic Films of the Era*, ed. Noah Isenberg (New York, 2008), 138.
16. Murray G. Hall, *Der Fall Bettauer* (Vienna, 1978), 34.
17. Linking Jews with prostitution in central Europe was common, although likely overstated, in the early to mid-twentieth century. See Elizabeth Loentz, *Let Me Continue to Speak the Truth: Bertha Pappenheim as Author and Activist* (Cincinnati, 2007), 130–31. Moreover, the figure of the Jewish madam was a common literary trope in the novels of Jewish and non-Jewish authors in Vienna. For one example, see Else Jerusalem, *Der heilige Skarabäus* (Berlin, 1909).
18. Beth Simone Noveck, "Hugo Bettauer's Vienna 1918–1925," in *Jura Soyfer and his Time*, ed. Donald Daviau (Riverside, CA, 1995), 368.
19. Atina Grossmann, "The New Woman and the Rationalization of Sexuality in Weimar Germany," in *Powers of Desire: The Politics of Sexuality*, ed. Ann Snitow. (New York, 1983), 167.
20. Darcy Buerkle, "Gendered Spectatorship, Jewish Women, and Psychological Advertising in Weimar Germany," *Women's History Review* 15, no. 4 (2006): 631.
21. Silverman, *Becoming Austrians*, 84–85.
22. Hugo Bettauer, *Viennese Love*, trans. F.H. Lyon (New York: Macaulay, 1929): 17–18.
23. Emily Bilski and Emily Braun, ed., *Jewish Women and Their Salons: The Power of Conversation* (New York, 2005), 5–7.
24. Bettauer, *Viennese Love*, 22.
25. Bettauer, *Viennese Love*, 23.
26. Alexandra Rabl, "Hugo Bettauer's Wien: Stadtromane der Zwischenkriegszeit," Diplomarbeit, Mag. Phil, University of Vienna, (2013), 57; Siegfried Mattl, "Geldentwertung und moralische Revolte. Zeitgenössiche Kontexte der 'freudlosen Gasse'" in *Wien, die Inflation und das Elend*, ed. Armin Loacker (Vienna: Filmarchiv Austria, 2008), 108 n.3, 120.
27. Bettauer, *Viennese Love*, 136.
28. Bettauer, *Viennese Love*, 121.
29. Bettauer, *Viennese Love*, 121.
30. Silverman, *Becoming Austrians*, 66–102.
31. Silverman, *Becoming Austrians*, 66–102.
32. Willy Haas, "Die Krise der deutschen Filmindustrie," *Die Literarische Welt*, no. 7, 12 February 1926.
33. Willy Haas, "Die Freudlose Gasse," Regiebuch handgeschr., Inv. no.8/67, undated. Sammlung G.W. Pabst. Filmmuseum München, 39–40. *Die freudlose Gasse*, DVD

(Filmmuseum München, 2009). Unless otherwise noted, the translations are all by author.
34. Haas, "Die Freudlose Gasse," 51–53.
35. The screenplay indicates that Rosenow knew Greifer well. Haas, "Die Freudlose Gasse," 78. Although uncredited, in the film Frau Greifer is played by Jewish performer Valeska Gert, who was already known for playing both a prostitute and procuress/madam on stage. See Valeska Gert, *Ich bin eine Hexe. Kaleidoskop meines Lebens* (Munich, 1968), 57.
36. Willy Haas, "Die Freudlose Gasse," Regiebuch handgeschr. #3, undated. Sammlung G.W. Pabst. Filmmuseum München, 115. *Die freudlose Gasse*, DVD (Filmmuseum München, 2009).
37. Willy Haas, "Die Freudlose Gasse," Regiebuch, undated, Mark Sorkin Collection, Film Study Center, Museum of Modern Art, New York, 28. *Die freudlose Gasse*, DVD (Filmmuseum München, 2009).
38. Haas, "Die Freudlose Gasse," Regiebuch, Mark Sorkin Collection, 29.
39. Haas, "Die Freudlose Gasse," Regiebuch handgeschr., Inv. no.8/67, 30. The film switches the site back to Melchiorgasse in the seventh district, however.
40. *Süddeutsche Film-Zeitung*, no. 27, 28 April 1925, 3.
41. Haas, "Willy Haas," in *Das Bin Ich*, ed. Ernst Deutsch, Hannes Reinhardt, et al. (Munich: Piper, 1970), 70–71.
42. Haas, "Die Krise der deutschen Filmindustrie," 24.
43. On Jewish women as femmes fatales, see Janis Bergman-Carton, "Negotiating the Categories: Sarah Bernhardt and the Possibilities of Jewishness," *Art Journal* 55, no. 2 (Summer, 1996); Bram Dijkstra, *Idols of Perversity: Fantasies of Feminine Evil in Fin-de-siècle Culture* (New York, 1986).
44. Patrice Petro, *Joyless Streets: Women and Melodramatic representation in Weimar Germany* (Princeton, NJ, 1992), 209–19.
45. "Errinerungen des Regieassistenten Mark Sorkin," *Die freudlose Gasse*, DVD (Filmmuseum München, 2009).
46. See Lisa Silverman, "Absent Jews and Invisible Antisemitism in Postwar Vienna: *Der Prozess* (1948) and *The Third Man* (1949)," *Journal of Contemporary History* 52:2 (2017): 211–28.
47. Valerie Weinstein, "Anti-Semitism or Jewish 'Camp'? Ernst Lubitsch's *Schuhpalast Pinkus* (1916) and *Meyer aus Berlin* (1918)," *German Life and Letters* 59, no. 1 (2006); Ashkenazi, *Weimar Film*, 173, n50.
48. Kerry Wallach, *Passing Illusions: Jewish Visibility in Weimar Germany* (Ann Arbor, 2017), 95.

Bibliography

Ashkenazi, Ofer. *Weimar Film and Modern Jewish Identity*. New York: Palgrave Macmillan, 2012.
Bachmann, Gideon. "Interview with Marc Sorkin." *Cinemages* 29 (1955): 23–40.
Bainbridge, John. "Greta's Haunted Path to Stardom: A Hypnotic Director Made Over Even 'Her Very Soul.'" *Life* 17 (January 1955): 76–90.
Bergman-Carton, Janis. "Negotiating the Categories: Sarah Bernhardt and the Possibilities of Jewishness." *Art Journal* 55 (2, Summer, 1996): 55–64.
Bettauer, Hugo. *Die freudlose Gasse*. Leipzig: Wien, 1924.

———. *Viennese Love*, trans. F.H. Lyon. New York: Macaulay, 1929.
Bilski, Emily, and Emily Braun, ed. *Jewish Women and Their Salons: The Power of Conversation*. New York: Jewish Museum New York, 2005.
Buerkle, Darcy. "Caught in the Act: Norbert Elias, emotion, and *The Ancient Law*." *Journal of Modern Jewish Studies* 8 (1, 2009): 83–102.
———. "Gendered Spectatorship, Jewish Women, and Psychological Advertising in Weimar Germany." *Women's History Review* 15 (4, 2006): 625–36.
Dijkstra, Bram. *Idols of Perversity: Fantasies of Feminine Evil in Fin-de-siècle Culture*. New York: Oxford University Press, 1986.
Eisner, Lotte H. *The Haunted Screen*. Berkeley: University of California Press, 1969.
"Errinerungen des Regieassistenten Mark Sorkin." *Die freudlose Gasse*, DVD, edition Filmmuseum München, 2009.
Gert, Valeska. *Ich bin eine Hexe. Kaleidoskop meines Lebens*. Munich: Schneekluth, 1968.
Grossmann, Atina. "The New Woman and the Rationalization of Sexuality in Weimar Germany." In *Powers of Desire: The Politics of Sexuality*, ed. Ann Snitow, Christine Stansell, and Sharon Thompson, 153–71. New York: Monthly Review Press, 1983.
Haas, Willy. "*Die Freudlose Gasse*." Regiebuch handgeschr., Inv. no. 8/67, undated. Sammlung G.W. Pabst. Filmmuseum München. *Die freudlose Gasse*, DVD, edition Filmmuseum München, 2009.
———. "*Die Freudlose Gasse*." Regiebuch handgeschr. #3, undated. Sammlung G.W. Pabst. Filmmuseum München. *Die freudlose Gasse*, DVD, edition Filmmuseum München, 2009.
———. "*Die Freudlose Gasse*." Regiebuch, undated. Mark Sorkin Collection, Film Study Center, Museum of Modern Art, New York. *Die freudlose Gasse*, DVD, edition Filmmuseum München, 2009.
———. "Die Krise der deutschen Filmindustrie." *Die Literarische Welt* 7 (12 February 1926).
———. "Willy Haas." In *Das bin Ich*, ed. Ernst Deutsch and Hannes Reinhardt, 54–83. Munich: Piper, 1970.
Hake, Sabine. *German National Cinema*. London: Routledge, 1993.
Hall, Murray G. *Der Fall Bettauer*. Vienna: Löcker, 1978.
Hall, Sara. "Inflation and Devaluation: Gender, Space, and Economics in G.W. Pabst's *The Joyless Street* (1925)." In *Weimar Cinema: An Essential Guide to Classic Films of the Era*, ed. Noah Isenberg, 135–54. New York: Columbia University Press, 2008.
Harmelin, Wilhelm. "Jews in the Leipzig Fur Industry." *Leo Baeck Institute Year Book* 9 (1, 1964): 239–66.
Horak, Jan-Christopher. "Film History and Film Preservation: Reconstructing the Text of *The Joyless Street* (1925)." In *Screening the Past* 5, ed. Ina Bertrand. Melbourne: La Trobe University, December 1998. www.screeningthepast.com/2014/12/film-history-and-film-preservation-reconstructing-the-text-of%C2%A0the-joyless-street%C2%A0 1925/ Accessed 22 April 2018.
Jerusalem, Else. *Der heilige Skarabäus*. Berlin: Fischer, 1909.
Joselit, Jenna Weissman. *A Perfect Fit: Clothes, Character and the Promise of America*. New York: Metropolitan Books, 2001.
Krobb, Florian. *Die schöne Jüdin: Jüdische Frauengestalten in der deutschsprachigen Erzählliteratur vom 17. Jahrhundert bis zum Ersten Weltkrieg*. Tübingen: Niemeyer, 1993.
Loacker, Armin. "Anmerkung zur Produktionsgeschichte von *Die freudlose Gasse*." In *Wien, die Inflation und das Elend*, ed. Armin Loacker, 9–27. Vienna: Filmarchiv Austria, 2008.
Loentz, Elizabeth. *Let Me Continue to Speak the Truth: Bertha Pappenheim as Author and Activist*. Cincinnati: Hebrew Union College Press, 2007.

Loewenstein, Andrea Freud. *Loathsome Jews and Engulfing Women: Metaphors of Projection in the Works of Wyndham Lewis, Charles Williams, and Graham Greene.* New York: New York University Press, 1993.

Mattl, Siegfried. "Geldentwertung und moralische Revolte. Zeitgenössiche Kontexte der 'freudlosen Gasse.'" In *Wien, die Inflation und das Elend,* ed. Armin Loacker, 107–29. Vienna: Filmarchiv Austria, 2008.

Noveck, Beth Simone. "Hugo Bettauer's Vienna 1918–1925." In *Jura Soyfer and his Time,* ed. Donald Daviau, 366–87. Riverside, CA: Ariadne, 1995.

Petro, Patrice. *Aftershocks of the New: Feminism and Film History.* New Brunswick, NJ: Rutgers University Press, 2002.

———. *Joyless Streets: Women and Melodramatic Representation in Weimar Germany.* Princeton, NJ: Princeton University Press, 1992.

Prawer, S.S. *Between Two Worlds: The Jewish Presence in German and Austrian Film, 1910–1933.* New York: Berghahn Books, 2005.

Rabl, Alexandra. "Hugo Bettauer's Wien: Stadtromane der Zwischenkriegszeit." Diplomarbeit, Mag. Phil. University of Vienna, 2013.

Schwarz, Egon. *Wien und die Juden: Essays zum Fin de Siècle.* Munich: C.H. Beck, 2014.

Seibel, Alexandra. "Vienna, Girls, and Jewish Authorship: Topographies of a Cinematic City, 1920–40." Doctoral dissertation. New York University, 2009.

Shapira, Elana. "Gaze and Spectacle in the Calibration of Class and Gender: Visual Culture in Vienna 1900." In *A History of Visual Culture: Western Civilization from the 18th to the 21st Century,* ed. Jane Kromm and Susan Benforado Bakewell, 157–68. Oxford: Berg, 2010.

Silverman, Lisa. "Absent Jews and Invisible Antisemitism in Postwar Vienna: *Der Prozess* (1948) and *The Third Man* (1949)." *Journal of Contemporary History* 52 (2, 2017): 211–28.

———. *Becoming Austrians: Jews and Culture between the World Wars.* New York: Oxford University Press, 2012.

Valman, Nadia. *The Jewess in Nineteenth-Century British Literary Culture.* Cambridge: Cambridge University Press, 2007.

Walk Cynthia. "Romeo with Sidelocks: Jewish-Gentile Romance in E.A. Dupont's *Das Alte Gesetz* (1923) and Other Early Weimar Assimilation Films." In *The Many Faces of Weimar Cinema: Rediscovering Germany's Filmic Legacy,* ed. Christian Rogowski, 84–101. Rochester, NY: Camden House, 2010.

Wallach, Kerry. "Buy Me a Mink: Jews, Fur, and Conspicuous Consumption." In *Jewish Consumer Cultures in Nineteenth- and Twentieth-Century Europe and North America,* ed. Paul Lerner, Anne Schenderlein, and Uwe Spiekermann. New York: Palgrave Macmillan, forthcoming.

———. *Passing Illusions: Jewish Visibility in Weimar Germany.* Ann Arbor: University of Michigan Press, 2017.

Weinstein, Valerie. "Anti-Semitism or Jewish 'Camp'? Ernst Lubitsch's *Schuhpalast Pinkus* (1916) and *Meyer aus Berlin* (1918)." *German Life and Letters* 59 (1, 2006): 101–21.

———. "Dissolving Boundaries: Assimilation and Allosemitism in E.A. Dupont's *Das alte Gesetz* (1923) and Veit Harlan's *Jud Süss* (1940)." *German Quarterly* 78 (4, 2005): 496–516.

Wischnitzer, Mark. "Origins of the Jewish Artisan Class in Bohemia and Moravia, 1500–1648." *Jewish Social Studies* 16 (4, 1954): 335–50.

Chapter 9

"THE WORLD IS FUNNY, LIKE A DREAM"

Franziska Gaal's *Verwechslungskomödien* and Exile's Crisis of Identity

Anjeana K. Hans

Es gibt kein herrlicheres Gefühl, als sozusagen am Webstuhl der Zeit mitzusitzen und für sein bescheiden Teil sagen zu können: "Wir waren dabei!" Allerdings ist der Publikumsgeschmack nicht so, wie er sich im Inneren eines jüdischen Regisseurs abspielt. Man kann kein Bild vom deutschen Volk im luftleeren Raum gewinnen. Man muß dem Volke aufs Maul schauen und selbst im deutschen Erdreich seine Wurzeln eingesetzt haben. Man muß ein Kind dieses Volkes sein. [There is no more wonderful feeling than to sit, so to speak, at time's loom and for one's humble part be able to say: "We were there!" Mind you, the audience's taste is not such as a Jewish director imagines. One cannot gain an understanding of the German people in a vacuum. One must listen to the man on the street and have oneself set one's roots in the German soil. One must be a child of the German people.]
—Gerd Albrecht, "Dr. Goebbels' Rede im Kaiserhof am 28. 3. 1933"

When Goebbels made his speech[1] on 28 March 1933 at the Hotel Kaiserhof to an audience of movie producers,[2] he was not only setting out the repressive National Socialist (Nazi) policy dictating who could take part in cultural production, but also suggesting something about the very nature of German and Jewish identity. The speech was the first step in a direction that would lead to the exclusion of an enormous number of those who made up the talent of the film industry because of their Jewish backgrounds: Horak puts the number at "over 2,000 German directors, producers, actors and technicians"[3] who were thus deprived both of their livelihoods and of the ability to contribute their talents to cultural production in Germany. If we were able to dig deeper, we could likely expand that number, to include those later affected by Nazi policy once their countries became allied or occupied, or those who never had the chance to break into the industry before becoming pariahs in the view of a government bent on defining all individuals either as German or as *unerwünscht* (undesired). The Nazi seizure of control over the film industry marks a traumatic and profoundly transformative moment, one in which the trajectory of German film history was irrevocably altered.

The path of film development was changed not only because of those who fled Germany, leaving Berlin's studios impoverished in so many ways, but also because of where those exiles went, in that their later work, when they were able to continue it, helped to shape other national film industries. Hollywood looms large as a destination, but the route to safety was often circuitous, and many exiles found themselves forced to keep moving.[4] Given especially linguistic issues, many of those blacklisted in Germany initially went (or returned) to Austria, where, at least until 1937, there was still some work to be found. Though the Austrian film industry was under pressure to conform to Berlin's antisemitic and ideological demands and though many of the main studios acquiesced, some independent studios, notably Universal, whose European arm was led by Joe Pasternak, continued to provide work for exiles up until 1937, though their films would not be shown in Germany.[5] While the precise number shifts depending on how one defines an exile film, Weniger states that 32 independent films—that drew on filmmakers, casts, and crews blacklisted by Berlin and by official Austrian studios—were produced in Austria before the complete alignment of the industry there with Berlin's directives.[6]

These Austrian films are in many ways especially interesting to analyze in the context of the effect of exile on the development of the medium. With the common language and the fact that German films would have been widely known in Austria and vice versa, there existed a certain cultural familiarity and even, in some sense, similarity that would suggest a more seamless integration of those exiled from Germany into the industry. Given this, the incongruities that we find, the moments in which expectations are disrupted, are especially telling, reflecting on the cultural background broadly as well as on the experience of exile itself. And that experience was one that was deeply and fundamentally traumatic, perhaps doubly so for those whose work in the film industry had accustomed them to popularity. Weniger suggests that the movie stars in particular, accustomed to being celebrated and revered by press and audience, were especially affected by the experience of exile: they "suffered agonies, when acclaim was followed first by the state boycott, then unemployment, and finally isolation, utter contempt, and oblivion."[7] The reality of life in exile, faced at best by the prospect of playing tiny roles, often in a foreign language, in front of indifferent audiences, at worst by unemployment, could certainly lead to agonies that would be the catalyst for a deep identity crisis for those who had known the peaks of popularity and cultural relevance. Consider Max Schmeling's recollection of a 1937 encounter with Otto Wallburg, the former star of theater and film, who had by then fled to the Netherlands and was working in a Jewish theater troupe: "According to him, Wallburg had complained to him, Schmeling, that he could not understand why he was suddenly being treated so badly by Germany and was unwanted there, and that he loved that country so much and had risked his neck for Germany in the World War. At that, he had noted in a tearful voice that he'd been awarded the Iron Cross for his bravery on the front in 1915."[8] Wallburg's heartbreaking statement—his continued love for his homeland and the fundamental fragmentation of his sense of identity that is evident in his insistence on still loving the country that had so cruelly rejected him—is testimony to the catastrophic and traumatic effect of exile on so many: their homeland no longer their own, their audiences turned against them, their work and past invalidated, it is little wonder that the very notion of their identity would be drawn in question. Wallburg was one of the many who were lost. He remained in the Netherlands until he was captured and sent to Auschwitz, where he was murdered in 1944.

Given the effect that expulsion from Germany had on the individual's sense of identity, the exile films that directly thematize questions of identity are especially interesting. The Austrian films fall into a fairly narrow range of genres, with musicals, historical/costume dramas, and comedies looming large. Among the latter, a significant number are *Verwechslungskomödien* (comedies of error), where the narrative hinges on the (deliberate or accidental) misapprehension of a key character's identity. This was, of course, not by any means a new plot device, going back to Shakespeare's *Comedy of Errors* (itself based on Plautus's play *Menaechmi*). But it takes on new significance when it becomes the narrative of films produced by filmmakers in exile, featuring casts, crews, and films no longer welcome in Germany.

Looking closely at the exile films produced in Austria allows us to trace the ways in which the traumatic experience of expulsion surfaced in the medium and, in doing so, drew on and often changed the tropes of a given genre. The *Verwechslungskomödie* in particular, in centering the disruptive potential of mistaken, misunderstood, and misrepresented identities, connects directly with a new world order in which the perception of one's identity no longer aligned with the sociocultural construction thereof. What might previously have been more purely a vehicle for humor becomes, in the context of post-1933 Austrian and German culture, a potentially tragic form; humor might well dominate, but beneath that lies the disconcerting realization that identity is not absolute, but rather subject to the whims of a bigoted regime. At the same time, a reevaluation of these films that are so often dismissed as purely entertainment films rather than the types of artistic or even overtly political films that would merit greater recognition might work, in some small way, to right the wrong done to so many of these filmmakers, actors, and crews. For, while some of those who were forced to flee the Nazi regime certainly were able to build on their success in the pre-Nazi era, too many were lost; too many, even when able to escape with their lives, found their stories consigned to obscurity. The Nazi policy that aimed to purge Germany's culture of Jewish participants thus proved remarkably successful even after their defeat. While we know of the Harry Kosters, Felix Jacksons, Peter Lorres, and Szöke Szakálls, who made it to—and also made it *in*—Hollywood, we have forgotten innumerable others who graced the European screens before being so cruelly expelled.

By the time that these comedies were being produced, the play with identity was already tied to the way in which German culture constructed Jewish identity. Ashekenazi suggests this in his analysis of Jewish identity in Weimar film, noting that many saw them as "an embodiment of the insoluble tensions that constitute the experience of modernity. . . . This discourse cultivated the image of 'the Jew' as an actor, a skillful master of appearance."[9] Examining a number of Lubitsch's comedies that hinge on identity confusion, Ashkenazi argues, "All these films depict the protagonists' desperate endeavors to integrate into a society that is reluctant to accept them."[10] He suggests that Lubitsch's films stage identity confusion as one step toward a resolution that acknowledges the impossibility of taking on a new identity even as it attempts to overcome these differences by resolving the narrative conflict through "true, blind love."[11] In this narrative move and in similar ones evident in films by other directors, Ashkenazi locates a sort of emancipatory and idealistic impetus that aimed at no less than "to construct and strengthen a liberal society into which they wished to assimilate."[12]

Ashkenazi draws attention to a significant point—namely, that these films and the ideological impetus behind their narratives were predicated on the context of a society in which a liberal bourgeoisie was yet a possibility. In his words, they "were concerned with *Jewish* identity inasmuch as it facilitated a profound discussion of the progressive bourgeois identity, its characteristics, and its boundaries."[13] With the end of German democracy and of the prospect of a sociocultural evolution toward a more liberal society, the significance of this type of identity play shifts radically, and that which we see in the *Verwechslungskomödien* of Austrian exile film works in a different way. No longer situated as squarely within a realistic context, they become progressively more melancholic, more of a representation of fantasy or wish fulfillment and a critique of real circumstances, as time passes.

We can trace the shift in this particular narrative motif by considering three Austrian films starring Franziska Gaal. Born in Budapest to a Jewish family and initially trained as a stage actress, Gaal's star rose seemingly overnight, when she debuted on Berlin screens in *Paprika* (dir. Carl Boese) on 4 November 1932. She had been discovered in Budapest by Joe Pasternak, who recalled in his autobiography, "In Budapest, on the way back to Berlin, I happened to see a play starring Franciska Gaal. She was one of Hungary's leading actresses but this was the first time I had seen her. I was enchanted. . . . In trying to describe Franciska Gaal's talent, one can only compare her with, say, Gertrude Lawrence or Mary Martin. She was perfect in whatever she did, song, dance, comedy, drama."[14] He convinced her to act in a German-language film, returning soon with the screenplay for *Paprika*. Pasternak's gamble—and it was certainly one, as Gaal spoke no German and thus had to learn her lines phonetically[15]—paid off: *Paprika* debuted to rave reviews. As one critic noted, "Franziska Gaal is already regarded as the coming big Berlin star."[16] Less than a year later followed *Gruß und Kuß, Veronika* (*Greetings and Kisses, Veronica*; 1933, dir. Carl Boese), for which Gaal earned equally rapturous accolades, with a critic in the *Vossische Zeitung* extolling her natural talent, her charm, even her idiosyncratic use of the German language in a way that often emphasized her foreignness.[17] For a short while, it looked as though her star could only rise, with a third success, *Skandal in Budapest* (*Romance in Budapest*; 1933, dir. von Bolváry/Székely), following close on the heels of the two films directed by Boese. Yet after 1933 and the Nazi rise to power, her meteoric success was cut short. True, she had several more films that were popular hits: *Csibi, der Fratz* (*Csibi, the Rascal*; 1934, dir. Neufeld), *Frühjahrsparade* (*Spring Parade*; 1934, dir. von Bováry), *Peter*

(1934, dir. Kosterlitz), *Kleine Mutti* (*Little Mother*; 1935, dir. Kosterlitz), *Katharina—die Letzte* (*Katharina—the Last*; 1936, dir. Kosterlitz) and *Fräulein Lilli* (*Miss Lilli*; 1936, dir. Behrendt/Wohlmuth). But only *Csibi* and *Frühjahrsparade* would be shown in Germany, while the arguably superior later films were banned. By the time she was making *Fräulein Lilli*, Pasternak had been recalled to Hollywood by Universal and the company's European arm had been shut down. When filming did not go smoothly—the original director, Hans Behrendt, was replaced by Robert Wohlmuth, supposedly because of Gaal's inability to work with him—the star found herself quite suddenly a target. As Brigitte Mayr notes, she was made "to feel the harshest reprisals and was defamed in campaigns of German-friendly papers as a greedy, capricious star."[18] Thus, *Der Wiener Film* wrote of the hitherto popular star:

> The way in which Ms. Franziska Gaal carries her unabashed movie star affectations to the extreme, how she disrupts normal work through unpredictable moodiness, gives film producers and financiers the runaround and, like a naughty and spoiled child wants to have her way at any price, cries out for redress and for the setting of a warning example. *Der Wiener Film* knows ... to correctly appreciate the significance of a Gaal-film for the Viennese film production; but if this production is only possible under the circumstances that Ms. Franziska Gaal now is dictating in her hysterical moodiness, then the business should rather forgo this kind of film and Ms. Franziska Gaal should look for a country in which such moods are perhaps the custom."[19]

That Gaal was ultimately made "a warning example" by being forced to "look for a country in which such moods are perhaps the custom" surely had less to do with her "unabashed movie star affectations" than with her Jewish background. Nevertheless, *Fräulein Lilli* would be her last European film. And yet, for a moment, it seemed she might land on her feet. In the fall of 1936 she went to Hollywood, brought there by DeMille himself, but, after acting in *The Buccaneer* (1938, dir. DeMille), *The Girl Downstairs* (1938, dir. Taurog), a remake of *Katharina—die Letzte*, and *Paris Honeymoon* (1939, dir. Tuttle), roles dried up for her. Mayr notes that Gaal mentions a Broadway role in 1940.[20] It seems not to have been promising, for Gaal, for incomprehensible reasons, chose to return to Hungary in 1941, where she had to hide from the Nazis until the end of the war. And even after the Third Reich fell, Gaal would not find success: a starring role in *Renée XIV*, a film planned by Hungarian director Akos Ráthonyi, fell through, and Gaal finally returned to the United States in 1947. The trajectory of her life after this is unclear: Mayr has traced only one additional Broadway role in 1951 and notes that Gaal, without the help of Hollywood insiders like her former colleagues, was unable to rebuild her career. When Gaal died in 1972, her passing went unremarked.[21]

And yet, Gaal, in those brief years between her debut in 1932 and the end of her European career in 1936, acted in films that were both popular successes and exemplary of some of the strongest exile films. While most of her films have some characteristics of *Verwechslungskomödien* and echoes of the screwball comedy, her Vienna films, in particular, center this question of mistaken identity. Comparing *Csibi der Fratz* (1934, dir. Neufeld) to *Peter* (1934, dir. Kosterlitz) and *Katharina—die Letzte* (1936, dir. Kosterlitz) lets us reflect on the differences in the way this topic is treated over time and speaks to the changing sociocultural background and the impact of continuing exile and marginalization on the actors and filmmakers.[22]

In *Csibi*, based on the 1924 play *Le fruit vert* (*Green Fruit*) by Régis Gignoux and Jacques Théry, Gaal plays Lucie Carol, a successful singer, who returns from an engagement in Paris to find that her mother's suitor, Dr. Lohnau, thinks she is in fact a young child. Rather than risk her mother's affair, she happily slips into that role. Complications arise when she falls in love with Lohnau's business partner, Dr. Werner. Believing him to be meeting another woman, she seeks him out at his home, then helps the woman (actually a client in a divorce case) avoid her husband's surveillance by "dressing up" as an adult, and finally lures Werner to a nightclub, where she proceeds to scandalize him by drinking and smoking. In the end, Werner discovers her true identity and Csibi and her mother both have happy endings with their respective suitors.

Csibi is perhaps the most straightforward of these comedies. It capitalizes on the talents the critic in the *Vossische Zeitung* had already praised in *Veronika*: Gaal's seemingly effortless charm, the "naturalness" of her performance (and of the characters she inhabits), and her ability to combine opposing traits, to embody a "mixture of impudence and shyness, abandon and roughness, drollness and wistfulness."[23] There is little here that is melancholy; rather, the social and geographical mobility that we see—Csibi's success as a performer, her unencumbered travel between France and Austria, and her unabashed pursuit of Werner—point to the relative freedom of pre-Nazi Europe. Filmed between 1933 and 1934 and premiering in Vienna on 2 February 1934, and in Berlin three weeks later, the film shows little evidence of the rapidly changing environment in which it was made.

In contrast, *Peter*, filmed in 1934 and premiering in Vienna on 20 December of that year, directly thematizes questions of exile, suffering, and identity. While it, too, ultimately is couched in terms of a love story, it begins with a traumatic event: Gaal's character, Eva, and her grandfather (Felix Bressart) are evicted from their home because they are unable to pay the rent. When they try to earn money as street performers, a thief takes Eva's dress as a disguise that allows him to escape police, leaving her only with his suit. Eva tries to sell newspapers, becomes involved in an altercation with Doktor Bandler (Hans Járay), and ends up in court, still dressed as a boy, for damaging his property. When Bandler feels sorry for "Peter," he arranges for a job at a gas station. As Peter, Gaal first despises, then comes to love Bandler; for his part, the doctor finally realizes the masquerade and the two end up happily together.

Several moments in *Peter* resonate with the experience of exile and articulate a crisis of identity that serves to reflect on the situation of the film's participants. The film opens on a long shot of a pile of furniture and other belongings, just as a chair is thrown onto the pile, then a table. The sequence cuts back and forth between the detritus and a second-floor window, from which the furniture is being thrown and we hear an unseen woman yelling indignantly at the unseen thrower of her belongings. She orders the culprit to "let go of Napoleon," just before a painting of the same joins the rest of her belongings, then argues that they should not be thrown out just because they have no money. Downstairs, a wild-haired, shabbily dressed man enters the courtyard just in time to catch a vase that is thrown from the window, only to have it break a moment later when a broom is thrown after it. We finally see the source of the voice, as a young woman comes to the window. Outraged at the broken vase, we hear her attack the unknown culprit before joining the old man.

The opening is at its basis comic, the actors' movements and lines choreographed perfectly, yet it contains key elements that are of interest in an exile film. Gaal and Felix Bressart, playing her grandfather, were both stars and would presumably have been recognized as Jewish exiles by viewers: the *Filmpolitik* (film politics) of the Third Reich was by this time well known,[24] and audiences surely would have recognized the reason why both actors had returned to take up work in Austria.[25] In spite of its comic rendering, their eviction and the destruction of their belongings thus represents the expulsion and expropriation experienced by exiles. We learn that they are poor, as they have no money to pay their rent, and yet their belongings seem to code them as bourgeois, with furniture joined by the painting and vase that stand in for cultural *Bildung* (personal cultivation and education) of some level. The introduction thus speaks to the way in which the exile of the Jewish community represented an unjust uprooting of a segment of society that was fundamentally integrated in the nation. The fact that the painting is of Napoleon might speak even more directly to antisemitism: if we see him as representative of a liberator of Jews (however unjustly so),[26] then the destruction of his portrait becomes a straightforward symbol of the attack on Jewish rights. That Gaal's character is so aptly named "Eva" reinforces the reading of their eviction as carrying larger symbolic significance: we can see it as no less than a metaphorical expulsion from paradise, Eva and her grandfather being doomed to suffer by unsympathetic powers.

The question of identity and belonging is raised even more directly later in the film. In a key scene, Gaal, in her incarnation as Peter, is recognized by the man who had earlier stolen her dress. In order to make up for his earlier transgression, he forces his female companion to take off her dress and gives it to Peter/Eva. In her room, Gaal's character changes from her boy clothes into the dress, then sings a telling song. The sequence starts with a long shot of Peter, who hurriedly undoes his overall and begins to unbutton his striped shirt, then, as the camera tracks to a close-up, pulls it over his head. It then dissolves to a close-up of Eva's face, boyish wig gone, as she smiles and smoothes the dress on her shoulders. The camera tracks out slightly before the shot dissolves to a long shot of her, then cuts to a shot of a mirror as she steps into view and admires herself. Already in this moment we see how constrained Eva is by the masquerade demanded from her: the shirt she takes off, with its striping, resembles nothing so much as a prison uniform, suggesting that she is imprisoned in the role required of her. The dissolve from Peter to Eva, as well as the multiple dissolves between shots of her and the presence of the mirror in which we watch her admiring herself, draw attention to the fluidity and indeterminacy of identity. In many ways, we no longer are entirely certain which identity is more representative of the character's true self. The song, then, is key to making sense of the moment, thematizing the question of identity and disguise, with its first lines posing Eva's dilemma: "Girl or boy, what am I?/ Won't anyone help me, what shall I do?/ If I knew what I really am/ How important that is./ I'm playing a false role." The repetition of one key line—"The world is funny, like a dream"—suggests that it is her environment forcing Eva into the disguise; as she notes, the world "wants/ for us to pretend," and happiness "goes by./ But one never knows if one will keep it."[27]

What the song emphasizes is a profound melancholy in the face of an environment that demands that Eva—and the Jewish exiles she stands in for—play a role that is incommensurate with her real identity. The gender crisis in which she finds herself, where she must ask herself, "What am I really?," symbolizes the profound identity crisis faced by exiles, forced to confront how strange the world is, and having experienced in the most fundamental ways how quickly that bit of happiness can disappear.

If the song clearly poses the key question at the root of this crisis of identity, the closing moments of the film reinforce the question that remains open for the exiles, even as it ostensibly resolves the narrative through romantic closure. Bandler discovers (or suspects) Peter's real identity after seeing Eva, but goes along with her insistence that she is in fact Peter's sister. Peter joins Bandler at a club, where he gains entry when he encounters the same thief who originally stole Eva's dress and demands his tuxedo. Once there, Peter tries to find patients for Bandler, whose medical practice is struggling, until the doctor begins to suspect that Peter is the thief of a pearl necklace. When confronted, Peter indignantly leaves. Back at the gas station, he and his grandfather are thrown out by his boss. The two—the grandfather and now Eva, as she leaves behind the tuxedo—pack their belongings and leave. As they pull their belongings down the road, Bandler arrives in his car and drives away with Eva, only to have a car accident as they kiss, returning full circle to the car accident that originally set their acquaintance in motion.

There are several elements of this final scene that are significant. The sequence starts with a vertical wipe to a shot showing Bandler driving along a road. The wipe, while overtly simply transitioning between settings and times, also is such a noticeable transition that it serves to remind the viewer of the film *as* film, and, in a sense, of the fantastic nature of the supposed resolution to Eva and her grandfather's destitution. We then cut to a medium shot of the two pulling a wagon loaded with furniture, with the painting of Napoleon on top (figure 9.1).

A chair falls and they stop to get it, the grandfather complaining about how their frequent moves destroy their belongings. We then see a medium shot of the wagon as Bandler drives into the frame and Eva moves to look at him, just as her grandfather notes, "It's really time that we finally know where we belong."[28] He resecures the chair, then turns to continue, only to find that Eva has joined Bandler in his car and they are driving off, presumably into a happier future. Key in this sequence is the imagery—of Eva and her grandfather pulling their wagon of belongings, firmly tying them to the image of the exile, expelled from their home and forced to become transient. The grandfather's suggestion that they have been repeatedly forced to move suggests that they

Figure 9.1. *Peter* (1934): Eva/Peter (Franziska Gaal) and her grandfather (Felix Bressart), once again expelled from their home. Screenshot courtesy of Film Archiv Austria.

are part of a larger diaspora, even resonating with the Old Testament's story of the forty-year search for the promised land. And his plaintive exhortation that "it's really time to know where one belongs" draws attention to both a longer history of antisemitism and the newly acute crisis brought about by the Nazi expulsion and persecution of Jews at the time. The resolution of the story, by contrast, is misleading at best. While the romance is drawn in a believable way, the car accident that Eva and Bandler are involved in suggests the concrete possibility of future difficulties (given Bandler's own financial insolvency and our awareness that they will have to pay for damages). Perhaps more importantly, with Eva's reappearance and the disappearance of Peter, a good amount of the air seems to go out of the love affair between her/him and Bandler. On one hand, this carries interesting implications for gender dynamics in the tale. More directly connected to the question of the exile experience, it suggests that the romance cannot be as satisfying once Eva is, again, herself. Indeed, the sequence is in many ways so very pat a resolution to the narrative crisis that it becomes unrealistic, a fantasy that actually serves to draw attention to itself (by, for example, the wipe at the sequence's start) and to comment in that way on the unresolvable situation of Jewish exiles.

What is effectively an acknowledgement of the depth of the crisis Jewish exiles found themselves in is even more clear in *Katharina—die Letzte* (1936), like *Peter* directed by Hermann Kosterlitz. Here, again, the narrative hinges on identity confusion, but this time it is not Gaal's character who is forced to masquerade. Gaal is Katharina, a lowly scullery maid in the home of the wealthy industrialist Sixtus Braun (Otto Wallburg). When Braun tries to prevent the relationship between his daughter and her lover, von Gerstikow (Hans Holt), by banning him from their home, the latter decides to gain access by pretending to be a chauffeur who has fallen in love with Katharina. She, however, falls in love with him, going so far as to spend all her money (which she was saving to buy a cow for her family farm in Hungary) on an ancient and barely functioning car that she hopes will enable him to become a taxi driver when she thinks he has been fired for defending her. Von Gerstikow, feeling guilty, initially tries to write her a letter to explain who he is, but Katharina, who is illiterate, never finds out what it says. Soon, he begins to develop feelings for her, but Braun decides to allow him to marry his daughter, until he discovers the relationship with Katharina and enlists her to serve cocktails in hopes of humiliating von Gerstikow (and, as collateral damage, Katharina) at the enormous engagement party by revealing the wealthy man's real identity to the maid. Katharina, however, gracefully denies him, then flees the home, intending to return to her family's farm. Desperate to find her, von Gerstikow tells the police that she's suspected of theft. Then, when they arrest her, he appears at the station and convinces her to leave with him.

One major change in *Katharina* is that here it is not Katharina, but rather von Gerstikow who is engaged in a masquerade. Indeed, the identity crisis is predicated not on the need for Katharina to play a specific role, but rather on the realization of deception by those around her. Katharina is depicted as fundamentally other. She is marginalized on multiple levels: by virtue of her social standing, as the last of the servants, who eats dinner alone in a corner of the kitchen while the remaining servants gather around a table and discuss who will take Katharina's days off and who is not even allowed to enter the rooms belonging to the *Herrschaften*; by virtue of her origin, from a town in Hungary so small and distant that the station master insists, when she tries to buy a return ticket, that it does not exist; and by virtue of her lack of even the most basic level of education, meaning that she cannot read even the explanation that von Gerstikow sends her. Yet, throughout the film, she is one of the most stringent enforcers of social status, insisting that she would never want "a posh gentleman"[29] and that social differences cannot be bridged. At the same time, her naïveté goes hand in hand with a fundamental honesty that contrasts sharply with the behavior of those around her. The servants who, as mentioned, isolate her; a crowd of people that gathers to laugh at the pitiful car she buys for von Gerstikow, their mockery filmed for an excruciatingly long several minutes; Braun, who sacrifices Katharina's pride in order to reveal von Gerstikow's infidelity to his daughter; even von Gerstikow himself, who not only cares so little for Katharina's feelings before knowing her that he is willing to use her to get to Sybill, but also, once in love with her, sends the police to arrest and humiliate her: *Katharina—die Letzte* meticulously stages the humiliation and suffering of its lead character. In the end, Katharina does not want to give in to von Gerstikow's suit, insisting, "We don't fit together."[30] He counters with a statement that embodies an idealized, and so very distant, liberal society: "I'm just like you. The clothes don't matter."[31] While superficially resolving the narrative crisis, this ending works so clearly on the level of fantasy that it can only be read as escapist. And, even then, one final moment injects an ominous overtone: as they kiss in the hallway of the police station to which Katharina had been brought, an old man enters and sees them, interrupting their kiss, then chases them away, shouting, "Say, where do you think that you are? See that you get out!"[32] In the end, their relationship opens them both up to abuse at the hands of bureaucracy, a hint at the ways in which the exile's identity, regardless of her inherent goodness, will always lead to problems for her and those who tie themselves to her.

What these films show is the way in which, in these films produced, directed, and starring exiles, the identity play we see no longer, as it did in earlier films, suggests how to create a progressive society in which even those marked as other have their equal place, but rather represents and reflects on the deeply traumatic experience of exile. Unlike the comedies of Lubitsch—unlike, even, the earlier films starring Gaal in similar roles—*Peter* and *Katharina—die Letzte* forgo any realistic idealism; instead, they draw clearly the connection between their persecuted and ostracized lead figures and the real exiles from Nazi Germany, and stage resolutions that are so unrealistic as to read as sheer wish-fulfillment in a historical moment in which the world seems turned upside down. A world in which an illiterate farm girl like Katharina could end up with the wealthy, titled young man who chooses her over the industrialist's daughter: this would surely be a world in which these exiles would be welcomed. Kosterlitz's films hearken back to an older tradition and remind the viewer of how recently that hoped-for progressive society seemed in reach, even as they exaggerate the identities at stake here—the underdog heroines and unsuitably socially superior men—so much as to rob any resolution of a claim to realism. Effective comedy they are, and yet, beneath the humor, these movies are documents to the anguish that resulted when identities were questioned and undermined, roots torn up, and lives shattered.

Anjeana K. Hans is associate professor of German studies at Wellesley College. She researches and has published on constructions of gender, sexual, national, and ethnic identity in film and culture. Her book, *Gender and the Uncanny in Films of the Weimar Republic* (Wayne State University Press, 2014), examined how these films engaged with anxieties emerging from women's emancipation. This chapter is part of a larger project in which she is examining the independent films produced in Austria between 1933 and 1937 by those forced into exile after Hitler's rise to power.

Notes

1. Unless otherwise noted, translations are my own.
2. Jan-Christopher Horak, "German Exile Cinema, 1933–1950," trans. Jennifer Bishop, *Film History* 8, no. 4 (1996), 373–89: 375.
3. Horak, "German Exile Cinema, 1933–1950," 373.
4. Kay Weniger, *"Es wird im Leben dir mehr genommen als gegeben . . . " Lexikon der aus Deutschland und Österreich emigrierten Filmschaffenden 1933 bis 1945: Eine Gesamtübersicht* (Hamburg: ACABUS Verlag, 2011), 14.
5. Weniger, *Lexikon der aus Deutschland*, 16–17.
6. Weniger, *Lexikon der aus Deutschland*, 18.
7. They "litt bisweilen Höllenqualen, als dem Jubel erst der staatliche Boykott, dann die Arbeitslosigkeit und schließlich Isolation, blanke Verachtung und Vergessenheit folgten." Weniger, *Lexikon der aus Deutschland*, 11.
8. "Demzufolge habe Wallburg ihm, Schmeling, sein Leid geklagt, dass er nicht verstehe, warum er von Deutschland plötzlich so schlecht behandelt werde und man ihn dort nicht mehr haben wolle und dass er doch dieses Land so sehr liebe und im Weltkrieg seine Knochen für Deutschland hingehalten habe. Dabei habe Wallburg mit tränenerstickter Stimme auf die Auszeichnung mit dem Eisernen Kreuz für seinen Mut an der Front 1915 hingewiesen." According to Weniger, Schmeling recounted this meeting decades later on an (unspecified) German talk show. Schmeling certainly visited the Netherlands in that year and met with Wallburg and others—photos of this exist. Weniger, *Lexikon der aus Deutschland*, 15.
9. Ofer Ashkenazi, *Weimar Film and Modern Jewish Identity* (New York: Palgrave Macmillan, 2012), 19.

10. Ashkenazi, *Weimar Film*, 22.
11. Ashkenazi, *Weimar Film*, 28.
12. Ashkenazi, *Weimar Film*, 41.
13. Ashkenazi, *Weimar Film*, 41.
14. Joe Pasternak and David Chandler, *Easy the Hard Way: The Autobiography of Joe Pasternak* (New York: Van Rees Press, 1956), 127.
15. Pasternak and Chandler, *Easy the Hard Way*, 127.
16. "Franziska Gaal gilt bereits jetzt als der kommende große Berliner Star." "Großer Berliner Tonfilm-Erfolg," *Das Kino-Journal* (5 November 1932), 11.
17. "Gruß und Kuß—Veronika," *Vossische Zeitung*, 30 August 1933, 7.
18. "Die Repressalien in aller Härte zu spüren und wurde in Kampagnen deutschfreundlicher Zeitungen als geldgieriger, kapriziöser Star diffamiert." Brigitte Mayr, "'Universal's European Money-Maker:' Franziska Gaal—von Budapest nach Hollywood," in Erika Wottrich, ed., *Deutsche Universal: Transatlantische Verleih- und Produktionsstrategien eines Hollywood-Studios in den 20er und 30er Jahren* (Munich: edition text+kritik, 2001), 100–10: 104.
19. "Die Art, wie Frau Franziska Gaal unverhohlene Starallüren auf die Spitze treibt, wie sie in unberechenbarer Launenhaftigkeit die normale Arbeit stört, die Filmproduzenten und Filmfinanciers an der Nase herumführt und wie ein böses und verzogenes Kind um jeden Preis ihren Kopf durchsetzen versucht, schreit nach Abhilfe und nach der Statuierung eines warnenden Exempels. Gerade 'Der Wiener Film' weiß... die Bedeutung eines Gaal-Films für die Wiener Filmproduktion richtig einzuschätzen; wenn aber diese Produktion nur unter solchen Bedingungen möglich ist, wie sie Frau Franziska Gaal jetzt in hysterischer Launenhaftigkeit diktiert, dann sollte die Produktion auf einen solchen Film doch lieber verzichten und Frau Franziska Gaal sich ein Land suchen, in dem solche Launen vielleicht Sitte sind." "Regie-Wechsel beim Gaal-Film" in *Der Wiener Film* 1.7 (23 June 1936), 1–2.
20. Mayr, "'Universal's European Money-Maker,'" 106.
21. Mayr, "'Universal's European Money-Maker,'" 108.
22. I was able to view these films during summers 2017 and 2018 at the Film Archiv Austria. Their help in accessing the films was invaluable.
23. "Mischung aus Frechheit und Schüchternheit, Hemmungslosigkeit und Sprödigkeit, Drolerie und Schwermut." "Gruß und Kuß—Veronika," *Vossische Zeitung* (evening edition, 30 August 1933), 7.
24. For example, in reporting on the Elisabeth Bergner film *The Rise of Catherine the Great* (1934, dir. Czinner/Korda) being banned in Germany, the magazine *Der gute Film* notes laconically, "Germany will in the future no longer allow foreign films with German-Jewish actors or Jewish actors who have left Germany to be screened." (Deutschland will künftig ausländische Filme, in denen deutsche jüdische Schauspieler oder aus Deutschland ausgewanderte jüdische Schauspieler auftreten, nicht mehr zur Vorführung zulassen.) *Der gute Film* 68 (16 March 1934), 4.
25. Newspapers and trade magazines frequently remarked on the many actors who returned or relocated to Vienna, though they often did not directly explain why. Referencing Bressart's relocation to Vienna, the newspaper *Der Wiener Tag* notes that he was "until a year and a half ago one of the busiest comics of Berlin theater and film" ("bis vor eineinhalb Jahren einer der meistbeschäftigten Komiker des Berliner Theaters und Films"), and implicitly references the forced expulsion from Germany that he and others experienced: "Like so many famous German actors, Bressart now lives in Paris, where he has been successful in film. He speaks French fluently since his childhood. At the French school in Berlin, where Bressart studied, he certainly could

have had no idea, how important this would one day be for him." ("Bressart hat jetzt, wie so viele bekannte deutsche Schauspieler, seinen ständigen Aufenthalt in Paris, wo er stark beim Film beschäftigt wird. Er spricht fließend französisch [sic] — schon seit seiner Jugendzeit. Am Französischen Gymnasium in Berlin, wo Bressart studierte, konnte er allerdings nicht ahnen, wie wichtig dies noch einmal für ihn werden sollte.") *Der Wiener Tag* 13.3996 (22 July 1934), 12.
26. See, e.g., Aubrey Newman, "Napoleon and the Jews," in *European Judaism: A Journal for the New Europe* 2:2 (Winter 1967), 25–32.
27. In the version available at the Film Archiv Austria, the bulk of this song is not included; instead, she sings only the final four lines. The full sequence is available on YouTube at https://www.youtube.com/watch?v=ws2TJkMQpUo. "Mädel oder Bub, was bin ich?/ Hilft mir niemand, was beginn ich?/ Wenn ich wüsst, was bin ich richtig,/ so wichtig ist das./ Eine falsche Rolle spiel ich." "Komisch ist die Welt, wie ein Traum." "Scheinbar will die Welt/ dass man sich verstellt." "Geht ein bisschen Glück durch den Raum./ Doch man weiss ja nie ob man es behält."
28. "Es wird wirklich mal Zeit, dass man endlich weiß, wo man hin gehört."
29. "Ein feiner Herr."
30. "Wir passen nicht zusammen."
31. "Ich bin genauso wie du. Auf den Anzug kommt's doch nicht an."
32. "Na sagen Sie, was glauben Sie eigentlich wo Sie sich hier befinden? Schauen Sie, dass Sie hinauskommen!"

Bibliography

Albrecht, Gerd. "Dr. Goebbels' Rede im Kaiserhof am 28. 3. 1933." In *Film im 3. Reich*, 26–31. Karlsruhe: Doku, 1979. www.filmportal.de/material/die-goebbels-rede-im-kaiserhof-am-2831933.
Ashkenazi, Ofer. *Weimar Film and Modern Jewish Identity*. New York: Palgrave Macmillan, 2012.
"Felix Bressart in Wien." *Der Wiener Tag*, 22 July 1934.
"Großer Berliner Tonfilm-Erfolg." *Das Kino-Journal*, 5 November 1932.
"Gruß und Kuß—Veronika." *Vossische Zeitung*, 30 August 1933.
Horak, Jan-Christopher, "German Exile Cinema, 1933–1950." trans. Jennifer Bishop, *Film History* 8 (4, 1996): 373–89.
Mayr, Brigitte. "'Universal's European Money-Maker:' Franziska Gaal—von Budapest nach Hollywood." In *Deutsche Universal: Transatlantische Verleih und Produktionsstrategien eines Hollywood-Studios in den 20er und 30er Jahren*, ed. Erika Wottrich, 100–10. Munich: Edition Text & Kritik, 2001.
"Neues vom Film: Deutschland." *Der gute Film*, 16 March 1934.
Newman, Aubrey. "Napoleon and the Jews." *European Judaism: A Journal for the New Europe* 2 (2, Winter 1967): 25–32.
Pasternak, Joe, and David Chandler. *Easy the Hard Way: The Autobiography of Joe Pasternak*. New York: Van Rees Press, 1956.
"Regie-Wechsel beim Gaal-Film." *Der Wiener Film*, 23 June 1936.
Weniger, Kay. *"Es wird im Leben dir mehr genommen als gegeben..." Lexikon der aus Deutschland und Österreich emigrierten Filmschaffenden 1933 bis 1945: Eine Gesamtübersicht*. Hamburg: ACABUS, 2011.

PART III

JEWISHNESS AS ANTISEMITIC CONSTRUCT

Chapter 10

CINEMATICALLY TRANSMITTED DISEASE

Weimar's Perpetuation of the Jewish Syphilis Conspiracy

Barbara Hales

> Wir wissen nun, warum der Jude mit allen Mitteln der Verführungskunst darauf ausgeht, deutsche Mädchen möglichst frühzeitig zu schänden. [We now know why the Jew, by all means of seduction, proceeds to disgrace the German girl as early as possible.]
> —Julius Streicher, "Deutsche Volksgesundheit aus Blut und Boden!"

In this chapter I consider how depictions of prostitutes functioned both consciously and unconsciously in Weimar cinema to perpetuate the longstanding conspiracy that the Jews were spreading syphilis.[1] The Jewish syphilis conspiracy can be traced back to as early as the fifteenth century, as attested by the phrase "Peste of the Marranos."[2] Sander Gilman notes how this prejudicial notion continued through the nineteenth century in popular German discourse, evident in the designation of certain skin conditions resulting from syphilis as *Judenkratze* (Jewish skin disease).[3] Adolf Hitler draws on the Jewish syphilis conspiracy in *Mein Kampf* (1925), claiming that Jewish men are contaminating the German people by spreading syphilis to prostitutes.[4] In light of this historical background and with an eye to how the National Socialists (Nazis) used this sort of antisemitic propaganda, I analyze how depictions of the prostitute in Weimar culture function unconsciously to perpetuate antisemitic discourse. This historical background helps us understand how we can interpret the films as invoking Jewishness. In what follows, I investigate Weimar medical works that advance the idea that Jews are responsible for spreading syphilis. I examine three medical films: Nicholas Kaufmann's *Die Geschlechtskrankheiten und ihre*

Folgen (*Sexually Transmitted Diseases and their Consequences;* 1919–20), Rudolf Biebrach's *Falsche Scham* (*False Shame;* 1926), and Walter Ruttmann's *Feind im Blut* (*Enemy in the Blood;* 1931). I contend that the syphilitic woman in these works is a metaphor for the maladies of modern culture, which encourages promiscuity at its own peril.[5] Along with the many other antisemitic myths, the Jewish syphilis conspiracy is part of the larger ideological propaganda that makes Jews responsible for the downfall of Western civilization. The coding of syphilis as Jewish in these films illustrates how film functioned as a venue for antisemitic constructions of Jewishness.

The Cultural Association of Jews, Prostitutes, and Syphilis

The connection between Jewish identity and sexuality as well as prostitution is evident in late-nineteenth and twentieth-century discourse. Jay Geller notes how sexuality is critical to constructions of Jewish identity in popular culture, substantiated through various associations of Jews with prostitutes.[6] In the nineteenth century, it was believed that the prostitute afflicted with syphilis was the victim of her Jewish pimp involved in the pernicious dealings of so-called "white slavery."

Jews were tied to illicit activity through their supposed lust for Christian women. The Jewish population in Vienna numbered 150,000 in 1900. Poor Jews from Galicia, Bohemia, and Moravia crowded into the Leopoldstrasse and other immigrant areas and became a target for prejudice, accusing them of criminal activity and engaging in various social vices.[7] Jewish men were accused of prowling amusement parks and boulevards in search of women that they could make into prostitutes.[8] Franz Schneider, an elected official of the Lower Austrian Assembly, provides the following report in 1899 before the Austrian parliament: "[There were] countless cases in which Christian servants employed by Jews disappear without trace, carried off to a dreadful fate in the brothels of Hungary, the Orient and South America, despite the vigilance of the legal authorities. These cases are connected with the incredible crimes committed by Jews because of their superstitions for the purpose of getting hold of Christian blood and calling to heaven for revenge."[9]

Jews were believed to prey on Christian women, who could be employed to work for them as prostitutes, as well as to sell on the slave trade. It is this sort of propaganda that held Jews accountable for defiling the body of the *Volk* (people).[10] In sum, Jews were seen to infect prostitutes with syphilis, passing the infection on to non-Jewish men. Jews were believed to be more susceptible to contracting this disease despite the simultaneous belief that they had a stronger immune system.[11]

Germany's economic depression following World War I created general social unrest, fueling the belief that Jews were responsible for all social ills. Reports of Jewish sexual misconduct including accusations of committing rape, procurement of women, and sexually transmitted diseases were common in antisemitic publications. In a discussion of *The Protocols of the Elders of Zion*, Nazi ideologue Alfred Rosenberg claimed that Jews used sexual freedom as part of their plot to demoralize other races: "The Jews had defiled the other races and made them rotten. On purpose."[12] Additionally, *Der Stürmer*'s lead article in the July 1926 issue, "Menschenfleisch Handel" (The Human Flesh Trade) charges the Jews, who supposedly abduct innocent blonde-haired German girls, as the sole party responsible for carrying out the white slave trade.[13] A 1930 edition of *Der Stürmer* published a cartoon entitled "Vom Juden Verseucht" (Infested by the Jew), which depicted a young German girl leaving the doctor's office with syphilitic sores marring her face. The doctor, who is identified as Jewish, scornfully comments, "Nothing is too bad for the *goya* [non-Jew]."[14]

Right-wing publications accused Jewish men of being involved in the white slave trade. Hitler draws on this in a section of *Mein Kampf*, "The Causes of Collapse," in which he describes the dangers of syphilis for mankind, warning his readers that even a single sexual encounter could result in denigration of one's genetic makeup for the next ten generations.[15] Moreover, Hitler blamed the Jews for spreading syphilis and permanently defiling the blood of the entire German race.[16] Hitler's Jewish syphilis conspiracy echoes the same sort of rhetoric that had been circulating for several hundred years in Europe, most notably antisemitic propaganda used during the Black Plague in 1348 and the Naples syphilis epidemic in 1495.[17] Hayden notes, "When the Black Death killed millions of Europeans and rotting bodies were piled in the streets, Jews were accused of poisoning wells as part of an international conspiracy to kill Christians."[18] Jews were also blamed as carriers during the Naples syphilis epidemic, having supposedly brought the disease from Spain.

Hitler claims that syphilis is caused by "prostitution of love" and the "Judaization of our spiritual life."[19] He argues that defeating syphilis begins with reining in prostitution in the larger metropolitan areas where the most contamination of culture has been experienced.[20] Hitler identifies Jews as the culprit behind the growth of prostitution in urban areas: "In no other city of western Europe could the relationship between Jewry and prostitution, and even now the white slave traffic, be studied better than in Vienna.... If you walked at night through the streets and alleys of Leopoldsstadt, with every step one could witness things which were unknown to the greater part of the German nation.... An icy shudder ran down my spine when seeing for the first time the Jew as a cool, shameless, and calculating manager of this shocking vice, the outcome of the scum of the big city."[21]

One should note Hitler's emphasis on the Jewish role in the "commercial exploitation" of prostitutes and the consequent "syphilization" of the German people.[22] He thus pleads with his readers to save the German race from the denigration of the German people through the Jewish syphilis conspiracy.[23] Hitler's pronouncements on Jews and commerce bring to mind the trope of the Jew and the prostitute as usurers: they are both seen as lending something for a large sum of money in order to gain illegitimate income.[24]

The topic of syphilis was further commented on by racial hygienists of the Weimar period who noted the grave dangers of sexually transmittable diseases. In Baur, Fischer, and Lenz (1921), the authors report that 10 percent of the contemporary German population was infected with syphilis and as much as 60 percent of men in Berlin had the disease.[25] Lenz reads these high numbers as a factor in disrupting the birth of healthy children. Many individuals with syphilis did not marry since they believed that any offspring would not be viable.[26] In addition, the perceived biological danger was that a syphilitic germ would change the progenitor's seed. One encounter with the syphilitic prostitute would condemn the man and his wife to children with disabilities or no children at all.[27]

Similarly, the cohabitation of the Jew and the Aryan woman was thought to poison the Aryan's blood forever. Julius Streicher, publisher of *Der Stürmer*, writes of an alien soul that is absorbed in this sexual interaction, which will never be discarded: the non-Jewish woman will not bear Aryan children.[28] These children will be bastards with two souls in their breast, easily identifiable as mixed race.[29] The pseudoscience of the period is not unlike the belief in breeding circles that an animal of superior stock, once bred with an inferior one, will always produce inferior offspring.[30] In all of these instances, the Jew is a carrier of disease that he passes on to the peril of unsuspecting individuals.

Notwithstanding Hitler and Streicher's outrageous claims, Weimar medical researchers were studying the rising rates of syphilis in the

Jewish population.[31] In *Zeitschrift für Demographie und Statistik der Juden*, Professor Hermann Strauß reports in 1927 of the staggering rates of syphilis found in the Jewish community, noting that there was an increase in Jews testing positive for the Wassermann reaction: "In the post-war years, syphilis became more common and increased relative to the Jewish population."[32] Examining late-stage syphilis, Strauss wants to know how often we find syphilis in the Jewish population and how these rates of infection compare with the non-Jewish population.[33]

Other doctors also corroborated the increase in syphilis among Jewish men.[34] In psychiatrist Max Sichel's article "Die Paralyse der Juden in sexualogischer Beleuchtung" (The Paralysis of Jews in a Sexual Context; 1919–20), he reports the increased rates of paralysis among male Jews suffering from syphilis in the past 50 years.[35] In Sichel's study, this attack on the central nervous system caused by syphilis occurred at just the time that Jews are moving from the land to the big cities. Sichel explains that materialistic Jews are drawn to urban areas, which they corrupt with their illicit sexual morality. He thus insists that Jews in these areas should move to the country in order to decrease the effects of sexually transmitted infection and obtain sexual hygiene.[36] According to Sichel, emancipated Jews in urban areas have a proclivity for loose morals, resulting in higher rates of sexually transmitted infection and paralysis.

Jewish newspapers like the popular *C.V.-Zeitung*, which claimed to represent 60 percent of the German Jews, and the *Jüdisch-liberale Zeitung* also carried stories about the problem of Jews contracting syphilis. In fact, a special issue of the *Jüdisch-liberale Zeitung* entitled "Die sexuelle Frage" (The Sexual Question) featured an article concerning Max Sichel's ideas on Jews and paralysis with emphasis on Jews who were patients at various asylums. The author of the article, W. Hanauer, mentions that the occurrence of Jews who contracted syphilis, the poisonous reaction of the disease in the Jewish population, together with Jews' supposed increased capacity of passing on the sexual infection were all attributed to the growing Jewish population in the metropolis. Hanauer remarks, "Syphilis amongst Jews is very common."[37]

In the *Jüdische Zeitung: National-Jüdisches-Organ*, Felix Resek discusses a brochure written by Rafael Becker on Jews and mental illness, noting that psychiatric patients who acquired their disease through an infection with syphilis were represented more commonly among Jews than among their non-Jewish counterparts. This statement was prefaced by the fact that while fewer Jews had contracted syphilis as compared with non-Jews, the disease attacked the central nervous system to a greater extent in the Jewish population. According to Resek's article, this was attributed to the Jew as a *geistige Arbeiter* (mental worker), who thus was predisposed to psychological maladies.[38]

Other Jewish newspapers like *Die Wahrheit: unabhängige Zeitschrift für jüdische Interessen* found that Jewish customs, namely circumcision, protected Jewish men from acquiring the disease of syphilis.[39] Family life was also a supposed protection against the disease as was the high level of education among Jews.[40] The *C.V.-Zeitung* similarly attributed a lower death rate caused by syphilis due to the strict religious laws that kept Jews morally bound to their marriage and to the laws of purity.[41]

In addition to the discussion of syphilis found in the medical journals as well as in Jewish newspapers, antisemitic diatribes like *Der Stürmer* featured pseudo-scientific articles such as *"Judenblut—Wissenschaftliche Blutforschung"* (Jewish blood—scientific blood research) to demonstrate the presence of Jewish disease. According to this piece, doctors have tested "Jewish blood" by injecting it into the body of a non-Jew. The non-Jews, according to the article, promptly had a high fever similar to having poison given to them. Even the color of this poisonous Jewish blood is reported to be different: pale blue instead of the normal red coloring of Gentile blood. This supposed observational difference leads the author to recommend further testing of Jewish blood to establish the percentage of "ape blood," "Mongolian blood," "Negro blood," and so on.[42] In Hans F.K. Günther's infamous Weimar study "Rassenkunde des judischen Volkes" (Racial Science of the Jewish People; 1930), he similarly regards Jewish blood as having a "different racial mixture" than Gentile blood.[43] Hitler could draw on these ideas in claiming that Jews were literally contaminating the German people through the spread of syphilis, spreading the "Jewish disease" resulting in the "poisoning of the soul."[44]

Weimar Medical Discourse Films

I turn now to an investigation of three Weimar medical discourse films to show the connection between the Jew, the prostitute, and syphilis: Nicholas Kaufmann's *Die Geschlechtskrankheiten und ihre Folgen* (1919–20), Rudolf Biebrach's *Falsche Scham* (1926) along with the accompanying Universum Film Aktiengesellschaft (UFA) book based on the film, and Walter Ruttmann's film *Feind im Blut* (1931).[45] With funding from the German government, UFA created an educational department devoted to medical discourse films. The earliest UFA film about syphilis was Nicholas Kaufmann's documentary *Die Geschlechtskrankheiten und ihre Folgen* (1919–20), which lacked narrative development and did not receive praise by critics. In contrast, Rudolf Biebrach's *Falsche Scham* (1925–26) and Walther Ruttmann's *Feind im Blut* (1931) integrated documentary and narrative elements and were, in turn, better received by audiences.[46] Curt Thomalla, a neurologist by training and head of UFA's Cultural Film Department, wrote the script for *Falsche Scham*, as well as the accompanying book, which included 109 stills from the film.[47] The UFA films were screened in university lecture halls, medical schools, and in more public settings as part of exhibitions dealing with health issues.[48] *Falsche Scham* and *Feind im Blut* even found a more popular audience in movie theaters in light of their integration of narrative elements. Because of longstanding and widespread discourses, syphilis, those who treat it, and those who spread it were culturally coded as Jewish; therefore, these didactic films, which were meant to scare people from catching sexually transmitted infections, also contributed to antisemitic constructions of Jewishness.

In considering the role of medical discourse films as a cultural artifact, we need to consider Weimar's sense of moral crisis. A series of enlightenment films were created and backed by government agencies such as the Reich Health Office, the Reich Committee for Hygiene Education, and the Prussian Welfare Ministry to combat this siege.[49] The Interior Ministry created a propaganda campaign in 1919 to use film as a means of combatting various moral and health concerns including alcoholism, prostitution, sexually transmitted diseases, and homosexuality. Although not explicitly about Jews, per se, these films shaped constructions of Jewishness and Jewish difference.

Weimar hygiene films varied in format from scientific documentaries meant to educate medical students and more popular films meant primarily as entertainment. Notable examples include E.A. Dupont's *Alkohol* (1919), Friedrich Zelnik's *Paradies der Dirnen/Leichtsinn und Lebewelt* (*Paradise of Whores/Recklessness and Fast Living*; 1919), and Richard Oswald's *Prostitution* (1919).[50] The popularity of hygiene films appears to have increased over the Weimar period. Films such as Adolf Trotz's *Fluch der Vererbung* (*Curse of Heredity*; 1927), Ulrich Schulz's and Wolfram Junghans's *Natur und Liebe: Vom Urtier zum Menschen* (*Nature and Love*; 1926–27), and Gustav Ucicky's *Vererbte Triebe: Der Kampf ums neue Geschlecht* (*Hereditary Instincts*; 1929) reflect a Darwinian perspective that health and illness are determined solely by genetic makeup, including constructions of Jewish difference and disease.

One perceived problem with cinema as an educative tool was that "deviant" subject matter could also lead to moral corruption. Killen articulates this fear concerning working-class viewers: "How were filmmakers to ensure the intended reading of their message by an audience perceived as lacking middle-class virtues of impulse control or discrimination."[51] As a means of counteracting the prurient aspect of the film, the screening of medical discourse films was often preceded by a scientific lecture providing a background of the pathology of the disease that will be presented.[52]

Nicholas Kaufmann's documentary film *Die Geschlechtskrankheiten und ihre Folgen* (1919–20) begins with a discussion of the growing problem of gonorrhea followed by gruesome depictions of people afflicted by syphilis in the second half of the film.[53] Despite the presentation of various medical facts, the film plays on the viewer's scopophilic curiosity when displaying naked bodies afflicted by open sores or human skulls of the deceased. One of the most disturbing of these images shows a paralyzed man unable to stand upright, requiring him to be institutionalized. The camera zooms in on the man as he is driven mad after making a feeble attempt to dress himself. The man's physiognomy (slightly bowed legs along with his stereotypical black hair) and belligerent nature signal the Jewish miscreant.[54] Gilman notes that antisemitism of the early twentieth century was based on physiognomy: "What had been an objection based on the Jew's religion came to be pathologized as an objection to the Jewish body."[55] The scene is also reminiscent of Max Sichel's work on the paralysis of male Jews who have contracted syphilis.

After the mention of the Wassermann blood probe, the film features a doctor (coded as Jewish by his pronounced nose), who advises his patients to get tested.[56] The fact that the film's doctor is associated with the Wassermann test calls to mind Jewish doctors who were prominent in the fields of dermatology and who defined the field of syphilology in the early twentieth century.[57] The Wassermann antibody test for syphilis was developed in 1906 by August Paul von Wassermann (1866–1925), a German-Jewish bacteriologist and hygienist. The test checks patients' blood for the syphilis bacterium antibody. Additionally, German-Jewish physician Paul Ehrlich (1854–1915) was responsible for the first effective treatment of syphilis in 1909.[58] Ehrlich discovered that Compound 606 Arsphenamine actively countered the spirillum-spirochaetes bacteria responsible for syphilis. The drug used to treat syphilis would be marketed as Salvarsan in 1910.

Die Geschlechtskrankheiten und ihre Folgen codes both the doctor and patient as Jewish, creating an ambiguous message that syphilis is a Jewish phenomenon. One scene shows a man parting a woman's lips in order to reveal her open syphilitic sores. In another scene, a man manually examines a woman's breast, which has a large wound on the nipple. Another scene shows a mentally ill woman without clothing writhing on a divan. The viewer is warned that syphilis is spread through contact with the genitals and the lips. The sexualization of these women afflicted by syphilitic sores reminds the audience of the prostitute's role in spreading sexually transmitted infection. It is also made clear that the disease can hide in plain sight, embedded in the lymph nodes of the genital area and the lower jaw in the second phase of the disease. This deception may allow the prostitute to practice her trade without being suspected of being a carrier of the disease.

Another prominent film that features the disease of syphilis and its connection to the prostitute and the Jew is entitled *Falsche Scham*. Written by Curt Thomalla and Nicholas Kaufmann and directed by Rudolf Biebrach, the film was initially screened during the Reichsgesundheitswoche (Imperial Health Week) 18–24 April 1926 and uses footage from psychiatric patients, as well as animated sequences and narrative scenarios to illustrate the consequences of the spread of syphilis and gonorrhea. (It was determined by the censoring authorities that the film did not contain any illicit content.)[59] *Falsche Scham* warns of the dangers posed by prostitutes who insidiously spread syphilis by enticing their unsuspecting patrons. There is also antisemitic coding through the characters of the pimp and the doctor. The film presents four cases of individuals suffering from syphilis. The *Sanitätsrat* (health counselor) figures as the central character, responsible for examining three of the venereal disease patients. In three of these cases, a prostitute is responsible for infecting the victims: a medical student who is seduced by a prostitute at a dance hall, a farmer who has an encounter with a prostitute during his war service, and a young salesman who contracts syphilis by sleeping with prostitutes. The film presents a doctor attempting to treat the disease while the final act includes a young couple dealing with the consequences of being infected. *Falsche Scham* also features inferential antisemitism, because of indirect and coded allusions to Jewishness.[60]

The film's first act, "Erste Versuchung" (First Temptation), begins with two students who are tempted by a prostitute on their visit to a state fair. With the flashing lights of the honky-tonk side shows, the school boys catch a glance at the seductive legs of the female boxers. The *Sanitätsrat*, who is at the fair to stop a roving prostitute from spreading venereal disease, spots the boys being propositioned by the prostitute. The film shows a blonde-haired woman making contact with the young boys who evidently have agreed to meet up with her later. The pimp (who is again coded as Jewish with stereotypical dark hair and eyes) spots the young boys as they are buying their tickets to the fair. The counselor comes to the rescue and diverts the boys to a multimedia exhibition near the boxing tent devoted to sexually transmitted infections. The boys are scared by the medical lecture and the accompanying gruesome models of syphilis sores. The first act ends with the boys exiting the exhibition just as the pimp and another prostitute are discussing how to entice them. At this point, the boys are propositioned by two prostitutes, leaving the audience uncertain whether they will accept their offer.

Thomalla expands on the importance of the prostitute and the pimp (coded as Jewish) in spreading disease in his accompanying book to *Falsche Scham*. He describes the doctor's search for the infected prostitute at the fair: "Already [the doctor] wants to hurry towards [the prostitute], . . . so that she does not spread new evil. His foot falters. He sees one of the typical night-figures of the city bowed to the girl's ear, he follows the lurking gaze of the lowly fellow, he sees the prostitute hurry away."[61] Thomalla identifies the community of prostitutes as "outbreaks . . . plague boils on the body of the entire *Volk*" (Krankheitsherde . . . Pestbeulen am Körper des Volksganzen).[62] In a passage that reads like *Mein Kampf*, Thomalla states that the individual must finally work for the good of the *Volk* to cure venereal disease, a task that is worthy of a "großen starken und gesunden Kulturvolkes" (great, strong and healthy people of culture).[63] It may be of some interest that Thomalla's next film script was considered the first German film on eugenics, *Der Fluch der Vererbung* (*The Curse of Heredity*; 1927), which proposes the sterilization of those with "hereditary diseases," in order to strengthen the *Volk*.

The film *Falsche Scham* as well as Curt Thomalla's narrative book based on the film provide evidence that the prostitute and her accompanying pimp are dangerous to unsuspecting members of the community. In the final act of the film entitled "Durch Wissen zur Heilung" (Through Knowledge for Healing), we see the dangers of syphilis played out on multiple generations. The young woman from the country, Anna, leaves her syphilitic uncle in an asylum and moves to the city to find a livelihood (figure 10.1). She is befriended by a young man, Karl Mertens, who infects her with syphilis, the disease he has picked up from frequenting prostitutes that he meets at nightclubs. Anna chases after Karl to the nightclub where she encounters young men and women dancing with abandon. Thomalla describes the scene as "disgusting menfolk and painted women, all half-naked."[64]

Figure 10.1 Scene from *Falsche Scham* (1925–26, dir. Rudolf Biebrach). Source: DFF-Deutsches Filminstitut & Filmmuseum.

Falsche Scham's first act is echoed in the final one, which presents pimps and prostitutes preying on unsuspecting young men—the prostitutes lie in wait in front of the nightclub as a dancer inside is applying lipstick, possibly to hide her mouth sores. The dancer and another prostitute swarm Karl as he sits down at the table. Death is symbolized in an apparition seen by Anna on the face of one of these women of the night. Karl and Anna escape the nightclub and watch a medical documentary film about the role of certain "strange races" (presumably the Jews) that have been responsible for the transmission of venereal disease since the time of the Crusades. The people in the medical documentary possess notably deformed facial features.[65] The suggestion that these "strange races" stand in for Jews is what Valerie Weinstein describes elsewhere as "subtle, coded, or covert representations of Jewish difference" that reinforce antisemitism.[66] This inference is embedded in social, historical, and institutional contexts: Jews were accused by the Genoese ambassador to Charles VIII in 1492 of transmitting the disease of syphilis, and are certainly meant as the target of the documentary film's "strange races" that were historically responsible for spreading syphilis. Finally, an image of the devil appears above Anna's head as she exits the theater, suggesting the evil borne by this syphilitic scourge.

Falsche Scham illustrates the danger of the prostitute and by relationship the Jewish pimp in the spread of syphilis and lays the groundwork for the later film *Feind im Blut* in its connection to the disease. *Feind im Blut* was commissioned by both the Deutsche Gesellschaft zur Bekämpfung der Geschlechtskrankheiten (German Society for the Fight Against Sexual Diseases) and the Schweizerische Gesellschaft zur Bekämpfung der Geschlechtkrankheiten (Swiss Society for the Fight Against Sexual Diseases) and premiered in Berlin on 17 April 1931.[67] The film presents three cases of individuals inflicted with syphilis and offers the physician delivering a detailed lecture about the symptoms of syphilis before an auditorium of university students. Within the frame of this pseudo-documentary is a dramatic story of three intertwined individuals and their fight against syphilis. The film builds on what Anita Gertiser calls the importance of *Abschreckung* (deterrence) in these medical discourse films through the salacious details of disease and its dissemination.[68] The coding of syphilis as Jewish included a malicious historical undercurrent that meant such *Abschreckung* could be mobilized for antisemitic purposes.

Feind's opening montage features diseased and deformed wax faces. This rendition of illness is followed by a history of the spread of syphilis. Extra diegetic sounds of "Hilfe! Hilfe!" (Help! Help!) accompany a historical summary of the spread of syphilis from the discovery of America to the present day of 1931.[69] Large dates on the screen are interspersed with a bubbling black puddle meant to suggest the festering disease. A narrator describes the disease's unstoppable path, carried by sexual desire that seems to be a permanent historical fixture.

In *Feind*, sexual urges are illustrated by a simple kiss that leads to the infection with syphilis of the medical student, his friend, and a machinist. Examples of the prostitute's deadly kiss include the scene with the friend and a young girl in his train compartment, the medical student in a girl's apartment, and a subsequent scene with both men on a night out in the city's dancehalls and taverns. The audience is granted an ominous clue of the prostitute's danger since a syphilitic sore can be detected on her lips as she looks at herself in the mirror. The viewer is privy to this in a transition shot that moves from the wax forms provided for the medical students with oozing sores on the lips to a close up of the prostitute, who services both the medical student and the mechanic. The syphilitic prostitute's degeneracy is signaled by her makeup as she masquerades as a healthy individual despite the fact that she is responsible for spreading the disease.[70] The evening ends with the friend leaving the nightclub with a local prostitute. The dingy winding streets seen in the early morning hours suggest the evening's illicit activities, which are made explicit as a street walker removes money from her garter to pay her pimp.[71]

Although the pimp in *Feind* seems to stand in the typical relationship with the prostitute, we might consider another reading of his relationship with her in light of the 1930s medical discourse literature. Geller argues that the Jewish doctors on the forefront of medical breakthroughs in the field of syphilology were targeted for ridicule by right-wing groups.[72] Albert Neisser and Paul Ehrlich were looked on with suspicion due to their scientific methodology: Neisser supposedly infected young prostitutes in his research, and Ehrlich used arsenic-based Salvarsan that caused various trial participants to die in the process. The serum used to prevent syphilis was suspected as a way to disseminate the disease: the serum inoculation was perceived as a Jewish plot to spread the disease and to contaminate Aryan blood.[73]

The negative press surrounding Jewish scientists led individuals like Martin Staemmler to blame the Jews for the spread of syphilis.[74] Hans Reiter in his article "Nationalsozialistische Revolution in Medizin und Gesundheitspolitik" (National Socialist Revolution in Medicine and Health Policy) notes the *Überfremdung* (foreign infiltration) in the field of dermatologists and gynecologists who are influenced by their own dangerous instinct and desires.[75] These doctors supposedly come in contact with young girls and defile the German soul by soiling German honor and committing *sittliche Vergewaltigung* (moral rape).[76] The insinuation is that Jewish doctors violate German women, recalling the violation of German women by Jews in the white slave trade.

Jewish doctors were believed to dominate the fields of dermatology and syphilology, and were said to sell quack cures to treat these diseases.[77] Parish notes that Jewish physicians were prohibited from practicing jobs that were more popular and financially beneficial in medicine and surgery: "Because dermatology was not held in high regard by the medical establishment, the specialty was available to Jewish physicians."[78] Individuals of Jewish descent were forced to practice in some of the less respected fields of medicine such as dermatology, which was known as *Judenhaut* (Jew skin); in the process, they were demonized for their service.[79]

Feind indirectly references Jewish doctors and their nefarious relation to syphilis in the awkward interaction between the medical professor and the prostitute in the scene in the lecture hall. In order to demonstrate the second stage of syphilis, the professor parades a living patient at the head of the classroom so the students may inspect her infectious sores and blisters. Hiding behind dark colored glasses (no "respectable woman" would do this), the prostitute removes her dress so the students may examine her red pock-marked skin and blistered breasts. The scene ironically creates sexual tension in both the male medical students and the film's audience, in spite of the fact that the woman's body is marred by the infectious sores. The Jewish doctor, who is supposed to help in curing disease, represents the pimp pandering prostitutes who are spreading the disease.

The ambiguity of the naked woman paraded through an academic lecture hall symbolizes the cognitive dissonance of the Weimar period. The dermatology professor is no less ambiguous because he is both exposing the young men to the infectious disease and warning them about its harmful effects. It should be noted that about 25 percent of Weimar dermatologists were of Jewish descent. Moreover, it was the Jewish physician and scientist Paul Ehrlich who was credited with the Magic Bullet cure for syphilis.[80] Like the doctor in *Feind im Blut*, Jews were not only responsible for treating and curing syphilis, but also would be blamed by Hitler and the Nazis for spreading the dreaded "Jewish disease."

The racial hygiene films of the Nazi era took their cues from late Weimar hygiene films like *Feind im Blut*, reflecting political support for separating the sick from the healthy, and for tracing disease to the degenerate Jew. The early Third Reich racial hygiene films included *Sünden der Väter* (*Sins of the Fathers*; 1935), *Abseits vom Wege* (*Off Track*; 1935), *Erbkrank* (*Hereditarily Ill*; 1936), *Alles Leben ist Kampf* (*All Life Is Struggle*; 1937), among others, with these films directed and produced by Herbert Gerdes from the Rassenpolitischen Amt (Racial Political Office). The Nazis' fear of the "Jewish scourge" is also documented in the Gesetz zum Schutze des deutschen Blutes und der deutschen Ehre (Law for the Protection of German Blood and German Honor, 15 September 1935),[81] the prohibition of marriage between Jews and Germans, and the Law for the Protection of the Hereditary Health of the German Volk, 18 October 1935 (Gesetz zum Schutze der Erbgesundheit des deutschen Volkes),[82] the prohibition of marriage on hereditary grounds. With the close proximity of these laws passed in 1935, the insinuation was that race was indicative of disease, and that the immediate threat was the Jew. Racial hygiene films provided a medium of propaganda for advancing eugenic policies during the Weimar and Nazi periods and was a tool for indoctrinating the wider German populace in spreading "racial purity."

Conclusion

The Weimar revival and propagation of the Jewish syphilis conspiracy theory (which had been circulating for several hundred years throughout Europe) would serve as a crucial part of Hitler's eugenic propaganda that regarded Jews as hereditarily diseased. During the Weimar period, the conspiracy alleged that Jews exhibit loose morals and engage in sexually promiscuous behavior. Immigrant Jews were particularly stereotyped for being morally bankrupt as evidenced by their attraction to larger urban areas where they could partake in the indulgences found in Weimar's cabaret scene. In addition to overindulging in alcohol and risky sexual behavior, Jews were believed to spread their corrupt morality and thus to pose an imminent threat to the physical and psychological health of the German populace. Drawing on a longstanding association of Jews with the white slave trade, Jews were believed to be responsible for orchestrating and profiting from the German sex work industry.

Weimar narrative film depictions of prostitutes thus make subtle allusions to the role of Jews such as are evident in Rudolf Biebrach's *Falsche Scham* and Walter Ruttmann's *Feind im Blut*. This association, further established in medical documentaries like Nicholas Kaufmann's *Die Geschlechtskrankheiten und ihre Folgen*, attempts to vilify the many Jewish physicians such as Albert Neisser and Paul Ehrlich that were working to cure syphilis and other diseases as pimps responsible for corrupting innocent Germans girls and infecting healthy men. *Feind im Blut* thus shows the physician parading a pock marked woman before his medical students as if she is a cabaret dancer who is attempting to titillate the audience. Syphilis was historically coded as Jewish, particularly by antisemites. Therefore, antisyphilis films, even when they do not explicitly refer to Jews, resonate with those historical discourses and reinforce antisemitic notions.

Acknowledgments

For feedback on the manuscript, I would like to thank Dr. Philipp Stiasny (CineGraph Babelsberg), Dr. Valerie Weinstein (University of Cincinnati), and Dr. Kerry Wallach (Gettyburg College). All translations, unless otherwise noted, are my own.

Barbara Hales is a Professor of History and Humanities at the University of Houston-Clear Lake. Her publications focus on film history of the Weimar Republic and the Third Reich. She is the author of *Black Magic Woman: Gender and the Occult in Weimar Germany* (Peter Lang, Oxford, 2021). She has also co-edited a volume entitled *Continuity and Crisis in German Cinema 1928-1936* for Camden House in 2016 (with Mihaela Petrescu and Valerie Weinstein). Dr. Hales is President of the Houston based organization, Center for Medicine After the Holocaust.

Notes

1. The epigraph is from Julius Streicher, "Deutsche Volksgesundheit aus Blut und Boden!" *Nürnberg* 3, no.1. 1 January 1935, 1. Although the main focus of my analysis is how the syphilis conspiracy was used to fuel antisemitic propaganda during the Weimar period, it is important to debunk various ideas that were asserted by the medical discourse of the period. First, there are limited statistics regarding the religious breakdown on people testing positive for syphilis during this period. How do we deconstruct the propagandistic elements of the antisemitic rhetoric? One must further consider the bifurcation (or trifurcation) of Jews during this period between traditional observant Jews and nontraditional or secular Jews. The syphilis conspiracy attempts to represent all Jews as being sexually promiscuous and generally possessing loose morals. It should be noted that observant Jews adhere to strict laws regarding modesty and sexual purity and are forbidden by religious law (*halacha*) from any physical contact with members of the opposite sex prior to marriage. That said, there was an increasing number of Jews during the late-nineteenth and early-twentieth centuries that were breaking away from tradition. Many of these Jews were seeking a more spiritual approach that was less governed by the restrictions of the Mosaic law. A third group of Jews sought to lose their Jewish identity and attempt full integration into Germany society. One can imagine that some individuals who make the conscious decision to disassociate themselves from a strict religious upbringing might engage in libertine behavior as a means of exercising their newfound freedom from the restrictions of their upbringing. These liberated Jews would obviously be more attracted to urban areas, which afforded them greater ability to engage in the emerging nightclub scene. Efron notes that, by the turn of the century in Europe, the crashing of the ghetto walls ensured that Jews were taking on Christian morals, which led to a subsequent rise in syphilis, paralysis, and feeblemindedness. John M. Efron, *Medicine and the German Jews: A History* (New Haven, CT: Yale University Press, 2008), 176–77.
2. In the fifteenth century, Genoese ambassador to Charles VIII of France dubbed syphilis the "Peste of the Marranos," highlighting the disease's association with Jews. Efron, *Medicine and the German Jews*, 227–28.
3. Sander Gilman, *The Jew's Body* (New York & London: Routledge, 1991), 96, 100.
4. Adolf Hitler, *Mein Kampf*, trans. Alvin Johnson et. al. (New York: Reynal & Hitchcock, 1940), 247.
5. See Peter Baldwin, "Syphilis between prostitution and promiscuity," in *Contagion in the State of Europe, 1830–1930* (Cambridge: Cambridge University Press, 1999), 355–523.

6. Jay Geller, "Bloodsin: Syphilis and the Construction of Jewish Identity," *Faultline: Interdisciplinary Approaches to German Studies* 1 (1992): 23.
7. Edward J. Bristow, *Prostitution and Prejudice: The Jewish Fight against White Slavery* (New York: Schocken Books, 1983), 75–76. See also Daniel M. Vyleta, *Crime, Jews and News: Vienna, 1895–1914* (New York: Berghahn Books, 2007).
8. For the definitive study of prostitutes in Viennese society, see Karin Jusek, *Auf der Suche nach der Verlorenen: Die Prostitution im Wien der Jahrhundertwende* (Vienna: Löcker Verlag, 1994). Also see Jill S. Smith, "Working Girls: White-Collar Workers and Prostitutes in Late Weimar Fiction," *German Quarterly*, 81–84 (2008): 449–70.
9. "Auch jene unzähligen Fälle, in welchen christliche Dienstmädchen, die bei Juden bedienstet sind, spurlos verschwinden, um in Freudenhäusern in Ungarn, im Orient, in Südamerika einem gräßlichen Schicksale entgegengeführt zu werden, fordern die Aufmerksamkeit der gesetzgebenden Körperschaften herauß. Zu diesen Fällen gesellen sich noch jene unglaublichen Verbrechen, welche von Juden auf Grund ihres Aberglaubens an Christen zu dem Zwecke begangen werden, um sich in den Besitz von Christenblut zu setzen und die zum Himmel um Rache emporrufen." W. Giese, ed., *Anti-Semitisches Jahrbuch* (Berlin: W. Giese Verlag, 1903), 64, quoted in Bristow, *Prostitution and Prejudice*, 82. There was Jewish crime, procurement, and prostitution in many eastern European countries at the beginning of the twentieth century. In villages and cities, pauperism and economic marginality weakened Jewish life and well-being. Bristow, *Prostitution and Prejudice*, 91.
10. Bristow, *Prostitution and Prejudice*, 82. Viennese tabloids at the turn of the century noted that the city's prostitutes were a consequence of seduction by Jewish employers. Jay Geller, *The Other Jewish Question. Identifying the Jew and Making Sense of Modernity* (New York: Fordham University Press, 2011), 108.
11. Gilman, *The Jew's Body*, 100. The Jew was known as a mixed race in the 1930s and was deemed impure, unlike the pure Aryan race. With a weakened body, the Jew was prone to diseases like syphilis. Gilman, *The Jew's Body*, 102.
12. "Die Juden hätten die andern Rassen geschändet und morsch gemacht. Mit Absicht." Alfred Rosenberg, *Die Protokolle der Weisen von Zion und die Judische Weltpolitik* (Munich: Deutscher Volks Verlag, 1923), 106.
13. "Mädchenfleisch Handel," *Der Stürmer: Nürnberger Wochenblatt zum Kampf um die Wahrheit* 30 (1926): lead story.
14. "Vom Juden Verseucht," cartoon, *Der Stürmer: Nürnberger Wochenblatt zum Kampf um die Wahrheit* 44 (1930).
15. Hitler, *Mein Kampf*, 339. A 20 June 2007 news release on the *Medical News Today* website entitled "Did Hitler Have Syphilis" speculates that Hitler may have contracted syphilis from a Jewish prostitute, fueling his animosity toward the Jews. The article was provoked by a paper presented by Bassem Habeeb at the Royal College of Psychiatrists, in which Habeeb speculates that if Hitler indeed had syphilis, as is believed in popular legend, he may have experienced subsequent mental illness leading to his actions in masterminding the Holocaust. Although this may be an enticing argument, one should be careful both because of the lack of evidence of the claim, and as another attempt to diminish culpability for the Holocaust on account of a single individual's mental state. https://www.medicalnewstoday.com/releases/74776.php.
16. Hitler, *Mein Kampf*, 336.
17. Deborah Hayden, *Pox: Genius, Madness, and the Mysteries of Syphilis* (New York: Basic Books, 2003), 265.
18. Hayden, *Pox*, 265.

19. Hitler, *Mein Kampf*, 337.
20. Hitler, *Mein Kampf*, 338, 342, 347.
21. Hitler, *Mein Kampf*, 78. For a discussion, see Hayden, *Pox*, 266; Alison Rose, *Jewish Women in Fin-de-Siècle Vienna* (University of Texas Press, 2009), 144.
22. Hitler, *Mein Kampf*, 337–39.
23. Hitler, *Mein Kampf*, 339, 343.
24. Geller, *The Other Jewish Question*, 111.
25. Fritz Lenz, *Grundriß der menschlichen Erblichkeitlehre und Rassenhygiene. Band II: Menschliche Auslese und Rassenhygiene* (Munich: J. F. Lehmanns Verlag, 1921), 25–26; Erwin Baur, Eugen Fischer, and Fritz Lenz, *Grundriß der menschlichen Erblichkeitlehre und Rassenhygiene. Band I: Menschliche Erblichkeitslehre* (Munich: J.F. Lehmanns Verlag, 1921).
26. Lenz, *Grundriß der menschlichen*, 26.
27. Geller, *The Other Jewish Question*, 115.
28. Streicher notes, "Ein einziger Beischlaf eines Juden bei einer arischen Frau genügt, um deren Blut für immer zu vergiften. Sie hat mit dem 'artfremden Eiweiß' auch die fremde Seele in sich aufgenommen. Sie kann nie mehr, auch wenn sie einen arischen Mann heiratet, rein arische Kinder bekommen, sondern nur Bastarde, in deren Brust zwei Seelen wohnen und denen man körperlich die Mischrasse ansieht. Auch deren Kinder werden wieder Mischlinge sein, das heißt häßliche Menschen von unstetem Charakter und mit Neigung zu körperlichen Leiden." "Deutsche Volksgesundheit," 1.
29. Streicher, "Deutsche Volksgesundheit," 1.
30. Geller, *The Other Jewish Question*, 115. Artur Dinter, *Die Sünde wider das Blut* (Leipzig: Matthes and Thost, 1920) was extremely popular in the Weimar period. In this dark text, the Jewish seed ensures the destruction of progeny for several generations and through separate marriages.
31. Hermann Strauß was a German-Jewish internist at the Jewish Hospital in Berlin. He perished at Theresienstadt Ghetto in 1944.
32. "In den Nachkriegsjahren ist [die Syphilis] häufiger geworden und bei den Juden auch relative gewachsen." Hermann Strauss, "Erkrankungen durch Alkohol und Syphilis bei den Juden," *Zeitschrift für Demographie und Statistik der Juden* 4/3–4 (1927): 35, 39.
33. "Wie häufig die Syphilis unter den Juden überhaupt und im Vergeich mit den Nichtjuden ihres Beobachtungsmilieus ist." Strauss, "Erkrankungen durch Alkohol," 34.
34. Max Sichel was an assistant psychiatrist at the Frankfurt am Main City Mental Asylum, and was of Jewish descent.
35. Max Sichel, "Paralyse der Juden in sexualogischer Beleuchtung," *Zeitschrift für Sexualwissenschaft*, Band VI (1919–20): 98.
36. Sichel, "Paralyse der Juden," 99–100.
37. W. Hanauer, "Die sexuelle Frage von jüdisch-biologischen Standpunkte," *Jüdischliberale Zeitung* 34: 21 August 1925. "Die Syphilis bei Juden [ist] sehr verbreitet."
38. Felix Resek, "Das Sanitätswesen." *Jüdische Zeitung: National-Jüdisches-Organ (Wien)* 38 (20 September 1918): 5.
39. "Ursachen und Zweck der Beschneidung," *Die Wahrheit: unabhängige Zeitschrift für jüdische Interessen; Deutschösterreichische Wochenschrift für jüdische Interessen* 20 (May 16, 1924), 5.
40. "Die Sterblichkeit unter den Juden," *Die Wahrheit: unabhängige Zeitschrift für jüdische Interessen; Deutschösterreichische Wochenschrift für jüdische Interessen* 4 (February 9, 1922): 14.
41. Binjamin Segel, "Die Judenheit in Ziffern," *Central Verein Zeitung* 14 (5 April 1923): 113.

42. "Judenblut: wissenschaftliche Blutforschung und ihre Ergebnisse," *Der Stürmer: Nürnberger Wochenblatt zum Kampf um die Wahrheit* 35 (1926).
43. Hans F.K. Günther, *Rassenkunde des judischen Volkes* (Munich: J.F. Lehmann, 1930), 267.
44. Hitler, *Mein Kampf*, 345–46.
45. For a discussion of sexuality in Weimar cinema, see Malte Hagener, *Geschlecht in Fesseln: Sexualität zwischen Aufklärung und Ausbeutung im Weimarer Kino 1918–1933* (Edition Text + Kritik, 2000).
46. C. Bonah and A. Laukötter, "Introduction: Screening Diseases. Films on Sex Hygiene in Germany and France in the First Half of the 20th Century," *Gesnerus* 72–1 (2015): 8.
47. In a letter from Professor Adam, Generalsekretär des Reichsausschusses fur hygienische Volksbelehrung, published in the introduction to the *Falsche Scham* book, he writes how the film could draw in cinema viewers, who might not be interested in dense lectures on the topic of syphilis. Curt Thomalla, *Falsche Scham* (Berlin: Film Bücherei, 1926), 5.
48. Anja Laukötter, "Listen and Watch: The Practice of Lecturing and the Epistemological Status of Sex Education Films in Germany," *Gesnerus* 72–1 (2015): 66.
49. Andreas Killen, "What Is an Enlightenment Film? Cinema and the Rhetoric of Social Hygiene in Interwar Germany," *Social Science History* 39–1 (Spring 2015): 111.
50. See Jill Suzanne Smith, "Richard Oswald and the Social Hygiene Film: Promoting Public Health or Promiscuity?" in *The Many Faces of Weimar Cinema: Rediscovering Germany's Filmic Legacy*, ed. Christian Rogowski (Rochester, NY: Camden House, 2010), 13–30 on Richard Oswald's early hygiene films. Also note S.S. Prawer, *Between Two Worlds: The Jewish Presence in German and Austrian Film, 1910–1933* (New York: Berghahn Books, 2005), 72–81 on Weimar Enlightenment Films.
51. Killen, "What Is an Enlightenment Film?" 111.
52. Censorship was abolished in Germany in 1918 and reinstated in 1920. During that brief time, 150 films with sexual themes were released. The fear was that the common people could be overwhelmed by the supposed sensationalism in these films. Critics marked films like *Anders als die Andern* (*Different from the Others* 1920) as deviant; this particular film by Richard Oswald was eventually banned by the censors for the depiction of homosexuality. Killen, "What Is an Enlightenment Film?," 110.
53. Nicholas Kaufmann's documentary film *Die Geschlechtskrankheiten und ihre Folgen* was released in Berlin and shown in 13 German villages and cities. The film was also screened both in Japan and the United States. The film did quite well with the public due to low ticket prices. It was, however, censored in Germany in 1920 and could be shown to adolescents only with gender segregation. Laukötter, "Listen and Watch," 60.
54. Gilman, *The Jew's Body*, 43–46.
55. Gilman, *The Jew's Body*, 43.
56. The hooked nose was known as the *Judennase*; the saddle nose with the sunken bridge was attributed to Jews and was also a characteristic of congenital syphilitics in nineteenth-century medical literature. Geller, *The Other Jewish Question* 110.
57. A different doctor appears in Part I, who instructs a patient how to wash his hands; this same doctor appears at the end of Part II. It is interesting then that a separate doctor is introduced after the mention of the Wassermann test.
58. Sahachiro Hata was Ehrlich's assistant for the discovery of Salvarsan.
59. The state of Baden demanded that the film be banned for young audience members (Killen, "What Is an Enlightenment Film?," 114). These objections were eventually overridden. Thomalla worried about the genre of medical discourse films; that the "kitsch and trash" circulating in the contemporary German film industry was a result of the public's desire for sensationalism. It is interesting that Curt Thomalla was ap-

pointed to Joseph Goebbels's Ministry of Popular Enlightenment and Propaganda, in the fields of public health, welfare, and population policy. *Falsche Scham* was taken out of circulation in 1933. Killen, "What Is an Enlightenment Film?" 115, 117.
60. For more on inferential antisemitism, see Valerie Weinstein, *Antisemitism in Film Comedy in Nazi Germany* (Bloomington: Indiana University Press, 2019): 14–16, 36–37.
61. "Schon will er eilig auf sie zu, . . . damit sie nicht etwa neues Unheil verbreite. Da stockt sein Fuß. Er sieht eine der typischen Nachtgestalten der Großstadt an das Ohr des Mädchens gebeugt, er folgt dem lauernden Blick des niedrigen Gesellen, er sieht die Dirne davoneilen und zwei jungen Bürschen anreden." Thomalla, *Falsche Scham*, 10.
62. Thomalla, *Falsche Scham*, 10.
63. Thomalla, *Falsche Scham*, 54.
64. Thomalla describes the scene with "widerliches Mannsvolk und bemalte und geschminkte Weiber, alle halbnackt." Thomalla, *Falsche Scham*, 195.
65. The film-within-a-film foregrounds the technology of filmmaking, illustrating the ability of modern science to tell the truth.
66. Weinstein, *Antisemitism in Film Comedy*, 15. Weinstein notes, "Inferential antisemitism reinforces assumptions, values, tropes, and language fundamental to overt antisemitism without targeting Jews explicitly and without necessarily intending to target them at all." Weinstein, *Antisemitism in Film Comedy*, 37.
67. For an extensive coverage of Ruttmann's *Feind*, see Michael Cowan, *Walter Ruttmann and the Cinema of Multiplicity: Avant-Garde-Advertising—Modernity* (Amsterdam: Amsterdam University Press, 2014), 102–17. The film was also accompanied by a prerecorded lecture by Hermann Roeschmann. Roeschmann had already given the same lecture at the Berlin premiere of the film.
68. Anita Gertiser, *Falsche Scham: Strategien der Ueberzeugung in Aufklärungsfilmen zur Bekämpfung der Geschlechtskrankheiten (1918–1935)* (Göttingen: V & R unipress, 2015), 214.
69. The date of the discovery of America is significant because Jews were accused in 1492 by the Genoese ambassador to Charles VIII of transmitting the disease of syphilis.
70. Geller notes that the syphilitic prostitute may be spotted by the gold leaf covering her lesions. Geller, *The Other Jewish Question*, 110.
71. This is supported by the fact that the friend is found to have contracted a sexually transmitted disease.
72. Geller, "Bloodsin," 25–26.
73. Geller, *The Other Jewish Question*, 96.
74. Martin Staemmler, "Aufgaben und Ziele der Rassenpflege," *Ziel und Weg* 3–14 (1933): 417, 21.
75. Hans Reiter, "Nationalsozialistische Revolution in Medizin und Gesundheitspolitik," *Ziel und Weg* 14 (1933): 424.
76. Reiter, "Nationalsozialistische Revolution," 425.
77. Gilman, *The Jew's Body*, 97.
78. Lawrence Charles Parish, "Review of *Death of Medicine in Nazi Germany: Dermatology and Dermatopathology under the Swastika*," *New England Journal of Medicine* 340-24 (1999): 1931.
79. Geller, *The Other Jewish Question*, 96.
80. Ehrlich at age 54 was an assistant professor when he won the Nobel Prize in 1908 for his work in immunology. He would have to wait until 1914 to be promoted to full professor at the University of Frankfurt. Climbing the academic ladder was a matter of religion: most Jews with professorships had been baptized. Efron, *Medicine and the German Jews*, 240.

81. "Law for the Protection of German Blood and German Honor," in *The Third Reich Sourcebook*, eds. Anson Rabinbach and Sander L. Gilman (Berkeley: University of California Press, 2013), 209.
82. "Law for the Protection of the Hereditary Health of the German Volk," in *The Third Reich Sourcebook*, eds. Anson Rabinbach and Sander L. Gilman (Berkeley: University of California Press, 2013), 329–30.

Bibliography

Baldwin, Peter. "Syphilis between Prostitution and Promiscuity." In *Contagion in the State of Europe, 1830–1930*, 355–523. Cambridge: Cambridge University Press, 1999.

Baur, Erwin, Eugen Fischer, and Fritz Lenz. *Grundriß der menschlichen Erblichkeitlehre und Rassenhygiene. Band I: Menschliche Erblichkeitslehre*. Munich: J.F. Lehmanns, 1921.

Bonah, C., and Laukötter, A. "Introduction: Screening Diseases. Films on Sex Hygiene in Germany and France in the First Half of the 20th Century." *Gesnerus* 72 (1, 2015): 5–14.

Bristow, Edward J. *Prostitution and Prejudice: The Jewish Fight against White Slavery*. New York: New York: Schocken Books, 1983.

Bullough, Vern and Bonnie. *Women and Prostitution: A Social History*. Amherst, NY: Prometheus Books, 1987.

Cowan, Michael. *Walter Ruttmann and the Cinema of Multiplicity: Avant-Garde-Advertising—Modernity*. Amsterdam: Amsterdam University Press, 2014.

"Did Hitler Have Syphilis?" *Medical News Today*, 20 June 2007. https://www.medicalnewstoday.com/releases/74776.php

"Die Sterblichkeit unter den Juden." *Die Wahrheit: unabhängige Zeitschrift für jüdische Interessen; Deutschösterreichische Wochenschrift für jüdische Interessen* 4 (9 February 1922): 14–15.

Dinter, Artur. *Die Sünde wider das Blut*. Leipzig: Matthes and Thost, 1920.

Efron, John M. *Medicine and the German Jews: A History*. New Haven, CT: Yale University Press, 2008.

Geller, Jay. "Bloodsin: Syphilis and the Construction of Jewish Identity." *Faultline: Interdisciplinary Approaches to German Studies* 1 (1992): 21–48.

———. *The Other Jewish Question. Identifying the Jew and Making Sense of Modernity*. New York: Fordham University Press, 2011.

Gertiser, Anita. *Falsche Scham: Strategien der Ueberzeugung in Aufklärungsfilmen zur Bekämpfung der Geschlechtskrankheiten (1918 1935)*. Göttingen: V & R unipress, 2015.

Giese, W., ed. *Anti-Semitisches Jahrbuch*. Berlin: W. Giese, 1903.

Gilman, Sander. *The Jew's Body*. New York: Routledge, 1991.

Günther, Hans F.K. *Rassenkunde des judischen Volkes*. Munich: J.F. Lehmann, 1930.

Hagener, Malte. *Geschlecht in Fesseln: Sexualität zwischen Aufklärung und Ausbeutung im Weimarer Kino 1918–1933*. Munich: Edition Text & Kritik, 2000.

Hanauer, W. "Die sexuelle Frage von jüdisch-biologischen Standpunkte." *Jüdisch-liberale Zeitung* 34 (21 August 1925).

Hayden, Deborah. *Pox: Genius, Madness, and the Mysteries of Syphilis*. New York: Basic Books, 2003.

Hitler, Adolf. *Mein Kampf*, trans. Alvin Johnson. New York: Reynal & Hitchcock, 1940.

"Judenblut: wissenschaftliche Blutforschung und ihre Ergebnisse." *Der Stürmer: Nürnberger Wochenblatt zum Kampf um die Wahrheit* 35 (1926).

Jusek, Karin. *Auf der Suche nach der Verlorenen: Die Prostitution im Wien der Jahrhundertwende*. Vienna: Löcker, 1994.

Killen, Andreas. "What Is an Enlightenment Film? Cinema and the Rhetoric of Social Hygiene in Interwar Germany." *Social Science History* 39 (1, Spring 2015): 107–27.

Laukötter, Anja. "Listen and Watch: The Practice of Lecturing and the Epistemological Status of Sex Education Films in Germany." *Gesnerus* 72 (1, 2015): 56–76.

"Law for the Protection of German Blood and German Honor." In Rabinbach and Gilman, *The Third Reich Sourcebook*, 209.

"Law for the Protection of the Hereditary Health of the German Volk." In Rabinbach and Gilman, *The Third Reich Sourcebook*, 329–30.

"Mädchenfleisch Handel." *Der Stürmer: Nürnberger Wochenblatt zum Kampf um die Wahrheit* 30 (1926).

Parish, Lawrence Charles. Review of *Death of Medicine in Nazi Germany: Dermatology and Dermatopathology under the Swastika*. *New England Journal of Medicine* 340 (24, 1999): 1931.

Prawer, S.S. *Between Two Worlds: The Jewish Presence in German and Austrian Film, 1910–1933*. New York: Berghahn Books, 2005.

Rabinbach, Anson, and Sander L. Gilman, ed. *The Third Reich Sourcebook*. Berkeley: University of California Press, 2013.

Reiter, Hans. "Nationalsozialistische Revolution in Medizin und Gesundheitspolitik." *Ziel und Weg* 14 (1933): 422–27.

Resek, Felix, "Das Sanitätswesen." *Jüdische Zeitung: National-Jüdisches-Organ (Wien)* 38 (20 September 1918): 5–6.

Rose, Alison, *Jewish Women in Fin-de-Siècle Vienna*. Austin: University of Texas Press, 2009.

Rosenberg, Alfred. *Die Protokolle der Weisen von Zion und die Judische Weltpolitik*. Munich: Deutscher Volks, 1923.

Segel, Binjamin. "Die Judenheit in Ziffern." *Central Verein Zeitung* 14 (5 April 1923): 113–14.

Sichel, Max. "Paralyse der Juden in sexualogischer Beleuchtung." *Zeitschrift für Sexualwissenschaft*, Band 6 (1919–20): 98–104.

Smith, Jill Suzanne. "Richard Oswald and the Social Hygiene Film: Promoting Public Health or Promiscuity?" In *The Many Faces of Weimar Cinema: Rediscovering Germany's Filmic Legacy*, ed. Christian Rogowski, 13–30. Rochester, NY: Camden House, 2010.

———. "Working Girls: White-Collar Workers and Prostitutes in Late Weimar Fiction." *German Quarterly* 81 (4, 2008): 449–70.

Staemmler, Martin. "Aufgaben und Ziele der Rassenpflege." *Ziel und Weg* 3 (14, 1933): 415–22.

Strauss, Hermann. "Erkrankungen durch Alkohol und Syphilis bei den Juden." *Zeitschrift für Demographie und Statistik der Juden* 4 (3–4, 1927): 33–39.

Streicher, Julius. "Deutsche Volksgesundheit aus Blut und Boden!" *Nürnberg* 3–1 (1 January 1935): 1–3.

Thomalla, Curt. *Falsche Scham*. Berlin: Film Bücherei, 1926.

"Ursachen und Zweck der Beschneidung." *Die Wahrheit: unabhängige Zeitschrift für jüdische Interessen; Deutschösterreichische Wochenschrift für jüdische Interessen* 20 (16 May 1924): 4–5.

"Vom Juden Verseucht." Cartoon. *Der Stürmer: Nürnberger Wochenblatt zum Kampf um die Wahrheit* 44 (1930).

Vyleta, Daniel M. *Crime, Jews and News: Vienna, 1895–1914*. New York: Berghahn Books, 2007.

Weinstein, Valerie. *Antisemitism in Film Comedy in Nazi Germany*. Bloomington: Indiana University Press, 2019.

Chapter 11

THE EINSTEIN FILM

Animation, Relativity, and the Charge of "Jewish Science"

Brook Henkel

On 2 April 1922, in celebration of the opening of the Frankfurter Messe, a lengthy educational film on Albert Einstein's theory of relativity premiered in a large auditorium at the Universität Frankfurt am Main. Produced by the Colonna Filmgesellschaft of Berlin, *Die Grundlagen der Einsteinschen Relativitätstheorie* (*The Basic Principles of the Einstein Theory of Relativity*) ran more than two hours long and featured extensive, painstakingly constructed animation sequences, alongside photographic images and live-action shots, plus live commentary (in lieu of intertitles) to explain key principles of classical relativity, the theory of light, and Einsteinian relativity, which were illustrated on screen.[1] The film's director and commentator Hanns Walter Kornblum had considerable experience producing educational films for schools—including simple animated films on mathematical concepts—as head of the Kulturfilm department at the Deutsche Lichtbild-Gesellschaft (Deulig) founded in 1916. With his 1922 Einstein-Film, as it was popularly known and advertised, Kornblum reached a much larger audience outside the classroom and provoked a minor sensation in Germany and abroad. For both admirers and detractors of Einstein and his theories, Kornblum's film was notable for its efforts to make Einstein's abstract and counterintuitive theories of time and space more tangible for the viewer through the technical resources of cinema, especially animation. Promotional materials for the film stressed both the considerable time and effort required to produce its numerous trick sequences, as well as the fact that animation was indeed necessary to depict the strange phenomena theorized by Einstein and to transform his abstract scientific thoughts into *greifbare Vorstellungsbilder* (graspable images) for a popular audience.[2]

Appearing as it did in 1922, Kornblum's film entered the Weimar scene at a time of severe political conflict in the young republic. Just a few months after the film's premiere, foreign minister Walther Rathenau was assassinated by right-wing nationalists amid a German political climate dominated by antisemitism and violent attacks on the liberal and internationalist direction of the new democratic government. Einstein, a well-known Jewish scientist and outspoken supporter of left-leaning politics, pacifism, and both cosmopolitanism and Zionism, was a frequent target at the time of right-wing nationalists and suffered politically motivated attacks on the very validity of his scientific theories, considered to be "Jewish science" by his antisemitic detractors.[3] While Einstein's first publication on special relativity dated back to 1905, the early 1920s brought on a highly public and politicized interest in his theories as, alternatively, a source of national pride for the young republic in the groundbreaking work of a German scientist, or as espousing a perceptual, political, and ethical relativism that threatened the worldview of German nationalists.[4]

The antisemitic charge of Einstein's Jewish science in the 1920s involved several overlapping right-wing anxieties. Beyond personal attacks on Einstein himself, his theory of relativity came to symbolize a profound and destabilizing challenge to German national and cultural identities. Appearing in a 1922 issue of the Berlin film journal *Kino-Rat*, one review of *Die Grundlagen der Einsteinschen Relativitätstheorie*, with the headline "Der Film des physikalischen Nihilismus" (The Film of Physical Nihilism), declared that Einstein's theories not only made the public doubt their perception of physical reality, but also bolstered a broader nihilistic view of the world that relativized all sense of national honor and allegedly aligned with Einstein's leftist political affiliations.[5] The overtly antisemitic author goes on to condemn relativity theory as a Bolshevik-Zionist conspiracy to destroy a fixed, "absolute understanding of the universe."[6] With such attacks largely centered on Einstein's personal politics and Jewish identity, the broader charge of Jewish science lumped together his radical scientific theories with the post–World War I political, cultural, and social upheavals that German right-wing nationalists viciously and falsely blamed on the Jews of Europe. More recently, by contrast, there has been an attempt to reclaim the label Jewish science from its antisemitic origins by affirming Einstein's own suggestions of links between his Jewish heritage and patterns of intellectual thought. While denying that there is anything inherently Jewish about the scientific theory of relativity, new scholarship on Einstein has suggested a certain Jewish style in his scientific thought, which assumes that "an absolute truth exists, but is unavailable to any particular frame of reference," and is thus "formally similar [to] Talmudic interpretation, in which a larger metaphysical truth, God's truth, is presumed to exist, but which is as a whole beyond our capacity to grasp, but elements of which are illuminated, uncovered, exposed, by seemingly contrasting human interpretations."[7]

This chapter on the 1922 Einstein film cannot do justice to the extensive scholarship on the political and antisemitic responses to Einstein's theories themselves during the Weimar period, nor will it address the difficult question of an authentic connection between Einstein's Jewish identity and beliefs, on the one hand, and his work as a scientist, on the other. Instead, the present analysis will focus on Kornblum's film itself and the roles that animation played in the representation, experience, and divergent receptions of Einstein's theories through the popular medium of cinema in the 1920s. As numerous reviewers noted at the time, the famous personality of Einstein the man is conspicuously absent in Kornblum's film.[8] As a result, critical responses to the film focused less on Einstein himself than on the variously destabilizing, suggestive, and illuminating effects of Kornblum's animation sequences. As is well known, animation as a genre and set of techniques has a longstanding and problematic relationship to representations of racial, ethnic, and gendered difference. While the Einstein film entirely lacks the cartoon figuration that made Felix the Cat and early Mickey Mouse ciphers of Blackness and Jewishness during the interwar years, the aesthetic effects of Kornblum's animated images provoked uneasy responses in many German viewers and reinforced their antisemitic beliefs in the destabilizing influence of Einstein's Jewish science. In this sense, Kornblum's Einstein film lends itself less to a reading of a conscious and affirmative Jewish identity on the part of cultural producers and more of Jewishness as an antisemitic construct that emerges in the reception of the film's animated images and concepts. Most surprising is how this response comes about in relation to moving images that are seemingly neutral, abstract, and diagrammatic.

The following sections will explore the convergence of science, antisemitism, and cinematic experience in the reception of Kornblum's Einsteinian animations in the 1920s, beginning with a reconstruction of the film's relationship to the broader artistic, cinematic, and popular-scientific culture of the Weimar Republic. Exact analysis of *Die Grund-*

lagen der Einsteinschen Relativitätstheorie itself proves difficult since the 1922 film has been lost and exists only in contemporaneous promotional stills and as the basis for a similar but much shorter American film, Max and Dave Fleischer's *The Einstein Theory of Relativity*, released a year later.[9] This chapter nevertheless ventures a close reading of Kornblum's original film by reconstructing its animation sequences based on published stills, promotional materials, and the Fleischers' 1923 film. In addition to analyzing the antisemitic reception of Einstein's Jewish science in the film, the sections that follow document the perceived affinities between relativity theory and animation in the 1920s and show how German responses to Kornblum's film reveal unconscious connections to both early avant-garde cinema and the racially explicit figurations of contemporaneous cartoon animation. In this reading, animation becomes central for understanding the connections between cinematic experience and a range of antisemitic discourses that coalesce around the reception of relativity in 1920s Germany.

Relativity as Mass Suggestion

One of Einstein's staunchest detractors during the Weimar period, the German physicist Ernst Gehrcke, is to thank for an exhaustive collection of early-1920s newspaper articles on Einstein and relativity theory, including numerous clippings on the Kornblum film.[10] When Gehrcke famously and repeatedly derided the acceptance of Einsteinian relativity by popular audiences as the result of mass suggestion via media, it was not only newspapers, but also educational science films like Kornblum's that were supposedly the culprit.[11] Gehrcke's primary interest was the deluge of popular reporting on the theory of relativity in the 1920s, which irritated Einstein himself and was weaponized by his opponents to discredit his work, whose popularity and acceptance was allegedly predicated on mass propaganda and advertising that supposedly hypnotized both scientists and the general public.[12]

In the case of Kornblum's film, the accusation of hypnotic suggestion has a particular historical resonance with the representations and reception of German expressionist and avant-garde cinema of the Weimar period.[13] While Gehrcke's language of mass suggestion should be read first and foremost as a suspect strategy to attack Einstein and his theories, it also provides a productive link between popular media representations of relativity theory and broader anxieties about cinema and hypnosis in the 1920s. Alongside prominent close-ups of eyes staring out at the audience in films such as Fritz Lang's *Dr. Mabuse, der Spieler* (*Dr. Mabuse, the Gambler*, 1922), cinema's hypnotic powers were frequently evoked in Weimar cinema through the appearance of spinning circles and discs, from hypnotic whorls on the original posters and advertisements for Robert Wiene's *Das Cabinet des Dr. Caligari* (*The Cabinet of Dr. Caligari*, 1920) to rotating spirals in shop windows in Walter Ruttmann's city symphony film *Berlin* (1927) and Lang's *M* (1931). According to Siegfried Kracauer, the swirling spirals in Weimar cinema symbolized a wavering between anarchic chaos and authority that he saw in both the period's films and society at large.[14] Gehrcke's twin anxieties about the destabilizing nature of Einstein's theories and a supposed mass media conspiracy in their dissemination fits neatly into this reading of Weimar culture. Kornblum's film, for its part, features numerous spinning discs, which might be read as both a symbolic materialization of Gehrcke's fears and a visual motif that links the Einstein film to the suggestively hypnotic images of Weimar cinema at large.

Due to the nature of the physical phenomena depicted, the Einstein film indeed relied on numerous animations of spinning circular objects like clocks, wheels, and planets to demonstrate time dilation, the relative trajectories of material objects and light, and a general unmooring of temporal and spatial location, such as in one of the film's images of a rotating Earth receding into the darkness of space. In a sequence likely borrowed from Kornblum's original 1922 film, the Fleischers' 1923 version *The Einstein Theory of Relativity* features a spinning cutout animation of Earth with an arrow extended perpendicular to the planet's surface to indicate an observer's location. "To the man on earth the arrow always points up," reads a block of text above the image of the spinning planet. "To us out here in space it points in all directions." As the image of Earth continues to spin, the film suggests to the viewer the disorienting relativity and instability in our comfortable sense of direction—up, down, left, right, north, south, and so on—when unmoored from Earth's gravity and left floating in space. Despite the educational aims of the film, the general impression left on the viewer, as many contemporaneous critics noted, was a feeling of profound uncertainty in our familiar perceptions and secure place in the world.[15]

The Einstein film's affinities with the disorienting and hypnotic effects of Weimar cinema were already prominently announced in the film's own promotional materials. The cover illustration of a four-page film program distributed at initial screenings of *Die Grundlagen der Einsteinschen Relativitätstheorie* primed viewers for a cinematic experience that blended expressionist film aesthetics, abstract animation, and scientific theory (figure 11.1). Dominating the top half of the image, an explosion of jagged shapes recalls the distorted set design and writing in early expressionist films like *Das Cabinet des Dr. Caligari*, evoking associations, likely unintentional, between Einstein's theories and Caligarian themes of psychological delusion and manipulation by authorities. Surrounding these abstract shapes, a halo of energetic looping lines adds to the image the suggestion of animation, both the recent innovations of Ruttmann's and Hans Richter's abstract films, as well as the figurative line-drawing animations of Felix the Cat and Mutt and Jeff cartoons, recently imported to Germany.[16] Completing the cover illustration, the abbreviated title "The Einstein-Film" appears below in a matching jagged style, thus further associating relativity theory with expressionist film aesthetics, while blurring any clear distinction between Einstein being the subject of the film or the creative force behind it.[17] In comparison with the program cover, the Fleischer film and the surviving images and descriptions of Kornblum's original seem utterly tame and didactic. Nonetheless, the sensationalism of such promotional materials colored and shaped the reception of the film, which was attributed a suggestive and disorienting power that, for antisemitic reviewers, could be traced back to Einstein himself.[18] Perhaps inadvertently, the hyphen in the abbreviated title used in promotional materials and film reviews fused together in the minds of German viewers the manipulations of cinema with relativity theory and Einstein's personal identity.

Although Gehrcke's antisemitic tendencies were not the primary motivation behind his public attacks on Einstein,[19] his mistrust of both relativity and mass media fit into a general pattern of right-wing antisemitic thought in the Weimar period. Crystallizing by 1930 in the vague and notoriously flexible term *Kulturbolschewismus* (cultural Bolshevism), progressive aspects of modernist art, science, media, and mass culture were decried by right-wing Weimar commentators and Nationalsozialistische Deutsche Arbeiterpartei (National Socialist German Workers' Party; NSDAP) members as a dangerous foreign influence and enemy of a supposedly authentic German culture. As many Jewish and leftist critics were quick to note, the accusation of cultural Bolshevism had little to do with revolutionary communism in the Soviet Union and was more a veiled antisemitic *Schlagwort* (buzzword) to encompass the broad cultural developments seen as Jewish by the far right: from psychoanalysis and sexual reform to avant-garde art and architecture, left-leaning newspapers, pacifism, and the distinctly Ameri-

Figure 11.1. "The Einstein-Film." Cover illustration of the four-page film program for *Die Grundlagen der Einsteinschen Relativitätstheorie*, Colonna-Filmgesellschaft, 1922. Source: Filmmuseum München/Edition Filmmuseum, used with permission.

can mass-cultural products of jazz and Hollywood.[20] Interestingly, for the present argument, the widespread critical reporting on the topic of cultural Bolshevism around 1930 frequently included mentions of Einstein's relativity theory alongside popular cinema and animation as belonging to this loose constellation of cultural phenomena that were the focus of antisemitic attacks.[21] The following sections will analyze how science, cinematic experience, and animation converge in the construction of this antisemitic response to Kornblum's film.

Disorientations

According to the author of a critical 1922 review of Kornblum's film in the *Casseler Allgemeine Zeitung*, it was "all the illusions of animation" that were especially suspect in the film's attempt "to cram the world-wonder [of relativity] into the minds" of viewers.[22] Like Kornblum's original film, the Fleischer version dedicates its early sections to demonstrating not Einstein's theories, but rather the basic principles of classical relativity that date back to Newton and earlier: the relativity of motion, direction, size, and speed as dependent on different frames of reference. Ironically, it seems to be these sections of the film that draw the most ire of Einstein's explicitly antisemitic critics, who blamed the Jewish scientist for undermining their sense of absolutes and stable standpoints.

While the author of the review "Der Film des physikalischen Nihilismus" was able to dismiss as frivolous a live-action scene demonstrating the relativity of motion, it is the animation sequences that prove the most disconcerting and provocative. For a live-action scene appearing in both the Kornblum and Fleischer versions, a camera was mounted first on a barge and then along the shore of the canal to demonstrate that a working boatman can appear fixed in relation to the shore while moving across the boat.[23] Due to the wealth of indexical information in the photographic image, the demonstrated relativity of motion is scarcely disorienting or troubling. Based on foreground and background details, viewers can easily identify the stable location and viewpoint of the camera, whether mounted on the moving barge or along the fixed shore of the canal. The situation is not so clear in the case of animation, where the experience of perspective, foreground–background relations, and movement can be freely manipulated at the animation table. While Kornblum's and the Fleischers' animation sequences often include a stationary object (a cutout of the sun, a planet, or earthly landscape), which serves as a fixed referent for the type of relativity being demonstrated, this is not always the case. In one sequence illustrating the counterintuitive fact that the movement of the Earth around the sun is significantly faster than a flying bullet, the Fleischer film displays cutouts of the Earth and a bullet, both animated and moving against a black background. The deceptively simple depiction of the relativity of speed is in fact highly disorienting for viewers, as we are denied a fixed and stable viewpoint and can easily imagine another factor of relativity in our own speeding trajectory through space. In contrast to the inferred camera location in live-action shooting, the camera fixed atop the animation table disappears as a presence in the animated image. Without the inferred camera-eye easily located in live-action shots, the viewer of animation is left adrift in the image. Are the animated lines and objects alone moving, or are we as viewers to feel that we are moving, too? The experience of animation denies any easy answer and fits nicely with the lesson of classical relativity, "that the stillness or movement of an object can only be determined in relationship to another," as one reviewer of Kornblum's film put it.[24]

With the complaint of lacking absolutes and stable viewpoints—found in many critical German reviews of Kornblum's film at the time—the experience of animation intersects with the antisemitic response to Einstein's theories. Even sympathetic reviewers noted with dismay what Einstein's teachings suggested to the layperson—that is, the shattering of "basic mechanical, physical, and mathematical principles," that "two times two is no longer four"—declaring further that cinematic animation was indeed a fitting technique for communicating this new reality, for it made "the apparently impossible possible."[25] Often, it was less the particulars of Einstein's theories themselves that provoked reactionary writers and more what they metaphorically suggested in areas outside of physics. In explicitly antisemitic terms, Austrian writer Arthur Trebitsch's 1921 book *Deutscher Geist—oder Judentum!* (*German Spirit—or Jewishness!*) claimed, "When applied to life, the theory of relativity means nothing other than the loss and forfeiture of all definite standards for comprehending the world, whether that has to do with justice, ethics, science, or knowledge of any kind."[26] This Trebitsch relates formally to the shape of an "ever-rolling sphere, lacking in fixed standpoints," which he took as symbolic of the "Jewish . . . worldview."[27] With such antisemitic anxieties already articulated in terms of dynamic and disorienting geometric forms, it is perhaps less surprising that they would be directly projected onto the experience of abstract animation in Kornblum's film. The *Casseler Allgemeine Zeitung* review quoted above similarly decried the ethical relativism and loss of absolutes implied by Einstein's theories. For this reviewer, Kornblum's film not only functioned as a general *Reklame* (advertisement) for such broadly relativistic views, but also purposely used "all the illusions of animation" to astound, bewilder, and manipulate the audience into accepting them.[28]

In addition to the antisemitic prejudices of such German reviewers, the paranoid reception of Kornblum's animations as disorienting and manipulative depended on at least two other historical factors. First, the distinction between lay and expert viewers, mentioned repeatedly in reviews of the film, made the medium of cinema itself a conflicted site for the representation and communication of scientific theories in the 1920s. While many lay reviewers affirmed the tradition of German visual pedagogy in relation to the film with terms like *Anschaulichkeit* (vividness) and *Veranschaulichung* (visualization),[29] just as many expressed confusion over the concepts and their relationship to the moving images, confirming fears of expert scientists that complex physical and mathematical concepts could not be successfully communicated to a mass audience via film.[30] In the explicitly antisemitic reception of the film, this concern over lay spectatorship was exploited to suggest that the film failed to teach a delimited set of scientific ideas and instead suggested broader notions of ethical, political, or perceptual relativity to an uninformed viewer (mainly projections, of course, of these critics' own fears). When focusing on expert opinion, opponents cast doubt on the theories themselves and the *Klüngel* (cabal) of scientists that espoused them, by highlighting the recourse to the mass medium of cinema to propagate scientific ideas, when the core of relativity theory, if valid, should be summarizable in "ten to twelve short theses."[31] In both cases, animation was suspect for its manipulative and suggestive effects that exceeded purely illustrative and educational purposes.

The second more-general factor in this reception of Kornblum's film was a broader discourse in the 1920s linking the experience of cinema and animation with Einstein's theories of relativity. Already in 1922, Dziga Vertov remarked that "drawings in motion" were especially suited for showing "the theory of relativity on the screen."[32] In his book *Der sichtbare Mensch* (*Visible Man*; 1924), Béla Balázs describes how the flexible manipulations of movement and proximity in cinema give the impression of bending time and space in ways comparable to Einstein's thought experiments.[33] Making the connection to animation explicit, a British educator in a 1927 *Observer* article reflected on the pedagogical value of the elastic animated line, which could bring together "the joys of Felix [the Cat], Professor Einstein, and the Zoo simultaneously."[34] Repeatedly in the 1920s, critics and filmmakers saw a strong affinity between animation and Einsteinian relativity with its elastic dilations of time, bendings of space, and collapsing black holes, which corresponded well with what Sergei Eisenstein would later call the plasmaticness of animation.[35]

Interestingly, in contrast to Kornblum's animated demonstrations of classical relativity, which so vexed critics, the images presenting aspects of Einstein's own theories of special and general relativity toward the end of the film were far less dynamic and disorienting—at least visually. An illustration of space-time curvature, first empirically observed during the May 1919 solar eclipse by Arthur Eddington, for example, simply shows the observed displacement of stars around the eclipsed sun through the superimposition of two static images. For an illustration of the time dilation of interstellar travel in the 1923 Fleischer film, a spaceship races against an animated background text of yearly dates emanating from a fixed image of the planet Earth.[36] Although the very idea of a relative slowing down of time or contraction of length at great speeds made one "actually begin to sweat," according to one German reviewer, the accompanying images were largely stable and static, even more so in Kornblum's film, which showed, for example, rectangular shapes moving against a fixed grid and clock to illustrate relativistic length contraction.[37] With the limitations of early film technologies, the affinities between animation and Einsteinian relativity existed more as an imaginative possibility than a cinematic reality. Nevertheless, the discourse linking the two contributed to a sense that Einsteinian physics were somehow immanent in film animation itself and, for antisemitic critics, that a Jewish influence was somehow behind it.

Abstraction and Figuration

On 24 August 1920 Gehrcke delivered a lecture on relativity theory as "mass suggestion" at an anti-Einstein rally and meeting of the Arbeitsgemeinschaft deutscher Naturforscher zur Erhaltung reiner Wissenschaft (Working Society of German Scientists for the Preservation of Pure Science) at the Berlin Philharmonic. At the same event, the organization's founder, overt antisemite Paul Weyland, also gave a talk in which he famously derided Einsteinian relativity as scientific Dadaism, thus equating Einstein's theories with avant-garde works later condemned by the National Socialists as degenerate art.[38] The implications would have been clear to the assembled audience. Like the Berlin Dadaists, Einstein and his theories were taken as a direct threat to morality, rationality, traditional institutions, stable perspectives, and one's very perception of the world. While Weyland's mention of Dada was meant to be purely derogatory, the comparison also underscores a credible link between the popular reception of Einstein's theories in the early 1920s and contemporaneous developments in the avant-garde. For experimental filmmakers, in particular, there indeed seemed an inherent connection between Einsteinian relativity and avant-garde cinema, both of which upended stable perspectives and perceptual orientation. Viking Eggeling and Hans Richter, both familiar figures in Berlin Dadaist circles, must have sensed this connection when in 1920 they solicited Einstein himself for a letter of support when applying for technical assistance from Universum Film Aktiengesellschaft (UFA) for their early experiments in abstract animation. While their request likely went unanswered, clearly relativity theory had a strong appeal for artists like Eggeling and Richter, and perhaps Ruttmann, too, all erstwhile painters, who looked to cinema to add the Einsteinian fourth dimension of time to the visual arts.[39] With the Einstein film, this loose connection between abstract animation and relativity was substantially realized.

Keeping Weyland's own agenda at a critical distance, this concluding section takes his equation of relativity theory and avant-garde art at face value as encouragement to read Kornblum's *Die Grundlagen der Einsteinschen Relativitätstheorie* not only as an educational film, but also as a work of abstract animation not unlike the early 1920s absolute film. At the same time, a comparison between the Einstein film and contemporaneous avant-garde cinema underscores how Einstein's public persona along with the popular reception of his theories shaped the experience of Kornblum's seemingly neutral, abstract, and diagrammatic animations in explicitly antisemitic terms. While the disorienting and hypnotic effects of abstract animation in Ruttmann's *Opus* films (1921–25), for example, did provoke some consternation among contemporary critics, it was not in the politically and racially charged way that critics responded to Kornblum's film.[40] For antisemitic critics in the early 1920s, Einstein's Jewish identity was somehow manifest in the destabilizing lines and motions of cinematic animation itself. Or, more accurately, the neutral scientific film provided the animated space for projecting antisemitic fears and anxieties about various unrelated instabilities, whether political, cultural, perceptual, or socioeconomic. A comparison with avant-garde cinema will help to bring out the interplay between abstraction and figurative meaning in the reception of the Einstein film.

In addition to the antisemitic discourses that saw relativity theory as a metaphor for "Jewish" manipulation and disorientation, as analyzed above, Jews were frequently linked in German racialist thinking to the modernity of cities, new technologies, and market exchange.[41] In the 1920s the avant-garde abstract animation film seemed to embody these new technological rhythms. Richter's abstract *Rhythmus* (*Rhythm*) films (1923–25) related not only to the dynamic movements of other art forms like dance and music, but also to the rhythms of urban traffic, advertising, industry, and media technologies.[42] Ruttmann made these connections explicit when he reworked his earlier *Opus* animations into advertisement films and with his 1927 *Berlin* city symphony film, which begins with accelerating, animated abstractions giving way to a rapid photographic montage of trains speeding toward the metropolis.[43] In Kornblum's film a similar connection between abstract animation and technological modernity is complicated by the explicit focus on relativity and the implied presence of Einstein behind these theories. While not strictly necessary for its pedagogical aims, Kornblum's more abstract, diagrammatic animations are filled with simple images of trains, cars, towers, modern bridges, clocks, and guns, which taken together suggest a connection between relativity theory and the dynamic structures of modern technology and the city. The Fleischers' American version is even more direct. After introducing the concept of relativity, the film begins with a photographic montage of technologies, from steam engines, cars, suspension bridges, skyscrapers, and airplanes to wireless telegraphy and x-rays. The invention of the latter, we are told, required us to overcome the deception of our senses, much like Einstein's theories. In the minds of antisemitic detractors, this could only have confirmed their dubious associations of modernity and deception with Einstein's Jewish science.

Like the abstract animations of avant-garde cinema, Kornblum's film not only evoked the ideas and images of technological modernity, but also embodied and approximated its dynamic movements and rhythms through the experience of animated forms. Striking in the Einstein film, as discussed above, is how this experience of largely abstract animation mapped onto existing antisemitic discourses. In this sense, the Einstein film perhaps has just as much in common with the reception of 1920s animated cartoons, which were often racially explicit in their figurative representations. As recent scholarship has shown, even less racially explicit characters like Felix the Cat and Mickey Mouse were not only taken as representations of Jewishness or Blackness by viewers, but were also directly inspired by preexisting performances and caricatures of racial otherness in music, dance, folktales, and theater.[44] In Germany, "early Mickey Mouse cartoons featur[ing] a pesky, ratty creature creating mischief, indulging in vaudeville and low-life," fit easily into racist ideas and caricatures of both Jews and African Americans, often centered on racist projections of the cartoons' animated movements and syncopated rhythms as supposedly representative of both a degenerate mass culture and the racial or ethnic other.[45] By contrast, for Walter Benjamin, who downplayed the racial overtones in animation, early Mickey Mouse not only embodied and reproduced the animating rhythms of modernity, but also functioned as a figure of survival in a dehumanizing world.[46] In short, modernity and race were deeply and ambiguously intertwined in early cartoon animation.

Lacking any clear figurative representations of racial or ethnic identity, Kornblum's educational science film excludes the possibility of both a positive expression of Einstein's Jewishness, as well as a critique of overt or latent antisemitism in the film itself. Instead, well outside its intended pedagogical function, the Einstein film appeared historically as an abstract animated surface for projecting antisemitic anxieties about modernity, mass media, and social, political, and moral disorientations, which coalesced around the loose and multivalent metaphor of relativity. In this case, among Kornblum's antisemitic viewers, even abstract lines and objects in their animatedness produced what theorist Sianne Ngai calls an ambiguous ugly feeling of racial otherness in animation.[47] Whereas various 1920s cartoon figures exhibited outward markers of racial and ethnic difference, the perceived Jewishness of Kornblum's animated lines and objects emerged only in relation to the external factors of Einstein's Jewish identity, combined with the antisemitism and nationalism of German right-wing viewers, who found in Kornblum's disorienting animations not only a symbol but also an approximate experience of the tumultuous early years of the Weimar Republic.

Brook Henkel is assistant professor of German and film studies at St. Lawrence University. His research focuses on twentieth-century German literature and film with a special interest in German modernism, early and avant-garde cinema, and interrelations between art and science. His recent publications include "Kafka's Animations: Trick Films, Narrative, Reification" (2018) in *New German Critique*, as well as articles on Hans Richter, Stan Brakhage, and Nikolaus Geyrhalter. He is currently completing his first book, *Animistic Fictions: Literary Modernism, Animation, and Early Film*, and is developing a new research project on the functions of astronomy in postwar German film, literature, and critical theory.

Notes

1. The complete 1922 version of *Die Grundlagen der Einsteinschen Relativitätstheorie* is considered lost. Its original length and basic structure, however, can be inferred from the censorship card, which lists three sections to the film: "1. Das Relativitätsprinzip; 2. Die Lichttheorie; 3. Die spezielle Relativitäts-Theorie." The censorship card and a wealth of other archival documents related to the film can be accessed as digital files on the DVD release, *Wunder der Schöpfung* (1925, dir. Hanns Walter Kornblum). This feature-length *Kulturfilm* with the translated title "Our Heavenly Bodies" follows Kornblum's narrowly educational Einstein film and attempts a more expansive visualization of contemporary scientific knowledge and humans' place in the universe.
2. See the original four-page film program, Der Einstein-Film, for *Die Grundlagen der Einsteinschen Relativitätstheorie* (Colonna-Filmgesellschaft, 1922), included on the *Wunder der Schöpfung* DVD. Translations from the original German are mine unless otherwise noted.
3. The term "Jewish science" I borrow from Steven Gimbel as shorthand for the broad antisemitic assessment of Einsteinian relativity in 1920s and 1930s Germany. While clearly a Nazi construction, Gimbel has taken up the label to explore possible authentic connections between Einstein's Jewish identity and his scientific thought. As Gimbel himself acknowledges, however, positive connections between Einstein's Jewishness and relativity theory were not evident in contemporaneous writings of Jewish intellectuals and the German-Jewish press, where interest was more in Einstein's public politics and support for Zionism. See Steven Gimbel, *Einstein's Jewish Science: Physics at the Intersection of Politics and Religion* (Baltimore: Johns Hopkins University Press, 2012). I thank Kerry Wallach for sharing with me her notes on references to Einstein in the Weimar Jewish press.
4. For detailed reconstructions and analysis of the politically charged reception of Kornblum's film and Einstein's theories more generally in the 1920s, see Milena Wazeck, "The 1922 Einstein Film: Cinematic Innovation and Public Controversy," *Physics in Perspective* 12 (2010): 163–79; and Wazeck, *Einstein's Opponents: The Public Controversy about the Theory of Relativity in the 1920s*, trans. Geoffrey S. Koby (Cambridge: Cambridge University Press, 2014).
5. "Der Film des physikalischen Nihilismus," *Kino-Rat* 9–10 (1922): "Einstein baut ein Weltgebäude auf den Unvollkommenheiten unserer Sinneswahrnehmungen auf. Er predigt uns: Alle deine Wahrnehmungen sind relativ, folglich musst du dir ein relatives Weltall nach meinem Rezept zurechtzimmern. Das ist nichts anderes als *wissenschaftlicher Nihilismus* unfruchtbarster Art im Einklang mit der politischen Vergangenheit des Professors, der Parteien angehört, die die *Relativität des nationalen Ehrgefühls* auf ihre Fahne geschrieben haben" (emphasis in original).
6. "Der Film des physikalischen Nihilismus": "Alle Einsteinler mitsamt ihrem Verständnis heuchelnden bolsche-zionistischen Klüngel können die Tatsache nicht aus der

Welt schaffen, daß Zeit, Raum und Materie unendlich bestehen und daß man von einem gegebenen Mittelpunkt aus sehr wohl ein absolutes Weltbild konstruieren kann."

7. Gimbel, *Einstein's Jewish Science*, 213. Gimbel references Einstein's own writings that assert a connection between Jewish identity and intellectual work (4). See Albert Einstein, "Antisemitismus: Abwehr durch Erkenntnis" [c. 1920], in *The Collected Papers of Albert Einstein*, vol. 7, *The Berlin Years: Writings, 1918–1921*, ed. Michel Janssen (Princeton, NJ: Princeton University Press, 2002), 294: "man merkt an ihrer geistigen Produktion die jüdische Abstammung."
8. See, e.g., "Ein Einstein-Film," *Deutsche Allgemeine Zeitung* (Berlin), 4 April 1922.
9. The idea to purchase and bring a version of Kornblum's film to the United States was likely the work of Edwin M. Fadman, director of Equity Films of New York City. In adapting the film for an American audience, the popular science writer Garrett P. Serviss also put together a short book publication, *The Einstein Theory of Relativity* (New York: Edwin Miles Fadman, 1923), illustrated with images inspired by Kornblum's film and taken directly from the Fleischer version. For a more detailed account, see Stewart Tryster and Ronny Loewy, "The Kornblum Puzzle," in the *Wunder der Schöpfung* DVD booklet.
10. The 1922 articles "Der Film des physikalischen Nihilismus" and "Ein Einstein-Film," referenced above, plus the many other newspaper articles quoted in the pages to follow, are now easily accessible online among complete scans of Ernst Gehrcke's surviving collection of newspaper clippings, made available at http://echo.mpiwg-berlin.mpg.de/content/modernphysics/gehrcke/ by the Max-Planck-Institut für Wissenschaftsgeschichte. I am indebted to Milena Wazeck for identifying and contextualizing many of the key articles on Kornblum's film in Gehrcke's collection. See Wazeck, "The 1922 Einstein Film."
11. Ernst Gehrcke, *Die Relativitätstheorie, eine wissenschaftliche Massensuggestion* (Berlin: Arbeitsgemeinschaft deutscher Naturforscher zur Erhaltung reiner Wissenschaft, 1920). On Gehrcke's newspaper-clipping scrapbooks and conception of mass media influence, see also Anke te Heesen, "Albert Einstein in Papier: Die Zeitungsausschnittsammlung des Physikers Ernst Gehrcke," in *Der Zeitungsausschnitt: Ein Papierobjekt der Moderne* (Frankfurt am Main: Fischer, 2006), 137–74.
12. Wazeck, *Einstein's Opponents*, 219–27.
13. On the historical discourses and representations linking early cinema and hypnotic suggestion, see Stefan Andriopoulos, *Possessed: Hypnotic Crime, Corporate Fiction, and the Invention of Cinema* (Chicago: University of Chicago Press, 2008).
14. Siegfried Kracauer, *From Caligari to Hitler: A Psychological History of the German Film* (Princeton, NJ: Princeton University Press, 2004), 186, 222.
15. See, for example, "Der Einstein-Film über die 'Grundlagen der Relativitäts-Theorie,'" *Württemberger Zeitung* (Stuttgart), 14 September 1922: "Sicher . . . , dass Einstein an den Grundfesten unserer altgewohnten Anschauungen rüttelt . . . , dass wir uns unsicher fühlen, auf dem Fleckchen Erde, das uns stets so festgegründet erschien."
16. On the influence of American cartoon animation on the German avant-garde toward the end of World War I, see Andrés Mario Zervigón, "'A Political Struwwelpeter?' John Heartfield's Early Film Animation and the Wartime Crisis of Photographic Representation," in *John Heartfield and the Agitated Image: Photography, Persuasion, and the Rise of Avant-Garde Photomontage* (Chicago: University of Chicago Press, 2012), 95–135.
17. Einstein himself publicly denied any involvement in the film, which was produced rather in consultation with others, among them physiologist Georg Friedrich Nicolai

and writer Otto Buek of Berlin. See Einstein's statement in "Professor Einstein und der Einstein-Film," *Berliner Tageblatt*, 2 June 1922. Kornblum's later remembrances, however, suggest that Einstein may have in fact looked over the screenplay, though he did not want his contributions made public due to concerns over political attacks on himself and his theories. See Wazeck, "The 1922 Einstein Film," 165, 175–76.

18. In his collection of newspaper clippings, Gehrcke highlighted with red pencil a brief article reporting that advertisement posters for the film had been ripped down from the walls of train stations in the area of Zehlendorf in Berlin. See "Demonstrationen gegen den Zehlendorfer Einsteinfilm," *Groß-Lichterfelder Lokalanzeiger* (Berlin), 12 May 1922.
19. Wazeck, *Einstein's Opponents*, 230–31.
20. Hermann Gundersheimer, "Jüdischer Kulturbolschewismus," *Gemeindeblatt der Israelitischen Gemeinde Frankfurt am Main* 11, no. 5 (January 1933): 133–34.
21. An article by Hans Bach from 1932, for example, lists "Einstein's relativity theory," "Chaplin films," and "Mickey Mouse," alongside Bauhaus architecture and Piscator's drama, as examples of so-called cultural Bolshevism attacked by right-wing critics. See "'Kulturbolschewismus'?," *C.V.-Zeitung: Blätter für Deutschtum und Judentum* (Berlin) 11, no. 8 (19 February 1932): 65.
22. "Einstein und kein Ende!" *Casseler Allgemeine Zeitung*, 18 May 1922. The author condemns "der Einstein-Film, der alle Bluffs der Trickzeichnung spielen läßt, um, von mehr oder weniger passenden Worten begleitet, das Weltwunder in die Gehirne einzupauken."
23. This scene, mentioned in many reviews and reproduced both in the Fleischer version and in promotional materials for Kornblum's film, was described most dismissively in "Der Film des physikalischen Nihilismus" as frivolous pedantry (*belanglose Tüfteleien*).
24. "Der Einstein-Film: Bildliche Darstellung der Relativitätstheorie," *Vossische Zeitung* (Berlin), 6 April 1922. An American review of Kornblum's film suggested that even more might have been done to avoid static backgrounds in the animation sequences in order to preserve the disorienting "paradoxes and puzzles of relativity" in cinema. See J. Malcolm Bird, "Relativity in the Films," *Scientific American* (August 1922): 92.
25. "Der Einstein-Film," *Württemberger Zeitung* (Stuttgart), 18 September 1922.
26. Arthur Trebitsch, *Deutscher Geist—oder Judentum! Der Weg der Befreiung* (Berlin: Antaios, 1921), 256.
27. Trebitsch, *Deutscher Geist*, 256: "Denn hier wäre Relativität . . . nichts anderes als die dem tiefsten Wesen der jüdisch beweglichen Kugelgestalt konforme und angepasste Weltanschauung. Denn wahrlich! die Kugel, die ewig rollende, standpunktlose, wie sollte sie als denkendes Wesen anders als relativistisch orientiert sein?"
28. "Einstein und kein Ende!"
29. See, e.g., the reviews "Einstein im Film," *Vorwärts* (Berlin), 1 September 1921; and "Ein Einstein-Film," *Deutsche Allgemeine Zeitung* (Berlin), 4 April 1922, respectively.
30. One reviewer complained of a vexing discrepancy (*Zwiespalt*) between the verbal explanations and illustrative images in Kornblum's film. See "Kein Aufklärungsfilm: Philosophische Betrachtungen eines Unphilosophen," *B.Z. am Mittag* (Berlin), 4 April 1922. For a broader reconstruction of expert and lay audiences of Kornblum's film, see Wazeck, "The 1922 Einstein Film," 172–74. Scott Curtis has argued persuasively for taking up the expert/lay distinction as a key category for theorizing early film spectatorship, which he explores in detailed readings of German scientific films before World War I, including the tradition of visual means of instruction (*Anschauungs-*

unterricht) in pedagogical theory and cinema. See Scott Curtis, *The Shape of Spectatorship: Art, Science, and Early Cinema in Germany* (New York: Columbia University Press, 2015).

31. See "Einstein und kein Ende!" and, quoted above, "Der Film des physikalischen Nihilismus."
32. Dziga Vertov, "WE: Variant of a Manifesto," in *Kino-Eye: The Writings of Dziga Vertov*, ed. Annette Michelson (Berkeley: University of California Press, 1984), 9.
33. Béla Balázs, *Visible Man or the Culture of Film*, in *Béla Balázs: Early Film Theory*, ed. Erica Carter, trans. Rodney Livingstone (New York: Berghahn Books, 2010), 40.
34. Quoted in Huntly Carter, *The New Spirit in the Cinema* (London: Harold Shaylor, 1930), 30.
35. See Sergei Eisenstein, *Eisenstein on Disney* [c. 1941], ed. Jay Leyda, trans. Alan Upchurch (Calcutta: Seagull Books, 1986). For a multifaceted theorization of the plasticity of film animation, see the essays collected in Karen Beckman, ed., *Animating Film Theory* (Durham, NC: Duke University Press, 2014). The notion of a fit or correspondence between cinematic form and scientific theory and practice has been expertly analyzed in Curtis, *The Shape of Spectatorship*.
36. This episode appearing in both the Fleischer film and the accompanying book by Garrett Serviss in fact depicts the impossible occurrence of a spacecraft traveling faster than the speed of light and thus moving backward in time relative to the Earth, a speculative scenario first popularized in the 1846 text *Die Gestirne und die Weltgeschichte* by German jurist and amateur astronomer Felix Eberty and again current with a new 1923 edition including a prominent introduction by Einstein himself. For commentary and versions of Eberty's original text, see Karl Clausberg, *Zwischen den Sternen: Was Einstein und Uexküll, Benjamin und das Kino der Astronomie des 19. Jahrhunderts verdanken* (Berlin: Akademie, 2006).
37. "Der Einstein-Film," *Württemberger Zeitung* (Stuttgart), 18 September 1922. For the relevant stills, see the four-page film program, Der Einstein-Film, 4.
38. See Jeroen van Dongen, "Reactionaries and Einstein's Fame: 'German Scientists for the Preservation of Pure Science,' Relativity, and the Bad Nauheim Meeting," *Physics in Perspective* 9 (2007): 212–30.
39. On the connections between Einstein and the 1920s avant-garde, see Linda Dalrymple Henderson, "Einstein and 20th-Century Art: A Romance in Many Dimensions," in *Einstein for the 21st Century: His Legacy in Science, Art, and Modern Culture*, ed. Peter L. Galison (Princeton, NJ: Princeton University Press, 2008), 101–29, especially 112–13.
40. Ruttmann's abstract animation film *Lichtspiel Opus II* (1922), for example, was restricted by German censors for its allegedly "hypnotic effect on the viewer." Jeanpaul Goergen, *Ruttmann: Eine Dokumentation* (Berlin: Freunde der deutschen Kinemathek, 1987), 23. Richter, who unlike Ruttmann had a Jewish background, claimed that Nazis in the late 1920s attacked both him and his films for their cultural Bolshevism, but there was no immediate antisemitic response to his earlier *Rhythmus* work that was comparable to the Einstein film's reception.
41. In the words of historian David Blackbourn, Jews became the "symbol of the disturbingly modern" by the 1870s, a decade that saw the emergence of a systematic scapegoating of "Semites" and the coinage of "antisemitism" as a term. David Blackbourn, *The Long Nineteenth Century: A History of Germany, 1780–1918* (New York: Oxford University Press, 1998), 307–8.
42. See Forschungsnetzwerk BTWH, ed., *Hans Richters* Rhythmus 21: *Schlüsselfilm der Moderne* (Würzburg: Königshausen & Neumann, 2012).

43. For detailed analysis of the relationship between avant-garde abstraction, advertising, and technological modernity in Ruttmann, see Michael Cowan, *Walter Ruttmann and the Cinema of Multiplicity: Avant-Garde—Advertising—Modernity* (Amsterdam: Amsterdam University Press, 2014).
44. See, e.g., Christopher P. Lehman, *The Colored Cartoon: Black Representation in American Animated Short Films, 1907–1954* (Amherst: University of Massachusetts Press, 2007).
45. Esther Leslie, *Hollywood Flatlands: Animation, Critical Theory and the Avant-Garde* (London: Verso, 2002), 81. For more extensive documentation, see J.P. Storm and M. Dressler, *Im Reiche der Micky Maus: Walt Disney in Deutschland, 1927–1945* (Berlin: Henschel, 1991).
46. Walter Benjamin, "Mickey Mouse" [1931], in *Selected Writings*, vol. 2, part 2, 1931–34, ed. Michael W. Jennings, Howard Eiland, and Gary Smith, trans. Rodney Livingstone (Cambridge, MA: Harvard University Press, 1999), 545. For a brilliant explication of Benjamin's scattered writings on Disney, see Miriam Bratu Hansen, "Micky-Maus," in *Cinema and Experience: Siegfried Kracauer, Walter Benjamin, and Theodor W. Adorno* (Berkeley: University of California Press, 2011), 163–82.
47. Sianne Ngai, "Animatedness," in *Ugly Feelings* (Cambridge, MA: Harvard University Press, 2005), 89–125.

Bibliography

Andriopoulos, Stefan. *Possessed: Hypnotic Crime, Corporate Fiction, and the Invention of Cinema*. Chicago: University of Chicago Press, 2008.
Balázs, Béla. *Visible Man or the Culture of Film*. In *Béla Balázs: Early Film Theory*, ed. Erica Carter, trans. Rodney Livingstone. New York: Berghahn Books, 2010.
Beckman, Karen, ed. *Animating Film Theory*. Durham, NC: Duke University Press, 2014.
Benjamin, Walter. "Mickey Mouse." In *Selected Writings*, vol. 2, part 2, 1931–34, ed. Michael W. Jennings, Howard Eiland, and Gary Smith, trans. Rodney Livingstone, 545–46. Cambridge, MA: Harvard University Press, 1999.
Blackbourn, David. *The Long Nineteenth Century: A History of Germany, 1780–1918*. New York: Oxford University Press, 1998.
Carter, Huntly. *The New Spirit in the Cinema*. London: Harold Shaylor, 1930.
Clausberg, Karl. *Zwischen den Sternen: Was Einstein und Uexküll, Benjamin und das Kino der Astronomie des 19. Jahrhunderts verdanken*. Berlin: Akademie, 2006.
Cowan, Michael. *Walter Ruttmann and the Cinema of Multiplicity: Avant-Garde—Advertising—Modernity*. Amsterdam: Amsterdam University Press, 2014.
Curtis, Scott. *The Shape of Spectatorship: Art, Science, and Early Cinema in Germany*. New York: Columbia University Press, 2015.
Der Einstein-Film. Four-page film program. *Die Grundlagen der Einsteinschen Relativitätstheorie*. (Colonna-Filmgesellschaft, 1922). *Wunder der Schöpfung*, DVD. Munich: Edition Filmmuseum, 2009.
Einstein, Albert. "Antisemitismus: Abwehr durch Erkenntnis." In *The Collected Papers of Albert Einstein*, vol. 7, *The Berlin Years: Writings, 1918–1921*, ed. Michel Janssen, 294–97. Princeton, NJ: Princeton University Press, 2002.
Eisenstein, Sergei. *Eisenstein on Disney*, ed. Jay Leyda, trans. Alan Upchurch. Calcutta: Seagull Books, 1986.
Fleischer, Dave, and Max Fleischer. *The Einstein Theory of Relativity*. Out of the Inkwell Films, 1923. *Wunder der Schöpfung*, DVD. Munich: Edition Filmmuseum, 2009.

Forschungsnetzwerk BTWH, ed. *Hans Richters* Rhythmus 21: *Schlüsselfilm der Moderne*. Würzburg: Königshausen & Neumann, 2012.

Gehrcke, Ernst. *Die Relativitätstheorie, eine wissenschaftliche Massensuggestion*. Berlin: Arbeitsgemeinschaft deutscher Naturforscher zur Erhaltung reiner Wissenschaft, 1920.

Gimbel, Steven. *Einstein's Jewish Science: Physics at the Intersection of Politics and Religion*. Baltimore: Johns Hopkins University Press, 2012.

Goergen, Jeanpaul. *Ruttmann: Eine Dokumentation*. Berlin: Freunde der deutschen Kinemathek, 1987.

Hansen, Miriam Bratu. "Micky-Maus." In *Cinema and Experience: Siegfried Kracauer, Walter Benjamin, and Theodor W. Adorno*, 163–82. Berkeley: University of California Press, 2011.

Heesen, Anke te. "Albert Einstein in Papier: Die Zeitungsausschnittsammlung des Physikers Ernst Gehrcke." In *Der Zeitungsausschnitt: Ein Papierobjekt der Moderne*, 137–74. Frankfurt am Main: Fischer, 2006.

Henderson, Linda Dalrymple. "Einstein and 20th-Century Art: A Romance in Many Dimensions." In *Einstein for the 21st Century: His Legacy in Science, Art, and Modern Culture*, ed. Peter L. Galison, 101–29. Princeton, NJ: Princeton University Press, 2008.

Kornblum, Hanns Walter, dir. *Wunder der Schöpfung*. 1925. Munich: Edition Filmmuseum, 2009. DVD.

Kracauer, Siegfried. *From Caligari to Hitler: A Psychological History of the German Film*. Princeton, NJ: Princeton University Press, 2004.

Lehman, Christopher P. *The Colored Cartoon: Black Representation in American Animated Short Films, 1907–1954*. Amherst: University of Massachusetts Press, 2007.

Leslie, Esther. *Hollywood Flatlands: Animation, Critical Theory and the Avant-Garde*. London: Verso, 2002.

Ngai, Sianne. "Animatedness." In *Ugly Feelings*, 89–125. Cambridge, MA: Harvard University Press, 2005.

Serviss, Garrett P. *The Einstein Theory of Relativity*. New York: Edwin Miles Fadman, 1923.

Storm, J.P., and M. Dressler. *Im Reiche der Micky Maus: Walt Disney in Deutschland, 1927–1945*. Berlin: Henschel, 1991.

Trebitsch, Arthur. *Deutscher Geist—oder Judentum! Der Weg der Befreiung*. Berlin: Antaios, 1921.

van Dongen, Jeroen. "Reactionaries and Einstein's Fame: 'German Scientists for the Preservation of Pure Science,' Relativity, and the Bad Nauheim Meeting." *Physics in Perspective* 9 (2007): 212–30.

Vertov, Dziga. "WE: Variant of a Manifesto." In *Kino-Eye: The Writings of Dziga Vertov*, ed. Annette Michelson, 5–9. Berkeley: University of California Press, 1984.

Wazeck, Milena. "The 1922 Einstein Film: Cinematic Innovation and Public Controversy." *Physics in Perspective* 12 (2010): 163–79.

———. *Einstein's Opponents: The Public Controversy about the Theory of Relativity in the 1920s*, trans. Geoffrey S. Koby. Cambridge: Cambridge University Press, 2014.

Zervigón, Andrés Mario. "'A Political Struwwelpeter?' John Heartfield's Early Film Animation and the Wartime Crisis of Photographic Representation." In *John Heartfield and the Agitated Image: Photography, Persuasion, and the Rise of Avant-Garde Photomontage*, 95–135. Chicago: University of Chicago Press, 2012.

Chapter 12

"A CLARION CALL TO STRIKE BACK"

Antisemitism and Ludwig Berger's
Der Meister von Nürnberg (1927)

Christian Rogowski

On 7 October 1927 one of the largest movie theaters in Germany, the newly built Phoebus Palast, with more than 2,000 seats, was supposed to open in Nuremberg. Its owner, the Berlin-based Phoebus Film A.G., had selected what it deemed a suitably glamorous film for the festive opening, a film with a local connection, Ludwig Berger's *Der Meister von Nürnberg* (*The Master of Nuremberg*). Yet in the run-up to that opening, Berger's light-hearted historical costume drama, loosely associated with Richard Wagner's most popular opera, *Die Meistersinger von Nürnberg* (1868), became the target of a vehement propaganda campaign, prompting protests from the southern German city and from right-wing groups elsewhere. Two days before the projected opening, representatives from various cultural organizations in the Franconian city published an *einmütig* (unanimous) Nuremberg Protest against the film that in the eyes of the signatories defiled Wagner's masterpiece, that *deutscheste* (most German) of German cultural achievements.[1] The agitation prompted the Phoebus company to replace it with what it hoped would be a more innocuous feature. What was it that made Berger's film such a thorn in the eye of German nationalists in general, and the burghers of Nuremberg in particular?

The polemical campaign surrounding the film took place in the context of various political and cultural currents in the Weimar Republic—including discourses of highbrow art versus popular culture, film versus opera, cosmopolitan Berlin versus provincial parochialism, Prussian federalism versus Bavarian particularism, national(-ist) tradition versus modernity, adherence to convention versus creative license, ethnic "purity" versus outside "contamination," a vehemently anti–Weimar Republic cultural conservatism, and the peculiar significance of Wagner in post–World War I German culture. Most importantly, the polemics were triggered by issues of antisemitism festering below the surface of the supposedly quiet middle period of the Weimar Republic—between the economic consolidation in the wake of hyperinflation (1923) and the onslaught of the Great Depression (1929). Jewish-born director Berger and his film got caught in a web of various minor social, political, and cultural crises facing its production company as well as other contextual issues that affected its reception. What was at stake with Berger's film, I will argue, were questions about what (and who) was German: who did and who did not belong to certain definitions of a national community, and who did and who did not have the right to speak for a nationally defined culture. Ultimately, as I will show, Berger's film raised questions about the position of Jews within the Weimar German national community and culture.

In many ways it is surprising that the planned screening of Berger's film in Nuremberg provoked such controversy. Its production company, Phoebus, had what seemed to be impeccably patriotic credentials. In the summer of 1927, when the company announced its program for the upcoming season, the trade journal *Film-Kurier* noted the "purely German character" of its roster, singling out Berger's project as the presumed crowning highlight.[2] That same summer, however, Phoebus became embroiled in a scandal that casts a somewhat sinister light on the patriotic films produced by the company. In August of the year, a liberal Berlin daily, *Berliner Tageblatt*, broke the story that Walter Lohmann, a captain of the German naval transportation division, had used Phoebus as a front to funnel money into clandestine armament projects for the German Navy and Luftwaffe, such as submarine or aircraft design, illegally circumventing restrictions imposed by the Versailles Treaty. Secret infusions of money arranged by Lohmann had propped up the ailing film company, on condition that Phoebus "produce films of a 'national' character designed to stimulate the 'fatherland consciousness' of the German people."[3] As we shall see, the fact that the right-wing self-appointed protectors of German culture chose as their target a film produced by a company that had ostensibly been only too eager to contribute to making Germany great again, was not the only irony surrounding the propaganda campaign.

When Berger's *Der Meister von Nürnberg* premiered on 5 September 1927, at the glamorous Capitol Theater in Berlin, in a special charity event to benefit the Bühnengenossenschaft (an organization of theater artists), there were no signs of impending trouble: the film scored a huge success with the audience and was greeted with enthusiastic accolades by the press. Even reviewers who voiced certain reservations, such as Felix Henseleit of the *Reichsfilmblatt*, who thought that Berger had delved too much into *Einzelheiten* (details), conceded that "everywhere one could sense the hand of a tasteful, accomplished director."[4] Most reviewers acclaimed Berger's film precisely for what they regarded as its uniquely German qualities. *Film-Kurier* hailed the Berlin gala premiere on its title page as "another great day for Phoebus" as well as "a day of honor for German film."[5] Similarly, the *Berliner Lokalanzeiger* called it "a German film, a pleasure because what is German about it is genuine and not contrived," and *Abendpost-Nachtausgabe* proclaimed Berger's film to be "the best and grandest film of the year" (this in a year that also saw the release of Fritz Lang's *Metropolis*!).[6] Even communist critics conceded, grudgingly, that although it was a bourgeois film, it was *"sehenswert"* (worth seeing).[7]

Across the political spectrum critics were unanimous in their praise for Rudolf Rittner, the actor who portrayed Hans Sachs and who was one of the coauthors of the film script. A veteran of stage and screen who had brought some of acclaimed playwright Gerhart Hauptmann's most significant characters to life, Rittner provided German audiences with a "model of German manliness"—"good, loyal, straightforward and, when necessary, heroic and noble in renunciation"—that German youth should flock to and emulate.[8] The film was subsequently shown with equally great success in other major German cities such as Frankfurt am Main, Dresden, and Cologne, as well as in the Austrian capital, Vienna.[9] It ran for several months throughout the German provinces, continued its "triumphal march through Europe" and was successfully exported to various countries.[10]

To a certain extent, the presentation surrounding the film's Berlin premiere, as well as aspects of the film itself, invite a misreading of the film as a mere rendering of Wagner's opera. At the Capitol Theater premiere, for instance, leading singers from the Berlin Staatsoper, including legendary dramatic soprano Frieda Leider, presented arias from various operas. Acclaimed Heldentenor Fritz Soot sang Walther's "Preislied" from *Die Meistersinger*, and the film was launched to the sounds of the chorus of the Städtische Oper singing the "Wach auf" chorus from the opera. The film revolves around episodes in the life of Nuremberg's shoemaker-poet Hans Sachs that were invented by Wagner, and it borrows all major characters from the opera as well as several plot lines and dramatic conflicts: Sachs is attracted to Eva, the daughter of goldsmith Veit Pogner; Walther von Stolzing, a young aristocrat, appears in town and falls in love with Eva; Sixtus Beckmesser, a pedantic town scribe, schemes to prevent this union, because he also harbors designs on Eva; Sachs has an apprentice, David; and Eva has a friend and companion, Magdalene. Some critics, perhaps understandably, thus actually mistook the film's title to be *Die Meistersinger von Nürnberg*.[11] Moreover, the music created for the premiere by Willy Schmidt-Gentner mixed Wagnerian themes with a pastiche taken from various sources, including Haydn and Schubert.[12]

So how did the controversy get started? The perceived closeness to the Wagnerian original provoked the ire of a prominent Berlin-based music critic, Hugo Rasch, who launched an indignant attack in the *Allgemeine Musikzeitung* against "that exploitative frivolity that now flickers by at the Capitol theater night after night." The film, he argues, maliciously distorts the image of Hans Sachs, a universally beloved figure, who, in the Wagner opera, "displays genuine German virtues." Interestingly, Rasch frames the issue in terms of copyright legislation. Italy and Czechoslovakia, he notes, had just passed legislation to protect significant works of art beyond the expiration of a certain time limit. Berger's deplorable film, Rasch claims, makes it clear that similar legal protection is necessary in Germany, too, where ruthless hands have appropriated a "masterpiece that is the envy of the entire globe, that is the common property of the German people and that is, or should be, subject to protection as a national treasure—Wagner's *Meistersinger*." In barely controlled outrage, Rasch calls for protective measures that shield important works of art from *Verunstaltung* (disfigurement) and *Verstümmelung* (mutilation). Rasch's moralistic rhetoric echoes much of the disdain of film as a mass medium that characterized the *Kinoreform* debates of the 1910s and 1920s. Rasch refrains from spelling out whose hands he is referring to, adding the cryptic phrase, "hands, which unfortunately however I cannot call out by their proper name without making myself subject to being charged with libel."[13]

Rasch's ranting against reckless *Geschäfts-'tüchtigkeit'* (business 'acumen') that "tramples our most precious possessions" (Rasch 958) recalls the dog-whistling code that extremist right-wing circles used in their critique of the German film industry after World War I. When one considers that Rasch in 1931 joined the National Socialist (Nazi) party and would become music critic for the Nazi paper, *Völkische Beobachter*, the subtext of his polemic about an insidious threat that is already operating from within is clear: without saying so directly, Rasch insinuates that it is the Jews who are assaulting one of Germany's most significant "national cultural treasures."[14] The film's director, Berger (1892–1969), and one of his co-script-writers, Robert Liebmann (1890–1945), were of Jewish extraction; the Capitol Theater in Berlin was owned by David Oliver (1880–1947), who hailed from Galicia. Rasch's incensed rhetoric implies that these Jews had maliciously appropriated Wagner's masterpiece not only for personal gain but also in order to undermine German culture as a whole.

In his polemic zeal, Rasch conveniently overlooks many crucial aspects of what, perhaps not entirely disingenuously, was billed not as a version of Wagner's opera but as a "Hans Sachs Film." As a medium bereft of sound, silent film could not possibly render a four-and-a-half-hour musical drama on the screen in a straightforward manner—even Richard Strauss and Hugo von Hofmannsthal made substantial changes to their film version of *Der Rosenkavalier* (1926) to accommodate the different logic of the medium, altering the musical score for the live orchestral accompaniment and adding scenes that round out and illustrate the background of the main action. Various efforts at producing film operas, mostly as early-twentieth-century short films that combined live singers in the auditorium with images of actors on screen lip-synching the *Tonbilder* (score), had failed, sometimes for technical reasons, but also on account of the unsuitability of the spatially restricted stage dramaturgy of opera for the movie screen.

From the outset, Berger's film introduces locations not featured in Wagner's opera and outlines the respective psychological dispositions of the main characters before the plot proper sets in: in the film, Eva tries to escape the pressure her father puts on her to marry town scribe Beckmesser by seeking help from Hans Sachs, who loves her, too, but who recognizes that he is too old for her as a partner and wisely refrains from exploiting her emotional vulnerability. Likewise, the film's Walther runs away from his ancestral castle when his family council tries to force him into marrying a drab relative—the oddly named Edelgundis von Katzenellenbogen. By way of creating a prehistory for the two young lovers, Berger's film provides a motivation for their susceptibility to falling in love with one another at first sight. Their meeting at a church service in Nuremberg, which starts the opera, is delayed until the middle of the third of the film's eight reels. Moreover, the gist of the central conflicts is modified: the film revolves around a rivalry between goldsmith Pogner and shoemaker Sachs for the post of mayor of

Nuremberg in upcoming elections. The annual singing contest among art-loving guild members that the opera hails as a long-standing local tradition, is eliminated and replaced by a spontaneous poetry competition that Beckmesser suggests to Pogner as a political expediency to win over votes and that is rigged to ensure that it will be Beckmesser who gets the prize—Eva's hand. In fact, what is perhaps most striking about this film supposedly based on Wagner's *Die Meistersinger* is that it contains no "*Meistersingers*" at all! In the film there is not a single reference to the existence of an association of citizens who practice poetry and song and who compete with one another for the advancement of art. There is no conflict between the adherents of established rules and the forces of artistic innovation. In the opera, Beckmesser's heavy-handed insistence on tradition is contrasted with Walther's impulsive creative genius, put into stark relief in the first act in David's lengthy explanations concerning the complex regulations that govern the Meistersinger guild's craftsman-like approach to the manufacture of poetry. In Wagner's opera, Sachs mentors Walther to channel the young maverick's raw creativity into appropriate form, enabling Walther to produce the *Preislied*, with which in the third act he wins a singing competition by public acclaim. In Berger's film it is Sachs who writes a superior poem and gives it to Walther, encouraging him to claim it as his own, thus helping the young aristocrat win a poetry competition and Eva's hand (figure 12.1).

Hans Rudolf Vaget has highlighted the appeal that Wagner's *Die Meistersinger von Nürnberg* had for *völkisch* circles in early twentieth-century Germany: Wagner's opera offers a seductive, utopian vision of an organic, classless community (*Gemeinschaft*) as a countermodel to contract-based, conflict-ridden forms of polity (*Gesellschaft*). Wagner's world is centered on the voluntary, spontaneous submission to a charismatic leader (Hans Sachs), whose authority is based on his personality and validated by public acclaim (rather than subject to electoral rules and regulations). That this self-governing community necessitates the marginalization or elimination of undesirable individuals—the exclusion of the pedantic Beckmesser—is something the inhabitants of Wagner's Nuremberg willingly accept for the affirmation of the common good. In the context of the political conflicts and socioeconomic crises that riddled the Weimar Republic, Wagner's opera could be seen as foreshadowing the Nazi notion of a classless, homogeneous ethnic community (*Volksgemeinschaft*), united under a charismatic leader who delivered the ailing nation to political, economic, and, above all, spiritual redemption.[15]

Figure 12.1. Evchen (Maria Matray) appeals to Hans Sachs (Rudolf Rittner) for support. *Der Meister von Nürnberg* (1927, dir. Ludwig Berger). Courtesy of DFF—Deutsches Filminstitut & Filmmuseum, Frankfurt.

Berger's film undercuts such quasi-religious idealizations of Renaissance Nuremberg. It starts with a visual joke: after the opening credits, we see a title card that reads, "Nuremberg was awaiting a mayoral election." We then see what looks like the inside of an assembly room with a large table, which we assume is where a meeting of the city council is to take place. Suddenly, someone's—shockingly big—arm reaches into the frame from top left, placing figurines of councilors on the chairs at the table. What we took to be a long shot of a council chamber is revealed to be a close-up of a kind of doll house filled with toy-sized figurines. A puppeteer appears, jovially chatting with children who gather around him. The whimsical gesture, reminiscent of the opening of Ernst Lubitsch's silent film comedy, *Die Puppe* (*The Doll*; 1919), introduces the motif of manipulation, setting the stage for the political machinations surrounding the mayoral elections that follow. Wagner's backward-looking utopia of a self-regulating community united by a common devotion to culture and art is replaced in Berger's film by a world of political maneuvering and corruption, where petty, narrow-minded people jostle for power and prestige, governed by self-interest and ambition.

Rasch's polemic, then, paradoxically finds fault with the film precisely for what it did not set out to be, simply a rendering of Wagner's opera. The film's treatment of the figure of Beckmesser is a particularly significant deviation from Wagner. The pedantic, conceited, and scheming town scribe has often been taken as a "most blatantly anti-Semitic" caricature.[16] Interestingly enough, the film removes the reference to the antisemitic German fairy-tale, "The Jew in the Brambles" that in the opera occurs in reference to Beckmesser in Walther's first attempt at song writing in act one.[17] While Berger's Beckmesser is still a buffoon and an intriguer (and is played by German-Jewish comedian Julius Falkenstein), the film casually makes the point that he is as good and upstanding a Christian burgher as anybody else: he is the central figure sitting at the table during the first actual council meeting we see in the film, and he is placed in one of the pews during the church service at which Eva and Walther meet; a Roman Catholic service, no less—somewhat incongruous in arch-Lutheran Renaissance Nuremberg. The film's character Beckmesser is thus shown as an integral part of the fabric of the tight-knit local elite, an elite that is outwardly righteous but internally corrupt. Here, Beckmesser is in cahoots with Nuremberg's civic leaders, Veit Pogner (Max Gülstorff), the goldsmith who aspires to become lord mayor, and with the president of the city council (Hans Wassmann), who agrees to mark Beckmesser's submission to the poetry contest with an "x" so that it can be picked as the winning poem—an arrangement that becomes necessary when the council is inundated with so many submissions that the councilors find it impossible—or, after looking at a few dismally inane samples, even not desirable—to read them all.

Berger's tongue-in-cheek comedy eliminates the opera's self-reflective debates concerning the nature and function of art and creativity and replaces them with a gently indulgent portrayal of a fundamentally flawed and latently corrupt community. The sets created by Berger's brother Rudolf Bamberger (1888–1945) convey a sense of theatrical artificiality—not a single scene is filmed in a real outdoor location. Bamberger's Nuremberg, with its narrow, crooked lanes and dark interiors, is reminiscent of the medieval fantasy architecture familiar from Paul Wegener's *Golem* films, as well as other period dramas filmed entirely in studio settings, such as F.W. Murnau's *Faust* (1926) and Hans Kyser's *Luther* (1928). Some critics compared the film's evocation of an idyllic if somewhat claustrophobic past to nineteenth-century *Biedermeier* period paintings artists such as Carl Spitzweg.[18] Like Spitzweg, Berger points without harsh judgment to the foibles of the characters in this provincial world, in a gentle satire akin in spirit, as critics noted, to the ironic portrayal of German myopic philistinism in August von Kotzebue's comedy, *Die deutschen Kleinstädter* (1802).[19] Nuremberg's liberal daily, *Nürnberger Zeitung*, noted matter-of-factly that Berger's film, instead of sharing Wagner's idealized vision of an ideal, art-loving community in a kind of utopia turned backward, shows the city "as it really could have been," with all its human—all-too-human—limitations.[20]

The film parallels the plot of Wagner's opera most closely in what is the equivalent of Act 2—Beckmesser's abortive nighttime serenade to Eva and the general mayhem that ensues, as crowds of burghers appear in the city's narrow lanes and engage in an all-out public brawl. Berger's Walther is no untrained artistic genius whose creativity has to be molded into the proper channels but instead shows himself to be a reckless, impulsive young cad who, after the brawl, ends up in prison, for his attempt at running away with Eva. Berger's Sachs is no philosopher poet—there is no equivalent of the famous "Wahn-Monolog" from the beginning of Act 3, in which Wagner's hero reflects on the outbreak of violence of the previous night. And Berger's Sachs is not above bending the truth a bit to achieve his ends—donning a monk's habit, he smuggles a love poem he has written into Walther's prison cell and urges him to pretend that it is own so that the young knight can win the competition and be united with Eva.

Significantly, the film differs most pronouncedly with regard to its handling of the denouement: what would be the third act in the opera is transformed and stripped of the national(istic) undertones conveyed by Wagner's communal festivities: Berger eliminates the sun-drenched festival meadow (*Festwiese*) celebrations in which the various city guilds march to assemble outdoors in a display of civic pride and wealth and during which the townspeople are won over by the brilliance of Walther's entry into the song contest. Instead, the rigged poetry competition takes place in the dark and foreboding space of the city council's assembly hall, where Sachs unmasks the collusion between Beckmesser and the city officials and helps Walther win Eva's hand. Perhaps most importantly, gone are the infamous musings of Sachs from the opera's finale, in which the shoemaker-poet exhorts his fellow-citizens to honor German traditions and their German masters (*Ehrt Eure deutschen Meister*) and guard everything that is "German and genuine" (*deutsch und echt*) against "foreign frivolousness" (*welschen Tand*). Berger's film dispenses both with the celebration of a German cultural community and with the paean to "sacred German art" (*heilge deutsche Kunst*) that culminate in a rousing chorus that ends the opera on a gloriously sonorous final chord of C major. Instead, Berger's film ends on a quiet note with a wistful Sachs, who has sacrificed his own happiness by bringing Eva and Walther together, at home admonishing his apprentice David to close the shutters so that he can be alone in silent resignation.

It is perhaps the removal of the celebratory tone of the opera that right-wing critics of the film such as Rasch found most unsettling. Berger's film does not buy into the idealization of a self-regulating *Volksgemeinschaft* that is united by a common interest in the arts and willingly accepts the "leadership principle" (*Führerprinzip*) based on public acclaim. Nor does the film subscribe to quasireligious fantasies of German cultural superiority in a Wagnerian apotheosis of sacred German art. Instead we see a polity ruled by a codified system of laws and populated by individuals not averse to violating rules and codes when it serves their own interests. Under the heading, "Schutz dem Urheber!" (Protect the Copyright Holder!), Hugo Rasch railed against what he viewed as the willful distortion of Wagner's idealizing portrayal of Renaissance Nuremberg. Conflating the historical Hans Sachs (1494–1576), who was always shown sporting a beard, and Wagner's cobbler-poet-turned-national-hero in *Die Meistersinger*, Rasch bemoaned that Berger's film portrays Sachs as a "thoroughly mendacious, clean-shaven comedian," that goldsmith Pogner "appeared repugnant beyond all measure," and that the plot revolved around "disgusting bribery" among Nuremberg's city officials.[21]

Rasch's charge that Berger had deliberately and cynically set out to exploit a treasured piece of German musical high art was, to say the least, somewhat baffling: born Ludwig Bamberger in 1892 in Mainz, Berger came from a highly assimilated, upper-middle-class Jewish family that played a prominent role in the cultural and civic life of that southwest German city. His mother was a classically trained pianist who had been a student of Clara Schumann; his father was a local politician and a passionate amateur violinist; Ludwig himself played the piano and was an excellent cellist. In 1914 he had obtained a doctorate at Heidelberg in art history with a dissertation on an eighteenth-century German painter. His 1915 theater debut was with a performing version of Mozart's early opera, *Die Gärtnerin aus Liebe*, which he and his brother Rudolf had edited. In his early days as a theater director in Mainz and Hamburg, Berger had directed several shrove tide farces (*Fastnachtsspiele*) by Hans Sachs, suggesting that he perhaps knew the historical Sachs, with his robust, often bawdy, sense of humor, better than many of his critics who viewed the figure through Wagner's idealizing lens. A gifted playwright himself and an experienced film director with several critically acclaimed and commercially successful films to his credit, Berger had, over the years, also directed a number of operas, canonical plays by Goethe, Schiller, Kleist, and Shakespeare, and modern dramas by Ibsen, Strindberg, von Unruh, and Zuckmayer at some of Germany's leading theaters. With such credentials, Ludwig Berger could credibly claim that he approached Germany's cultural patrimony with the requisite respect and sensitivity, and—more importantly—that he had every right to consider himself a fitting representative of German high culture. Yet all these qualifications count for nothing in Rasch's antisemitically tinged broadside attack.

The gauntlet thrown down by Rasch in the *Allgemeine Musikzeitung* some two weeks after the Berlin premiere of *Der Meister von Nürnberg* was picked up by a Nuremberg-based colleague, Wilhelm Matthes, an occasional contributor to the same musical journal. His main job was as music critic for the right-leaning local paper, *Fränkischer Kurier*. In an article published on 29 September 1927, Matthes excerpts much of Rasch's text, adding an introduction that frames Rasch's argument in explicitly ethnic (*völkisch*) terms. Under the alarmist heading, "Another Defilement [*Neue Schändung*] of a German Cultural Monument," Matthes complains that Berger's film is only the latest, most egregious, example of what he views as a concerted effort of the so-called destructives to undermine German culture.[22] Cultural Bolshevists had, Matthes suggests, deviously appropriated seemingly innocuous forms of popular culture such as illustrated magazines, newspaper articles, novels, and theater plays in a systematic effort to weaken the German spirit. In Matthes's estimation, Berger's film is a particularly devious effort to sully *Die Meistersinger von Nürnberg*—"the most popular [*volkstümlichste*], the most German work of Richard Wagner," by using the popular mass medium of film to indoctrinate the German populace. Something must be done, Matthes warns, before these subversive forces have completely destroyed "all that the *Volk* [people] has until now held as sacred ideals."

Lest there is any doubt concerning his ideological allegiances, Matthes uses key concepts familiar from post–World War I German right-wing agitation: in speaking of "insidious backstabbing" (*heimtuckischen Dolchstöße*) destroying German culture, he creates a cultural version of a familiar political myth, the stab-in-the-back legend (*Dolchstoßlegende*). The tropes Matthes uses center around the same notions of compromised health (*eingeimpft*), pollution (*verseucht*), and sexualized violence

(*Schändung*) that dominated the paranoid rhetoric of right-wing ideologues who argued that Germany had been defeated not on the battlefield but through treason, subversion, and sabotage from within. Like Rasch, Matthes does not explicitly name whom he deems responsible, yet his coded references to the "greedy destructive furor of these reckless businessmen" mobilize tropes from the repertory of antisemitism. Rasch had called for legal measures to protect German works of art through comprehensive copyright legislation. Matthes argues that the time has come for more-concrete action, for the nation to resort to self-help (*Selbsthilfe*): "Let us take this monstrous crime against the *Meistersinger* as a clarion call to strike back. The pushback has to originate from Nuremberg!"[23]

Matthes's feverish call to arms, with the notion of striking back that emanates from a sense of victimhood at the hands of an international conspiracy, reflects a politically charged situation in his hometown: a few weeks before he penned his broadside, the Nazis had for the first time (after Munich in 1923 and Weimar in 1926) held their Reichsparteitag in Nuremberg, which would become an annual event in the city. In an oblique reference to the "Wach auf" chorus from Wagner's *Meistersinger*, the rally's opening day, Friday 19 August, 1927, was declared a day of awakening. The Nazis eagerly adopted Nuremberg as the site where the alleged need to defend an imperiled Aryan race through mass action was being articulated.[24] In this context, Matthes's incendiary article, though still phrased in largely metaphorical terms, acquired an all-too literal subtext, insinuating that the time had come for the imperiled *Volk* to defend itself through the use of physical violence.

In a manner reminiscent of the spread of current-day memes—unsubstantiated claims that go viral online—the impassioned call for militancy by Matthes exploded via the social media of the day—the various clubs, corporate entities, and social groups involved in Nuremberg's cultural life. Matthes's invective resonated among local elites with prejudices long held among the Bildungsbürgertum—the educated German upper-middle class—against modern mass media in general, and against film as an uncouth, frivolous form of mass entertainment in particular. A sense of the cherished high culture of personal cultivation and education (*Bildung*) under threat from smut (*Schund*) aligned with a sense of precious regional traditions being trampled on by unscrupulous Berlin-centered business interests. More broadly, Matthes also spoke to fears concerning the potential negative economic repercussions that Berger's supposedly distorted representation of the city might have for Nuremberg's tourist industry. Within days, the appeal for a revision of copyright law to protect German cultural products beyond a thirty-year limit was endorsed by large segments of Nuremberg's cultural elite, across a broad political spectrum. Under the heading "Nürnberger Protest," and subtitled, "A Unanimous Spiritual Uprising," some twenty local corporate entities and cultural associations endorsed the initiative in Matthes's paper, *Fränkische Kurier*.[25]

On 5 October Nuremberg's city council debated a motion brought forward by council member Fritz Schuh on behalf of Fraktion Schwarz-Weiß-Rot—the right-wing Deutsch-nationale Volkspartei—that the city issue an official declaration condemning the film. In presenting the motion, Schuh reminded the council of its duty to protect Wagner's "most German" and "most valuable" opera from the "denigration" (*Verunglimpfung*) by the film. He approvingly noted that Phoebus had actually already withdrawn Berger's film from the planned opening of the Nuremberg Phoebus Palast and replaced it with a film version of the comedy *Die Hose* (The Underpants). This prompted the sarcastic interjection, "by a Jew by the name of Sternheim" from fellow city councilor Julius Streicher, who was the notorious editor of *Der Stürmer*, the Nazi propaganda paper based in Nuremberg.[26] In response, councilor Max Süßheim, the Jewish-born representative of the majority Social Democratic Party and an experienced professional lawyer, wryly noted that, while he shared the esteem for Wagner's masterpiece, he found it odd that the council was asked to judge a film that none of its members had seen, a task that anyway lay outside its jurisdiction. Schuh insisted that what was at stake here went beyond mere legal considerations—it was an emotional matter (*Gefühlssache*) for Nuremberg and "a question of honor that concerned every art-loving German" (Stadtarchiv Nürnberg C7/IX, no. 412). All the same, Süßheim's countermotion prevailed that the council defer its collective judgment by taking up Phoebus-Film's offer for a private screening of Berger's film at a later date, and a decision concerning Schuh's motion was postponed.

Even without the official intervention, the controversy spread to Munich, the Bavarian state capital, where Matthes found support from various cultural organizations ahead of the film's Munich premiere scheduled for 6 October. The film was discussed by Munich's city council, and the protest received the endorsement by many of the city's leading figures, including Lord Mayor Karl Scharnagl (Bayrische Vaterlandspartei), Clemens von Franckenstein (director of the Bavarian State Opera), and conservative composer Hans Pfitzner.[27] Yet the protest also prompted resistance in Nuremberg itself, for instance with the liberal *Nürnberger Zeitung*, the newspaper with the highest local circulation

(90,000). The paper argued, in an article published the same day as the Munich declaration, that given that none of the critics had actually seen the film, the agitation campaign ran the risk of exposing the city to ridicule. In the paper's opinion, the attacks only revealed the ignorance of the local dignitaries, especially concerning the caliber and standing of the film's director, Ludwig Berger: "He is—and outside the city of Sixtus Beckmesser there is general consensus—a top-notch director, he is the man who created Germany's most beautiful films."[28]

Phoebus-Film, for its part, did not take the assault from self-appointed guardians of German culture lying down. The company launched legal action against the *Fränkische Kurier* for malicious libel and issued a press release that defended the film as a thoroughly patriotic effort, stating that it "sprung from the serious desire to produce a purely German film" and that the Berlin censorship board had officially recognized it as "culturally valuable" (*kulturell wertvoll*, a designation that exempted the film from entertainment tax).[29]

While Matthes was still collecting signatures for his petition, the Bavarian protests were unmasked as largely disingenuous: newspapers noted that the film had actually been screened to Munich's cultural leaders as early as August, when they had found no fault with it, weeks before they joined the Nuremberg petition.[30] Papers also raised the question of who exactly initiated the controversy, offering various speculations: Was it forces at Wagner's stronghold Bayreuth or fanatically *völkisch* orthodox Wagnerians in Munich, or did it involve a conspiracy by right-wing media mogul Alfred Hugenberg, head of Universum Film Aktiengesellschaft (UFA), aimed at discrediting the Phoebus Film company as an unwelcome competitor?[31] Outside Bavaria the quixotic anti-Meisterfilm campaign raised eyebrows, too. Oscar Geller, writing for the *Österreichische Filmzeitung*, mocked the Nuremberg controversy as a manifestation of an irrational anti-Prussian "particularism of the royal republic of Bavaria."[32] Berger's film differed so substantially from Wagner's opera, Geller argued, that the controversy missed the point. Moreover, the protests were logically inconsistent: either Wagner's opera was a work of such grandeur that it could not be diminished by a mere film, or, if the film posed such a challenge to the work, then Wagner's opera could not be the timeless, sublime work of art it was hailed to be.

For his part, Ludwig Berger, who in early October 1927 was preparing to follow a call to Hollywood, was clearly taken aback by the vehement backlash against his film. Before his departure to the United

States, he defended himself against his critics in an open letter published in the *Berliner Börsen-Courier*: after pointing to the enthusiastic reviews the film had received in Berlin and elsewhere, Berger takes issue with the fact that none of the signatories had actually seen the film, singling out Nuremberg's liberal Lord Mayor Luppe and Ernst Heinrich Zimmermann, director of the city's Germanisches National-Museum, as men of reason and science, for abandoning the academic ideal of basing opinions on evidence rather than mere hear-say. Berger's letter culminates in an interesting rhetorical flourish that turns the tables against the protestors. In their day, Berger claims, Wagner's innovations had faced resistance on the part of self-appointed, philistine guardians of the status quo similar to the criticism leveled against his own efforts at advancing film as an art form: "One consolation: it is the sons and grandsons of those who used to boo Richard Wagner and fell over themselves reviling him in his ardent endeavors on behalf of the nature and renewal of German opera. Today, the nature and development of German film is at issue. And the naysayers promptly report for service again!"[33]

In the German press the polemical campaign against Berger's film had become a matter of considerable public ridicule. To put the controversy to rest for Nuremberg, the liberal paper *Nürnberger Zeitung* sent a critic to Munich to view the film there. Upon his return, on 12 October 1927, the paper published the apodictic verdict: "Result: The Nuremberg Protest against the film—which one hadn't seen!—was totally unjustified." Much of the opposition to Berger's film, the critic claims, stemmed from a general middle-class bias against film as a viable art form and from the mistaken assumption that Berger's film aimed at merely rendering the opera: "The very fact that a Wagnerian work was put on film was itself viewed as a desecration." When pointing out that film of necessity has to differ from a stage work, the reviewer argues that once the concerned citizens of Nuremberg were to see the film, they would have to agree that, "in filmic terms, everything turned out excellently, from beginning to end. Hans Sachs, the actual Hans Sachs did not live in some heavenly land [*Elysium*] but in little dung lane [*Kotgäßlein*] in Nuremberg. As he does in the film."[34]

Mainstream newspapers, if critical of the film, did not openly disclose the antisemitic subtext underlying the propaganda campaign, instead relying on coded language couched in patriotic sentiment. The *völkisch* press, however, was less squeamish: the *Münchener Beobachter* (the local precursor of the Nazi paper *Völkischer Beobachter*), for instance, complained that Berger's film did not feature a "German" Hans Sachs, but a "Jewish" one, a fact noted by Rudolf Kurtz, the editor of the trade journal *Lichtbild-Bühne* and author of the first study of filmic expressionism, who intervened in the debate. Interestingly enough, Kurtz chose as his venue the *C.V.-Zeitung*, the official newspaper of the Centralverein deutscher Staatsbürger jüdischen Glaubens, the largest organization representing Jewish Germans. Echoing many of the points made in the liberal *Nürnberger Zeitung*, Kurtz suggests that the campaign's vitriol was aimed at a director who is "suspected of not being one hundred percent Aryan." To counter such antisemitic prejudice, Kurtz emphatically and approvingly points to the central role that Jews had played in the growth of the German film industry from the very beginning.[35]

Perhaps it was Kurt Pinthus, writing for the Berlin *8-Uhr-Abendblatt*, who most succinctly summarized some of the many layers of irony that surrounded the campaign against Berger's film. In Pinthus's opinion, Berger, "the most musical of all film directors," had done more than almost any other director to elevate German film to the level of an art form. While *Der Meister von Nürnberg* may not be without flaws, Pinthus notes, it was particularly vexing that it was Berger of all people who had now, alongside his coscript writer and main actor, Rudolf Rittner, come under attack from reactionary circles: "So the grotesque situation has come to pass that Nuremberg's 'Beckmessers' are hurling abuse at the most German of all actors, Rittner; the most idealistic and most artistic German film director; the film that the entire Berlin press had deemed to be typically *deutsch* [German], indeed all-too *deutschtümelnd* [hyper-German]—for "denigrating German art," for "most recklessly violating Wagner," for "denigrating Nuremberg in the basest fashion."[36]

The disingenuous clamoring for copyright legislation to protect works of art against supposedly willful distortion, Pinthus argues, disregards the differences inherent in each art form, which necessitate that the transposition of an opera onto the screen has to involve changes specific to the filmic medium. Germans should bemoan the fact that Berger has been lured away to Hollywood rather than subjecting one of their most accomplished directors to a racially tinged smear campaign, especially when most critics, by their own admission, had not actually seen the film. It is necessary to protest against the Nuremberg protest, Pinthus proclaims, to come to the defense of the "now defenseless Berger" and "the freedom of German art."[37]

It is easy to dismiss the controversy surrounding Berger's film as a proverbial tempest in a tea pot. The hysteria was quickly unmasked as an absurd cocktail of misinformation, misinterpretation, and (racialized) prejudice, and, once debunked, it seemed to have little immediate effect. Not everybody who signed on to the protests and petitions can be labeled racist, antisemitic, or right-wing extremist. Yet the sense that traditional high cultural values were under threat from commercial mass culture for subversive ends obviously resonated with many signatories, even those with no direct sympathies for *völkisch* causes. The controversy exposed major fault lines within the political culture of the Weimar Republic and it was a symptom of the contested status of people of Jewish descent in Germany, characterized by an increasing marginalization and demonization of a minority defined as alien, years before the Nazis came to power.

By 1937 it was no longer necessary to use code to attack people of Jewish descent. In an openly antisemitic diatribe, entitled, *Film-"Kunst," Film-Kohn, Film-Korruption*, Berger's contributions to German film in general, and his *Meister von Nürnberg* in particular, were dismissed: he was declared—as a Jew—fundamentally incapable of tackling a German topic on account of his "racially conditioned sensibility" (rassisch bedingten Empfindung), that inevitably had turned his film into a "cynical affront" (zynische Herausforderung).[38]

The mindset that manifested itself in nascent form in the controversy over Berger's film in 1927 had real, and tragic, consequences: Berger, who returned to Germany in 1931 after his stint in Hollywood, lost his job at UFA film in 1933, as part of a purge of Jewish talent. Forced into exile, to Amsterdam, he miraculously survived the German occupation. Robert Liebmann, the coauthor of the film script, was also dismissed by UFA in 1933 and fled to France. He was arrested in 1942 and murdered in Auschwitz in July 1942. Berger's brother Rudolf Bamberger was arrested in Luxembourg, where the Bamberger family owned a brewery, in 1944, and deported to Auschwitz, where he was killed in January of 1945.

The symbolism surrounding the city of Nuremberg came full circle in 1949, when the victorious Allies chose the city as the site of the trials that sought to hold leading Nazi officials accountable for the genocidal madness of the Third Reich, attesting to the constantly changing status of the city, described by Stephen Brockmann as "an imaginary space in which conceptions of Germany and Germanness came into being over many centuries."[39] The controversy surrounding Berger's *Der Meister von Nürnberg* of 1927 suggests that, for some, the conception of Germanness did not include German citizens of Jewish descent.

Acknowledgments

This research was supported by a grant from the Amherst College Faculty Research Award Program, funded by the H. Axel Schupf '57 Fund for Intellectual Life. I would like to thank Mr. Siegfried Kett (Nuremberg) and Ms. Michaela Kett (Berlin) for generously making materials collected by Mr. Kett in various local archives available to me. I am grateful to the staff at the Ludwig Berger Archiv (Akademie der Künste, Berlin), the Deutsche Kinemathek (Berlin), and the Performing Arts Library (New York Public Library) for their support. Thanks are also due to Dr. Philipp Stiasny (CineGraph Babelsberg) for useful input, Joan Murphy and Ulrich Nowka (Berlin) for their gracious hospitality, and Nona Monáhin (Amherst) for valuable feedback. All translations, unless noted otherwise, are my own.

Christian Rogowski is G. Armour Craig Professor in Language and Literature and chair of the Department of German at Amherst College. His publications comprise two books on Austrian author Robert Musil, a CD-ROM on teaching German studies, an edited volume, *The Many Faces of Weimar Cinema: Rediscovering Germany's Filmic Legacy*, as well as numerous essays on Germanophone literature, opera, film, drama, and intellectual history, with a focus on the cinema and popular culture of the Weimar Republic. Most recently, he authored a monograph on Wim Wenders's film, *Wings of Desire* (2019), for the newly launched series German Film Classics.

Notes

1. L.W., "Der Nürnberger Protest gegen den Film *Der Meister von Nürnberg*. Eine einmütige geistige Erhebung," *Fränkischer Kurier* (5 October 1927).
2. "Deutsche Großfilme!" *Film-Kurier* 178 (30 July 1927): 1.
3. James H. Belote, "CIA-Report: The Lohmann Affair," *Studies in Intelligence* 4, no. 2 (Spring 1960): A35. See also "Die Phoebus-Affäre," *Österreichische Filmzeitung* 48 (26 November 1927): 12.
4. Felix Henseleit, "*Der Meister von Nürnberg*," *Reichsfilmblatt* 36 (1927): 45.
5. "Wieder ein großer Tag der Phoebus—der gleichzeitig ein Ehrentag für den deutschen Film bedeutet: die Uraufführung des *Meisters von Nürnberg* im Capitol," *Film-Kurier* 210 (6 September 1927): 1.
6. Press review quotes taken from an ad in the trade journal, *Lichtbild-Bühne* 217 (10 September 1927), 3: "ein deutscher Film, eine Freude darum, weil das Deutsche an

ihm echt ist und nicht gewollt" (*Berliner Lokalanzeiger*); "der beste und größte Film des Jahres" (*Abendpost-Nachtausgabe*).
7. B., "Die Filme der Woche," *Die rote Fahne* 10, no. 214 (11 September 1927).
8. Henseleit, "*Der Meister von Nürnberg*," 45.
9. L.W., "Eröffnung des Gloria-Palastes. Saisonbeginn in Frankfurt a. M.," *Film-Kurier* 219 (19 September 1927): 2; "*Der Meister von Nürnberg*-Film als Festvorstellung in Köln," *Film-Kurier* 224 (22 September 1927): 2; "*Der Meister von Nürnberg*," *Österreichische Filmzeitung* 49 (3 December 1927): 16.
10. Press-clipping entitled "*Meistersinger*-Film mit zweisprachigen Titeln," *New Yorker Staatszeitung* (undated, presumably, after the December 1929 U.S. premiere), Ludwig Berger Archiv, Akademie der Künste, Berlin, folder 18.
11. For instance, Oscar Geller, "Münchner Notizen," *Österreichische Filmzeitung* 43 (22 October 1927): 32.
12. A.W., "*Der Meister von Nürnberg*. Festvorstellung im Capitol," *Deutsche Allgemeine Zeitung* 66, no. 416 (6 September 1927): 1–2.
13. Hugo Rasch, "Schutz dem Urheber!" *Allgemeine Musikzeitung* 38 (23 September 1927): 958.
14. See Gerhard Splitt, "Richard Strauss und die Reichsmusikkammer—im Zeichen der Begrenzung von Kunst?" In Albrecht Rietmüller and Michael Custodis, eds., *Die Reichsmusikkammer. Kunst im Bann der Nazi-Diktatur* (Cologne: Böhlau, 2015): 21.
15. Hans Rudolf Vaget, "Das *Meistersinger*-Land," "*Wehvolles Erbe.*" *Richard Wagner in Deutschland. Hitler, Knappertsbusch, Mann* (Frankfurt am Main: S. Fischer, 2017): 175–80.
16. Marc A. Weiner, *Richard Wagner and the Anti-Semitic Imagination* (Lincoln: University of Nebraska Press, 1995): 84.
17. "Der Jud' im Dorn" was published in the first edition of the Grimm's famous collection of German fairytales, *Kinder- und Hausmärchen* (1815). See Vaget, "Das *Meistersinger*-Land," 176.
18. L.H., "Capitol: *Der Meister von Nürnberg*," *Berliner Tageblatt* 56: 435 (11 September 1927); and Herbert Ihering, "*Der Meister von Nürnberg*," *Berliner Börsen-Courier* (6 September 1927).
19. Ernst Jäger, "Film-Kritik. *Der Meister von Nürnberg*. (Capitol)," *Film-Kurier* 210 (6 September 1927).
20. "Reise zum *Meister von Nürnberg*." *Nürnberger Zeitung* (12 October 1927).
21. Rasch, "Schutz dem Urheber!" 958.
22. Wilhelm Matthes, *Der Meister von Nürnberg*. Neue Schändung eines deutschen Kunstdenkmals," *Fränkischer Kurier* 269 (29 September 1927): 3.
23. "Doch nehmen wir dieses ungeheure Verbrechen an den 'Meistersingern' als endliches Signal zum Losschlagen. In diesem Fall muß der Gegenstoß von Nürnberg kommen!" Matthes, *Der Meister von Nürnberg*, 3.
24. Alfred Rosenberg and Wilhelm Weiß, *Reichsparteitag der NSDAP Nürnberg 19. /21. August 1927* (Munich: F. Eher, 1927).
25. "Der Nürnberger Protest," *Fränkischer Kurier* (5 October 1927).
26. Stadtarchiv Nürnberg, Stadtratsprotokolle C 7/IX, no. 412 (5 October 1927), item 19.
27. "Auch München protestiert gegen den Film *Der Meister von Nürnberg*. Schärfster Einspruch des Münchener Theaterausschusses und Musikbeirates. Forderung eines gesetzlichen Schutzes für deutsches Kulturgut," *Fränkischer Kurier* (6 October 1927).
28. "Skandal in einer kleinen Residenz?" *Nürnberger Zeitung* (6 October 1927).
29. "Die Phoebus A. G. klagt." *Nürnberger Zeitung* (7 October 1927).

30. L.W., "Nürnberger Chronik. Lampe gibt seine Unterschrift zu einer lächerlichen Angelegenheit?" *Fränkische Tagespost* (6 October 1927).
31. There is no mention of Berger's film or the propaganda campaign in the official organ of the Bayreuth Festival, *Bayreuther Blätter*, in the 1927/28 period.
32. Geller, "Münchner Notizen," 32.
33. "Ein Trost: es sind die Söhne und Enkel derer, die Richard Wagner auspfiffen und nicht genug schmähen konnten, als er sich heiß um das Wesen und die Erneuerung der deutschen Oper bemühte. Heute geht es um das Wesen und die Entwicklung des deutschen Films. Und die Pfeiffer stellen sich wieder pünktlich ein!" Quoted in"Reise zum *Meister von Nürnberg.*"
34. "Reise zum *Meister von Nürnberg.*
35. Rudolf Kurtz, "*Der Meister von Nürnberg.* Völkischer Protest gegen die Nürnberger Uraufführung," *Central Verein-Zeitung* 41 (14 October 1927): 582.
36. Kurt Pinthus, "Nürnberg gegen die Meistersinger. Ludwig Bergers Abschied," *8 Uhr-Abendblatt* 236 (8 October 1927): 234.
37. Pinthus, "Nürnberg gegen die Meistersinger," 234.
38. Carl Neumann, Curt Belling and Hans-Walther Betz, *Film-"Kunst", Film-Kohn, Film-Korruption; ein Streifzug durch vier Film-Jahrzehnte* (Berlin: Hermann Scherping, 1937): 38–39.
39. Stephen Brockmann, *Nuremberg. The Imaginary Capital* (Rochester, NY: Camden House, 2006): 9.

Bibliography

A.W. "*Der Meister von Nürnberg.* Festvorstellung im Capitol." *Deutsche Allgemeine Zeitung* 66 416 (6 September 1927): 1–2.
B. "Die Filme der Woche." *Die rote Fahne* 10 214 (11 September 1927).
Belote, James H. "CIA-Report: The Lohmann Affair." *Studies in Intelligence* 4:2 (Spring 1960): A31–38.
Brockmann, Stephen. *Nuremberg. The Imaginary Capital.* Rochester, NY: Camden House, 2006.
"*Der Meister von Nürnberg.*" *Lichtbild-Bühne* 217 (10 September 1927): 3.
"*Der Meister von Nürnberg.*" *Österreichische Filmzeitung* 49 (3 December 1927).
"*Der Meister von Nürnberg*-Film als Festvorstellung in Köln." *Film-Kurier*, 22 September 1927.
"Der Nürnberger Protest gegen den Film *Der Meister von Nürnberg.* Eine einmütige geistige Erhebung." *Fränkischer Kurier*, 5 October 1927.
"Deutsche Großfilme!" *Film-Kurier*, 30 July 1927.
"Die Phoebus A.G. klagt." *Nürnberger Zeitung*, 7 October 1927.
"Die Phoebus-Affäre." *Österreichische Filmzeitung* 48 (26 November 1927).
"Eröffnung des Gloria-Palastes. Saisonbeginn in Frankfurt a. M." *Film-Kurier*, 19 September 1927.
Geller, Oscar. "Münchner Notizen." *Österreichische Filmzeitung* 43 (22 October 1927).
Henseleit, Felix. "*Der Meister von Nürnberg.*" *Reichsfilmblatt* 36 (1927).
Ihering, Herbert. "*Der Meister von Nürnberg.*" *Berliner Börsen-Courier*, 6 September 1927.
Jäger, Ernst. "Film-Kritik. *Der Meister von Nürnberg.* (Capitol)." *Film-Kurier*, 6 September 1927.

Kurtz, Rudolf. "*Der Meister von Nürnberg*. Völkischer Protest gegen die Nürnberger Uraufführung." *C.V.-Zeitung*, 14 October 1927.

L.H. "Capitol: *Der Meister von Nürnberg*." *Berliner Tageblatt* 56, 435 (11 September 1927).

L.W. "Auch München protestiert gegen den Film *Der Meister von Nürnberg*. Schärfster Einspruch des Münchener Theaterausschusses und Musikbeirates. Forderung eines gesetzlichen Schutzes für deutsches Kulturgut." *Fränkischer Kurier*, 6 October 1927.

Matthes, Wilhelm. "*Der Meister von Nürnberg*. Neue Schändung eines deutschen Kunstdenkmals." *Fränkischer Kurier*, 29 September 1927.

"*Meistersinger*-Film mit zweisprachigen Titeln." *New Yorker Staatszeitung* (undated, presumably after December 1929 U.S. premiere). Ludwig Berger Archiv, Akademie der Künste, Berlin, folder 18.

n. "Reise zum *Meister von Nürnberg*. Ergebnis: Der Nürnberger Protest gegen den Film— den man nicht gesehen hatte!—war völlig unberechtigt." *Nürnberger Zeitung*, 12 October 1927.

n. "Skandal in einer kleinen Residenz?" *Nürnberger Zeitung*, 6 October 1927.

Neumann, Carl, Curt Belling, and Hans-Walther Betz. *Film-"Kunst," Film-Kohn, Film-Korruption; ein Streifzug durch vier Film-Jahrzehnte*. Berlin: Hermann Scherping, 1937.

"Nürnberger Chronik. Lampe gibt seine Unterschrift zu einer lächerlichen Angelegenheit?" *Fränkische Tagespost*, 6 October 1927.

Pinthus, Kurt. "Nürnberg gegen die Meistersinger. Ludwig Bergers Abschied." *8 Uhr-Abendblatt* 236 (8 October 1927). Reprint Rolf Aurich and Wolfgang Jacobsen, eds., *Kurt Pinthus*, 233–34. *Filmpublizist*. Munich: Edition Text & Kritik, 2008.

Rasch, Hugo. "Schutz dem Urheber!" *Allgemeine Musikzeitung* 38 (23 September 1927).

Rosenberg, Alfred and Wilhelm Weiß, *Reichsparteitag der NSDAP Nürnberg 19/21. August 1927*. Munich: F. Eher, 1927.

Splitt, Gerhard. "Richard Strauss und die Reichsmusikkammer—im Zeichen der Begrenzung von Kunst?" In *Die Reichsmusikkammer. Kunst im Bann der Nazi-Diktatur*, ed. Albrecht Rietmüller and Michael Custodis, 15–32. Cologne: Böhlau, 2015.

Stadtarchiv Nürnberg. Stadtratsprotokolle 7/IX, 412 (5 October 1927).

Vaget, Hans Rudolf. "Das *Meistersinger*-Land." "*Wehvolles Erbe*." In *Richard Wagner in Deutschland. Hitler, Knappertsbusch, Mann*, 175–80. Frankfurt am Main: S. Fischer, 2017.

Weiner, Marc A., *Richard Wagner and the Anti-Semitic Imagination*. Lincoln: University of Nebraska Press, 1995.

"Wieder ein großer Tag der Phoebus—der gleichzeitig ein Ehrentag für den deutschen Film bedeutet: die Uraufführung des *Meisters von Nürnberg* im Capitol." *Film-Kurier*, 6 September 1927.

Chapter 13

BANNING JEWISHNESS

Stefan Zweig, Robert Siodmak, and the Nazis

Andréas-Benjamin Seyfert

In the first months of 1933 the German democratic government of the Weimar Republic was undergoing a significant political transition to National Socialism (Nazism). After Adolf Hitler was named chancellor on 30 January, the Nazi Party faced the challenge of gaining a clear majority in the Reichstag, the German parliament. In an effort to achieve complete sovereignty in Germany, the Nazi Party proceeded to weaken and do away with its political and ideological opponents. The arson attack on 27 February gave legitimacy to the Reichstag Fire Decree adopted the following day, a decree that temporarily repealed the rights of German citizens and allowed the Nazis to pursue and arrest members of the Communist Party. Further emergency decrees were introduced to impede meetings, activities, and publications of left-wing parties. On 24 March the Enabling Act was passed that gave Hitler the power to enact laws without the approval of parliament, effectively redrawing legislative cornerstones of democracy for the purpose of benefiting the Nazi totalitarian agenda. This major milestone finally led Hitler to declare the success of the National Socialist Revolution with the dissolution of all political fractions excluding the Nazi Party on 6 July.[1]

For years before Hitler's rise to power, the Nazis had blamed Germany's "degeneration" on the destructive influence of Weimar culture, with particular attention given to the alleged negative impact of "the film-Jews of Berlin."[2] An important task the government leaders set out to complete in the early weeks and months of the Third Reich was inspiring change within the psycho-political climate inherited from Weimar Germany. Joseph Goebbels, Nazi district leader in Berlin for more than six years, was put in charge of the Reich Ministry of Enlightenment and Propaganda and formally entrusted with the responsibility to implement and supervise the ideological transition. Seeking to simultaneously convey an impression of revolution and conservative stability, the ministry took it upon itself to navigate the fine line between determination and activism through mass propaganda and to silence what they perceived as politically and ideologically dissident voices. The ministry sought to emphasize the Nazi struggle against communists, foreign influences and "Jewish subversion." Swiftly, plans were laid out to restructure the means of communication in alignment with party policies: literature, art, music, theater, radio, and film were all targeted for government control with a notable emphasis on the cinematic medium.[3]

Robert Siodmak's adaptation of *Burning Secret*, Stefan Zweig's 1911 bestselling novella at the tail end of the Weimar Republic, and the film's reception shortly after the Nazi takeover reveal two different definitions of Jewishness that coexisted in early 1933 Germany. In adapting the novella for the screen, its Jewish makers airbrushed visible traits and mentions of Jews out of the picture. The film left out the novella's noted Jewish overtones and never acknowledged that two of its protagonists—as was Zweig—are Jews. This embrace of Jewish invisibility on the part of the film's creators points to a first definition of Jewishness as visibility, in the tradition of passing, an intrinsic component of early efforts of Jewish assimilation.[4] Like other films produced in the wake of the Third Reich with a heavy involvement of Jewish talent, *Burning Secret* came under attack from the German antisemitic press. Armed with brand new weapons of propaganda and censorship, the film was banned despite having been lauded as a cinematic achievement of the very highest order by all but the Nazi Party newspapers. This backlash in reaction to the film suggests a second definition of Jewishness as essence—unalterable, biological, and deep-rooted—in response to which antisemitic supporters proposed the "solution" of removing the Jewish body from its domain of influence over the non-Jewish, "Aryan" one.

Under more careful inspection of the context in which *Burning Secret* was finally removed from the German film circuit, however, there are several indications that even Nazi ideologues initially remained uncertain about how precisely to excise Jewishness from the film industry. They resorted first to removing the names of Jewish talent from *Burning Secret*'s opening credits, allowing this redacted version of the film to premiere before they finally demanded its ban in an article laden with fascist innuendo. Not only were there two coexisting definitions of Jewishness (visibility and essence) but also the tensions in and around the release of this film reveal the Nazis' own lack of success in identifying clear distinctions in what could qualify as Jewish and non-Jewish codes in the cinematic medium. Faced with the inability to locate and define Jewishness in the context of cinema, they proceeded to eliminate Jews from the industry altogether and to appoint a Nazi Party spokesperson who would decide what was acceptable in movies and what was not. Caught in the midst of film industry transformations and debates around Jewish passing, *Burning Secret*, its process of adaptation, and its reception provide critical insight into the changing outlook on Jewishness during the transitional period.[5] Beyond the commonly held explanation that German-Jewish filmmakers saw the writing on the wall and preemptively left the Third Reich for other countries in order to avoid the extreme persecution that was to come, this chapter offers instead a close look at mechanisms that were effectively used by the Nazi government to propagate and implement their definition of Jewishness as essence, compelling artists of Jewish background to seek out exile as the only way to ensuring their livelihood and continuation of a professional as well as artistic career in the cinematic medium.

Burning Secret's Erasure of Jewish Visibility from the Page to the Screen

The 1933 film *Burning Secret* was adapted from the eponymous 1911 novella by Austrian-Jewish writer Stefan Zweig. The story involves three characters: a bachelor,[6] a young married woman, and her twelve-year-old son. Interested in the mother, the young man befriends the son to get closer to her. His scheme succeeds and the two adults engage in a secret and adulterous love affair, leaving the boy betrayed, used, and confused. In the novella, Jewishness is foregrounded both directly through explicit mention of its Jewish characters and indirectly by focusing on a difficult transition into adulthood that can be read as an investigation of the Jewish assimilation process. Zweig explores the psychological development of the teenage son who is determined to figure out what the two adults are hiding from him; it is only when he abandons his childish idealism and adopts a worldview more tolerant of the complexity of human nature (along with its fallibility, its capacity for hate, love, and deception) that the boy is granted access to the hegemonic group of the adults. The story allows a parallel between the othered child in the adult world and Jewish difference. In both cases, assimilation can be used as a strategy to overcome prejudice and further fulfill the marginalized person's fantasy of finding acceptance and productively engaging with the hegemonic group. In his desire to pass as an adult, the young Jewish boy in Zweig's novella reflects the assimilationist predicament. While screenwriter Frederick Kohner saw a "sense of urgency" in telling this story "especially, of course [for] those who were Jewish,"[7] he also removed explicitly Jewish-coded features from the novella, suggesting an awareness of the rise in antisemitism since the novella's initial publication. The erasure of Jewish visibility by *Burning Secret*'s makers showcases how self-effacing certain German Jews had become of their own identity in order to garner a semblance of social acceptance in the Weimar Republic. The importance given to Jewish invisibility in the adaptation process reveals a definition of Jewishness quite different from that of Jewish essence which antisemitic Nazi ideologues would propagate in the Third Reich.

A guiding principle of Nazi racist politics was the condemnation of people based on predetermined guilt rather than individual actions. As the Nuremberg Trials later established, Nazi policy was to arrest people identified as possibly opposing the regime as a preemptive measure.[8] Nazis deemed certain groups of people, especially communists and Jews, guilty until proven innocent. This Kafkaesque absurdity led Stefan Zweig to write in 1933, "Whatever a Jew may venture to do nowadays, it will always be the wrong thing."[9] With the establishment of Nazi anti-Jewish policies, efforts of acculturation, which could have still seemed useful in the Weimar Republic, became increasingly futile. The understanding of what constitutes Jewishness moved increasingly from surface to essence. As scholars have pointed out, the elimination of certain "Jewish" traits or behaviors did not suffice to eliminate what was seen more and more as biological and unredeemable in a Third Reich context.[10] In pre-Nazi times, a great number of Jews felt pressured to appear non-Jewish, concealing and minimizing physical traits or modes of behavior, which would have been considered Jewish-coded, in order to garner favor and satisfy non-Jews. Recent scholarship has attempted to consider the extent to which Jews were aware of heightened discrimination against them and what strategies they developed in order to acculturate to a pervasively antisemitic society, which they recognized as hostile to their existence.[11] Although Jewish identity cannot be defined by any particular observable trait per se, as Kerry Wallach notes, Jewish visibility was constantly emphasized in

Weimar culture and society, reinforcing both the notion that Jewishness could be made visible and the desire of some German Jews to pass as non-Jewish.[12] In times before the adoption of an authoritative racist discourse of Jewishness as essence in the Nazi context, assimilation did not necessarily entail giving up on Jewish identity but rather recognizing the conditions to which one was required to hide it in exchange for social participation, individual growth, and eventual integration.

Traces of Zweig's own acculturated Jewish experience were implicitly reflected in his fiction, neither seeking to conceal nor to emphasize the Jewish markers of his characters. A few connections can be drawn between the author's life and his early bestseller *Burning Secret*, despite the fictional nature of this text. Zweig and the teenage protagonist of his story share a common Austrian Jewish background: "Edgar was the only son of a Viennese lawyer, obviously a member of the prosperous Jewish middle class."[13] Zweig's father was a Jewish textile manufacturer in Vienna, and his mother's wider family included lawyers, merchants, and bankers across Europe and America. He was thus part of the same Jewish middle class as the one he depicts in his novella. In addition, despite what some have argued,[14] Zweig saw his Jewish identity as crucial to his own thinking: "I have been vitally interested in Jewish problems all of my life, vitally aware of the Jewish blood that is in me ever since I have been conscious of it."[15] Despite his professed personal engagement with the Jewish condition and a number of Jewish characters in his fiction, he was all but outspoken about Jewish causes and anti-fascism. He saw his role as an artist who would capture the resistance of the oppressed who fell victim to their beliefs.[16]

Edgar, the Jewish teenager at the center of *Burning Secret*, occupies the position of the marginalized character in this particular Zweig story. He is othered and alienated in the novella not because of his Jewishness, but instead because of his place as a minor surrounded by adults. He wishes nothing more than to be "tall and strong, a man, a grown-up like the others."[17] Overcoming his initial suspicion as to why the bachelor would wish to befriend him "when no one else bothered about him,"[18] Edgar begins to revel in his dream of having been granted the keys to adulthood, believing for a time that he actually passes for an adult with his new friend.[19] Encouraged by the bachelor and his mother, he begins to perform adulthood to the best of his abilities and "it was not surprising that his deceptive feeling of being grown up himself grew and flourished."[20] The effort of passing is not successful, however. Initially trying to emulate adult behavior and seeking acceptance from his elders, Edgar is met with the ultimate realization that neither the bachelor nor his mother considered him their equal, that he was used as part of a scheme motivated by the interests of adult desires with which he cannot relate. It is this realization of his deception (and the Jewish boy's coming to terms with it) that Zweig frames as the real awakening and move toward adulthood, as Edgar loses his illusions about the grown-up world.

Edgar is a stranger to the adult world of desire and passion that the bachelor and his mother inhabit; however, it is not their affair and not the adultery that pains the young boy and forces him into an intellectual awakening. It is rather the deep-felt betrayal at having been lied to and deceived by the two adults that he trusted: "His rage and impatience, his anger, curiosity, helplessness, and the betrayal of the last few days all repressed in his childish struggle to live up to his delusion of being an adult . . . he wept everything out of him: trust, love, belief, respect—his entire childhood."[21]

In the last few chapters of the novella, Edgar realizes that everyone has their own struggles in life, and sometimes people will deceive, lie, and take advantage of others to achieve their goals; ultimately, though, adults are complex individuals, driven by the need for connection despite their hostile appearance—they are part of "the rich variety of life."[22] The novella closes this lesson with Edgar's ability to forgive the man who took advantage of his childish innocence to seduce his mother and with his acceptance of the rules imposed on him as a child.[23] Rather than attempting to change his identity, to pass as an adult and modify the way in which he is perceived by the adult world that alienates him, the Jewish boy begins to dream about the potential that lies in his own future, he starts to "dream . . . his own life."[24] Edgar has thus moved from a shy character, unaware of his place in the world and manipulated by his elders, to a place of knowledge and power, capable of pursuing ambitions with an understanding of the current limitations due to his status as a child in an adult world.

In Zweig's novella, the Jewish background of characters is not problematized nor is their oppression as a marginalized group made thematically explicit; they are rather both discreetly embedded into the narrative. The themes of otherness and alienation that underpin Edgar's interaction with the two adult protagonists are not explicitly linked with his Jewishness. Instead, his status as a child and his description as a Jew coexist side by side, allowing the reader to view them as two separate unrelated aspects of the character or to establish a relation between the two. Hanni Mittelmann is among those readers of Zweig's works who see a connection, arguing that the author's representation of outsiders in his fiction occupies an analogous function to the assimilationist Jewish condition. Zweig's outsiders and assimilationist Jews, Mittelmann suggests, struggle to understand a secret that escapes and alienates them from the world they seek to be a part of: "The 'Geheimnis' [secret] that they are so desperately trying to solve for themselves is basically the puzzlement at their rejection by a world whose rules and norms they are constantly trying to recognize and emulate, only to be met with prejudice and misgivings which keep them from entering and becoming part of this world."[25] In *Burning Secret*, Edgar is the character that Mittelmann describes, the one who feels a sense of alienation, not for being Jewish but because he is being manipulated and ignored by the adults around him whose motivations remain a mystery to him. His realization that "the words he'd thought reality behind them were just bright bubbles, swelling with air then bursting, leaving nothing behind,"[26] his acceptance of the condition he is in, and his dreams of a better future ahead bring Edgar closer to entering the world he so desires to be a part of.

Reading Zweig's outsiders as implicitly reflecting the assimilationist predicament is particularly convincing in Edgar's case since he also happens to be Jewish in the novella; however, it is important to keep in mind that the Jewishness of his character and the alienation that marks his coming-of-age positionality are presented as distinct in Zweig's text. With Mittelmann's approach, *Burning Secret* gains an added layer of meaning. In other words, it allows a parallel between two experiences of alienation: a universal one (that of being the othered child in a society that privileges adults) and a specific one (that of being a Jew in a country that stigmatizes Jewish people). In his various efforts to assimilate to the adult world, Edgar seeks to pass as an adult by imitating their behavior. As Kerry Wallach has noted, downplaying markers associated with Jewishness, thereby trying to blend in and pass as non-Jewish was a constant feature of dealing with one's Jewish identity in pre-Nazi times.[27] In Zweig's novella however, this rejection of one's own identity and performance of the marginalizing other does not prove effective in the ultimate goal to integrate into the targeted hegemonic group. Instead, what is presented as the solution or the secret to fulfilling the desire for connection inherent in all humans, is gaining an understanding for the basic features that drive human psychology: everyone you meet has their own struggles and goals, yet all people share the capacity for failure and a fundamental need to feel connected to one another. This realization helps the young protagonist to figure out where he fits into society, the function he serves for others, and the freedom he has to develop his own goals, no matter which struggles he may face in life. Zweig does therefore not embrace invisibility and passing, which he identifies as the rejection of one's identity in favor of another, but rather encourages a keen awareness of the prejudice against and the limitations imposed on one's identity, a consciousness he sees as key to a productive, mature engagement with the rest of the world.

While Edgar's Jewishness and his status as a child appear alongside each other in the text, two distinct features of his character, the 1932 screenplay adaptation of *Burning Secret* airbrushed all visible signs and references to Jews out of the picture. Edgar is still a child with no mention made of his religion. The effacement of Jewish signs from the novella to the screenplay points to a tradition of passing enacted on the page. In Zweig's novella, Edgar and his mother are both labelled as Jews. The mother's Jewishness is even fetishized through the point of view of the desiring bachelor as he first notices her: "The lady on whom alone the young Baron's attention was bent, was very soignée, dressed with obvious good taste, and what was more, she was the type he liked very much, one of those rather voluptuous Jewish women just before the age of over-maturity. . . . [He] admired the beautifully traced brows, a pure curve above a delicate nose that did in fact betray her race."[28] In this section of the novella, Zweig, through the perspective of the bachelor, defines the mother's voluptuousness and the shape of her nose as signs of Jewish visibility. This, as well as the explicit mention of Edgar's Jewish family background, identifies the mother as distinctly Jewish. In the process of adapting the novella for the screen, the character of the mother loses concrete features of her identity, her Jewishness but also her name, Mathilde. In the screenplay, she is simply referred to as "an elegant lady, Edgar's mother," and mentioned from here on out as *Die Frau* (the woman).[29] With these changes, all traces of Jewish visibility were excised from the original text, removing to some extent the interpretive layer that Mittelmann had helped to point out.

The screenwriters' embrace of Jewish invisibility points to a tradition of passing previously mentioned, an underlying aspect of Jewish assimilation. It further suggests an awareness of the rise in antisemitism since the novella's initial publication, since Kohner wrote of a sense of urgency among the Jewish talent involved in making the film at the onset of Hitler's takeover. The erasure of Jewish visibility also showcases how self-effacing certain German Jews had become of their own identity in order to garner a semblance of social acceptance in the Weimar Republic. A film needs to do well at the box office: the makers cannot necessarily afford to target and discriminate between specific audiences with which the film would be likely to resonate. Removing explicit mentions of Jews from a film in times of unprecedented antisemitism would therefore have made strategic sense as well. Removing Jewishness from the story disconnects the author Stefan Zweig from his creation, since Edgar and the author no longer share the same background of Jewish middle class. What remains in the film is a universal sense of alienation experienced by the child, with the second half of the analogy, the marginalized Jewish experience, left unmentioned. Hired along with Austrian Jewish critic Alfred Polgar, who had counted among the same coffeehouse literati as Stefan Zweig, Frederick Kohner expressed his wish to keep the story's essence unchanged, being of the firm belief that "[Zweig's] raw material would be understood and appreciated by any audience."[30] Considering this universal understanding as a guiding principle for translating the novella into the form of a screenplay, one of the decisions along the way may therefore very well have been one of resonating more with a universal sense of alienation rather than a specifically Jewish one, offering a point of empathetic access to any viewer of the film who may have felt othered in some way throughout their life (figure 13.1).

The casting of the mother with stage actress Hilde Wagener further avoided any comparison between the character in the novella: Christian, slim, blonde, straight-nosed, she displayed none of the elements that Zweig had mentioned as visible signs of Jewishness in his description of the mother and satisfied all the requirements to be considered a true "Aryan," in Nazi terms.[31] In the film, either the mother was meant as a Jewish woman who could pass perfectly as a non-Jew or, more likely, the intention was to eliminate her Jewishness from the story altogether. Those who had read Zweig's bestseller and would have chosen to read it as an analogy for the Jewish experience would have still been able to see it as such. The importance given to Jewish invisibility in the adaptation process reveals a preoccupation with Jewishness as defined by specific visible traits, that can be shown or removed at will, in order to pass or reveal Jewish identity. This definition was fundamentally contradictory with a Nazi view on race.

The "Aryanization" of German Cinema and the Attack on Robert Siodmak's Film

On the early Spring night of 20 March 1933, the lucky few who had received an invitation for the premiere of *Burning Secret* flocked to the

Willi Forst und Hilde Wagener in „Brennendes Geheimnis".

Figure 13.1. Willi Forst and Hilde Wagener in Robert Siodmak's *Burning Secret* (1933). Courtesy of Kreisky-Archiv, Vienna.

Capitol Theater near the Kurfürstendamm, electric lights reflecting on the Kaiser Wilhelm Memorial Church across the street, this monumental construction from a different time, before the hustle and bustle of speeding automobiles, neon advertisements, and flashy film posters. Entering the Capitol Theater, the audience would not only have had a chance to admire the octagonal ceiling of its interior, embellished with ninety lights like the innumerable incandescent bodies on a clear night sky, but some living stars as well: Willi Forst and Hilde Wagener in the company of the creatives responsible for the night's big sensation; director Robert Siodmak, screenwriter Frederick Kohner, and composers Allan Gray and Max Colpe were all in attendance.

As the theater darkened and the main titles hit the screen, something unusual happened: the credits were incomplete. Except for the title card and full cast, most names had been omitted, specifically the names of Jewish talent. As if nothing major had just transpired, the film continued its steady run through the projector. When the theater lights came back on, the spectators spontaneously began to clap and cheer; the applause went on for an unusual amount of time. After the show, the people responsible for *Burning Secret* spent a good part of the night together, wondering what kind of career lay before them in a world where Jews no longer received recognition for their work.

In the adaptation process, Siodmak and his collaborators had removed all references to the Jewishness of the story's protagonists; yet what had been taken out of Zweig's novella was not enough for the Nazis. Testimonies suggest that Goebbels's office, if not the minister of propaganda himself, had a part to play in the censored opening credits of *Burning Secret*.[32] According to the head of the Deutsche Universal Max Friedland, the editor-in-chief of a powerful Nazi newspaper, *Der Angriff*—literally the attack—had threatened the distribution company that they would ban the film in Germany if they did not agree to erase the names of all Jewish individuals featuring in the opening credits.[33] At a loss, the distributors agreed and ordered the film to be recut along those lines.

Responsible for all film-related matters at *Der Angriff* was a certain Willi Krause, writing under the pseudonym of Peter Hagen, who would become *Reichsfilmdramaturg* (the Reich's dramatic adviser for films) in 1934, the person appointed by the Ministry of Enlightenment and Propaganda in order to decide which materials were fit to be turned into movies in an effort to prevent films from being produced that were not in line with Nazi Party policies. Valerie Weinstein notes, "Krause's position both reflects the confidence Goebbels had in his political and artistic judgment and illustrates that in the crucial transitional period, scripts were controlled by an ideologue who wanted to purge Jewish moral, financial, and aesthetic corruption from German film."[34] Since Hitler's appointment in late January 1933, Krause's power had been steadily on the rise. As the example of *Burning Secret*'s censored opening credits suggests, his word already counted for a great deal. Only a few days after the premiere of *Burning Secret*, Krause would take over *Film-Kurier*, the only daily film trade newspaper, and lay off its entire Jewish personnel (which included its owner Alfred Weiner), part of the generalized effort of *Gleichschaltung*, the process through which the Nazi Party sought to gain uniform control over all aspects of German life.[35] By the summer of 1933 the Ministry of Enlightenment and Propaganda had taken control of the national press; after letting go of any opposing voices, it proceeded to tighten its control over journalism professionals.

On the day immediately following *Burning Secret*'s premiere, the time at which reviews for the film appeared in Berlin's major newspapers, Krause's publishing privileges were still limited to the columns of *Der Angriff*. On 21 March most Berlin newspapers featured many left-leaning liberal journalists and these individuals found nothing but praise for the film and its topic: Lotte Eisner, Curt Riess, and Herbert Ihering not only praised the film for its artistic merit but also were careful to mention the achievements of the Jewish creative staff whose names had been omitted in the opening credits.[36] Not only did Willi Krause write the only negative review of *Burning Secret* amidst what was otherwise a unanimously favorable critics' consensus, but *Der Angriff* also went back on its word, calling for the film to be banned. The review itself remains vague as to what makes the film unacceptable, referring instead to a cluster of unsound values, "Doubly dangerous because of the captivating form in which it is presented. . . . As I said: The issue at hand is not the beautiful exterior form but the film's content in terms of ideas and its content in terms of innermost constructive values. In that spirit, we recommend banning."[37] Given Krause's previous efforts to remove the names of Jewish creatives from the film's opening credits, allusions to dangerous values can only be interpreted in terms of fascist innuendo, an indirect method to convey antisemitic feeling defined by Theodor Adorno as a common practice of Nazi discourse in which negative forces are alluded to without directly being mentioned, and yet the target "audience at once understands that his remarks are directed against the Jews."[38] This assessment is also consistent with the virulent antisemitism ever-present in the columns of the *Angriff* that invariably blamed the Jewish community for the ills befalling the German nation.[39]

The press's mostly favorable echoes of *Burning Secret*, with the exception of Krause's suggestion of a ban, quickly reached Stefan Zweig who wrote a letter to Kohner two days later, thanking him for the faithful and sensitive adaptation of his novella, and attempting to reassure him as to the possibility of a ban that Krause had mentioned. In this letter Zweig uses language in quotation marks that reflects the changing outlook on Jewishness within the context of the Third Reich: "All that I have heard so far about the film is conceivably pleasing and your subtlety in the details was praised, the way in which you preserved the essence of the story. Furthermore, I do not believe in the possibility of a ban. It has to be a shot in the air to warn and avoid 'foreign' material in the future."[40] In the German original of this letter, Zweig uses the word *"fremdstämmig"* in quotation marks. This word does not simply mean foreign but of foreign origin (literally of foreign stock), a term that was extensively used in antisemitic circles to qualify Jews as *kulturfremd* (culturally foreign).[41] Zweig's use of the word and the quotation marks around it is indicative of the larger semantic difficulty of defining exactly what it was within the film that was problematic in light of the new regime ideology.

Indeed, the Nazi language about race emphasized a notion of Jewishness as biological and deep-rooted; in one word: essence. To Zweig and other acculturated Jews, this definition seemed strange, which explains Zweig's reluctance in using the language as his own, preferring to add the quotation marks instead. With Nazi belief in race becoming the authoritative stance for public policy. As historians have pointed out, "those stamped as of lesser value were left with the puzzle of trying to make sense of ideas and practices that marked them as less than human."[42] An emphasis on visibility as the denominating factor for Jewishness had given Jews the possibility to try and pass as non-Jewish and chose the moment when to emphasize it. Jewishness as essence, however, left no space for Jews to maneuver in society. Their very existence was enough to be deemed offensive to an antisemite, since it was construed as a polar opposite identity to the German "Aryan" race. How this racist ideology of Jewishness as essence translated to film practice however was still unclear to many people in the early Nazi regime.

The same day that Lotte Eisner's review for *Burning Secret* appeared in the movie industry trade paper *Film-Kurier*, so did an editorially authoritative article entitled *"Zensurklärung"* (Clarifying Censorship), seemingly speaking on behalf of the entire national film production. The article requested "a clarification and an official statement concerning directives to follow by the German film industry after this period of uncertainty." This request was addressed to Joseph Goebbels, newly appointed minister of propaganda. It recommended that "an official or semi-official instance" should at least issue "transitional measures by which the studios could be maintained, yes even revitalized, to fulfill the demands of a new era—through the elimination of questionable materials."[43] The article illustrates not only how difficult it must have been for the film industry to gauge what film would be banned or not, and therewith the danger of financial bankruptcy, but also the problem of clearly defining what was considered un-German or objectionable according to the new government. Words such as *volksfremd* (alien to a people or race), *kulturfremd* (culturally foreign), and *fremdstämmig* (of foreign origin), may well have worked as rhetorical devices to inflame the masses against the Jews and engrain in the general consciousness of Nazi followers the idea of Jewishness as essence, however both this article and the two-step process that Krause undertook in terms of addressing *Burning Secret* suggest that both the implementation of antisemitic ideology and its consequences for the cinematic medium were open to question at this time, even to Nazi ideologues themselves.

The response to this plea for clarity came a week later in the form of a speech in front of members of the German film industry at the Kaiserhof on 28 March 1933. Goebbels did not answer the question of what qualifies as objectionable under the new state policies. Indeed, these criteria would never come to be clearly defined in the remainder of the Nazi period. Instead, they would be constantly reassessed on a case-by-case basis by a person of authority, the *Reichsfilmdramaturg*, and—from 1934 to 1936—this was none other than Willi Krause himself. Rather than offering a clear answer as to what *would* constitute German cinema under the swastika, Joseph Goebbels clarified what it *would not* be: "In any case, public taste is not as it is conceived in the mind of a Jewish director. It is impossible to gain an idea of the German people while living in a vacuum. One must take an honest look at the German people and for this one must have one's own roots firmly embedded in the German soil. One must be a child of this nation."[44] In his diaries, Goebbels wrote that day: "Developed program in front of film creatives. Riotous success! Everyone will help," and "Call for boycott made public today. Panic amongst the Jews."[45] While Goebbels did not define what criteria should be followed to make sure that films would be guaranteed permission to be shown in Germany under Nazi rule, he did announce the elimination of Jews from the film industry as the first concrete step toward attaining such security, the implementation of which was not long deferred.

Two days following Goebbels's speech, on 1 April (the date announced by the ministry for a general boycott of Jewish businesses), its effects became unmistakable. Conditions drastically changed for Jews involved in the film industry, as the example of *Burning Secret* illustrates. In his memoirs, *The World of Yesterday*, Stefan Zweig described the events that followed: "Policemen raced around on motorbikes, further showings of the film were banned, and by the next day the title of my novella *Burning Secret* had vanished without trace from all newspaper advertisements and all the advertising pillars where posters went up."[46] The head of Deutsche Universal, Max Friedland, was stopped by his secretary when trying to enter his office with the explanation that no Jew was allowed to enter.[47] In that vein, German branches of six American companies received notices from the Nazi cells within their company to discharge all employees of Jewish "race," emphasizing the definition of Jewishness as essence, stating explicitly that this meant all people of Jewish background whether of faith or Christianized.[48] Witnesses reported that Nazis beat up Jews in the open street while others wrote antisemitic slogans on the storefronts of Jewish-owned businesses.[49] Only a week after the premiere of *Burning Secret*, the exodus of Jewish talent from the film industry was in full swing.

Conclusion: Jewishness Ostracized

In considering *Burning Secret*'s adaptation process and its reception, this chapter reveals two different definitions of Jewishness that coexisted in early 1933 Germany: Jewish visibility and essence. As the end of the story shows, only one definition survived with the growth of antisemitism in Nazi Germany: Jewish invisibility, which was a method of acculturation open to Jews in the Weimar Republic, passing for non-Jewish, was not enough as well as beside the point for Nazi ideologues who believed in a concept of race as deep-rooted, inborn, and unalterable. Goebbels's speech at the Kaiserhof in late March 1933 gave an answer to the uncertainties as to an immediate course of action concerning Jewishness: German films in the Nazi spirit meant a film industry without Jews. Beyond the unsatisfactory explanation sometimes offered that Jews in the German film industry sensed early on what was to come and sought refuge elsewhere, the story of *Burning Secret* sheds light on a particular moment in which questions of Jewishness were negotiated between the Nazis and the movie industry, setting up the guidelines that would compel German-Jewish film artists to leave the Third Reich to continue their careers elsewhere.

To varying degrees, the Jewish talent behind *Burning Secret* fell victim to the Ministry of Enlightenment and Propaganda's crusade to remove the Jewish body from its domain of influence over the "Aryan," non-Jewish one. Robert Siodmak and Frederick Kohner finally found refuge in Hollywood and went on to have successful careers, Siodmak as the master of a genre that would become known as film-noir. For his part, Kohner wrote a treatment for an American remake of the 1933 film that was never made—he would become famous for inventing the prototypical beach bunny Gidget instead. Others would not make it as far as the screenwriter and the director. According to research assembled by their son Pierre Lellouch, Alfred and Ruth Sternau, the producer and set designer of *Burning Secret*, respectively, left Berlin in October

1933. Their exile through Europe took them to Spain and Italy in 1937, and France in 1939. They were finally caught by the Gestapo in Nice in the Fall of 1943. Sternau wrote to the Kohners pleading for an affidavit; they would have no such luck. After multiple arrests, they were deported from Drancy to Auschwitz in October 1943 where they finally died on 13 October. Their son Pierre survived in hiding. More than a year prior to their deaths, on 22 February 1942, Stefan Zweig had given into his despair seeing the Europe he once knew disappear from afar, in his South American exile. He committed suicide.

Caught in the wheels of political transition, Robert Siodmak's *Burning Secret*, the story of its adaptation, release, and reception, resounds with the debates around Jewish difference occurring at the time. In January 1934, less than a year after the release of the film, a patriotic front page of the *Film-Kurier* celebrated the achievements of the "rebirth" of German cinema since Hitler's takeover, speaking of a "change in the destiny of the German film" and advocating "in the spirit of National Socialism, [for] films that can conquer the world as German objects of cultural value in their highest form of completion."[50] Always looking toward the future, the *Film-Kurier* was ready to forget that the question of defining Jewishness in German film had been unclear in early 1933, before having been worked out on the side of both the government and the film industry. From the perspective of Nazi ideologues this hesitation did not matter; all that was of importance was that what had been seen as *kulturfremd* (culturally foreign), had been excised, splitting apart the German *Volk* and the Jewish people. Jewishness was banned, and "culturally foreign" books burnt; among the pages seized by the flames were Stefan Zweig's works. By taking a close look at *Burning Secret*'s fate, we come closer to understanding how it came to be that, a few months after Hitler seized power, the German filmic medium had been drained of its Jewish population, allowing for racist culture to prevail and stifling the voices of this oppressed social group.

Andréas-Benjamin Seyfert is a Ph.D. candidate at the Department of Germanic Languages at the University of California, Los Angeles (UCLA). He completed the Gender Studies Concentration and holds a Digital Humanities Graduate Certificate. His work includes *The Weimar Talkies Project*, a Digital Humanities project supported by the UCLA Digital Library Program, as well as a chapter in the German-language volume *Goethe als Literatur-Figur* (Wallstein, 2016). His dissertation focuses on the filmic production of the late Weimar Republic.

Notes

1. In early 1933 Hitler was far from having obtained such breadths of power as the second round of elections on 5 March determined: the Nazi Party achieved only a small majority of votes and had to settle for a coalition. The election results are one of the signs that mark the transitional period as one of great uncertainty, resisting the straight deterministic line that has sometimes been drawn from Weimar liberalism directly into the Holocaust. Excellent and thorough historical overviews on the subject of the passage from Weimar to Nazi Germany can be found in Richard J. Evans's *The Coming of the Third Reich*; and Benjamin Carter Hett's *The Death of Democracy*.
2. Martin Loiperdinger, "Filmzensur und Selbstkontrolle," *Geschichte des deutschen Films*, ed. Wolfgang Jacobsen, Anton Kaes, and Hans-Helmut Prinzler (Stuttgart and Weimar: J.B. Metzler, 2004), 525–44; here, 534.
3. To stress the importance and priority of film as a means for propaganda in the view of Nazi leaders, one should only mention that the Reich Film Chamber, the statutory corporation controlled by the Ministry of Enlightenment and Propaganda, was set up before the Reich Chamber of Culture that would later house it. See David Welch, *The Third Reich: Politics and Propaganda* (London, New York: Routledge, 2002), 28–57.
4. See Kerry Wallach, *Passing Illusions: Jewish Visibility in Weimar Germany* (Ann Arbor: University of Michigan Press, 2017).
5. For further reading on the films of this transitional period, see, especially, Barbara Hales, Mihaela Petrescu, and Valerie Weinstein, eds. *Continuity and Crisis in German Cinema, 1928–1936* (Rochester, NY: Camden House, 2016). The collection of essays examines various turning points and continuities from the late Weimar Republic into the first years of Hitler's regime, challenging the easy answer of 1933 as a decisive break but rather defining the period between 1928 and 1936 as a transitional period in which changes of a social, political, and cinematic significance began to take shape and firm up.
6. The young man, a baron in the novella, was adapted into a racecar driver, in keeping with the times, motorsports having become increasingly popular. The German Grand Prix, for example, had been introduced in 1931 and was held again the following year. This was perhaps an effort to capture some of the glamor represented by nobility in years preceding World War I that had been replaced to some degree with mass media stardom in the interwar years.
7. Frederick Kohner, *The Magician of Sunset Boulevard: The Improbable Life of Paul Kohner, Hollywood Agent* (Palos Verdes, CA: Morgan Press, 1977), 71.
8. On 18 March 1946, Hermann Goering testified: "People were arrested and taken into protective custody who had not yet committed any crime, but who could be expected to do so if they remained free." *Trial of the Major War Criminals before the International Military Tribunal*, vol. 9 (Nuremberg: International Military Tribunal, 1947), 422. In the German original: "Es sind Leute verhaftet worden, die noch kein Verbrechen begangen haben, von denen aber man es erwarten konnte, wenn sie in Freiheit blieben."
9. "Was ein Jude heute tut, ist immer falsch." Letter to Rudolf Kayser on 30 November 1933, cited in Stefan Zweig, *Stefan Zweig: Spiegelungen einer schöpferischen Persönlichkeit*, ed. Erich Fitzbauer (Vienna: Bergland Verlag, 1959), 76.
10. See especially Mark Roseman, "Racial Discourse, Nazi Violence, and the Limits of the Racial State Model," *Beyond the Racial State*, ed. Devin O. Pendas (Cambridge & New York: Cambridge University Press, 2017), 31–57.
11. See in particular Wallach, *Passing Illusions*.

12. See Wallach, "Introduction: Passing, Covering, Revealing," in Wallach, *Passing Illusions*, 1–26.
13. Stefan Zweig, *Burning Secret* (London: Pushkin Press, 2008), 22. "daß Edgar der einzige Sohn eines Wiener Advokaten sei, offenbar aus der vermögenden jüdischen Bourgeoisie." Stefan Zweig, "Brennendes Geheimnis," *Das Stefan Zweig Buch* (Frankfurt: S. Fischer Verlag, 1982), 23–81; here, 30.
14. This idea has been particularly influential as a result of Hannah Arendt's 1943 essay about Zweig. See Hannah Arendt, "Stefan Zweig: Jews in the World of Yesterday," *Reflections on Literature and Culture*, ed. Susannah Young-ah Gottlieb (Stanford, CA: Stanford University Press, 2007), 58–68.
15. Interview by David Ewen of Stefan Zweig in 1931, cited in Mark H. Gelber, *Stefan Zweig, Judentum und Zionismus* (Innsbruck: Studienverlag, 2014), 12. On this topic, see also Jasmin Sohnemann, "Umgang mit Antisemitismus und Judenverfolgung," *Arnold Zweig und Stefan Zweig in der Zwischenkriegszeit. Publizistisches Engagement und literaturwissenschaftliche Rezeption bis in das 21. Jahrhundert* (Berlin: Peter Lang, 2017), 354–93.
16. See interview by Thomas Curtiss of Stefan Zweig in 1939. Cited in Lionel B. Steiman, "The Worm in the Rose: Historical Destiny and Individual Action in Stefan Zweig's Vision of History," *The World of Yesterday's Humanist Today: Proceedings of the Stefan Zweig Symposium*, ed. Marion Sonnenfeld (Albany, NY: State University of New York Press, 1983), 151.
17. Zweig, *Burning Secret*, 28. "groß und stark, ein Mann, ein Erwachsener wie die andern." Zweig, "Brennendes Geheimnis," 34.
18. Zweig, *Burning Secret*, 19. "um den sich sonst keiner kümmerte." Zweig, "Brennendes Geheimnis," 28.
19. See Zweig, *Burning Secret*, 22–23.
20. Zweig, *Burning Secret*, 30. "es war nicht verwunderlich, daß in ihm das trügerische Gefühl üppig wuchernd wuchs, daß er ein Erwachsener sei." Zweig, "Brennendes Geheimnis," 35.
21. Zweig, *Burning Secret*, 68–69. "Die Wut, die Ungeduld, der Ärger, die Neugier, die Hilflosigkeit und der Verrat der letzten Tage, im kindischen Krampf, im Wahn seiner Erwachsenheit niedergehalten. . . . Er weinte in dieser Stunde fassungsloser Wut alles aus sich heraus, Vertrauen, Liebe, Gläubigkeit, Respekt—seine ganze Kindheit." Zweig, "Brennendes Geheimnis," 55.
22. Zweig, *Burning Secret*, 103. "Mannigfaltigkeit des Lebens." Zweig, "Brennendes Geheimnis," 74.
23. See Zweig, *Burning Secret*, 116.
24. Zweig, *Burning Secret*, 117. "es begann der tiefere Traum seines Lebens." Zweig, "Brennendes Geheimnis," 81.
25. Hanni Mittelmann, "Fragmentation and the Quest for Unity: Stefan Zweig's Novellas as Tales of the Assimilationist Jewish Predicament," in *Stefan Zweig Rediscovered, New Perspectives on his Literary and Biographical Writings*, ed. Mark H. Gelber (Tübingen: Niemeyer, 2007), 173.
26. Zweig, *Burning Secret*, 68. "er sah, daß die Worte, hinter denen er die Wirklichkeit vermutet hatte, nur farbige Blasen waren, die sich blähten und in nichts zersprangen." Zweig, "Brennendes Geheimnis," 55.
27. See Wallach, "Introduction," 1–26.
28. Zweig, *Burning Secret*, 13. "Die Dame—und nur auf sie hatte der junge Baron acht—war sehr soigniert und mit sichtbarer Eleganz gekleidet, ein Typus überdies, den er sehr liebte, eine jener leicht üppigen Jüdinnen im Alter knapp vor der Überreife . . .

[Er] bewunderte nur die schön geschwungene Linie der Augenbrauen, rein über einer zarten Nase gerundet, die ihre Rasse . . . verriet." Zweig, "Brennendes Geheimnis," 25–26.
29. Screenplay reprinted in Günter Knorr, "Robert Siodmak: Eine Dokumentation," *Filmkundliche Hefte* 1–2 (1973).
30. Kohner, *The Magician of Sunset Boulevard*, 71.
31. Hilde Wagener's Nazi sympathies are expressed in "Alle sagen Ja! Wiener Künstler zum 10. April," *Neues Wiener Journal* (7 April 1938), 13. According to an unpublished letter by F.K. Kaul to Günter Knorr on 14 May 1973 (scan courtesy of Jean-Philippe Boever), Willi Forst was responsible for the casting of Hilde Wagener. Since she had no prior experience in German talkies, it reinforced his claim to receive top-billing in the film.
32. See Kohner, *The Magician of Sunset Boulevard*, 72. Kohner believes this to have been Minister Goebbels himself. This is unlikely, however. Joseph Goebbels mentions nothing related to film censorship in his diaries that year prior to *The Testament of Dr. Mabuse* on 29 March 1933: "Film 'Dr. Mabuse' von Fritz Lang gesehen. Praktische Anleitung zum Verbrechen. Wird verboten." ("Saw film 'Dr. Mabuse' by Fritz Lang. Practical manual for crime. To be banned.") Joseph Goebbels, *Die Tagebücher von Joseph Goebbels Online* (Berlin & Boston: De Gruyter, 2012); entry of 29 March 1933. Retrieved 9 January 2020, from https://www.degruyter.com/view/TJGO/TJG-2473.
33. Werner Skrentny, "Bestellen Sie bitte Herrn Friedland einen Glückwunsch! Eine Begegnung im Stuyvesant Village, Manhattan," in *Deutsche Universal. Transatlantische Verleih- und Produktionsstrategien eines Hollywood-Studios in den 20er und 30er Jahren*, ed. Erika Wottrich (Munich: Edition Text + Kritik, 2001), 95.
34. Valerie Weinstein, *Antisemitism in Film Comedy in Nazi Germany* (Bloomington: Indiana University Press, 2019), 63.
35. "I urge all German theatre-owners, inasmuch as they have not as yet taken subscriptions, to do so at once after this take-over of the Film-Kurier has now become the real 'official organ' of the German film industry. Also I find it most important that German theatre-owners become interested to an even greater extent as until now in the Illustrierter Film-Kurier which is still being developed."—*Film-Kurier*, 6 April 1933. Cited and translated in Werner Sudendorf, "Film-Kurier 1919–1944," *FIAF Bulletin* 32 (1986), 15–17.
36. Mentioned responses to the premiere include Lotte H. Eisner, "Film-Kritik," *Film-Kurier* (21 March 1933); Curt Riess-Steinam, "Der Star Hans Joachim Schaufuss," *Das 12 Uhr Blatt* (21 March 1933); Herbert Jhering, "Das Brennende Geheimnis," *Berliner Börsen-Courier* (21 March 1933). Eisner and Riess fled Berlin for France. Eisner later wrote one of the most powerful books about Weimar cinema to date: *The Haunted Screen: Expressionism in the German Cinema and the Influence of Max Reinhardt*. Ihering remained in Germany, but his liberal left-leaning politics finally led to his exclusion from the National Writer's Chamber in 1936.
37. Peter Hagen, "Brennendes Geheimnis," *Der Angriff* (21 March 1933). "gerade wegen der bestechenden Form, in der sie dargeboten wird, doppelt gefährlich . . . Wie gesagt: Es geht hier nicht um die schöne äußere Form, sondern um den Ideengehalt des Films und sein Gehalt an inneren aufbauenden Werten. In diesem Sinne empfehlen wir das Verbot."
38. Theodor W. Adorno, "Anti-Semitism and Fascist Propaganda," *The Stars Down to Earth and Other Essays on the Irrational in Culture* (London & New York: Routledge, 2002), 218–31; here, 228.

39. See Russel Lemmons, *Goebbels and Der Angriff* (Lexington: University Press of Kentucky, 1994), 129. Throughout Adolf Hitler's rise to power (the *Kampfzeit*), *Der Angriff*, founded by Goebbels himself, had been an important player for the party. Many heads of the Berlin Nazi Party had started their political activism by working for *Der Angriff*, in the early years "the only legal means by which Goebbels could propagate Nazi ideas . . . always striving to create the atmosphere of battle or a ballroom brawl. He knew this type of nihilistic hooliganism appealed to his constituents." Willi Krause was its editor for cultural politics.
40. "Alles was ich bisher von dem Film hörte ist denkbar erfreulich und mir wurde im Einzelnen die Zartheit gerühmt, mit der Sie das Wesentliche der Erzählung bewahrt haben. Ich glaube auch nicht an die Möglichkeit eines Verbotes. Es ist dies wohl nur ein Luftschuss zur Mahnung, in Zukunft 'fremdstämmige' Stoffe zu vermeiden." Letter from Stefan Zweig to Frederick Kohner, Salzburg, 23 March 1933. Scan courtesy of the Deutsche Kinemathek.
41. For a definition of the word *fremdstämmig* in the Nazi context, see Ulrich Herbert, "Glossary and Abbreviations," *Hitler's Foreign Workers: Enforced Foreign Labor in Germany under the Third Reich* (Cambridge & New York: Cambridge University Press, 1997), xiii–xix; here, xv. For more-expansive work on the subject, see also Oliver Trevisol, *Die Einbürgerungspraxis im Deutschen Reich 1871–1945* (Göttingen: V & R unipress, 2006). This understanding of Nazi antisemitism as grounded in xenophobia rather than social Darwinism is also the conclusion Mark Roseman arrives at. See Roseman, "Racial Discourse," 31–57.
42. Roseman, "Racial Discourse," 51.
43. "Vor einer neuen Arbeits-Epoche Zensurklärung dringend! Eine Anregung der Produktion: wenigstens als vorübergehende Massnahme," *Film-Kurier* (21 March 1933). "Richtlinien nach der Periode der Ungewißheit geklärt und bekanntgegeben würden, nach denen der deutsche Film arbeiten darf," "eine amtliche oder halbamtliche Stelle," and "Uebergangs-Maßnahmen, durch die die Werkstätten erhalten bleiben, ja belebt werden und durch die Forderungen einer neuen Zeit—durch die Aussiebung bedenklicher Stoffe—erfüllt werden."
44. "Dr. Goebbels' speech at the Kaiserhof on 28 March 1933." Reprinted and translated in Welch, *The Third Reich*, 184–89; here, 188. "Allerdings ist der Publikumsgeschmack nicht so, wie er sich im Inneren eines jüdischen Regisseurs abspielt. Man kann kein Bild vom deutschen Volk im luftleeren Raum gewinnen. Man muß dem Volke aufs Maul schauen und selbst im deutschen Erdreich seine Wurzeln eingesetzt haben. Man muß ein Kind dieses Volkes sein."
45. Goebbels, *Die Tagebücher*. "Vor den Filmschaffenden Programm entwickelt. Bombenerfolg! Alle werden helfen," and "Boykott-Aufruf ist heute veröffentlicht. Panik unter den Juden."
46. Stefan Zweig, *The World of Yesterday* (Lincoln: University of Nebraska Press, 2013), 392. "jagten auf Motorrädern Polizisten herum, die Vorstellungen wurden verboten, vom nächsten Tage an war der Titel meiner Novelle 'Brennendes Geheimnis' aus allen Zeitungsankündigungen und von allen Plakatsäulen spurlos verschwunden". Stefan Zweig, *Die Welt von Gestern: Erinnerungen eines Europäers* (Frankfurt: S. Fischer Verlag, 2009), 378.
47. See Skrentny, "Bestellen Sie bitte," 94.
48. See "Nazi Orders Jews Dismissed by American Film Companies," *New York Times* (2 April 1933). Just as Stefan Zweig had predicted in his letter to Frederick Kohner, this stance was met with incomprehension and doubt from abroad. The *New York Times*

reprinted the notice verbatim on their front page, adding the concluding sentence: "American film interests believe the order unauthorized."
49. Kohner, *The Magician of Sunset Boulevard*, 73.
50. "Sieg Heil 1934!" *Film-Kurier* (1 January 1934). "eine Schicksalswende des deutschen Film ... wollen wir in nationalsozialistischem Geiste den neuen deutschen Film schaffen, der als ... deutsche Wertarbeit in höchster Vollendung sich wieder die Welt erobert."

Bibliography

Adorno, Theodor W. "Anti-Semitism and Fascist Propaganda." In *The Stars Down to Earth and Other Essays on the Irrational in Culture*, 218–31. London & New York: Routledge, 2002.
"Alle sagen Ja! Wiener Künstler zum 10 April." *Neues Wiener Journal*, 7 April 1938.
Arendt, Hannah. "Stefan Zweig: Jews in the World of Yesterday." In *Reflections on Literature and Culture*, ed. Susannah Young-ah Gottlieb, 58–68. Stanford, CA: Stanford University Press, 2007.
Eisner, Lotte H. "Film-Kritik." *Film-Kurier*, 21 March 1933.
———. *The Haunted Screen: Expressionism in the German Cinema and the Influence of Max Reinhardt*. Berkeley: University of California Press, 2008.
Evans, Richard J. *The Coming of the Third Reich*. New York: Penguin Press, 2004.
Fitzbauer, Erich, ed. *Stefan Zweig: Spiegelungen einer schöpferischen Persönlichkeit*. Vienna: Bergland, 1959.
Gelber, Mark H. *Stefan Zweig, Judentum und Zionismus*. Innsbruck: Studienverlag, 2014.
Goebbels, Joseph. *Die Tagebücher von Joseph Goebbels Online*. Berlin: De Gruyter, 2012. Retrieved 9 January 2020 from https://www.degruyter.com/view/db/tjgo
Hagen, Peter. "Brennendes Geheimnis." *Der Angriff*, 21 March 1933.
Hales, Barbara, Mihaela Petrescu, and Valerie Weinstein, eds. *Continuity and Crisis in German Cinema, 1928–1936*. Rochester, NY: Camden House, 2016.
Herbert, Ulrich. "Glossary and Abbreviations." In *Hitler's Foreign Workers: Enforced Foreign Labor in Germany under the Third Reich*, xiii–xix. Cambridge: Cambridge University Press, 1997.
Hett, Benjamin Carter. *The Death of Democracy: Hitler's Rise to Power and the Downfall of the Weimar Republic*. New York: Henry Holt, 2018.
Jhering, Herbert. "Das Brennende Geheimnis." *Berliner Börsen-Courier*, 21 March 1933.
Knorr, Günter. "Robert Siodmak: Eine Dokumentation." *Filmkundliche Hefte* 1–2 (1973).
Kohner, Frederick. *The Magician of Sunset Boulevard: The Improbable Life of Paul Kohner, Hollywood Agent*. Palos Verdes, CA: Morgan Press, 1977.
Lemmons, Russel. *Goebbels and Der Angriff*. Lexington: University Press of Kentucky, 1994.
Loiperdinger, Martin. "Filmzensur und Selbstkontrolle." *Geschichte des deutschen Films*, ed. Wolfgang Jacobsen, Anton Kaes, and Hans-Helmut Prinzler, 525–44. Stuttgart: J.B. Metzler, 2004.
Mittelmann, Hanni. "Fragmentation and the Quest for Unity: Stefan Zweig's Novellas as Tales of the Assimilationist Jewish Predicament." In *Stefan Zweig Rediscovered: New Perspectives on his Literary and Biographical Writings*, ed. Mark H. Gelber, 163–74. Tübingen: Niemeyer, 2007.
"Nazi Orders Jews Dismissed by American Film Companies." *New York Times*, 2 April 1933.

Riess-Steinam, Curt. "Der Star Hans Joachim Schaufuss." *Das 12 Uhr Blatt*, 21 March 1933.
Roseman, Mark. "Racial Discourse, Nazi Violence, and the Limits of the Racial State Model." In *Beyond the Racial State*, ed. Devin O. Pendas, 31–57. Cambridge: Cambridge University Press, 2017.
"Sieg Heil 1934!" *Film-Kurier*, 1 January 1934.
Skrentny, Werner. "Bestellen Sie bitte Herrn Friedland einen Glückwunsch! Eine Begegnung im Stuyvesant Village, Manhattan." *Deutsche Universal: Transatlantische Verleih- und Produktionsstrategien eines Hollywood-Studios in den 20er und 30er Jahren*, ed. Erika Wottrich, 88–99. Munich: Edition Text & Kritik, 2001.
Sohnemann, Jasmin. "Umgang mit Antisemitismus und Judenverfolgung." *Arnold Zweig und Stefan Zweig in der Zwischenkriegszeit: Publizistisches Engagement und literaturwissenschaftliche Rezeption bis in das 21. Jahrhundert*, 354–93. Berlin: Peter Lang, 2017.
Sudendorf, Werner. "Film-Kurier 1919–1944." *FIAF Bulletin* 32 (1986): 15–17.
Trevisol, Oliver. *Die Entbürgerungspraxis im Deutschen Reich 1871–1945*. Göttingen: V & R Unipress, 2006.
Trial of the Major War Criminals before the International Military Tribunal, vol. 9. Nuremberg: International Military Tribunal, 1947.
"Vor einer neuen Arbeits-Epoche Zensurklärung dringend! Eine Anregung der Produktion: wenigstens als vorübergehende Massnahme." *Film-Kurier*, 21 March 1933.
Wallach, Kerry. "Introduction: Passing, Covering, Revealing." In Wallach, *Passing Illusions*, 1–26.
———. *Passing Illusions: Jewish Visibility in Weimar Germany*. Ann Arbor: University of Michigan Press, 2017.
Weinstein, Valerie. *Antisemitism in Film Comedy in Nazi Germany*. Bloomington: Indiana University Press, 2019.
Welch, David. *The Third Reich: Politics and Propaganda*. London: Routledge, 2002.
Zweig, Stefan, "Brennendes Geheimnis." *Das Stefan Zweig Buch*, 23–81. Frankfurt: S. Fischer, 1982.
———. *Burning Secret*. London: Pushkin Press, 2008.
———. *Die Welt von Gestern: Erinnerungen eines Europäers*. Frankfurt: S. Fischer, 2009.
———. *The World of Yesterday*. Lincoln: University of Nebraska Press, 2013.

Chapter 14

DETOXIFICATION

Nazi Remakes of E.A. Dupont's Blockbusters

Ofer Ashkenazi

Since its early days, cinema was a major venue for the negotiation of Jews' experiences and aspirations in modern Germany. Particularly after 1918, men and women of Jewish ancestry played a significant role in the German film industry.[1] Jewish producers, directors, and scriptwriters, as well as set designers, cameramen, actresses, and actors contributed to many of the most significant critically acclaimed as well as popular genre films of the era, and Jewish critics and magazine editors played a major role in the reception of these films.[2] Yet, with a few notable exceptions, pre-1933 German films generally shied away from explicitly Jewish-related themes, Jewish characters, and spaces associated with modern Jewish life. Recent studies have demonstrated how—by using strategies such as appropriation of anti-Jewish stereotypes and undermining generic expectations—Weimar Jewish filmmakers reflected on the prospect of acculturation from the perspective of the outsider who yearns to belong.[3] The dual encoding of characters and motivations as both typical of the bourgeois experience and stereotypically Jewish enabled these filmmakers to evoke German-Jewish aspirations and fears, while at the same time being relevant and attractive to a wider audience. Jewish critics frequently spotted this dual encoding and associated these films with major concepts in the German-Jewish identity discourse.[4] The study of Jewish filmmaking in Weimar, however, still requires a better understanding of the ways non-Jewish filmmakers and viewers perceived the Jewish aspects of these films.

National Socialist (Nazi) remakes of films that were originally made by Jewish filmmakers during the Weimar Republic tend to isolate and highlight these Jewish aspects. In her analysis of the similarities between E.A. Dupont's pro-acculturation film *Das alte Gesetz* (*The Ancient Law*; 1923) and Veit Harlan's notoriously antisemitic *Jud Süss* (1940), Valerie Weinstein showed that Nazi filmmakers sought to revisit and "correct" certain aspects of Weimar films.[5] In line with Weinstein's argument, this article considers continuities and dialogues between Jewish and non-Jewish German filmmakers across the 1933 watershed. Yet I focus here on the Nazi remakes of films that, although made by Jewish filmmakers, neither featured obviously Jewish protagonists nor showed explicit interest in Jewish assimilation. As the discussion below indicates, the makers of the post-1933 versions nevertheless felt the need to revise significantly various elements of the plot and of the imagery. Comparisons between the different versions of the same film reveal the elements of the earlier versions that Nazi filmmakers deemed incompatible with Nazism.

Many of the revisions to the earlier versions pertained to what adherents of Nazism perceived to be the Jewish aspects of the pre-1933 films. In the Nazi imagination, Jewish filmmaking was not confined to specific themes, styles, or genres. Rather, the analysis below suggests that this concept referred to the propensity of certain Jewish filmmakers to subvert notions of German nationality that were consistent with Nazi views. In dismissing exclusive notions of German identity and advocating a heterogeneous modern community—in which belonging is based on a shared habitus rather than on the innate blood and soil—Jewish filmmakers challenged fundamental premises of Nazi ideology. Consequently, the remakes discussed below had little use for overtly antisemitic imagery. In confronting the Jewish facet of Weimar cinema, they sought to eradicate the Jewish model of German identity that was propagated in pre-1933 films rather than to support anti-Jewish violence.

In a pair of case studies of such Nazi remakes, I focus here on the re-production of two films that were written and directed by the Jewish filmmaker Ewald Andre Dupont before Hitler's rise to power, namely *Die Geier-Wally* (1921) and *Peter Voss, der Millionendieb* (*Peter Voss, Who Stole Millions*; 1931–32). Instead of a close reading of Dupont's films, I underscore here the differences between his versions and their remakes under Nazism. The two films differ widely in their themes and styles, and were produced in very different historical and biographical circumstances.

Made in the early years of the Weimar Republic, Dupont's *Die Geier-Wally* (hereafter *Wally*) is generally regarded by scholars as a prototypical *Heimatfilm*, a pioneering (or proto-generic) contribution to the transition of sentimental *Heimat* culture to cinema.[6] The comic adventure film *Peter Voss, der Millionendieb* (hereafter *Peter Voss*) was released in the spring of 1932, during the final months of the Weimar Republic. By contrast to *Wally*, which evoked a premodern rural environment, *Peter Voss*'s protagonists are modern urbanites who enjoy and exploit modern technology and customs. And, by contrast to *Wally*, the plot of *Peter Voss* unfolds in foreign lands, far distant from the serene landscape of the German *Heimat*. Dupont directed *Wally* early in his career, before achieving international acclaim in the later 1920s.[7] *Peter Voss* was his homecoming film, after spending a few years in London where he directed popular and critically acclaimed films such as *Piccadilly* (1928–29) and *Moulin Rouge* (1928).[8] Yet there are also some notable similarities between the two films. Both *Wally* and *Peter Voss* are cinematic renditions of popular novels. Both were considered particularly suitable for the screen and, consequently, were remade several times during the twentieth century: in Weimar, during the Third Reich, and in postwar West Germany. Both films are manifestly different from Dupont's popular productions of the mid- and late 1920s, which portrayed the urban entertainment milieu. Both of them, however, demonstrate his exceptional talent for creating a blend of melodrama and irony, viewer-pleasing imagery and a sense of melancholia.[9]

As adherents of Nazism, the directors Hans Steinhoff and Karl Anton sought to change what they viewed as the faults of Dupont's films in their remakes of *Wally* and *Peter Voss*, respectively. The different context notwithstanding, the desire to re-produce these particular films is consistent with the Hollywood studios' logic of remakes. Studies of Hollywood productions show that studios opt to remake films when certain preconditions are met: the target audience is aware of the previous production (or, at least, of the original story behind the previous film); the original version should and can be modernized—in terms of technology or the worldview it advocates—to fit the expectations of current viewers; and the original story is considered relevant to contemporary audiences (i.e., it should have significance beyond the time of its original production).[10] Hans Steinhoff's 1940 remake of *Wally* clearly conforms to this scheme: It was produced as part of the Nazi adaptation of the timeless concept of *Heimat* to its blood-and-soil ideology. It used the new technology of sound and cinematography. And it capitalized on viewers' awareness of the popular previous version.[11] As demonstrated below, Karl Anton's remake of *Peter Voss* exploited viewers' familiarity with Dupont's film as well, and likewise endeavored to modernize it in tune with the conditions and conventional views of the final years of the Third Reich.[12]

The study of remakes often focuses on the context of their reception, pointing out where the divergences between the films highlight differences in the expectations, preferences, and desires of viewers in two different historical circumstances. Yet recent studies have challenged the dichotomy between the original and the remade versions and their audiences. The international acclaim gained by certain films—both originals and remakes—refutes the association of a version with the expectations and experiences of a specific, well-defined, audience.[13] Moreover, as Robert Eberwein has asserted, remakes inherently involve a "re-reading of the original," namely, a process that confers new meaning on the original by virtue of the cultural and political perspective at the moment of remaking.[14] My reading of the 1940s remakes of Dupont's films considers them in this vein, as an attempt to explain and correct—from a Nazi point of view—all that was wrong in the original (figure 14.1).

Figure 14.1. A visit by the regional nobility connects the village with the outside world in Hans Steinhoff's 1940 *Die Geierwally*.

Reclaiming *Heimat*: Hans Steinhoff's Response to Dupont's *Die Geier-Wally*

Written in the mid 1870s, Willhelmine von Hillern's novel *Die Geier-Wally* is a sentimental melodrama that narrates the passionate, forbidden affair between the free-spirited Wally and her beloved Josef, the brave hunter who challenges her father's dominance in the community. In line with the emerging *Heimat* culture of the time, the novel situates the melodrama in an unspecified, premodern era, in a small rural community.[15] In the novel, Wally's village is located in Ötztal, a southern region of Tyrol (which would become part of Austria after World War I). Amid snow-capped mountains, sheer cliffs, and avalanches, the extremes of the Alpine scenery reflect the roughness of the novel's characters and their varying moods. The story is partly narrated by a traveler who spies Wally on the mountain and recounts her adventures to a fellow tourist. According to his story, Wally is an odd woman, half-boy, whose indifference to conventional gender-related norms prevents her from fully integrating into the community, namely finding a mate and marrying.[16]

The traveler explains that the locals call her Geier-Wally (Vulture Wally) after the vulture she occasionally nestles in her arms. Wally obtained the scavenger by courageously climbing down a cliff to the nest, where she killed the mother vulture and adopted its fledgling. Wally is in love with Bear Josef, whose nickname derives from his daring hunt of a bear that had terrorized the village. Josef, however, challenges Wally's father's dominant position in the village and humiliates him in front of all the locals. Instead of Josef, therefore, the father tries to marry Wally off to a neighboring farmer, Vincenz. When Wally refuses, he sends her away to a remote hut on the mountain. One day, during a fierce snowstorm, Josef arrives at the hut, but—to Wally's chagrin—with another woman, named Afra, on his arm. An avalanche destroys the hut, and the mortified Wally returns to the village. After her father dies, she takes over his role in managing the estate. A chance encounter with Afra brings suppressed emotions to the surface, and Wally viciously curses her rival. The passionate assault on Afra appears to strike a chord with Josef, who finally invites Wally to be his partner at the local summer festival, the Feast of Saint Peter and Saint Paul. Yet during the festival Josef pushes her away in disgust and, in view of all the villagers, castigates her for the way she has behaved toward Afra. Humiliated, Wally urges Vincenz to avenge her honor, and he shoots Josef. Fortunately, Josef's wound is not lethal. Now repentant, Wally vows to care for Josef until he recovers. Once he is finally able to walk again, Josef laboriously climbs up the mountain, where he finds Wally sitting alone, filled with remorse (and self-pity). Josef approaches and clarifies a terrible misunderstanding: Afra is his sister, not his lover; his heart belongs to Wally. At the end, when all misunderstandings are cleared up, Josef invites Wally to come home with him. The novel ends with their wedding, and with an assurance that they lived happily thereafter, even though they had no children.

Von Hillern's melodramatic storytelling and the book's picturesque settings were eminently suited to cinema and its growing audience.[17] The first rendition of the story in film was produced by Dupont in 1921, in the wake of Germany's catastrophic defeat in World War I and the political turmoil of the war's aftermath. The 1940 remake premiered in Berlin in mid-September, at a time when Hitler had declared a blockade of the British Isles and British aircraft had attacked Berlin for the first time.[18] Both versions appear to owe their box-office success in part to the detachment of the serene Alpine landscapes of *Wally* from life outside the theater.[19] The critical discussion of the two films in the press was remarkably similar, particularly in its praise of the film's realism. The reviewers of Dupont's 1921 *Wally* recurrently highlighted its realist approach to the landscapes and to the people of the German provincial communities. The term "realism" here did not refer to a naturalist depiction of rural houses and villagers' routines—which, according to one reviewer, no longer exist—but rather to the spirit of *Heimat*, its essence.[20] Reviewers of Hans Steinhoff's 1940 remake similarly lauded its realist approach. Here, however, realism was associated with the on-location shooting of the film. As a result of the Anschluss, Ötztal had come into the realm of the German Reich and *Wally* could be filmed on location where the story was originally conceived.[21] Contrary to the reviewers of Dupont's film, the critics in 1940 highlighted the steadfastness of the community's way of life: Steinhoff's approach displayed the components of *Heimat* "as they have endured for ages."[22] Consequently, the lengthy on-location shooting had transformed the actors into organic dwellers in the provincial landscape, who move confidently in it rather than merely playing their roles. Finally, the reviewers noted that the authenticity of the place and of the characters had resulted in the Nazification of the *Heimatfilm* genre, alongside the Nazification of the landscape itself.[23]

As some enthusiastic reviewers asserted in 1940, Steinhoff's aspiration to use *Wally* as a vehicle for a Nazi vision of *Heimat* suited his talent and reputation.[24] While he had collaborated with Jewish filmmakers before 1933,[25] Steinhoff was one of the most prominent filmmakers of the Third Reich, and directed films that outlined the varying interests, views, and aesthetics of Nazi cinema, such as *Hitlerjunge Quex* (*Hitler Youth Quex*; 1933) and *Der alte und der junge König* (*The Old and the Young King*; 1935).[26] Shortly after making *Wally*, Steinhoff directed the maliciously antisemitic and anti-British *Ohm Krüger* (1941), the second-most-expensive propaganda film produced under Goebbels.[27] Unlike the freedom he enjoyed while working on the above-mentioned films, however, Steinhoff felt obliged to differentiate his *Wally* from the earlier cinematic rendition of the same plot.[28] In a promotional interview he gave, he declared that he had forbidden his actors to watch the previous version of the film, lest Dupont's vision influence the remake.[29]

At first glance, the many similarities between the two films appear to belie Steinhoff's ambition to create a new *Wally* that would meet the expectations of the Nazi worldview. By largely omitting the same elements of von Hillern's novel that Dupont had cut out, Steinhoff followed the main thrust of Dupont's plot. Despite shooting in a different location, Steinhoff's imagery of the Alpine scenery closely resembles that conceived in 1921 by Dupont and his (Jewish) set designer Paul Leni. Furthermore, Steinhoff's imagery makes no explicit references to the new political reality in Germany and displays none of the insignias of the Nazi movement. The main difference between the films seems to rest on technological advances—particularly the differences between silent and sound film—rather than on their ideological content. Yet a closer look at these seemingly minor differences between the films reveals Dupont's extraordinary understanding (and manipulation) of von Hillern's story—and its implications for the prospects of German-Jewish identity—as well as Steinhoff's endeavor to meet the challenges Dupont raised.

While he kept the general structure of the plot in place, Steinhoff added certain elements that significantly alter the story and its meaning. One such fundamental addition is a scene in which Josef attends a meeting in a nearby town, at which he is asked to assume parental responsibility for Afra, his illegitimate daughter (rather than his sister, as in the novel and in Dupont's film). This seemingly inconsequential scene shifts the focal point of the story. Unlike in Dupont's film, Steinhoff's viewers are party to Josef's knowledge about Afra's identity and cannot sympathize with Wally's rage. In the 1921 version the viewers see only what Wally knows, and thus identify with her point of view. The 1940 film narrates the story through Josef's perspective. Symbolically, Steinhoff even portrays Wally's tussle with the vulture—the source of both her nickname and the film title—from Josef's point of view (and in this version it is he, and not Wally, who kills the scavenger). Consequently, more so than in the novel and by contrast to Dupont's film, Wally's rage in Steinhoff's remake is clearly unwarranted and verges on the childish. It is moreover inconsequential: here Vincenz does not wound Josef and Wally does not burn down her father's house; like a rebellious adolescent, she is stubborn and passionate yet presents no danger to the existing social order. By the end of the film Josef has domesticated her and channeled her unfettered spirit into the role of a conventional housewife.

Dupont's Wally, by contrast, is no immature juvenile in need of guidance, but a powerful woman who is hurt and lashes out. In line with her description in the novel as half boy, Dupont depicts her as someone who transcends fixed biological and social categories (gender).[30] She is not domesticated, but rather actively fights for her place within the village's society. Dupont's visualization of Wally closely resembles the depiction of the female monster Alraune in the films of Weimar Jewish directors Henrik Galeen (1927) and Richard Oswald (1931): a stand-in for the acculturation-seeking Jew, the protagonist of these films was marked as a stranger by the intolerant society to which she belonged.[31] Unlike the urban, bourgeois Alraune, however, Wally seeks acceptance within a rural community, in a setting that played a significant role in the German national identity discourse.[32]

The provincial German landscape lies at the core of both films, and both portray it through constant use of *Heimat*-culture clichés: the wide-angle image of a small village amid snow-capped mountains, the church spire towering above the farmers' dwellings, traditional local festivities, locals dressed in traditional Tracht clothing, and so on. An early attempt at translating *Heimat*-culture to film, Dupont's *Wally* borrowed its imagery from pre-1918 illustrated books, paintings, photographs, and poems.[33] Steinhoff complemented the earlier images by borrowing from the cinematic iconography that developed during the two decades that followed Dupont's production (partly influenced by the 1921 *Wally*).[34] In using conventional *Heimat* iconography, Steinhoff linked the cinematic landscape with the sentiments and ideas that were conventionally associated with *Heimat* in the early twentieth century (such as the sense of being at home, the organic connection between the land and its dwellers, and continuity in times of crisis).[35] In line with typical *Heimat* novels and paintings and with earlier films, Steinhoff underscores the village's connection to other landscapes of the land and to the political structure of the time.[36] His version displays the roads that lead into and out of the village and features scenes of visits—such as that of the regional count—from the outside. It also includes the above-mentioned sequence that follows Josef on his journey to a nearby town, where the local council places Afra in his custody. The long sequence of their hike on the narrow mountain trails back to the village further emphasizes the topography of the film, which connects the village to other regions within a hierarchical political system. Steinhoff complements this traditional *Heimat* depiction with images of electricity wires stretched across the skyline that blend into the mountain scenery. On top of their function as a further emphasis on the connection of the village and its landscape to the greater national geography and social structure, the wires advertise the nondestructive modernization of *Heimat* under Nazism.[37] By using this recurring theme in the visualization of *Heimat* in the 1930s, Steinhoff shows how the essence of *Heimat* has remained unchanged despite the intrusion of modern technology.[38] Finally, in highlighting the on-location shooting in post–Anschluss Austria, Steinhoff makes a direct reference to the current regime and celebrates the restoration of *Heimat* as its achievement.

Steinhoff's construction of the film's landscape underscores Dupont's strange topography. While, like Steinhoff, Dupont based his imagery on *Heimat*-culture clichés, the village of his *Wally* is utterly detached from other landscapes. No road leads into or out of the village, no river connects it with other regions. In fact, the film acknowledges no landscape beyond the immediate vicinity of the village. No one visits from outside the rural community, and no one leaves. There is no sign of the march of time and no indication of the political structure or social organization that exists beyond the village. This complete isolation detaches the settings of the film from the matrix of reality. Dupont thus uses conventional iconography to locate his film within the German *Heimat*, only to reveal that the *Heimat* is detached from reality.

A similar strategy is evident in Dupont's approach to the functions of home in Wally's world. The concept of home is central to von Hillern's novel: Wally is expelled from her home because of her love for Josef, and her reacceptance into the village community is completed when she returns home and assumes her father's place; the novel's happy ending depicts Wally and Josef as they go home together.[39] Steinhoff's film goes farther than the novel in its depiction of home as a metaphor for rootedness and a sense of security. Not only does the director end the story with the restoration of home, but he also erases the dread that von Hillern's Wally feels at home under her father's strict domination. His images of home appear to have been derived from popular early twentieth-century paintings and from the early cinematic adaptation by Peter Ostmayr of Ludwig Ganghofer's *Heimat*-novels.[40] The rooms are bright with sunlight, the (often-open) windows display Alpine scenery, and—with rare and brief exceptions—the villagers cheerfully conduct their domestic interactions and go about their chores.

By contrast to this serene image, Dupont's depiction of Wally's home is reminiscent of the domestic imagery of the contemporary expressionist film genre—in particular the films of Paul Leni, Dupont's set designer—rather than of conventional *Heimat* imagery. The early depiction of Wally and her father in their living room is telling: shot from a diagonal low angle, the room is dark and the closed windows are concealed; the lines of shadow cast on the floor tiles and the walls are diagonal and curved. The recurring use of this style in the film's indoor scenes associates home with the emotional distress and threat of violence that characterize contemporaneous expressionist films (including Leni's renowned 1923 *Das Wachsfigurenkabinett*).

Moreover, the key theme of Dupont's film—unlike Steinhoff's and far more explicit than in von Hillern's book—is the recurrent loss of home. Wally is first expelled from her home in the village, then from her cabin on the mountain when it is destroyed by an avalanche. When she first returns to her childhood home, she burns it down while seeking to escape her father's rage. Even when her home is not wrecked by natural forces or human recklessness, Dupont's indoor scenes situate Wally amid signifiers of alienation, such as broken mirrors. Finally, contrary to the plot of the novel, Dupont ends the film away from home, on the mountain. The happy ending notwithstanding, the association of the film's settings—the cliché *Heimat* imagery—with homelessness and *Unheimlichkeit*, prevails.

A third palpable difference between Steinhoff's and Dupont's renditions of the story is their treatment of violence. Von Hillern's novel depicts violence as part of everyday life in the rural community: the tensions between different social groups and different generations occasionally erupt into brutal conflict; and, similarly, the need to survive in the rough terrain necessitates aggression against wild animals. Steinhoff follows this logic and depicts several acts of violence on the screen. Yet conflicts between members of the community—between Josef and Wally's father, and between Josef and Vincenz—are short-lived. Asserting his unrivaled superiority, Josef gets rid of his adversaries quickly, almost effortlessly. Steinhoff staged the conflicts outdoors on sunny days, using a medium-length shot that reveals the mountains in the background. Integrated with the bright scenery, the violence in Steinhoff's film is devoid of gore or misery. As in the novel, Steinhoff's plot portrays the union between Wally and Josef after Wally's father dies as bringing about the reconciliation of all the conflicts in the community, and restoring the natural harmony of life in the rural province.

In Dupont's film, however, a ubiquitous violence dominates the village's life. The film contains several instances of violence that erupts between members of the community: first Wally's father and Josef fight each other in front of the church; then the humiliated father beats Wally to the ground with a wooden stick on the way back from church. When they return home, he beats her again, leaving her lying helpless on the living room floor. Vincenz assaults one of the farmers, and Wally immediately retaliates by striking him on the back with an axe (and shortly thereafter she burns her house down). After her verbal confrontation with Afra, Josef assaults and humiliates Wally in the presence of all the villagers; Vincenz responds to Wally's call for revenge and shoots Josef in the back. Dupont portrays these acts by using close-ups that underscore the physical and emotional pain of the victims. This emphasis on the gory aspect of violence is evident from the beginning of the film, when Wally kills the vulture and steals its flegling. Dupont displays the killing from close and medium range, showing in detail how Wally repeatedly stabs the scavenger with her long knife until the mother bird perishes. In the novel the vulture attacks Wally as she hangs from a rope with the young bird in her arms, on her way back up the cliff; she kills the vulture only because it endangers both her and the fledgling. In Dupont's film she is standing firmly on a rock and is in no such danger. The comparison with the equivalent scene in Steinhoff's film, where Josef, rather than Wally, kills the vulture by shooting her with his rifle at long range, is particularly interesting. In Dupont's film Wally is a product of her environment; much like the other—mostly male—villagers, she is constantly alternating between perpetrating violence and falling victim to it. Dupont's film impresses on the audience that in a community beset by constant violent interactions, there is no room for solidarity and trust. In a lengthy scene that does not feature in Steinhoff's film, Dupont portrays a bull rampaging through the village; in face of the threat all the members of the community rush to save their own lives, abandoning a vulnerable child.

Thus, beyond its reading of Wally as an outsider in her own land, Dupont's film is important by virtue of its attack on *Heimat*. In appropriating *Heimat* iconography, the 1921 *Wally* sought to address the meaning of the concept and its implications. In Dupont's vision, *Heimat*, as imagined in German national culture, is detached from real life and has no place in the experienced world. Moreover, it is a dangerous fantasy: it allows one no sense of being at home, it is built on constant violence, it leaves no room for a sense of solidarity, and it provides no basis for a functional community. It is no coincidence that the *Heimat* that Dupont displays is a primarily Christian space, in which Christian symbols abound and communal gatherings are regulated by the church calendar. Allowing no place for Jews, Dupont's homogenous *Heimat* is a dreadful illusion rather than a foundation for German nationality. By introducing subtle yet significant amendments, Steinhoff sought to construct his remake as a response to Dupont's challenge. His *Heimat* is once again homogenous and harmonious, provincial and national, traditional and modern. It is the building block of the Nazi notion of German identity.

From Jewish Experience to German Escapade: Karl Anton's *Peter Voss*

The first cinematic rendition of Ewald Gerhard Seeliger's 1913 novel *Peter Voss der Millionendieb* (*Peter Voss Who Stole Millions*) was released in March 1921, a few months before the premiere of Dupont's *Wally*. It marked a career breakthrough for the film's director and cowriter Georg Jacoby, who—after completing several wartime patriotic productions—used Seeliger's thrilling plot to display his talent for creating viewer-pleasing imagery and pace.[41] Jacoby turned Seeliger's story into six consecutive films (under the overall title *Der Mann ohne Name* [*The Man Without a Name*]), that narrate a hunt spanning the globe for a bank teller who had allegedly stolen millions from the bank's safe and disappeared. Yet in fact Voss, the protagonist, has merely staged the robbery in a bid to save the bank. When the wealthy industrialist Frederik Nissen comes to withdraw the capital he deposited in the bank—to cover losses he incurred by making poor investments—Voss volunteers to rob the empty vault and provide his uncle, the bank manager, with a convincing pretext for his inability to pay out the money. The resourceful detective Bobby Todd (in later versions, Bobby Dodd) sets out to pursue him and artfully manages to follow Voss's tracks. However, Todd is constantly one step behind Voss, who crosses borders and oceans, hides among natives of various cultures, and eventually makes it safely back to his hometown. There, in the final episode of Jacoby's series, he marries Nissen's daughter. At the same time his uncle makes a fortune in a smart stock-market investment, repays the debt to Nissen, and clears Voss's name.

Like von Hillern's *Wally*, Seeliger's *Peter Voss* took the fancy of various German filmmakers over several decades. With minor amendments of detail, the remakes by E.A. Dupont (1931–32), Karl Anton (1943–46), and Wolfgang Becker (1958) retained the general structure of the story: the staged robbery, the battle of wits between Voss and Todd, the international scale of the chase after Voss, and the resolution, in which Voss and the patron's daughter fall in love and Voss clears his name.[42] Each rendition, however, reflected the circumstances of its production and emphasized different aspects of the story. Karl Anton's Nazi version of *Voss* was shot between September 1943 and March 1944, but the post-production was delayed and the music-editing of the film was not completed before the end of the war.[43] In his attempt to answer Dupont's understanding of Voss's motivation, Anton adapted his character to fit into the late Nazi era and sought to shed the film of its Jewish aspects.

Born in Prague in 1898, Karl Anton began his filmmaking career during World War I as an assistant to the Czech director Karel Lamač. During the 1920s he directed various documentaries and slapstick comedies in Prague, followed by local productions of German-language sound films and German versions of Hollywood productions. When the Nazi movement assumed prominence in Germany, Anton was living in Paris, directing light comedies. He relocated to Berlin in 1936, where he worked for Tobis on "lavish revue musicals [and] sophisticated crime capers," reminiscent of *Peter Voss*.[44] At first glance, Anton appears to be an indifferent or opportunistic filmmaker who exploited the resources accessible under Goebbels, as opposed to Hans Steinhoff, who openly sought to promote Nazi views and objectives. Yet Anton was no stranger to Nazi ideology and Goebbels's propaganda efforts. In 1936 he directed the bitter anti-Communist film *Weisse Sklaven. Panzerkreuzer "Sewastopol,"* which was designed to take up Goebbels's call for a new German cinematic aesthetic. In 1941 he was credited as codirector—working together with Steinhoff—of the notorious propaganda film *Ohm Krüger*. Consequently, his remake of *Peter Voss* was a blend of wartime escapism and an advertisement of Nazi views.

As was the case with *Wally*, it seemed appropriate to remake *Peter Voss* during the war. The escapist qualities of Peter Voss's story—the thrilling fast-paced chase, the multiple locations (evoking prewar imperialist fantasies), and the inevitable happy ending—evidently held a particular appeal in war-ridden Germany. Moreover, Voss's elegant maneuvering of his powerful opponents most likely struck a chord with audiences during the prolonged national struggle (particularly in the aftermath of the devastating defeat at Stalingrad).[45] Furthermore, as he traverses the globe Voss comes across representatives of several different cultures, nations, and races. These encounters highlight a racial-cultural hierarchy, displayed through a series of dichotomies: the proactive, rational, and physically robust Voss is set against the weak, passive, and superstitious indigenous people. In addition, the natives Voss meets function essentially as means to achieve his goals. In his constant endeavor to outsmart Dodd, wherever he goes Voss either ignores or exploits the natives' desires, needs, and distress. Anton's film takes full advantage of this setting and exploits it to demonstrate the weaknesses of non-German societies and political systems: India, Tahiti, Lisbon, and Brazil, are all part of a global playground for the suave German protagonist.[46]

In addition to the film's effective use of the contrast between the protagonist and the various indigenous peoples he encounters, Anton appropriates the story to reflect more directly on contemporary affairs. The most explicit reference to the current conflict appears in the American episode of the film, which depicts the Wild West, in this case Texas, as an emblem of Americanism: the foolish, belligerent, and greedy mindset against which the Germans were pitted in 1943. While his film is set in the pre–World War I era, Anton's depiction of the Americans clearly refers to the current conflict and downplays its threat. The comparatively lengthy episode that plays out in Texas, the longest of all those that take place away from the protagonist's hometown, features Voss's visit to his uncle, who is both the priest and the sheriff of a small American town. Voss considers his American relative to be a natural ally; he confesses to him the entire scheme—including his love for the patron's daughter—and asks for his help. Yet the American uncle has different priorities.

The uncle appears first in church, where he leads the service and absentmindedly alternates between religious hymns and a kitschy Yankee Doodle Dandy melody. When several sheriff's deputies come rushing in to announce the escape of a local criminal, Big Bill, the pastor-sheriff draws his pistols and fires into the air before proceeding with the service. Unsurprisingly, having concluded the service, Voss's uncle nonchalantly negotiates with Dodd the reward he will receive for betraying his relative. Blood relations are, for the American, merely a bargaining chip: he cannot be expected to hand over his flesh and blood, he declares, for less than $10,000. Shortly thereafter the viewers learn that the uncle is conducting a secret love affair with his black maid; his willingness to trade blood for money is thus associated with intimate interracial relations. Naturally, Voss outsmarts his uncle and exposes the foolishness of the American justice system, which mistakenly arrests Big Bill rather than Peter Voss.

In using the generic clichés of pre-1933 adventure films to offer his audiences escapism and reassurance in times of crisis, Anton's film, although more amusing and wittier than most, is nothing if not conventional. A more interesting aspect of the film is its ongoing endeavor to confront and defuse the challenge raised in Dupont's 1931–32 adaptation of *Peter Voss*. Born into an acculturated German-Jewish family in 1891, Dupont tried his hand at journalism—his parents' profession—before turning to filmmaking during World War I.[47] By the early 1930s he had directed and written several dozen films in Berlin, Hollywood, and London.[48] Renowned for his flair for appealing imagery and narration, Dupont won international fame with box-office hits such as *Varieté* (Berlin, 1925), *Moulin Rouge* (London, 1927–28), and *Piccadilly* (London, 1928), which focused on the melodrama and excitement of modern urban entertainment. Yet unlike many of his Jewish peers, Dupont also wrote and directed films that explicitly contemplated the difficulties and rewards of Jewish acculturation. In films as such *Das alte Gesetz* (*The Ancient Law*; 1923) and *Zwei Welten* (*Two Worlds*; 1930) he depicted Jewish protagonists who wrestle with the anti-Jewish biases of modern society and struggle for the integration of Jews within the bourgeois environment.[49] As his above-mentioned adaptation of *Wally* demonstrates, Dupont's interest in German and German-Jewish identity extended beyond films that explicitly addressed Jewish-related themes.

In the face of the ascent of Nazism and the renewed popular appeal of antisemitic convictions, Dupont's *Peter Voss* brings his coded discussion of Jewish integration to its climax. The *Peter Voss* he directed and cowrote was not merely the ultimate vehicle for escapist entertainment; it was also the embodiment of the stereotypical Jew, his ambitions, and his struggles in early 1930s Germany. In using Seeliger's novel to negotiate modern Jewish experience, Dupont highlights Voss's manipulation of the tension between appearance and identity on the one hand and, on the other hand, Dupont radically alters the plot's structure and gives the story a different ending.

The starting point of Dupont's film resembles that of Anton's, albeit with a few notable differences. Here Voss is a resourceful clerk working in Hamburg's banking district who is blamed for losing the money in a sloppy investment, even though he merely followed the instructions of his boss, the bank manager. After staging the robbery of the vault, he flees to Marseilles, and then on to Morocco (Dupont's Voss never makes it to Latin America, East Asia, or the United States). Bobby Dodd and the millionaire's daughter, Polly, set off in pursuit of him. From the initial act of the fake robbery to the end of the film, almost every scene involves deception, disguise, and role-playing on the part of all the three principal characters. To escape Dodd, Voss assumes the appearance and acts the part of various different characters, from a French police officer and a female dancer to a native Moroccan, and Dodd and Polly go to great lengths to disguise their identity from Voss. It soon becomes apparent that Voss is far better at adapting to new environments and emulating the appearance and habitus of others. In the streets of Marseilles he speaks fluent French; as a singer at a variety performance he turns into the star of the show; dressed up as a girl, he is not recognized as a man (despite his evidently ungraceful gestures); and he even feels at home among the natives in North Africa, where—although his otherness is conspicuous—he quickly adapts to the local practices. By virtue of his talent for blending in, Voss recurrently manages to elude Dodd. Moreover, disguised as a local within various foreign cultures, he repeatedly exposes Dodd as a dangerous stranger. At the end of the film, after he stages his own death, a telegram that arrives from Hamburg to Morocco clears Voss's name (and, thanks to a fortunate stock-market turn, the bank regains the lost funds and is able to repay the deposit). Now Voss can come clean, and he and Polly fall in love.

To put it simply, Dupont's Voss is a caricature of the acculturated Jew. He is a native of Hamburg's banking district, a place stereotypically associated with Jews, who falls victim to a false allegation that forces him into exile and condemns him to constant wandering across borders and oceans, just like "the wandering Jew of history."[50] Echoing the Jewish identity discourse of the time, Voss constructs his persona by changing his appearance and behavior to match his social environment.[51] And, echoing the lament of certain contemporary antisemitic commentators, his talent for adaptation through emulation facilitates his assimilation with many different national and cultural contexts.[52] Yet, by contrast to the antisemitic depictions of Jewish deception, by simulating his environment Dupont's Voss is able to survive and, eventually, discover his authentic self. Symbolically, had it not been for the array of deceptions and simulations he would not have found his true love Polly. An embodiment of the contemporaneous discourse about Jewish identity, Dupont's Voss conspicuously resembles Baruch, the Jewish protagonist of his 1923 *Das alte Gesetz*.[53] In this fairytale of assimilation, Baruch leaves the Jewish ghetto in Galicia to become an actor on the stage of the Viennese Burgtheater in the late nineteenth century. Like Voss, Baruch excels at assuming different roles and embodying different characters; like Baruch, Voss exploits his talent in order to assimilate within modern society. In fact, in *Peter Voss* Dupont combines the symbolism he developed in *Das alte Gesetz* with the symbolism that dominated the early adventure films of the Jewish director Joe May, who used the encounters between different ethnic groups to challenge the concept of fixed, inborn identities.[54]

Yet unlike Baruch and Maud, the protagonist of Joe May's *Herrin der Welt* (*Mistress of the World*; 1919–20), Voss does not make his way back home to the modern (German) city. Contrary to all other productions of *Peter Voss*, Dupont's film does not end with Voss's triumphant return to Germany. Instead, after his name is cleared, he chooses to remain in North Africa with Polly. Dupont's film therefore alters the structure of the story from a world tour that begins and ends at home, to a tale of migration (or exile)[55]: the (stereotypically Jewish) protagonist's one-way journey from central Europe to the Orient. Set against the political circumstances of the time, Dupont's *Voss* is a pessimistic fable about the prospects of German-Jewish acculturation.[56]

Anton's *Peter Voss* should be read, therefore, as an attempt to reclaim Voss's story and restage it as a German escapade, rather than as a reflection on Jewish experience in early 1930s Germany. In Anton's remake Voss is no longer a resourceful victim of circumstances, but rather a mastermind who pulls all the strings from the very beginning.[57] Even before he concocts the fake robbery scheme he is determined to find a way to convince Polly to marry him and, hence, make him a millionaire. Hiring the arrogant Bobby Dodd is part of Voss's initial plan, a clever ploy to avoid confrontation with the police. And, while the betrayal of his American uncle compels him to improvise, he nevertheless returns to his home town just as his name is cleared. In accordance with his calculations, the market eventually moves, and the bank now has sufficient funds to pay Polly, who hands her check back to Voss, her husband and the new codirector of the bank. Rather than exploring exclusion and exile, Anton narrates an imperial fantasy in which the Aryan protagonist overcomes both the natives and the European villains in various colonial settings and eventually returns home to enjoy the colonial loot.

Deception and disguise are likewise central to Anton's remake, albeit with several essential amendments. In this version it is Bobby Dodd—rather than Voss—who is the master of disguise. Dodd is the first character in the film to alter his appearance (he enters the banker's room already disguised as a bank teller); his plan to catch Voss, as he explains to Polly, involves multiple changes of appearance and name.

Unlike Voss, Dodd consistently assumes the stereotypical appearance and behavior of the residents of the nation in which he finds himself: a caricature of an English aristocrat, a Portuguese adventurer, an American cowboy, and an Indian yogi. Unlike Voss, whose false beard falls off in the middle of his act, Dodd is a true chameleon, who can even trick Polly into believing that he is Voss. In Dupont's film, when he tries to disguise himself Dodd sports a Hitler mustache; in Anton's film, he comes close to the stereotypical Jew, who speedily adapts to every social environment by merging with its appearance and habitus. Fortunately, his talent notwithstanding, Voss does not fall for Dodd's subterfuges and easily identifies him.

Unlike in Dupont's film, where Voss struggles alone to clear his name, in Anton's version Voss confides his plan to Polly early on and—after initial misgivings—she helps him outmaneuver Dodd. Shortly before the end of the film, on Paradise Island in the South Sea, Polly and Voss humiliate Dodd by staging a ritual orgy at a local temple, which Dodd is eager to join. Stripped of his clothes and money, he is caught, literally with his pants down, by the local authorities as Voss and Polly sail tranquilly back home.[58]

Conclusions

As the above discussion demonstrates, the Nazi filmmakers who sought to remake Dupont's films wrestled with his remarkable ability to narrate the popular themes of German national culture from the perspective of the (Jewish) outsider. Dupont's version of *Wally* cries out against the ideas that linked *Heimat* with a homogenous, exclusive notion of German identity that had gained popularity during and after World War I. It was Jewish inasmuch as it portrayed this *Heimat*—in which Jews have no place—as a dangerous fantasy, isolated from the fabric of reality, violent and devoid of solidarity. Dupont's *Voss* was Jewish in its association of Peter Voss's behavior with key elements in the Jewish identity discourse (as well as the antisemitic perception of the Jewish threat). Steinhoff and Anton—who, between their respective remakes of Dupont's films, met on the set of the notorious *Ohm Krüger* (together with Dupont's cameraman Friedl Behn-Grund)—retold the same stories while introducing seemingly minor yet fundamental revisions. Their remakes indeed included direct references to principles of Nazi ideology, and they enlisted in Goebbels's endeavor to provide escapist entertainment in times of crisis. No less remarkable, however, was their effort to reverse Dupont's interpretations of these stories—namely, to erase from them all reference to Jews' experiences and aspirations. Reading Dupont backwards, through the eyes of the Nazi filmmakers who watched his films during the Weimar years, underscores his success in integrating Jews' experiences, ambitions, and fears with mainstream German culture.

Ofer Ashkenazi is associate professor of history and director of the Koebner-Minerva Center for German History at the Hebrew University of Jerusalem. He is the author of three monographs on German and German-Jewish film: *A Walk into the Night: Reason and Subjectivity in Weimar Film* (2010); *Weimar Film and Modern Jewish Identity* (2012) and *Anti-Heimat Cinema: The Jewish Invention of the German Landscape, 1918–1968* (scheduled for summer 2020).

Notes

1. Siegbert Salomon Prawer, *Between Two Worlds: the Jewish Presence in German and Austrian Film, 1910–1933* (New York: Berghahn Books, 2005).
2. The distinctive presence of Jewish filmmakers and critics in both classic and popular genre films of the Weimar era is evident also in recent anthologies, including Christian Rogowski (ed.), *The Many Faces of Weimar Cinema* (Woodbridge: Camden House, 2010); and Noah William Isenberg (ed.), *Weimar Cinema: An Essential Guide to Classic Films of the Era* (New York: Columbia University Press, 2009).
3. Ofer Ashkenazi, *Weimar Film and Modern Jewish Identity* (New York: Palgrave-MacMillan, 2012).
4. Ofer Ashkenazi, "Rethinking the Role of Film in German History: The Jewish Comedies of the Weimar Republic." *Rethinking History* 14, no. 4 (2010): 569–85.
5. Valerie Weinstein, "Dissolving Boundaries: Assimilation and Allosemitism in E.A. Dupont's *Das alte Gesetz* (1923) and Veit Harlan's *Jud Süss* (1940)," *German Quarterly* 78, no. 4 (2005): 496–516.
6. Johannes von Moltke, *No Place Like Home: Locations of Heimat in German Cinema* (Berkeley: University of California Press, 2005), 28–30.
7. For a review of Dupont's life and work, see J. Bretschneider and E. Hampicke, "Biographie," in J. Bretschneider (ed.), *Ewald Andre Dupont. Autor und Regisseur* (Munich: Text+Kritik, 1992), 111–26.
8. P.M. St Pierre, *E.A. Dupont and His Contribution to British Film: Varieté, Moulin Rouge, Piccadilly, Atlantic, Two Worlds, Cape Forlorn* (Cranbury, NJ: Fairleigh Dickinson University Press, 2010), 11–26.
9. Dupont wrote about the director's need to comprehend and satisfy the viewers' desires: E.A. Dupont, *Wie ein Film geschrieben wird und wie man ihn verwertet* (Berlin: Reinhold Kühn, 1919).
10. Björn Bohnenkamp, Ann-Kristin Knapp, Thorsten Hennig-Thurau, and Ricarda Schauerte, "When Does It Make Sense to Do It Again? An Empirical Investigation

of Contingency Factors of Movie Remakes." *Journal of Cultural Economics* 39, no. 1 (2015): 15–41.
11. On the changes to the concept of *Heimat* that the Nazi regime advocated, see C. Applegate. *A Nation of Provincials: the German Idea of Heimat* (Berkeley: University of California Press, 1990), 149–96. The discussion of Steinhoff's film in contemporary film magazines repeatedly referred to its novelties in comparison with the earlier version. See, e.g., f.h., "Menschen aus dem Bergen. Charakter, Erlebniswelt und Schicksalmelodie im Film / Der Filmschöpfer auf neuen Wegen," *Film-Kurier*, 180, 3 August 1940.
12. Notably, while Anton's film clearly grapples with Dupont's adaptation, contemporaneous reviewers mentioned neither the two earlier versions of the film nor the novel on which it is based (e.g., "Aufnahmenschluss bei *Peter Voss Der Millionendieb*," *Film-Kurier* 18, 3 March 1944).
13. Constantine Verevis, "Re-Viewing Remakes," *Film Criticism* 21, no. 3 (1997): 1–19.
14. Robert Eberwein, "Remakes and Cultural Studies," in *Play it Again, Sam: Retakes on Remakes*, Andrew S. Horton and Stuart Y. McDougal (eds.), (Berkeley: University of California Press, 1998), 15–33, here 15.
15. Alon Confino, *The Nation as a Local Metaphor: Württemberg, Imperial Germany, and National Memory, 1871–1918* (Chapel Hill: University of North Carolina Press, 1997).
16. Wilhelmine von Hillern, *Die Geier-Wally: Eine Geschichte aus den Tiroler Alpen* (Berlin: BoD, 2016), 5.
17. Beate Bechtold-Comforty, Louis Bedeck and Tanja Marquardt, "Zwanziger Jahre und Nationalsozialismus. Vom Bergfilm zum Bauernmythos," in *Der deutsche Heimatfilm der fünfziger Jahre. Motiven, Symbole und Handlungsmuster* (Cologne: Teiresias Verlag, 1998), 33–67, especially 44–45.
18. The Munich premiere was held a month earlier, shortly after the beginning of the Battle of Britain.
19. As is evident from the advertisement for Dupont's film (Archive of the Stiftung deutsche Kinemathek [SdK], folder 2902) and in the early reviews of Steinhoff's film: "*Die Geierwally* mit grossem erfolg München und Innsbruck gestartet," *Film-Kurier* 191, 16 August 1940.
20. "Die Geier-Wally," *LichtbildBühne*, 38, 17 September 1921;"Die Geier-Wally," *Acht UhrAbendblatt*, [n.d.], SdK, 1920;"Die Geier-Wally," *FilmKurier*, 214, 14 September 1921.
21. "Geierwally. Die Handlung des Films," *Illustrierte Film-Kurier*, August 1940.
22. "Geierwally kommt als Tonfilm wieder," *Illustrierte Film-Kurier*, August 1940.
23. "Geierwally kommt als Tonfilm wieder."
24. Georg Herzberg, "Hans Steinhoff über *Geierwally* und allgemeine Filmfragen," *Film-Kurier*, 114, 18 May 1940.
25. Ashkenazi, "Rethinking the Role of Film."
26. For instance, Eric Rentschler, "Emotional Engineering: Hitler Youth Quex," *Modernism/Modernity* 2:3 (1995): 23–44; Linda Schulte-Sasse, *Entertaining the Third Reich: Illusions of Wholeness in Nazi Cinema* (Durham, NC: Duke University Press, 1996), 127–42.
27. Christian W. Hallstein, "Ohm Kruger: The Genesis of a Nazi Propaganda Film," *Literature/Film Quarterly* 30:2 (2002): 133–39.
28. The Nazi press did not mention the Jewish filmmakers of the 1921 *Wally*, but rather attributed it to the work of (the non-Jewish) leading actors, Hans Dieterle and Henny Porten. The success and the (allegedly albeit dated) artistic merits of the early film were nonetheless mentioned in the discussion of Steinhoff's production (e.g., "Geierwally kommt als Tonfilm wieder").

29. Herzberg, "Hans Steinhoff über *Geierwally*."
30. Intriguingly, contrary to the modern femme fatale that, according to Barbara Hales, fascinated post–World War I (male) filmmakers, Wally does not exploit her sexuality to achieve her goals (Barbara Hales, "Projecting Trauma: The Femme Fatale in Weimar and Hollywood Film Noir," *Women in German Yearbook* (2007): 224–43).
31. Ashkenazi, *Weimar Film*, 77–110.
32. Wally seems to resemble Junta, the female protagonist of the 1932 film *Das blaue Licht* (directed by Lenni Riefenstahl and written by Béla Balázs). As the following discussion argues, the 1940 production of *Wally* replaces this type of Alpine femme fatale with a domesticated protagonist, misunderstood rather than dangerous to the existing power structure.
33. Compare this imagery, for instance, with Fedor von Köppen, *Unser deutsches Land und Volk. Bilder aus den deutschen Alpen, dem Alpenlande und aus Oberbayern* (Leipzig: Otto Spamer, 1878); Moritz von Schwind, Carl Spitzweg, and Heinrich Wölfflin, *Bilder der Heimat: je 6 farbige Blätter nach Carl Spitzweg und Moritz von Schwind; 4 einfarbige Blätter nach Moritz von Schwind* (Tübingen: Furche-Verlag, 1917 [1916]).
34. For instance, Albert Hetzger, *Bilder der Heimat* (Zörbig: zörbiger Bote, 1937); Hans Ostwald, *Deutschland. Ein Buch der Heimat* (Berlin: Paul Franke Verlag, 1938). Steinhoff's imagery is also heavily influenced by the mountain-film (*Bergfilm*) genre of the 1920s and 1930s (Bechtold-Comforty, Bedeck, and Marquardt, "Zwanziger Jahre und Nationalsozialismus."
35. Peter Blickle, *Heimat: A Critical Theory of the German Idea of Homeland* (Rochester, 2002); Andrea Bastian, *Der Heimat-Begriff: eine begriffsgeschichtliche Untersuchung in verschiedenen Funktionsbereichen der deutschen Sprache* (Tübingen: Niemeyer, 1995).
36. Karlheinz Rossbacher, *Heimatkunstbewegung und Heimatroman: Zu einer Literatursoziologie der Jahrhundertwende* (Stuttgart: Ernst Klett, 1975), 139–40.
37. Ofer Ashkenazi, "Improbable Twins: The Bifurcating Heritage of Weimar Culture in Helmar Lerski and Walter Frentz's Kulturfilms," *German Studies Review* 40:3 (2017): 527–48.
38. Compare with Eric Rentschler, "Mountains and Modernity: Relocating the Bergfilm," *New German Critique* 51, 1990: 137–61.
39. von Hillern, *Die Geier-Wally*, 143.
40. von Moltke, *No Place Like Home*, 36–45.
41. Hans-Michael Bock and Tim Bergfelder, *The Concise CineGraph: Encyclopaedia of German Cinema* (Berghahn Books, 2009), 222–23.
42. Another Peter Voss film was directed by Georg Marischka in 1959 (*Peter Voss—Held des Tages*), but its plot begins after the original story ends. Rudolf Meinert's *William Voss, Der Millionendieb* (1915) narrates an unrelated story about the mind games played between a smart thief and a smarter detective.
43. The film was eventually released in East Germany in1946 as a DEFA production (Falk Schwarz, "Das Spiel mit der Illusion." https://www.filmportal.de/film/peter-voss-der-millionendieb_868e4f8fdd0449f4b807e2b74a106ba4.
44. Bock and Bergfelder, *Concise CineGraph*, 15.
45. Reports on the forthcoming film in the German press emphasized the gap between impression and reality: between the universal belief that the criminal Voss was doomed, and the actual state of affairs, in which Voss was a benevolent victim who had outmaneuvered his rivals. See, e.g., "Geschichte mit dem Clown. Oder: Vom eingebildeten Wert des Geldes," *Film-Kurier* 143, 18 November 1943.

46. Siegfried Kracauer famously depicted Weimar adventure films, which often shared the above motifs, as fantasies of the prisoners of the mutilated, blockaded Germany after World War I. According to Kracauer, this was the mindset that encouraged and facilitated Hitler's rise to power. Siegfried Kracauer, *From Caligari to Hitler: A Psychological History of the German Film* (Princeton, NJ: Princeton University Press, 2004 [1947]), 57.
47. I. Stratenwerth. "Ewald A. Dupont." in I. Stratenwerth, H. Simon (eds.), *Pioniere in Celluloid: Juden in der frühen Filmwelt* (Berlin: Henschel, 2004), 289–91.
48. T. Bergfelder. 2008. "Life Is a Variety Theater—E.A. Dupont's Career in German and British Cinema," in T. Bergfelder and C. Cargnelli (ed.), *Destination London: German-Speaking Emigrés and British Cinema, 1925–1950* (New York: Berghahn Books, 24–35).
49. Cynthia Walk, "Romeo with Sidelocks: Jewish-Gentile Romance in E.A. Dupont *Das alte Gesetz* and Other Early Weimar Assimilation Films," in Rogowski, *The Many Faces of Weimar Cinema*, 84–101.
50. The trope of the wandering Jew of history played an important role in the German-Jewish discourse about acculturation before 1933 (e.g., Meyer Kayserling, *Die Juden als Patrioten* (Berlin: Albert Katz, 1898), 4).
51. The German-Jewish identity discourse of the late nineteenth and early twentieth centuries recurrently addressed the relations between acculturation and emulation of the habitus of the non-Jewish (mostly bourgeois) society: Kerry Wallach, *Passing Illusions: Jewish Visibility in Weimar Germany* (University of Michigan Press, 2017); Simone Lässig, *Jüdische Wege ins Bürgertum: kulturelles Kapital und sozialer Aufstieg im 19. Jahrhundert* (Vandenhoeck & Ruprecht, 2004).
52. For instance, Oskar Panizza, "The Operated Jew," (trans. Jack Zipes), *New German Critique*, no. 21 (Autumn 1980): 63–79; Hans Blüher, *Secessio Judaica. Philosophische Grundlegung der historischen Situation des Judentumes und der antisemitischen Bewegungen* (Berlin: Der Weisse Ritter, 1921), 19–20, 55. Nazi-era films, such as *Jud Süss* (*Jew Süss*; 1940, dir. Veit Harlan) and *Der Ewige Jude* (*The Eternal Jew*; 1940, dir. Fritz Hippler), demonstrate the paralyzing fascination of Nazi ideology with the Jewish ability to be invisible—namely, to blend into hegemonic cultures.
53. Ofer Ashkenazi, "Jewish Displacement and Simulation in the German Films of E.A. Dupont," Simone Lässing and Miriam Ruerupp (eds.), *Space and Spacelessness in German-Jewish History* (New York: Berghahn, 2017), 88–106.
54. Ashkenazi, *Weimar Film*, 111–47.
55. This extraordinary decision was not overlooked by the reviewers of the film. See, e.g., Fritz Olimsky, "*Peter Voß*," *Berliner Börsen-Zeitung*, 26 March 1932.
56. The mixed reviews of the film seem to reflect this blend of cheerful comedy and pessimistic undertones ("*Peter Voß*," *Morgenpost*, Berlin, April 1932).
57. Voss outsmarts Dodd by excelling in the art of disguise and manipulation. The use of such stereotypically Jewish talents, however, is not exceptional for Nazi comedies. As Valerie Weinstein showed, it was an effective strategy in the antisemitic comedy *Robert und Bertram* (1939, dir. Hans H. Zerlett). See Valerie Weinstein, *Antisemitism in Film Comedy in Nazi Germany* (Bloomington: Indiana Uniersity Press, 2019), 184–212.
58. Notably, despite its antisemitic connotations, the isolation and humiliation of the Jewish Dodd does not lead to his annihilation in Anton's film. The ridiculed Dodd eventually returns to the bank and is compensated for the work he was hired to do (although not for the disgrace and suffering he endured).

Bibliography

Applegate, Celia. *A Nation of Provincials: the German idea of Heimat*. Berkeley: University of California Press, 1990.

Ashkenazi, Ofer. "Improbable Twins: The Bifurcating Heritage of Weimar Culture in Helmar Lerski and Walter Frentz's Kulturfilms." *German Studies Review* 40 (3, 2017): 527–48.

———. "Jewish Displacement and Simulation in the German Films of E.A. Dupont." In *Space and Spacelessness in German-Jewish History*, ed. Simone Lässing and Miriam Ruerupp, 88–106. New York: Berghahn Books, 2017.

———. "Rethinking the Role of Film in German History: The Jewish Comedies of the Weimar Republic." *Rethinking History* 14 (4, 2010): 569–85.

———. *Weimar Film and Modern Jewish Identity*. New York: Palgrave-MacMillan, 2012.

"Aufnahmenschluss bei *Peter Voss Der Millionendieb*." *Film-Kurier*, 3 March 1944.

Bastian, Andrea. *Der Heimat-Begriff: eine begriffsgeschichtliche Untersuchung in verschiedenen Funktionsbereichen der deutschen Sprache*. Tübingen: Niemeyer, 1995.

Bechtold-Comforty, Beate, Louis Bedeck, and Tanja Marquardt. "Zwanziger Jahre und Nationalsozialismus. Vom Bergfilm zum Bauernmythos." In *Der deutsche Heimatfilm der fünfziger Jahre. Motiven, Symbole und Handlungsmuster*, ed. Bechtold-Comforty, Bedeck, and Marquardt, 33–67. Cologne: Teiresias, 1998.

Bergfelder, Tim. "Life Is a Variety Theater—E.A. Dupont's Career in German and British Cinema." In *Destination London: German-Speaking Emigrés and British Cinema, 1925–1950*, ed. Bergfelder and Cargnelli, 24–35. New York: Berghahn Books.

Blickle, Peter. *Heimat: A Critical Theory of the German Idea of Homeland*. Rochester, NY: Camden House, 2002.

Blüher, Hans. *Secessio Judaica. Philosophische Grundlegung der historischen Situation des Judentumes und der antisemitischen Bewegungen*. Berlin: Der Weisse Ritter, 1921.

Bohnenkamp, Björn, Ann-Kristin Knapp, Thorsten Hennig-Thurau, and Ricarda Schauerte. "When does it make sense to do it again? An empirical investigation of contingency factors of movie remakes." *Journal of Cultural Economics* 39 (1, 2015): 15–41.

Bretschneider J. and Hampicke E. "Biographie." In *Ewald Andre Dupont. Autor und Regisseur*, ed. J. Bretschneider, 111–26. Munich: Edition Text & Kritik, 1992.

Confino, Alon. *The Nation as a Local Metaphor: Württemberg, Imperial Germany, and National Memory, 1871–1918*. Chapel Hill: University of North Carolina Press, 1997.

"*Die Geierwally* mit grossem erfolg München und Innsbruck gestartet." *Film-Kurier*, 16 August 1940.

"Die Geier-Wally." *Acht UhrAbendblatt*, [n.d.], SdK, 1920.

"Die Geier-Wally." *FilmKurier*, 14 September 1921.

"Die Geier-Wally." *LichtbildBühne*, 17 September 1921.

Dupont, Ewald A. *Wie ein Film geschrieben wird und wie man ihn verwertet*. Berlin: Reinhold Kühn, 1919.

Eberwein, Robert. "Remakes and Cultural Studies." In *Play it Again, Sam: Retakes on Remakes*, ed. Andrew S. Horton and Stuart Y. McDougal, 15–33. Berkeley: University of California Press, 1998.

f.h. "Menschen aus dem Bergen. Charakter, Erlebniswelt und Schicksalmelodie im Film / Der Filmschöpfer auf neuen Wegen." *Film-Kurier*, 3 August 1940.

"Geierwally kommt als Tonfilm wieder." *Illustrierte Film-Kurier*, August 1940.

"Geierwally. Die Handlung des Films." *Illustrierte Film-Kurier*, August 1940.

"Geschichte mit dem Clown. Oder: Vom eingebildeten Wert des Geldes." *Film-Kurier*, 18 November 1943.

Hales, Barbara. "Projecting Trauma: The Femme Fatale in Weimar and Hollywood Film Noir." *Women in German Yearbook* 23 (2007): 224–43.

Hallstein, Christian W. "Ohm Kruger: The Genesis of a Nazi Propaganda Film." *Literature/Film Quarterly* 30 (2, 2002): 133–39.

Hans-Michael Bock, and Tim Bergfelder. *The Concise CineGraph: Encyclopaedia of German Cinema*, 222–23. Berghahn Books, 2009.

Herzberg, Georg. "Hans Steinhoff über *Geierwally* und allgemeine Filmfragen." *Film-Kurier*, 18 May 1940.

Hetzger, Albert. *Bilder der Heimat*. Zörbig: zörbiger Bote, 1937.

Isenberg, Noah William, ed. *Weimar Cinema: An Essential Guide to Classic Films of the Era*. New York: Columbia University Press, 2009.

Kayserling, Meyer. *Die Juden als Patrioten*. Berlin: Albert Katz, 1898.

Kracauer, Siegfried. *From Caligari to Hitler: A Psychological History of the German Film*. Princeton, NJ: Princeton University Press, 2004 [1947].

Lässig, Simone. *Jüdische Wege ins Bürgertum: kulturelles Kapital und sozialer Aufstieg im 19. Jahrhundert*. Göttingen: Vandenhoeck & Ruprecht, 2004.

Olimsky, Fritz. "*Peter Voß*." *Berliner Börsen-Zeitung*, 26 March 1932.

Ostwald, Hans. *Deutschland. Ein Buch der Heimat*. Berlin: Paul Franke, 1938.

Panizza, Oskar. "The Operated Jew," trans. Jack Zipes. *New German Critique* 21 (Autumn 1980): 63–79.

"*Peter Voß*." *Morgenpost*, Berlin, April 1932.

Prawer, Siegbert Salomon. *Between Two Worlds: the Jewish Presence in German and Austrian Film, 1910–1933*. New York: Berghahn Books, 2005.

Rentschler, Eric. "Emotional Engineering: Hitler Youth Quex." *Modernism/Modernity* 2 (3, 1995): 23–44.

———. "Mountains and Modernity: Relocating the Bergfilm." *New German Critique* 51 (1990): 137–61.

Rogowski, Christian, ed. *The Many Faces of Weimar Cinema*. Woodbridge: Camden House, 2010.

Rossbacher, Karlheinz. *Heimatkunstbewegung und Heimatroman: Zu einer Literatursoziologie der Jahrhundertwende*. Stuttgart: Ernst Klett, 1975.

Schulte-Sasse, Linda. *Entertaining the Third Reich: Illusions of Wholeness in Nazi Cinema*. Durham, NC: Duke University Press, 1996.

Schwarz, Fal. "Das Spiel mit der Illusion." https://www.filmportal.de/film/peter-voss-der-millionendieb_868e4f8fdd0449f4b807e2b74a106ba4

St Pierre, P.M. *E.A. Dupont and His Contribution to British Film: Varieté, Moulin Rouge, Piccadilly, Atlantic, Two Worlds, Cape Forlorn*. Cranbury, NJ: Fairleigh Dickinson University Press, 2010.

Stratenwerth Irene. "Ewald A. Dupont." In *Pioniere in Celluloid: Juden in der frühen Filmwelt*, ed. Irene Stratenwerth and Hermann Simon, 289–91. Berlin: Henschel, 2004.

Verevis, Constantine. "Re-viewing remakes." *Film Criticism* 21 (3, 1997): 1–19.

von Hillern, Wilhelmine. *Die Geier-Wally: Eine Geschichte aus den Tiroler Alpen*. Berlin: BoD, 2016.

von Köppen, Fedor. *Unser deutsches Land und Volk. Bilder aus den deutschen Alpen, dem Alpenlande und aus Oberbayern*. Leipzig: Otto Spamer, 1878.

von Moltke, Johannes. *No Place Like Home: Locations of Heimat in German Cinema*. Berkeley: University of California Press, 2005.

von Schwind, Moritz, Spitzweg, Carl and Wölfflin, Heinrich. *Bilder der Heimat: je 6 farbige Blätter nach Carl Spitzweg und Moritz von Schwind; 4 einfarbige Blätter nach Moritz von Schwind*. Tübingen: Furche, 1917 [1916].

Walk, Cynthia. "Romeo with Sidelocks: Jewish-Gentile Romance in E.A. Dupont *Das alte Gesetz* and Other Early Weimar Assimilation Films." In Rogowski, *The Many Faces of Weimar Cinema*, 84–101.

Wallach, Kerry. *Passing Illusions: Jewish Visibility in Weimar Germany*. University of Michigan Press, 2017.

Weinstein, Valerie. *Antisemitism in Film Comedy in Nazi Germany*. Bloomington: Indiana University Press, 2019.

———. "Dissolving Boundaries: Assimilation and Allosemitism in E.A. Dupont's *Das alte Gesetz* (1923) and Veit Harlan's *Jud Süss* (1940)." *German Quarterly* 78 (4, 2005): 496–516.

CODA

Chapter 15

"*FILMRETTUNG*: SAVE THE PAST FOR THE FUTURE!"

Film Restoration and Jewishness
in German and Austrian Silent Cinema

Cynthia Walk

Two recent digital film restoration projects for *Das alte Gesetz* (*The Ancient Law*; 1923, dir. E.A. Dupont) at the Deutsche Kinemathek in Berlin and *Die Stadt ohne Juden* (*The City without Jews*; 1924, dir. Hans Karl Breslauer) at the Filmarchiv Austria in Vienna, bring new insights to our understanding of Jewishness in German and Austrian silent cinema.[1] But they also underscore the limits imposed by the absence of much documentation about the vintage nitrate sources.

The original release version shown at the premiere of a silent film usually represents the gold standard for its content. In the Weimar era that version was often corroborated by a written record with the list of intertitles in the government *Zensurkarte* (censor's certificate) approving its release. If there is no surviving camera negative or original release version, German silent film restoration must rely on the *Zensurkarte*, if available, together with any extant export prints with intertitles in different languages, which were often freely edited for distribution in other national markets. My chapter will attempt to show how the technical workflow of digital film restoration reveals diverging views of Jewishness in the surviving elements of *Das alte Gesetz* and *Die Stadt ohne Juden*.

Das alte Gesetz

Das alte Gesetz was the first major German film to thematize the quandaries of Jewish assimilation. It was widely distributed in adapted versions to accommodate national markets across Europe and America. While the camera negative and the original German release version are lost, the *Zensurkarte* and a series of vintage export prints from Sweden, America, Russia, Belgium, and Italy survive. For the restoration, first a written protocol of each source, viewed frame by frame on the editing table, was prepared in an Excel spreadsheet that also included a 1984 analog restoration of the film for comparison. Then all the elements were scanned and these digital image files served as the basis for a composite edit.[2] Following are two screenshots to illustrate the process.[3]

The first screenshot (figure 15.1) shows the timeline in a computer editing program called Avid Media Composer four minutes into the film. Act 1, scene 1: the shtetl sequence at the beginning introduces the rabbi (in the image on the upper left), as he dresses for the synagogue service on the morning of the Purim holiday. Four vintage sources are displayed at the bottom here in rows with overlaid patterns (and colors in the ebook): diagonal lines (yellow) for the Swedish version,[4] dark solid (red) for the Russian version, horizontal lines (blue) for the Belgian/French version; and vertical lines (green) for the Italian version. Dots (purple) designate the previous 1984 analog restoration. While

Figure 15.1. Avid Media Composer: five elements. Screenshot.

none of the surviving prints has complete images (large fields) or intertitles (small fields), the Russian version is notably the most selective with frequent omissions in the timeline.

A major task of this complex restoration was to compare, evaluate and combine the vintage elements of the film into a single composite edit, illustrated in the next screenshot (figure 15.2) at the end of Act 1. Here Baruch clutches the crown of King Ahasuerus, the costume of his role in the Purim play, while he dreams of becoming an actor. Using digital means beyond the limitations of analog technology, the primary objective of this project was to reconstruct the narrative continuity of the original release version as well as the *Unversehrtheit* (integrity) of each shot in every scene: a digital reconstruction on the macro and micro level that would restore *Das alte Gesetz* to its total length at the German premiere (3,028 meters).[5] Reviewing several hundred thousand frames in many versions of the film was a time-consuming process involving painful choices. And the fragility of 95-year-old film stock occasionally required tolerance of lesser image quality. The composite edit at the end of Act 1 shows material from all four sources and, because the available nitrate footage had disintegrated in some places, a rescan of those frames from the 1984 restoration, patterned here as light solid (and colored pink in the e-book).

Figure 15.2. Avid Media Composer: composite edit. Screenshot.

Once the digital reconstruction of the film by the team at the Deutsche Kinemathek was complete in a final edit, the next challenge was retouching and grading to blend the patchwork into a coherent whole. This task was delegated to experts in digital image restoration at the ARRI Media laboratory in Berlin.

Among many differences that surfaced in comparing the four export prints were cuts and other editing changes that indicate diverging national views of Jewishness. We have already observed, for example, that the Russian version is full of omissions in the shtetl sequence at the beginning of the film. The synagogue scene in particular is radically shortened and the entire religious service for the Purim holiday has been eliminated. Neither image displayed in the first screenshot is present, not the rabbi dressing for the service nor the insert shot of the Megillah scroll with the Book of Esther in Hebrew letters. Eliminating these positive allusions to religion is the kind of editing one might expect from government censors in Soviet Russia of the 1920s, whose job included conforming foreign films imported for domestic distribution to the secularism of Soviet ideology.

The fact that *Das alte Gesetz* was even brought to Soviet Russia points to active interest and support for Jewish culture in the Soviet Union after the Revolution and during the interwar period.[6] Tweaking this Jewish-themed film in a Soviet direction, the censors not only removed references to Judaism, but also remade the narrative through creative editing into an instructive fable, a story of personal transformation that promotes assimilation as the natural direction for the modern subject. Other export versions of *Das alte Gesetz* all conclude with a solemn family tableau, framing the deathbed reconciliation of father and son, which affirms the transition from tradition to modernity. However, in the Russian print an earlier scene is transposed and placed at the end of the film that now culminates in the embrace of the young couple in their sunny and comfortably furnished Vienna apartment (figure 15.3).[7]

This remarkable editing change in the Russian export print of *Das alte Gesetz* has powerful implications. Beyond the father-son melodrama in the Jewish milieu, it foregrounds and highlights the successful acculturation of Baruch and Esther in upper-middle-class Gentile society as the larger arc of the narrative. This is consistent with cuts in the visuals throughout the film that shorten the synagogue scenes and reduce or eliminate shots that include the menorah and the Star of David in the shtetl sequences. In this way the sites, rituals and emblems of Judaism become incrementally less visible. And, although Baruch

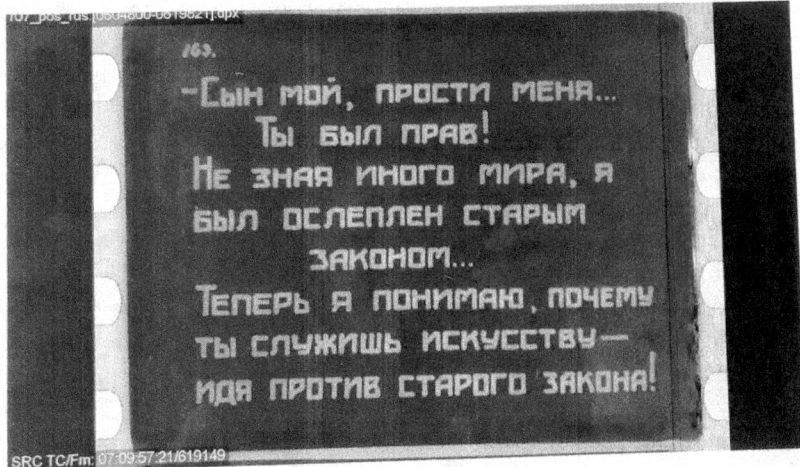

Figure 15.3. *Das alte Gesetz*, Russian export print. Title card on YouTube. Screenshot.

marries his childhood sweetheart from Galicia and Jewish endogamy is preserved, his secular career at the court theater requires that he cut off his sidelocks and (at least in his outward appearance) pass as non-Jewish. Eventually, even in the privacy of his home any trace of his religious heritage becomes invisible. Instead on display are the fashionable clothing and furnishings of the couple's private apartment in Vienna and their household servants, a completely acculturated non-Jewish bourgeois habitus. This trajectory is valorized by relocating the domestic scene to the conclusion of the film, where it seals the assimilation narrative with a classic happy ending.

Given the history of Soviet cinema in the 1920s with its investment in montage, it is not surprising that the Russian export print of *Das alte Gesetz* displays the most radical and consequential departures in editing changes that have the cumulative effect of displacing religion in a view of Jewishness without Judaism.

Die Stadt ohne Juden

In Austria the film adaptation of Hugo Bettauer's powerful satirical novel addresses public hostility toward immigrant and assimilated Jews in post–World War I Vienna in a film that directly targets exclusionary antisemitism. This restoration project had fewer vintage sources and even less evidence to work with: no camera negative, no original release print, and also no *Zensurkarte*. Indeed, for several decades the only known copy of *Die Stadt ohne Juden* was a fragmentary export print that had been held at the Nederlands Filmmuseum since 1933, known as the Amsterdam element. Recovered there in 1991, it became the basis of an analog restoration by the Filmarchiv Austria with 1,635 of a reported 2,400 meters in the original release version.[8] By a stroke of improbable good luck, previously missing footage was discovered more recently in a nitrate print found at a Paris flea market in 2015. This version includes a disturbing scene of antisemitic abuse on the streets of Utopia, a thinly disguised fictional reincarnation of 1924 Vienna (figure 15.4).[9]

While the representation of antisemitism in the first known source from Amsterdam is legal and bureaucratic, verbal and implicitly violent, in the Paris element there are graphic images of bullying, harassment, and physical abuse, most acutely in this unprovoked mob attack with shoving, hitting, and hair pulling. That such gratuitous violence for sport, accompanied by malicious laughter, was shocking and unacceptable to some contemporary audiences is suggested by its absence in the Amsterdam element. By contrast, the French were likely more wary of antisemitism—as a legacy of their own history during the Dreyfus Affair—and from that experience more inclined to recognize the danger and sound the alarm. This scene unequivocally displays the Jew as the innocent victim of group aggression in a mobbing. Without it the Amsterdam element (1926–27) appears to be a sanitized version of what surfaced sometime later in the Paris element (after 1928).[10] In their posture toward this scene, by including or omitting it, the two sources reveal subtly different views of Jewish vulnerabilty and the urgency of confronting antisemitism in interwar Europe during the late 1920s.

Today's post-Holocaust Austria puts the history of exclusionary antisemitic violence on display in the new and now almost complete digital reconstruction of *Die Stadt ohne Juden* by the Filmarchiv Austria. It launched the project in 2016 with a crowdfunding initiative, the first of its kind for film restoration in Austria, which drew wide support from 714 backers and overshot its campaign target of 75,500 Euro. Going forward with the campaign motto "Save the Past for the Future!," public sponsorship has included commitments from the city of Vienna as well as the National Fund of the Austrian Republic for a national tour of the film with screenings in cities throughout Austria as well as a multi-

Figure 15.4. *Die Stadt ohne Juden,* French export print. Frame scan of previously missing footage. Reproduction courtesy Filmarchiv Austria.

media exhibition at the Metro Kinokulturhaus in Vienna during 2018, the centennial of the First Republic: "Pride of place is to be given to the Austrian silent movie *The City without Jews* due to its highly charged symbolism."[11] No doubt the rise of the Freiheitliche Partei Österreichs (FPÖ; Freedom Party of Austria), the right-wing populist party, has lent this film and the project to restore it heightened contemporary relevance.

The recent digital restorations of *Das alte Gesetz* and *Die Stadt ohne Juden* under the auspices of national film archives in Germany and Austria have been well documented.[12] However, much is still unknown. Speculation about different national views of Jewishness based on the examination of export prints from the 1920s is fraught with unanswered questions. First: when, where, and by whom were these prints authorized? Specifically, were the editing changes noted here the work of the films' foreign exhibitors or a designated government agency? Then: before release in other countries, were the export prints subject to approval by a national censorship board as they were in Germany at the time? And finally: how were they received abroad in these countries? Perhaps we have reached the limits of historical documentation for these two films, although—as the sensational flea market discovery of a vintage nitrate print shows—hidden sources from the Weimar period are still surfacing. More material from the past waiting to be rescued and saved for the future! In any case, further research is necessary to support conclusions that are still tentative.

Cynthia Walk is Associate Professor Emerita of German Literature and Film Studies at the University of California, San Diego. Her research has focused on modern German drama, theater and film with publications on intermediality ("The Debate about Stage Tradition in Weimar Cinema: Murnau's *Herr Tartüff*" and "Cross-Media Exchange in Weimar Culture: *Von morgens bis mitternachts*"), race ("Anna May Wong and Weimar Cinema: Orientalism in Postcolonial Germany"), and ethnicity ("Romeo with Sidelocks: Jewish-Gentile Romance in E.A. Dupont's *Das alte Gesetz* (1923) and Other Early Weimar Assimilation Films") in Weimar cinema. Current work on the restoration of Jewish-themed films from the Weimar era is the subject of her chapter in this volume.

Notes

1. "*Filmrettung*: Save the Past for the Future!" was the motto of the crowdfunding campaign that launched the restoration of *Die Stadt ohne Juden* in 2016: https://wemakeit.com/projects/filmrettung-stadt-ohne-juden. For background, see my article on the historical context of these films and their related thematic focus on Jewish migration from eastern Europe, and the possibilities and limits of integration in post–World War I Germany and Austria. Cynthia Walk, "Romeo with Sidelocks: Jewish-Gentile Romance in E.A. Dupont's *Das alte Gesetz* (1923) and Other Early Weimar Assimilation Films," in *The Many Faces of Weimar Cinema: Rediscovering Germany's Filmic Legacy*, ed. Christian Rogowski (Rochester, NY: Camden House, 2010), 84–101. https://www.dropbox.com/s/ot0nnmaxp7m17y4/Walk_Romeo%20with%20Sidelocks_2010.pdf?dl=0.
2. Paul Read and Mark-Paul Meyer, eds., *Restoration of Motion Picture Film*, (Oxford: Butterworth-Heinemann, 2000). This is still the bible of film restoration used at the International Federation of Film Archives (FIAF) summer school on film restoration. More-recent articles on the subject appear regularly in the *Journal of Film Preservation* (FIAF) and *Moving Image* (Association of Moving Image Archivists; AMIA).
3. This account of the current restoration of *Das alte Gesetz* is based on my collaboration with the team at the Deutsche Kinemathek and the ARRI Media laboratory in Berlin. The screenshots here are records from these meetings.
4. There is a curious and unexplained anomaly in the history of *Das alte Gesetz*: some time after the first restoration of the film was completed in 1984, the American print was cut up and selectively edited into the Swedish print along with the German intertitles of the 1984 restoration. So now the Swedish version is really an amalgam of several different elements that could more properly be called the Swedish-American version with restored German intertitles. (The restoration team had an affectionate nickname for it: Frankenstein.) Today there are protocols in archives around the world that mandate the preservation of original elements without such manipulation. See the the first principle in the FIAF code of ethics (https://www.fiafnet.org/pages/Community/Code-Of-Ethics.html).
5. Daniel Meiller, "The Continuation of a Restoration with Digital Means," Booklet in the Flicker Alley DVD edition of *The Ancient Law*, 2018.
6. See Kenneth B. Moss, *Jewish Renaissance in the Russian Revolution* (Cambridge: Harvard University Press, 2009); and Anna Shternshis, *Soviet and Kosher: Jewish Popular Culture in the Soviet Union, 1923–1939* (Bloomington: Indiana University Press, 2006). With thanks to my colleague at University of California, San Diego, Amelia Glaser, scholar of Russian and modern Yiddish literature, for her insightful comments and these references.
7. See the transposed final scene in the Russian export print of *Das alte* Gesetz in a video clip on YouTube copied from a scan of the vintage source: https://www.youtube.com/watch?v=LD7AZ3djVyk&feature=youtu.be.
8. Guntram Geser and Armin Loacker, "Einleitung: Annäherungen an einen fragilen Torso," in Geser and Loacker, eds., *Die Stadt ohne Juden*, 11–15.
9. Newly discovered sequences aredisplayed in the crowdfunding campaign video of Filmarchiv Austria on wemakeit.com in support of "Saving *Die Stadt ohne Juden*. (https://wemakeit.com/projects/filmrettung-stadt-ohne-juden).

10. This dating of the sources A and P is offered in the 2020 Flicker Alley edition of *Die Stadt ohne Juden*, DVD booklet essay by Anna Dobringer, "Film sources and Reconstruction."
11. Fundraising document, "*The City without Jews* (A 1924): Restoration and Presentation," Filmarchiv Austria, 2017. On the Filmarchiv Austria website there is a link to the remarkable exhibition "*Die Stadt ohne . . . Juden Muslime Flüchtlinge Ausländer*" with a complete online digitorial (https://www.filmarchiv.at/program/exhibition/die-stadt-ohne/).
12. *Das alte Gesetz* (*The Ancient Law*) was published in 2018 as a DVD in Germany (absolut Medien ARTE Edition) and the United States (Flicker Alley). Both editions have bonus features that explain and illustrate the restoration process: an essay as well as a short film with raw scans of the elements. Similarly enhanced DVD editions of *Die Stadt ohne Juden* (*The City without Jews*) will be released in 2020:trailer and press release (https://www.youtube.com/watch?v=LTEfsVNy2fQ&feature=youtu.be&fbclid=IwAR2rbXOUirZloktqN_Q9HpA6xffk8RWKtNsumBgfepU1SsGIGebNsa2NRrY).

Bibliography

Archival Material

Deutsche Kinemathek
Zensurkarte for *Das alte Gesetz*.
Vintage nitrate sources used in the restoration of *Das alte Gesetz*.
Computer spreadsheet documenting them side by side (*Abgleich*).
DPX scan: mp4 video of Swedish, Russian, French, and Italian versions.
Screenshots of the reconstruction and final edit in Avid Media Composer.
Filmarchiv Austria
Scan: mp4 video of the recently discovered nitrate print of *Die Stadt ohne Juden*, the Paris element.
Written assessment and comparison of the two vintage sources, A (Amsterdam) and P (Paris).
Intertitle lists for A and P.
Fundraising document, "*The City without Jews* (A 1924): Restoration and Presentation." Filmarchiv Austria, 2017.
"Saving *Die Stadt ohne Juden*." Crowdfunding campaign sponsored by the Filmarchiv Austria. Retrieved 1 October 2018: https://wemakeit.com/projects/filmrettung-stadt-ohne-juden.
"DIE STADT OHNE . . . Juden Muslime Flüchtlinge Ausländer." Exhibit at the Metro Kinokulturhaus, Vienna,2 March–31 December 2018.

Secondary Sources

Cherchi Usai, Paolo. *Silent Cinema: A Guide to Study, Research and Curatorship*, 3rd edtn. London: The British Film Institute, 2019.
Dobringer, Anna. "Film sources and Reconstruction." Booklet in the Flicker Alley DVD edition of *Die Stadt ohne Juden*, 2020.

FIAF Code of Ethics. Retrieved 1 October 2018 from https://www.fiafnet.org/pages/Community/Code-Of-Ethics.html.

Fossati, Giovnna. *From Grain to Pixel: The Archival Life of Film in Transition*, 3rd rev. edtn. Amsterdam: Amsterdam University Press, 2018.

Geser, Guntram, and Loacker, Armin. "*Einleitung: Annäherung an einen fragilen Torso.*" In *Die Stadt ohne Juden*, Geser and Loacker, eds. Vienna: Filmarchiv Austria, 2000.

Meiller, Daniel. "The Continuation of a Restoration with Digital Means." Booklet in the Flicker Alley DVD edition of *The Ancient Law*, 2018.

Moss, Kenneth B. *Jewish Renaissance in the Russian Revolution*. Cambridge: Harvard University Press, 2009.

Read, Paul, and Meyer, Mark-Paul, eds. *Restoration of Motion Picture Film*. Oxford: Butterworth-Heinemann, 2000.

Shternshis, Anna. *Soviet and Kosher: Jewish Popular Culture in the Soviet Union, 1923–1939*. Bloomington: Indiana University Press, 2006.

Walk, Cynthia. "Romeo with Sidelocks: Jewish-Gentile Romance in E.A. Dupont's *Das alte Gesetz* (1923) and Other Early Weimar Assimilation Films." In *The Many Faces of Weimar Cinema: Rediscovering Germany's Filmic Legacy*, ed. Christian Rogowski, 84–101. Rochester, NY: Camden House, 2010.

Afterword

Barbara Hales and Valerie Weinstein

Rethinking Jewishness in Weimar Cinema sheds light on the cinematic portrayal of Jewishness in the critical period preceding the Holocaust. In Weimar cinema, Jewish difference intersected with gender, sexuality, class, and other vectors of identity, as well as other political and social concerns. In order to examine these intersections, the scholars in this volume consider both more well-trodden ground as well as many seemingly forgotten films and cultural artifacts. In the process of considering the important issue of Jewishness in Weimar cinema, we thus also hope to resuscitate scholarly interest in many great yet overlooked cinematic works.

The scholars in *Rethinking Jewishness in Weimar Cinema* excavate the oeuvre of once famous but now obscure Jewish film professionals. Many chapters emphasize important films that have received little scholarly attention, drawing on print and filmic sources to highlight their cultural significance. Even the few canonical films analyzed here are revived for a new purpose: our authors show how Jewishness was inextricable from other important elements of Weimar film and therefore reconsider its role in films best known for other qualities and interventions.

Rethinking Jewishness in Weimar Cinema illuminates neglected pathways for future scholars to follow. Several chapters in this volume begin a conversation about typecasting, stereotyping, gender, and Jewish difference that delves into the German-Jewish archive and draws salient comparisons with other ethnic performers. More research is needed into the lives and careers of Jewish actors and analysis of how their experiences of Jewishness affected their performances. Our contributors mine a variety of film genres, from melodrama to comedy, and other modalities of expression, including cabaret and expressionist theater, for Jewishness. These modes and genres are far from exhausted and offer rich opportunities to further analyze Jewishness and performance.

More work should also be done on the importance of Jewish film professionals besides actors and directors. Weimar film theory and criticism are well-studied, and some critics with Jewish origins, such as Siegfried Kracauer and Lotte Eisner, continue to have a central place in Weimar film scholarship.[1] In contrast, other critics, such as Alfred Rosenthal, whose career Ervin Malakaj scrutinizes in chapter 5, and their Jewishness have attracted little attention, perhaps because National Socialist (Nazi) antisemitism cut their lives and careers short, minimizing their postwar influence. In addition to now-forgotten critics, influential Weimar cinema owners, distributors, and publicists have also receded from view. Jewish screenwriters, cinematographers, designers, producers, and editors deserve renewed attention too. Despite their contributions and talents, many of these film professionals have not yet garnered enough scholarly attention. Admittedly, it requires persistence to trace forgotten careers through filmic, print, and archival evidence, yet more research along these lines would help us construct a fuller picture of the Weimar film industry, as well as the specific role of Jewish artists in that industry.

Many questions remain about how Jewish difference functions and is represented in both well-known and lesser-known Weimar films. Understanding how ethnicity operates in the cinema and how ethnoreligious identities are constructed by the media requires both historical and contemporary perspectives. As Weimar film scholars, we have much to contribute to these discussions. Because of the Nazis' virulent antisemitic backlash, the stakes in understanding ethnicity in the media environment of the Weimar Republic are high. The many close readings in this volume about the presence and absence of Jewishness and the functions of Jewish difference in individual films, their production, and their reception show various ways in which Jewish difference, acculturation, assimilation, and antisemitism were negotiated across and around Weimar cinema. Such debates extended well beyond the relatively few films that centered around Jewish characters and themes.

Several chapters in this volume illustrate how antisemitic discourses targeted Jewishness across sexual, scientific, and artistic cultures. Other chapters show how, in response to such debates, Jewishness was edited out of some films—protectively, maliciously, or in collaboration with political developments. As film preservation attempts to reconstruct lost film footage by restoring surviving fragments, the scholarship in this volume attempts to identify and restore some of Weimar cinema's Jewish remnants. We invite more research in German-Jewish film studies that continues to reconstruct Weimar cinema's Jewishness.

The loss of the Jews and Jewishness from Weimar cinema was manifold and catastrophic. To be sure, this loss includes the degradation and disappearance of film footage and film ephemera endemic to the medium. Such mundane and regrettable film studies losses are exacerbated by the more traumatic losses caused by Nazi violence. The majority of Jews in the Weimar film industry were exiled or murdered. As a symbolic ancillary to that violence, the Nazis excised Jewishness from German films and excluded Jewishness from German film historiography. Many of these losses can never be recovered. We nevertheless envision future scholarship that seeks to restore and comprehend what does remain of the Jewish contributions to Weimar cinema. Martin Pollak notes on the remains of the dead: "Most of the time, there is something, a dull idea, subtle hints, rumors, whispering that here or there something has happened ... certain material hints, archaeological finds."[2] Dead material is never truly dead. The work presented in this volume thus hopes to pay homage to those Weimar Jewish creatives and their contributions to cinematic history, particular those who suffered as a result of Nazi persecution.

Barbara Hales is a Professor of History and Humanities at the University of Houston-Clear Lake. Her publications focus on film history of the Weimar Republic and the Third Reich. She is the author of *Black Magic Woman: Gender and the Occult in Weimar Germany* (Peter Lang, Oxford, 2021). She has also co-edited a volume entitled *Continuity and Crisis in German Cinema 1928-1936* for Camden House in 2016 (with Mihaela Petrescu and Valerie Weinstein). Dr. Hales is President of the Houston based organization, Center for Medicine After the Holocaust.

Valerie Weinstein is Professor of Women's, Gender, and Sexuality Studies, Niehoff Professor in Film and Media Studies, and affiliate faculty in German Studies and Judaic Studies at the University of Cincinnati. She is the author of *Antisemitism in Film Comedy in Nazi Germany* (Indiana University Press, 2019) and numerous articles on Weimar and Nazi cinema. She is co-editor, with Barbara Hales and Mihaela Petrescu, of *Continuity and Crisis in German Cinema 1928-1936* (Camden House, 2016).

Notes

1. Examples of the rich scholarship on Weimar film criticism include Sabine Hake, *The Cinema's Third Machine: Writing on Film in Germany, 1907–1933* (Lincoln: University of Nebraska Press, 1993); Anton Kaes, Nicholas Baer, and Michael Cowan, eds., *The Promise of Cinema: German Film Theory, 1907–1933* (Oakland: University of California Press, 2016).
2. "Meist gibt es da etwas, eine dumpfe Ahnung, schwache Hinweise, Gerüchte, Geflüster, Geraune, das hier oder da etwas geschehen ist . . . irgendwelche materiellen Hinweise, Bodenfunde." Quoted in Reinhard Bernbeck, *Materielle Spuren des nationalsozialistischen Terrors: Zu einer Archäologie der Zeitgeschichte*. (Bielefeld: Transcript Verlag, 2017), 173.

Bibliography

Bernbeck, Reinhard. *Materielle Spuren des nationalsozialistischen Terrors: Zu einer Archäologie der Zeitgeschichte*. Bielefeld: Transcript, 2017.

Hake, Sabine. *The Cinema's Third Machine: Writing on Film in Germany, 1907–1933*. Lincoln: University of Nebraska Press, 1993.

Kaes, Anton, Nicholas Baer, and Michael Cowan, eds. *The Promise of Cinema: German Film Theory, 1907–1933*. Oakland: University of California Press, 2016.

Index

Abseits vom Wege (*Off Track*) (film), 228
Adorno, Theodor W., 289
Albert, Max, 120
Alexander, Kurt, 10
Alkohol (film), 221
Alles Leben ist Kampf (*All Life Is Struggle*) (film), 228
Allgemeine Musikzeitung, 260, 267
Allgemeine Zeitung des Judentums, 157
All Quiet on the Western Front (film), 141–42
Das alte Gesetz (*The Ancient Law*) (film), 12, 16, 78, 139; Dupont releasing, 301, 314, 316; Jewish assimilation in, 328; Jewishness in, 330; restoration of, 327–31, 335n4; Russian version of, 330–31
Altenloh, Emilie, 111
Amman, Betty, 79
Anders als die Andern (*Different from the Others*) (film), 137; conclusion, 168–69; critics of, 155–57, 161, 233n52; for educating about homosexuality, 153–56, 159, 162, 165–66; Enlightenment principles in, 162–64, 168; as gay rights film, 153, 155, 162, 167; gender inversion in, 165–66; homophobia, antisemitism and, 154–61; homosexual emancipation and, 161–63; Jewish difference decoded in, 15, 153–54, 161–68; Jewish visibility in, 162, 169; Oswald making, 153; outcries against, 158; overview, 152–54; restoration of, 171n11; as sexual hygiene film, 154
Der Angriff, 121–22, 288–89, 297n39
Ansky, S., 189
Antisemiten film project, 137–38
antisemitism, 2–3, 6, 14; *Anders als die Andern* and, 154–61; Arno and, 94–97; Buber on, 11; in *Falsche Scham* (film), 223; in *Familientag im Hause Prellstein*, 94; *Die freudlose Gasse* (film) and, 189; Granach on, 44–45; Jewish difference and, 225; Jewishness and, 15; of Jewish writers, 188; of Nazis, 339; in *Peter*, 206; response by Jewish filmmakers, 136–38; in *Die Stadt ohne Juden* (film), 332; *Die Stadt ohne Juden* (novel) and, 186; stereotypes and, 190; Wassermann, J., on, 10; in Weimar cinema, 15–16; in Weimar Republic, 95
"Antisemitismus und Zukunft" (Flake), 11
Anton, Karl, 302–303; *Peter Voss, der Millionendieb* (film) and, 311–17
Arnheim, Rudolph, 31
Arno, Siegfried, 14; antisemitism and, 94–97; Ashkenazi on, 93; in *Aufruhr in Jungesellenheim*, 98; in cabaret and sound film, 89, 97–102; on cabaret stage, 89; complaints against, 96–97; early career and film breakthrough, 90–93; exile of, 98, 102; in *Familientag im Hause Prellstein*, 92–93; Jewish coding

and, 100–101; Jewishness of, 101; Kracauer on, 91–93; as Lubitsch successor, 89–90; in *Moritz macht sein Glück*, 100–101; as movie star, 100–101; *Ostjude* and, 97; reviews of, 91–92; schlemihl type and, 91; soldier type and, 30, 96; Wollenberg on, 96–97
Aryanization of German cinema, 286–95
Ashkenazi, Ofer, 2, 28; on Arno, 93; on cosmopolitanism, 162; on integration of German Jews, 123; Jewish identity and, 4, 13, 114, 134, 147n9, 199; on Lubitsch, 190, 199; on Lulu type, 71; on *Verwechslungskomödien*, 199–200
Aufklärungsfilme (enlightenment films), 154–55, 158, 163–64
Aufruhr im Junggesellenheim (film), 98
Auschwitz concentration camp, 155, 198, 273, 293
Auslander, Leora, 8–9, 18n36
Austrian film industry, 197–98, 200
Avid Media Composer, 328–29

Baker, Josephine, 80
Balázs, Béla, 25, 40; on casting actors, 26–28
Bamberger, Rudolf, 264, 273
Bara, Theda, 67, 79–80
Baur, Erwin, 218
Becker, Rafael, 219
Becker, Wolfgang, 312
"Behind My Camera" (Freund), 27
Behrendt, Hans, 201
Beilinson, Mose, 7
Belling, Curt, 3
Benjamin, Walter, 7
Berber, Anita, 72
Berger, Grete, 78
Berger, Ludwig, 15, 257–58, 263; attacks on, 273; background of, 266; credentials of, 267; defense of, 270–71; exile of, 273; satire of, 265; tongue-in-cheek comedy of, 264

Ber-Gimpel, Jacob, 46, 62n5
Bergner, Elisabeth, 5, 77
Berlin (film), 241, 249
Berliner Börsen-Courier, 271
Bernauer, Rudolf, 69, 74
Bernhardt, Kurt, 50
Bernstein, Henry, 31
Die Bestie im Menschen (*The Beast in Man*) (film), 67, 76
Bettauer, Hugo, 16, 181–86, 331
Between Two Worlds (Prawer), 3–4, 133
Betz, Hans-Walther, 3
Bial, Henry, 13
Biebrach, Rudolf, 216, 220–21, 223, 229
Bildung (personal cultivation and education), 13
Black actors, 78, 81
blackface, 101
Bleichröder, Hans von, 72
Blüher, Hans, 160
Bogart, Humphrey, 27
Bois, Ilse, 101
Bolshevik-Zionist conspiracy, 238
Boyarin, Daniel, 159
Brand, Adolf, 160–61
Brennendes Geheimnis (*Burning Secret*) (film), 15; attack on, 286–92; banning of, 279, 289–90; censoring of, 288; Jewish difference in, 280–81; Jewish visibility erased from, 280–86; ostracization of Jewishness and, 292–93; premier of, 286–88; reviews of, 289
Brenner, Michael, 8
Bressart, Felix, 203, 206; exile of, 210n25
Brockmann, Stephen, 273
Brodnitz, Hanns, 74
Brooks, Louise, 71
Brown, Shane, 166
Brunner, Karl, 155
Buber, Martin, 7, 10; on antisemitism, 11
The Buccaneer (film), 201
Die Büchse der Pandora (*Pandora's Box*) (film), 71; Jewishness in, 143; menorah in, 142–43

Buerkle, Darcy, 12, 184
Burning Secret (novel) (Zweig, S.), 279; alienation in, 284; banning of, 291; film based on, 280–86; Jewish assimilation in, 285; Jewishness in, 283–85; Jewish visibility in, 285; plot of, 282–83

cabaret stage, 29; Arno on, 89, 97–102; campaign against, 96–97; transformation to film, 99–100
Das Cabinet des Dr. Caligari (*The Cabinet of Dr. Caligari*) (film), 166, 241, 242
Casseler Allgemeine Zeitung, 245–46
censor's certificate (*Zensurkarte*), 327, 328, 332
Centralverein deutscher Staatsbürger jüdischen Glaubens (Central Association of German Citizens of Jewish Faith), 95–97, 105n35, 134, 158, 272
Charell, Eric, 90
Colpe, Max, 287
comedies of error (*Verwechslungskomödien*), 198–200, 202
community (*Gemeinschaft*), 8, 10
concentration camps, 121, 122; Auschwitz concentration camp, 155, 198, 273, 293
consciousness industry, 113
cosmopolitanism, 4, 145, 162–63, 184, 238
Csibi, der Fratz (*Csibi, the Rascal*) (film), 200, 202
cultural Bolshevism (*Kulturbolschewismus*), 242
Currier, Ashley, 156
C.V.-Zeitung, 134, 219–20, 272; founding of, 158
Czinner, Paul, 5, 77

Dadaism, 247–48
Da geht ein Mensch (Granach), 36, 60
Dämon und Mensch (*Demon and Man*) (film), 73

Danton (film), 51
Darnton, Robert, 113
Deutsch, Ernst, 78
Deutscher Geist—oder Judentum! (Trebitsch), 245
Deutsches Theater, 47–48
Deutsche Zeitung, 74, 167, 168
Deutschvölkische Blätter, 158
Dickinson, Thorold, 1
Dieterle, Wilhelm, 50
Dietrich, Marlene, 64n29
Dirks, Christian, 112
Dr. Bessels Verwandlung (*The Transformation of Dr. Bessel*) (film), 163
Die Drei von der Tankstelle (*The Three from the Filling Station*) (film), 14; as German classic, 131; Jewish identity in, 145; labeling of, 133; story in, 132
Dreyer, Carl Theodor, 138
Dreyfus (film), 31, 137
Dreyfus, Alfred, 164, 332
Die dritte Eskadron (*The Third Squadron*) (film), 30, 96
Dr. Mabuse, der Spieler (*Dr. Mabuse, the Gambler*) (film), 241
dual legibility, 29
Du Maurier, George, 56–57
Dupont, Ewald André, 12, 16, 115–16, 131–32, 221; adaptation of *Peter Voss, der Millionendieb* (film), 312, 314–17; *Das alte Gesetz* released by, 301, 314, 316; background of, 314; *Die Geier-Wally* production, 305, 307–11; *Zwei Welten* released by, 139–41, 314
Der Dybuk (play) (Ansky), 189

eastern European Jew. *See Ostjude*
Eberwein, Robert, 303
Eddington, Arthur, 247
Edzard, Dietz, 71
Eggeling, Viking, 248
Ehrlich, Paul, 222, 227, 228, 229, 234n80

Eichberg, Richard, 50, 80, 169
8-Uhr-Abendblatt, 272
Ein ausgekochter Junge (film), 100, 101
Eine kleine Freundin braucht jeder Mann (film), 105n31
Einstein, Albert, 8; Dadaism and, 247–48; Jewish identity of, 238–39, 248; Jewish science and, 238, 249, 251n3; public attacks on, 242, 247–48
Einstein Film, 237, 242, 249–50. See also *Die Grundlagen der Einsteinschen Relativitätstheorie*
The Einstein Theory of Relativity (film), 240, 241
Eisner, Lotte, 1–2, 4, 133, 289–90; exile of, 3; film scholarship and, 339; on *Die freudlose Gasse*, 175–76
Enlightenment, 7; in *Anders als die Andern*, 162–64, 168
enlightenment films (*Aufklärungsfilme*), 154–55, 158, 163–64
Epistemology of the Closet (Sedgwick), 153
Erbkrank (*Hereditarily Ill*) (film), 228
Erdgeist (*Earth Spirit*) (play), 69–70
Erdgeist (film), 50
eugenics, 10, 224
exile: of Arno, 98, 102; of Berger, L., 273; of Bressart, 210n25; of Gaal, 15; of Granach, 60; of Kracauer and Eisner, 3; of Wallburg, 198

Falkenberg, Paul, 49
Falsche Scham (book) (Thomalla), 224
Falsche Scham (*False Shame*) (film): antisemitism in, 223; Jewish difference in, 225; prostitution in, 223–24, 226; as Weimar medical discourse film, 216, 220–21, 223–26, 229
Familientag im Hause Prellstein (film), 101, 104n19; antisemitism in, 94; Arno in, 92–93
fashion swellhead (*Modefatzke*), 30

Feige, Max, 117
Feind im Blut (*Enemy in the Blood*) (film): prostitution in, 226–28; as Weimar medical discourse film, 216, 220–21, 226–29
Feld, Hans, 91
Felix the Cat, 239, 242, 249
femme fatale type, 189; Orska as, 67, 73, 75, 77, 80, 81; vamp compared to, 79
femme fragile type, 77
Feuchtwanger, Lion, 31, 51
Filmarchiv Austria, 327, 332
Film "Kunst," Film Kohn, Film Korruption (Neumann, C., Belling, Betz), 3
Film-Kurier, 38–39, 91, 99–100, 112, 116, 258–59, 288; on rebirth of German cinema, 293
Film-Magazin, 112, 116, 117
film restoration, 16, 339; of *Das alte Gesetz*, 327–31, 335n4; of *Anders als die Andern*, 171n11; of *Die Stadt ohne Juden*, 327, 331–34
Fischer, Eugen, 10, 218
Flake, Otto, 11
Fleischer, Dave, 240–42, 244, 249
Fleischer, Max, 240–42, 244, 249
Fluch der Vererbung (*Curse of Heredity*) (film), 221, 224
"Forget Assimilation" (Spector), 7–8
Forst, Willi, 287
Franckenstein, Clemens von, 269
Fränkischer Kurier, 267, 270
Franzos, Karl Emil, 36
Die Frau von vierzig Jahren (film), 91
Fräulein Else (film), 72
Fräulein Else (novella) (Schnitzler), 72
Fräulein Lilli (*Miss Lilli*) (film), 201
Frenchness, 163
Freud, Sigmund, 8; on homosexuality, 159, 173n51
Die freudlose Gasse (novel) (Bettauer), 181; as film basis, 182–86; Jewish difference and, 185; misogyny in, 185–86, 188; plot of, 183–84;

prostitution in, 183, 185; screenplay from, 186–88
Die freudlose Gasse (*The Joyless Street*) (film): antisemitism and, 189; censoring of, 191n12; Eisner on, 175–76; fur symbolism in, 179–80; Garbo in, 175–79; Jewish coding of women in, 180; Jewish difference in, 15, 180–82, 189; making of, 188–90; novel as basis, 182–86; overview, 175–79; prostitution in, 175, 180; screenplay for, 186–88
Freund, Karl, 25, 27
Frick, Wilhelm, 141
Friedland, Max, 288, 291
Friedländer, Benedict, 160
Friedmann, Walther, 156–60
Fritsch, Willy, 143–44
From Caligari to Hitler (Kracauer), 1–4
Frühjahrsparade (*Spring Parade*) (film), 200
Le fruit vert (play) (Gignoux and Théry), 202
Führerprinzip (leadership principle), 266
Fulda, Bernhard, 116
Der Fürst von Pappenheim (*The Prince of Pappenheim*) (film), 169

Gaal, Franziska: in *Csibi, der Fratz*, 202; exile of, 15; in *Katharina—die Letzte*, 207–8; in *Peter*, 203–210; talent of, 200; as target, 201; in U. S., 201–2
Galeen, Henrik, 14, 25, 52–53, 307; as author, director, actor, 33; *Ostjude* portrayal, 32–35
Ganghofer, Ludwig, 309
Garbo, Greta, 28, 40, 51; in *Die freudlose Gasse*, 175–76
gay rights: *Anders als die Andern* and, 153, 155, 162, 167; erasure of, 159; as Jewish, 168; queerness and, 168
Gehrcke, Ernst, 240–42, 247
Die Geier-Wally (novel) (Von Hillern), 304–306, 309

Die Geier-Wally (*The Vulture-Wally*) (film), 15; Dupont production of, 305, 307–311; Nazi remake of, 301–14; Steinhoff response to, 304–314
Der gelbe Schein (*The Yellow Ticket*) (film), 78
Geller, Jay, 216
Geller, Oscar, 270
Gemeinschaft (community), 8, 10
Genini, Ronald, 79
Gerdes, Herbert, 228
German cinema, 30–31; Aryanization of, 286–92; *Film-Kurier* on rebirth of, 293; Jewish coding in, 81; Rosenthal on, 120–21
German-Jewish cooperation, 114–16
Germanness, 6, 9, 273; Jewishness compared to, 2–3
Gerron, Kurt, 98–99, 106n52, 145
Gert, Valeska, 79
Gertler, Viktor, 144
Die Geschlechtskrankheiten und ihre Folgen (*Sexually Transmitted Diseases and their Consequences*) (film), 215–16; Jewish coding in, 222–23; as Weimar medical discourse film, 220–23, 229
Geschlecht in Fesseln (*Sex in Chains*) (film), 169
Geschlecht und Charakter (Weininger), 152
Die Gezeichneten (film), 138
Gesetz zum Schutze der Erbgesundheit des deutschen Volkes (Law for the Protection of the Hereditary Health of the German Volk), 228
Gesetz zum Schutze des deutschen Blutes und der deutschen Ehre (Law for the Protection of German Blood and German Honor), 228
Gignoux, Régis, 202
Gilbert, Robert, 132, 144
Gilman, Sander, 5–6, 215
The Girl Downstairs (film), 201
Goebbels, Joseph, 3, 121, 142, 258, 306, 317; ideological transition and,

279, 290; speech of at the Hotel
Kaiserhof, 196–97, 291, 292
Goldberg, Heinz, 31
Goldstein, Moritz, 11
Der Golem (film), 32–35, 78, 138
Gorki, Maxim, 46–47
Graf, Wilhelm, 120
Granach, Alexander, 14, 25, 78; acting style of, 48–50; on antisemitism, 44–45; from apprentice baker to star actor, 46–48; escape from Germany, 51; exile of, 60; film career, 50–51; Jewishness shaping performances of, 44–60; Judas portrayal, 26, 38–40, 50; as Mehipsto, 49; in *Nosferatu*, 52–53; *Ostjude* and, 48; passing process and, 45; personal truths of, 39; in *Schatten*, 53–56; Shylock portrayal, 32, 37, 48–49; on Shylock type, 36; in *Svengali*, 56–59; *The Wall* and, 59–60
Grau, Albin, 53
Gray, Allan, 287
Great Depression, 258
Gregori, Ferdinand, 69
Die große Attraktion (film), 100–101
Großstadtschmetterling (Pavement Butterfly) (film), 50
Grünbaum, Fritz, 36
Die Grundlagen der Einsteinschen Relativitätstheorie (The Basic Principles of the Einstein Theory of Relativity) (film), 15; abstraction and figuration in, 247–50; animation in, 239, 244–47, 248; disorientations in, 244–47; overview, 237–40; program for, 241–43; relativity as mass suggestion in, 240–44; reviews of, 244–46, 253n30
Günther, Hans F.K., 220

Haas, Willy, 181, 182, 186–88
Hake, Sabine, 113, 116
Hanauer, W., 219

Hangmen Also Die (film), 51
Hansen, Max, 90
Harden, Maximilian, 157
Harden-Eulenburg affair, 157, 160
Harlan, Veit, 301
Hasidic tales, 8
Hauptmann, Gerhart, 259
Der Hauptmann von Köpenick (The Captain of Köpenick) (film), 31
Hays code, 78
Heimat culture, 302; under Nazis, 308; Steinhoff reclaiming, 304–314
Heimsoth, Karl, 160–61
Henseleit, Felix, 259
Herrnfeld, Anton, 94–95
Herrnfeld, Donat, 94–95
Herzberg, Georg, 94
Heymann, Werner Richard, 132, 144
Hirschfeld, Magnus, 153, 155–56, 160, 162; sexual intermediacy and, 166; slide show of, 165
His People (film), 135
Hitler, Adolf, 1, 141, 215, 217–18; on Jewish disease, 220, 228; power of, 241, 294n1; syphilis and, 231n15
Hofmannsthal, Hugo von, 188
Holländer, Ludwig, 9–10
Holocaust, 145, 231n15, 294n1, 338
homophobia, 152; *Anders als die Andern* and, 154–61; politicized, 156–59, 161
homosexual emancipation, 154; *Anders als die Andern* and, 161–63; Jewish community and, 156, 159–60, 167
homosexuality: *Anders als die Andern* for educating about, 153–56, 162, 165–66; discussions as taboo, 158; Freud on, 159, 176n51; Greek, 167; Jewishness and, 152, 159–60, 170n5; propaganda for combating, 221; as spectacle, 164, 166, 169
Horak, Jan-Christopher, 197
Die Hose (The Underpants) (film), 269
Hugenberg, Alfred, 117, 122–23, 270

Ich möchte kein Mann sein (*I Don't Want to Be a Man*) (film), 169
Ihering, Herbert, 64n28, 91, 289
Im Deutschen Reich publication, 158
I. N. R. I. (film), 27, 38–40, 50
Israelitischen Familienblatt, 30, 158

Jackson, Felix, 199
Jacoby, Georg, 311
Jahrbuch für sexuelle Zwischenstufen mit besonderer Berücksichtigung der Homosexualität, 159–60
Jargon theater, 29, 41n18, 94, 95
The Jazz Singer (film), 100–101, 134
Jelavich, Peter, 88
Jessner, Leopold, 50, 71, 74
Jew count (*Judenzählung*), 6
Jew farces (*Judenpossen*), 29
Jewish assimilation, 4, 6–7; in *Das alte Gesetz*, 328; in *Burning Secret* (novel), 285; Jewish identity and, 12–13; Jewish liberals supporting, 19n71
Jewish coding: Arno and, 100–101; in German cinema, 81; *in Die Geschlechtskrankheiten und ihre Folgen*, 222–23; Jewish identity and, 5–6, 13–14; of Orska, 73–77; of women, in *Die freudlose Gasse*, 180
Jewish difference, 3; in *Anders als die Andern*, 15, 153–54, 161–68; antisemitism and, 225; *Aufklärungsfilme* and, 155; in *Brennendes Geheimnis*, 280–81; debates around, 293; in *Falsche Scham* (film), 225; in *Die freudlose Gasse* (film), 15, 180–82, 189; *Die freudlose Gasse* (novel) and, 185; locating, 13–14; negotiation of, 338–39; operation of hidden, 190; Orska and, 79, 81; Silverman on, 4–5; in Weimar cinema, 338–39; Weimar medical discourse films and, 221
Jewish emancipation, 154, 159, 162–64, 168, 176n61

Jewish film print culture: fear of bias in, 115; German-Jewish cooperation and, 114–16; Rosenthal and, 116–17
Jewish Frontiers (Gilman), 5–6
Jewish identity: Ashkenazi and, 4, 13, 114, 134, 147n9, 199; construct of, 18n36; culture and, 8; in *Die Drei von der Tankstelle*, 145; of Einstein, 238–39, 248; of German Jews, 9; Jewish assimilation and, 12–13; Jewish coding, 5–6, 13–14; in long-term memory, 9–10; of Lubitsch, 133–34; sexuality and, 216; in Weimar cinema, 4, 6–11, 13, 133–35; Zweig, S., and, 282–85
Jewish liberals: Jewish assimilation supported by, 19n71; in Weimar cinema, 4, 8, 17n19
Jewish merchant (*Trödler*), 25, 31–33
Jewishness: in *Das alte Gesetz*, 330; antisemitism and, 15; of Arno, 101; as border zone, 5–6; in *Die Büchse der Pandora*, 143; in *Burning Secret* (novel), 283–85; concealment of, 12–13; as ethnoreligious identity and conceptual category, 4; exaggeration of, 29–30; exoticism and, 80; future analysis of, 339; Germanness compared to, 2–3; Granach performances shaped by, 44–60; homosexuality and, 152, 159–60, 170n5; locating of, 11–16; masking of, 15; Mickey Mouse and, 239, 249–50; Nazis and, 281, 289–91; New Woman and, 183–84; Orska and, 67–68, 74–81; ostracization of, 292–93; queerness and, 152–54, 159, 168–69; as racial identity, 9; of Rosenthal, 121–23; Wallach on, 284; in Weimar Republic, 2, 6
Jewish science, 238, 249, 251n3
Jewish skepticism (*jüdischer Skepsis*), 187
Jewish syphilis conspiracy: conclusion, 229; cultural

associations of Jews and prostitution, 216–20; debunking, 230n1; in *Mein Kampf*, 215, 217–18; overview, 215–16; Weimar medical discourse films and, 220–28

Jewish types: classical film types and, 26–28; Kolpenitzky on genuine, 30–31; negative stereotypes, 31–32; overview, 25–26; on Weimar screen, 28–32. *See also* typecasting; *specific Jewish types*

Jewish visibility: in *Anders als die Andern*, 162, 169; in *Burning Secret* (novel), 285; erased from *Brennendes Geheimnis*, 280–86; Rosenthal and, 112–13, 121–23; in Weimar cinema, 14

Judas type, 25, 30, 32; Granach portraying, 26, 38–40, 50

"Der Jude im Film" (Wollenberg and Kolpenitzky), 29–30, 96–97

Juden in der deutschen Literatur (Krojanker), 188

Judenpossen (Jew farces), 29

Judenzählung (Jew count), 6

jüdischer Skepsis (Jewish skepticism), 187

Jüdische Rundschau, 131–32, 134–35

Jüdisch-liberale Zeitung, 219

Jud Süss (film), 301

Jung, Uli, 38

Junghans, Wolfram, 221

kabalistic tradition, 7

Kabarett der Komiker (KadeKo), 95–101

Kaes, Anton, 37

Kameradschaft (film), 51

Karbach, Oskar, 7

Karlweis, Oskar, 143–45

Katharina—die Letzte (*Katharina—the Last*) (film), 201–2; Gaal in, 207–8

Kaufmann, Nicholas, 215–16, 220–23, 229

Keine Feier ohne Meyer (film), 101

Killen, Andreas, 221–22

Der Kinematograph, 5; lawsuits, 117; rhetoric of collaboration in, 117–21; Rosenthal at, 111–13, 116–23

Kleine Mutti (*Little Mother*) (film), 201

Kohner, Frederick, 281, 286, 287; escape to Hollywood, 292

Kolpenitzky, Max, 29; on genuine Jewish types, 30–31

Kornblum, Hanns Walter, 15, 237–40, 242, 244; animations of, 245–50

Kortner, Fritz, 45–47, 78, 142–43

Kosofky, Eve, 153

Koster, Harry, 199

Kosterlitz, Hermann, 207–9

Kotzebue, August von, 265

Kracauer, Siegfried, 1–4, 25, 40, 133; on Arno, 91–93; exile of, 3; film scholarship and, 339; on Garbo, 28; on Hollywood stars, 27; rotating spirals, 241; on *Schatten*, 53–54

Krafft-Ebing, Richard von, 162

Kramer, 158–59

Krause, Willi, 288–89, 291

Kreimeier, Klaus, 166

Krojanker, Gustav, 188

Kulturbolschewismus (cultural Bolshevism), 242

Kurtz, Rudolf, 272

Kyser, Hans, 264

Lamač, Karel, 312

Lang, Fritz, 5, 51, 241, 259

Die letzte Stunde (*The Last Hour*) (film), 76

Law for the Protection of German Blood and German Honor (*Gesetz zum Schutze des deutschen Blutes und der deutschen Ehre*), 228

Law for the Protection of the Hereditary Health of the German Volk (*Gesetz zum Schutze der Erbgesundheit des deutschen Volkes*), 228

lawyer type, 30

leadership principle (*Führerprinzip*), 266

Lehrhaus school, 7
Leichte Kavallerie (film), 78, 92
Leider, Frieda, 259
Lellouch, Pierre, 292–93
Leni, Paul, 306
Lenz, Fritz, 218
Lessing, Gotthold Ephraim, 158–59
Das letzte Fort (film), 50
Liebmann, Robert, 261, 273
Lieven, Lotte, 59–60
Linge, Ina, 165
Lohmann, Walter, 258
Lorre, Peter, 199
Lubitsch, Ernst, 5, 47, 51, 94, 114, 187; Arno as successor, 89–90; Ashkenazi on, 190, 199; comedy of, 88–89; Jewish identity of, 133–34; personal truths of, 39; versatility of, 28–29
Lulu type, 68–73
Lustig, H. G., 91

Mack, Max, 73
Madame Dubarry (film), 133–34
Mädchen in Uniform (*Girls in Uniform*) (film), 169
male femininity, 167
Mancini, Elena, 163
Marcus, Paul, 122
Massary, Fritzi, 90
Matray, Maria, 263
Matthes, Wilhelm, 267–70
Mayr, Brigitte, 201–2
McCormick, Richard W., 133–34
Meinhard, Carl, 69, 72
Mein Kampf (Hitler), 215, 217–18
Der Meister von Nürnberg (*The Master of Nuremberg*) (film), 15; condemnation of, 269–70; controversy over, 260–61; defense of, 270; propaganda campaign against, 257–58, 271–73; reviews of, 259; sets for, 264; Wagner opera compared to, 261–65
Mendelssohn, Moses, 163
menorah: in *Die Büchse der Pandora*, 142–43; in *Zwei Welten*, 142

Der Mensch am Wege (film), 50
Metropolis (film), 259
Meyer aus Berlin (*Meyer from Berlin*) (film), 28
Meyerinck, Hubert von, 74
Mickey Mouse, 239, 249–50
Millakowsky, Hermann, 132
misogyny, 160, 179, 184–86, 185, 188
Mittelmann, Hanni, 283–85
Modefatzke (fashion swellhead), 30
Morena, Erna, 71
Morgan, Paul, 96
Moritz macht sein Glück (film), 100–101
Mühsam, Kurt, 117
Münchener Beobachter, 271–72
Münsterberg, Hugo, 78
Murnau, Friedrich Wilhelm, 47, 50, 52–53, 264
My Life as a German and Jew (Wassermann, J.), 9

Die Nacht ohne Pause (film), 101
Napoleonic Code, 162–63
Nathan der Weise (*Nathan the Wise*) (film), 138–39
Nathan der Weise (play) (Lessing), 138, 158–59
"Nationalsozialistische Revolution in Medizin und Gesundheitspolitik" (Reiter), 227
Natur und Liebe (*Nature and Love*) (film), 221
Nazimova, Alla, 71–72
Nazis, 1, 95; antisemitism of, 339; arrests by, 49, 51, 273, 278, 281; criticizing Scherl media, 121; discourses of, 289; expulsion policy of, 199, 206; films re-made by, 301–320; *Heimat* culture under, 308; ideology of, 301, 317; Jewishness and, 289–91; Nuremberg trials of, 273, 281; predetermined guilt and, 281; Weimar Republic transition to Nazism, 278; *Zwei Welten* fighting against, 132, 141. *See also*

concentration camps; Hitler, Adolf;
Holocaust; Third Reich
Negri, Pola, 78, 134
Neisser, Albert, 227, 229
Neuländer-Simon, Else ("Yva"), 69, 70
Neumann, Carl, 3, 4
Neumann, Hans, 38
New Woman, 183–84
Ngai, Sianne, 250
Nielsen, Asta, 28, 71
Niewyk, Donald, 9
Ninotschka (film), 51
Nosferatu (film), 27, 36–38, 50; Granach character in, 52–53
Nürnberger Zeitung, 269–72

Ohm Krüger (film), 306, 312
Olimsky, Fritz, 67
Opfer der Leidenschaft (*Victim of Passion*) (film), 76–77
Orska, Maria, 14; addictions of, 72; animalistic style, 71; in *Die Bestie im Menschen*, 76; femme fatale type and, 67, 73, 75, 77, 80, 81; Jewish coding of, 73–77; Jewish difference and, 79, 81; life and acting career of, 68–73; in *Opfer der Leidenschaft*, 76–77; photo spreads of, 69–70; in *Die schwarze Loo, oder Die Komposition des Anderen*, 74–76; typecasting of and Jewishness, 67–81, 74–76
Ossietzky, Carl von, 122
Österreichische Filmzeitung, 270
Ostjude (eastern European Jew), 25, 30, 45, 136; Arno and, 97; Galeen portraying, 32–35; Granach and, 48
Ostmayr, Peter, 309
Oswald, Richard, 31, 114, 137, 152, 221, 307; *Anders als die Andern* made by, 153; *Aufklärungsfilme* and, 155, 163
Otte, Marline, 95, 123

Pabst, Georg Wilhelm, 140, 142; philosemitic portrayals and, 189. See also *Die freudlose Gasse* (*The Joyless Street*) (film)
pacifism, 238, 255
Paprika (film), 200
Paradies der Dirne (*Paradise of Whores*) (film), 221
Paragraph 175 (German legal code), 153–54, 156–65
"Die Paralyse der Juden in sexualogischer Beleuchtung" (Sichel), 219
Parish, Lawrence Charles, 227
Paris Honeymoon (film), 201
Parufamet Agreement, 120
Passing Illusions (Wallach), 12–13, 29
passing process, 12; Granach and, 45; politics of, 114–16; Rosenthal and, 121–23; Wallach on, 114–15, 145, 168–69
Pasternak, Joe, 197, 200
personal cultivation and education (*Bildung*), 13, 89, 203, 268
Peter (film), 200–2; antisemitism in, 206; Gaal in, 203–210
Peter Voss, der Millionendieb (novel) (Seegiler), 311–9
Peter Voss, der Millionendieb (*Peter Voss, Thief of Millions*) (film), 15; Anton and, 311–17; Dupont adaptation of, 312, 314–17; Jacoby production of, 311; Nazi remake of, 301–3, 311–17
Petro, Patrice, 189
Pfitzner, Hans, 269
"Pharisäertum" (Buber), 11
Phoebus Film company, 257–59, 270–71
Pick, David, 57
Pinthus, Kurt, 272
Pioniere in Celluloid (Stratenwerth and Simon), 3–4
Planer, Franz, 145
Der Pojaz (Franzos), 36
Polgar, Alfred, 286
Pollak, Martin, 340
Pommer, Erich, 132, 144
Porta, Elizza la, 78

Poslednij Tabor (film), 51
Prag sieht und hört, 122
Prawer, Siegbert, 3–4, 133, 139; on social justice, 163
"Das Princip der Assimilation" (Karbach), 7
Professor Mamlock (play) (Wolfe), 51
prostitution, 155, 192n17; cultural associations with Jews, 216–20; in *Falsche Scham* (film), 223–24, 226; in *Feind im Blut*, 226–28; in *Die freudlose Gasse* (film), 175, 180; in *Die freudlose Gasse* (novel), 183, 185; syphilis and, 215
Prostitution (film), 221
Putti, Lya de, 78

queerness: gay rights and, 168; Jewishness and, 152–54, 159, 168–69; male femininity and, 167; queer masculinity, 162, 166–68; queer theory, 153

racial hygiene films, 15, 18n47; *Abseits vom Wege* as, 228; *Alles Leben ist Kampf* as, 228; *Anders als die Andern* as, 154; *Erbkrank* as, 228; *Sünden der Väter* as, 228. See also Weimar medical discourse films
Radszuweit, Friedrich, 161
Rasch, Hugo, 160, 260, 266–67
"Rassenkunde des judischen Volkes" (Günther), 220
Ráthonyi, Akos, 201
Recovering Jewishness (Roden), 5
Reichsverband Deutscher Lichtspieltheater-Besitzer (Reich Association of German Movie Theater Owners), 120
Reinhardt, Max, 47, 69
Reinhardt Theater, 33, 36
Reiter, Hans, 227
The Renaissance of Jewish Culture in Weimar Germany (Brenner), 8
Rentschler, Eric, 42n40
Resek Felix, 219–20

Richter, Hans, 242, 248–49
Riess, Curt, 289
Righelli, Gennaro, 56
The Rise of Catherine the Great (film), 210n24
Rittner, Rudolf, 259, 263
Robeson, Paul, 80
Robison, Arthur, 45, 53
Robitschek, Kurt, 96, 99
Roden, Frederick, 5
Rosegger, Peter, 38
Rosenberg, Alfred, 155, 217
Rosenthal, Alfred, 14; as Aros, 112, 118, 122, 124n8; conclusion, 122–23; dismissal of, 121; on German cinema, 120–21; Jewish film print culture and, 116–17; Jewishness, 121–23; Jewish visibility and, 112–13, 121–23; at *Der Kinematograph*, 111–13, 116–23; media context in Jewish film print culture, 116–17; murder of, 121, 122; passing process and, 121–23; Scherl media and, 113, 126n35; stylizing as film industry expert, 117–21
Rosenzweig, Franz, 7
Roud, Richard, 2
Rühmann, Heinz, 143–44
Ruttmann, Walter, 216, 220–21, 229, 241–42, 248–49

Sacher-Masoch, Leopold, 179, 191n3
Sachs, Hans, 266, 271
Salmonova, Lyda, 78
Salome (play), 69
Salvarsan, 222, 227
Sanssouci (film), 51, 76
Scharnagl, Karl, 269
Schatten (film), 50; Granach character in, 53–56; Kracauer on, 53–54
Schatzberg, Walter, 38
Scheer, Ludwig, 120
Scherek, Jakob, 158–59
Scherl media: Hugenberg establishing, 117; Nazis criticizing, 121; Rosenthal and, 113, 126n45

Schicksalswende (film), 51
Schildkraut, Joseph, 47
Schildkraut, Rudolph, 73
The Schlemihl (film), 137
schlemihl type, 91
Schmeling, Max, 198
Schneider, Franz, 216
Schnitzler, Arthur, 72
Scholem, Gershom, 7–8
Der schönste Mann im Staate (film), 101
Schuh, Fritz, 269
Schulz, Franz, 132, 144
Schulz, Fritz, 154, 166–68
Schulz, Ulrich, 221
Schumann, Clara, 266
Schünzel, Reinhold, 114, 166–68
Die schwarze Loo, oder Die Komposition des Anderen (*The Black Dancer, or the Composition of the Other*) (film), 74–76
Scientific Humanitarian Committee, 153, 160–61
The Haunted Screen (Eisner), 1–4
Seeliger, Ewald Gerhard, 311–12
Die Sektwette (*The Champagne Bet*) (film), 73
"Die Sendung Semaels" (play) (Zweig, A.), 189
Sera-Manischedda, Gabriele, 72
The Seventh Cross (film), 51
sexual intermediacy theory (*sexualle Zwischenstufenlehre*), 160, 166–67
Shachar, Galili, 39
Shohat, Ella, 13, 31–32
Shylock type, 26, 30; Granach on, 36; Granach portrayal, 32, 37, 48–49
Sichel, Max, 219, 222
Der sichtbare Mensch (Balázs), 246
Sieburg, Helene, 139, 140
Silverman, Lisa, 4–5
Simmel, Georg, 13
Simon, Hermann, 3–4
Siodmak, Robert, 279; attack on film by, 286–92; escape to Hollywood, 292
soldier type, 30, 96

Soot, Fritz, 259
Sorkin, Marc, 179, 189
Spector, Scott, 7–8
Spitzer, Leo, 6
Spitzweg, Carl, 265
Sprevia, 10
Die Stadt ohne Juden (novel) (Bettauer), 184, 331; antisemitism and, 186
Die Stadt ohne Juden (*The City Without Jews*) (film), 16; antisemitism in, 332; restoration of, 327, 331–34
Staemmler, Martin, 227
Stalin, Joseph, 51
Stam, Robert, 31–32
Starke, Ottomar, 71
Steakley, James, 163–64
Steckel, Leopold, 31
Steinach, Eugen, 162, 165
Steinhoff, Hans, 302, 303; *Heimat* culture reclaimed by, 304–314; response to *Die Geier-Wally*, 304–314; Third Reich prominence, 306
Sternau, Alfred, 292–93
Sternau, Ruth, 292–93
Der Storch streikt (film), 101
Stratenwerth, Irene, 3–4
Strauß, Hermann, 219
Streicher, Julius, 215, 218
Der Streik der Diebe (*The Thieves' Strike*) (film), 76
Der Stürmer, 217–18
suicide, 72, 75, 77, 154, 171n10
Sumurun (film), 89
Sünden der Väter (*Sins of the Fathers*) (film), 228
Süßheim, Max, 269
Sutcliffe, Adam, 163
Svengali (film), 50; Granach character in, 56–59; Wegener in, 56–57
syphilis: coding of, 216; Hitler and, 231n15; prostitution and, 215; Salvarsan for, 222, 227; Wassermann antibody test for syphilis, 219, 222. *See also* Jewish syphilis conspiracy
Szakall, Szöke, 96, 199

Das tanzende Herz (*The Dancing Heart*) (film), 73
Tasiemka, Hans, 91
Theis, Wolfgang, 166
Theory of Film (Kracauer), 25
Théry, Jacques, 202
Thiele, Wilhelm, 132, 144
Third Reich, 16, 201, 278–79, 302–3; *Filmpolitik* of, 217; Jewishness and, 281, 289; prominence of Steinhoff in, 306; racial hygiene films, 228
Thomalla, Curt, 221, 223–24
Trebitsch, Arthur, 245
Trilby (Du Maurier), 56–57
Trödler (Jewish merchant), 25, 31–33
Trotz, Adolf, 221
Tucholsky, Kurt, 113, 122
typecasting: black actors and, 78, 81; history of, 77–79; of Orska, 67–81

Ucicky, Gustav, 221
Ude, Johann, 155–56
UFA. *See* Universum Film Aktiengesellschaft
Um eine Nasenlänge (film), 101
Universum Film Aktiengesellschaft (UFA), 30, 92, 149n46, 270; productions of, 99, 220–21; tactics of, 94, 104n18
"Untergang der Assimilation" (Beilinson), 7
Urgiß, Julius, 5

Vaget, Hans Rudolf, 262
Vallentin, Hermann, 140
vamp type, 79–80
Veidt, Conrad, 47, 166–67
Venus im Pelz (Sacher-Masoch), 179
Vererbte Triebe (*Hereditary Instincts*) (film), 221
Vertov, Dziga, 246
Verwechslungskomödien (comedies of error), 198–200, 202
Volkov, Shulamit, 168
Von Hillern, Willhelmine, 304–306, 309

Wagener, Hilde, 286, 287
Die Wahrheit, 220
Walk, Cynthia, 80
Wallach, Kerry, 12–13, 29, 97, 134–35, 163; on female characters, 190; on Jewishness, 284; on passing process, 114–15, 145, 168–69
Wallburg, Otto, 198
The Wall (film), 59–60
Wangenheim, Gustav von, 51
Wassermann, August Paul von, 222
Wassermann, Jakob, 9; on antisemitism, 10
Wassermann antibody test for syphilis, 219, 222
Wedekind, Frank, 69–70
Wegener, Paul, 32–33, 138, 264; in *Svengali*, 56–57
Weimar cinema: antisemitism in, 15–16; German national character in, 1; Jewish backgrounds in, 2–4; Jewish difference in, 338–39; Jewish identity in, 4, 6–11, 13, 133–35; Jewish liberals in, 4, 8, 17n19; Jewish types on, 28–32; locating Jewishness in, 11–16; Nazi narrative of, 3; visibility in, 14. *See also* German cinema; Weimar Republic
Weimar Film and Modern Jewish Identity (Ashkenazi), 4, 13, 134, 162
Weimar medical discourse films: *Alkohol* as, 221; as documentaries and popular entertainment, 221; *Falsche Scham* (film) as, 216, 220–21, 223–26, 229; *Feind im Blut* as, 216, 220–21, 226–29; *Fluch der Vererbung* as, 221, 224; *Die Geschlechtskrankheiten und ihre Folgen* as, 220–23, 229; Jewish difference and, 221; *Natur und Liebe* as, 221; *Paradies der Dirne* as, 221; *Prostitution* as, 221; *Vererbte Triebe* as, 221
Weimar Republic, 46, 73, 301; antisemitism in, 95; attacks on,

142; comedies in, 89, 94; creation of, 156; culture of, 239, 257–58, 273; ideology of, 138; Jewishness in, 2, 6; media environment of, 339; transition to Nazism, 278

Weininger, Otto, 152

Weinstein, Valerie, 29, 88, 190, 225, 288

Westfront 1918 (*Western Front*) (film), 140–41

Weyher, Ruth, 55

Weyland, Paul, 247–48

White, Patricia, 71–72

white slavery, 216

Wiene, Robert, 38, 50, 241

Der Wiener Film, 201

Wilde, Oscar, 69, 71, 164

Winkelstern, Marianne, 101

Wittner, Doris, 74

Wohlmut, Robert, 201

Wolf, Friedrich, 51

Wollenberg, Hans, 29, 31, 135; on Arno, 96–97; on exaggeration of Jewishness, 30

Wong, Anna May, 79–81

The World of Yesterday (Zweig, S.), 291

Yiddish-language films, 133, 135

Yiddish theater, 46–48, 51, 54, 62n5, 73, 202

Yuen, Nancy Wang, 81

Zeitschrift für Demographie und Statistik der Juden (Strauß), 219

Zelnik, Friedrich, 221

Zensurkarte (censor's certificate), 327, 328, 332

Zer-Zion, Shelly, 63n11

Zimmermann, Ernst Heinrich, 271

Zimmermann, Moshe, 136

Zinnemann, Fred, 51

Zionism, 7, 95, 251n3; Bolshevik-Zionist conspiracy, 238

Zola, Émile, 76, 163–64

Zuckmayer, Carl, 31, 267

Zweig, Arnold, 48–49, 189

Zweig, Stefan, 279–81; distancing of, 286; on film ban, 289–90; Jewish identity and, 282–85; memoirs of, 291

Zwei Welten (*Two Worlds*) (film), 14; depicting threat to eastern European Jews, 131; Dupont releasing, 139–41, 314; fight against Nazism and, 132, 141; menorah in, 142; popularity of, 143; reviews of, 141

Zwick, Reinhold, 38

www.ingramcontent.com/pod-product-compliance
Lightning Source LLC
Chambersburg PA
CBHW072044110526
44590CB00018B/3036